Bangkok

"All you've got to do is decide to go
and the hardest part is over.

So go!"

TONY WHEELER, COFOUNDER – LONELY PLANET

THIS EDITION WRITTEN AND RESEARCHED BY
Austin Bush

Contents

Plan Your Trip — 4

Explore Bangkok — 54

Understand Bangkok — 205

Survival Guide — 235

Bangkok Maps — 263

(left) **Golden Mount p83** Enjoy panoramic views from the peak.

(above) **Mae Nam Chao Phraya p10** Go sight-seeing by boat.

(right) **Sky Bar p136** Drink in the view – and the cocktails, too!

Greater Bangkok p156

Thewet & Dusit p91

Banglamphu p78

Ko Ratanakosin & Thonburi p58

Chinatown p99

Siam Square, Pratunam, Phloen Chit & Ratchathewi p108

Riverside, Silom & Lumphini p125

Sukhumvit p142

Welcome to Bangkok

Same same, but different. This Thailish T-shirt philosophy sums up Bangkok, where the familiar and the exotic collide like the flavours in a pàt tai.

Full-on Food

Until you've eaten on a Bangkok street, your noodles mingling with your sweat amid a cloud of exhaust fumes, you haven't actually eaten Thai food. It can be an intense mix: the basic flavours – spicy, sour, sweet and salty – aren't exactly meat and potatoes. But for adventurous foodies who don't need white tablecloths, there's probably no better dining destination in the world. And with immigration bringing every regional Thai and international cuisine to the capital, it's also a truly diverse experience.

Fun Folks

The language barrier may seem huge, but it's never prevented anybody from getting on with the Thai people. The capital's cultural underpinnings are evident in virtually all facets of everyday life, and most enjoyably through its residents' sense of *sà·nùk* (fun). In Bangkok, anything worth doing should have an element of *sà·nùk*. Ordering food, changing money and haggling at markets will usually involve a sense of playfulness – a dash of flirtation, perhaps – and a smile. It's a language that doesn't require words, and one that's easy to learn.

Urban Exploration

With so much of daily life conducted on the street, there are few cities in the world that reward exploration as handsomely as Bangkok. Cap off an extended boat trip with a visit to a hidden market. A stroll off Banglamphu's beaten track can lead to a conversation with a monk. Get lost in the tiny lanes of Chinatown and stumble upon a live Chinese opera performance. After dark, let the BTS (Skytrain) escort you to Sukhumvit, where the local nightlife scene reveals a sophisticated and dynamic city.

Contrasts

It's the contradictions that give the City of Angels its rich, multifaceted personality. Here, climate-controlled megamalls sit side-by-side with 200-year-old village homes; gold-spired Buddhist temples share space with neon-lit strips of sleaze; slow-moving traffic is bypassed by long-tail boats plying the royal river; and streets lined with food carts are overlooked by restaurants on top of skyscrapers. And as Bangkok races towards the future, these contrasts will never stop supplying the city with its unique and ever-changing strain of Thai-ness.

Why I Love Bangkok

By Austin Bush, Writer

Admittedly, there are some things – the hot weather, the pollution, the political instability – that make Bangkok a less-than-ideal city. But there's so much more that makes it amazing. I love the food. What other city has such a full-flavoured, no-holds-barred, insatiable, fanatical approach to eating? I love old Bangkok. Districts such as Banglamphu and Chinatown still carry the grit, charm and character of the city that used to be. And I'd be lying if I didn't also say that I love new Bangkok – don't we all have a soft spot for megamalls and air-con?

For more about our writer, see p288.

Top: Street-food vendor, Chinatown (p99)

Bangkok's
Top 10

Open-Air Dining *(p26)*

1 Bangkok's reputation as a polluted city belies its forte as an outdoor-dining capital. Despite the modern conveniences of air-conditioning and contemporary cafes, some of the most memorable meals in the city not coincidentally called the 'Big Mango' are had at the open-air markets and food stalls. Forget about three square meals: in Bangkok, locals snack throughout the day, packing away at least four meals before sunset. It would be rude not to join them.

✕ Eating

Jim Thompson House *(p110)*

2 The late American entrepreneur Jim Thompson used his traditional Thai-style home as a repository for ageing Thai traditions and artwork. Thompson mysteriously disappeared in 1967, and today his former home is a museum – one that every visitor secretly wishes to live in. Why? The rooms are adorned with his exquisite art collection and personal possessions, including rare Chinese porcelain pieces and Burmese, Cambodian and Thai artefacts, and the garden is a miniature jungle of tropical plants and lotus ponds. It's the epitome of the traditional Thai house.

◉ Siam Square, Pratunam, Phloen Chit & Ratchathewi

Banglamphu *(p78)*

3 Easily Bangkok's most charming neighbourhood, Banglamphu is the city's former aristocratic enclave, once filled with minor royalty and riverside mansions. Today the old quarter is dominated by antique shophouses, backpackers seeking R&R on famous Th Khao San, civil servants shuffling between offices and lunch spots, and bohemian artists and students. Vendor carts and classic restaurants also make a patchwork quilt of Banglamphu, offering ample options for a roving stomach, and the area is also home to some of the city's best bars. TOP LEFT: TH KHAO SAN (P84)

⊙ *Banglamphu*

Chatuchak Weekend Market *(p158)*

4 In a city obsessed with commerce, Chatuchak Weekend Market takes the prize as Bangkok's biggest and baddest market. Silks, sneakers, fighting cocks and fighting fish, puppies and souvenirs for the insatiable *fa·ràng* (Westerner) – if it can be sold in Thailand, you'll find it here. From everyday to clubby, clothes dominate much of the market but, this being Thailand, food and drink also have a strong – and refreshing – presence, making Chatuchak as much about entertainment and eating as it is about shopping.

⊙ *Greater Bangkok*

Wat Pho *(p65)*

5 The grounds of Wat Pho claim a 16th-century birthday, predating Bangkok itself. In addition to being the country's biggest temple, Wat Pho is home to a school of traditional Thai medicine, where on-site massage pavilions facilitate that elusive convergence of sightseeing and relaxation. Still not impressed? Let us not forget Wat Pho's primary Buddha – a reclining figure that nearly dwarfs its sizeable shelter. Symbolic of Buddha's death and passage into nirvana, the image measures 46m and is gilded with gold leaf, making it truly larger than life.

⊙ *Ko Ratanakosin & Thonburi*

Shopping *(p45)*

6 Even avowed anticonsumerists weaken in Bangkok. One minute they're touting the virtues of a life without material possessions, the next they're admiring the fake Rolex watches and mapping out the route to MBK Center. Bangkok's malls, however, are just a warm-up for the markets, the cardio workout of shopping. In this city, footpaths are for additional retail space, not for pedestrians. In addition to Chatuchak Weekend Market – one of the world's largest markets – Bangkok is an established destination for bespoke tailoring, and has its own emerging fashion scene. BELOW: MBK CENTER (P120)

📷 *Shopping*

Mae Nam Chao Phraya *(p134)*

7 Mae Nam Chao Phraya (the Chao Phraya River) is always teeming with activity: hulking freighter boats trail behind dedicated tugs, river-crossing ferries skip across the wake, and children practise cannonballs into the muddy water. You can witness this from the shore (ideally from Ko Ratanakosin or Thonburi), from a chartered long-tail boat or while on the deck of a river taxi. Regardless of your vantage point, as the blinding sun slips below the horizon in serene streaks of reds and golds, sooty Bangkok suddenly looks beautiful. TOP RIGHT: BOATS PASSING WAT ARUN (P69)

👁 *Ko Ratanakosin & Thonburi*

8

Chinatown (p99)

8 Forgive us for suggesting that Bangkok's Chinatown is something of an Asian El Dorado. The neighbourhood's main artery, Th Yaowarat, is crowded with gold shops – sealed glass-front buildings that look more like Chinese altars than downtown jewellers. Likewise, the Buddha statue at Wat Traimit has more gold than you've likely ever seen in one place. And the pencil-thin lanes that branch off Talat Mai are decked with gold-leaf-coated goods. Throw in the blazing neon signs and smoky, open-air kitchens and you have an urban explorer's fantasy.

👁 *Chinatown*

Thai Cookery Schools *(p52)*

9 Why let a plump tummy be the only sign of your visit to Thailand? Instead, spice up your life – and your dinner-party menus – by learning to create the kingdom's zesty dishes in your own kitchen. Cooking schools in Bangkok range from formal affairs for amateur chefs to home cooking for the recipe-phobic. Everyone always has a grand time, visiting a wet market, fumbling with ingredients, tasting the fruits of their labour and trotting home with new cooking techniques.

🏃 *Sports & Activities*

Songkran *(p22)*

10 If the idea of no-holds-barred water-based warfare appeals to you, make a point of being in Bangkok during April. With origins in an ancient religious practice of Buddha images being 'bathed', in recent decades the celebration of the Thai lunar New Year has evolved into a citywide water fight. Foreigners, especially well-dressed ones, are obvious targets, and the majority of the mayhem occurs on Th Khao San. In addition to water-throwing, festivities include open-air concerts and visits to Buddhist temples.

👟 *Month by Month*

What's New

Chinatown's Renaissance

It started with cool art spaces such as Soy Sauce Factory (p103). Since then, modern-feeling hostels such as Loftel 22 (p191) and surprisingly sophisticated bars like Tep Bar (p107) and Teens of Thailand (p107) have continued a slew of openings that may only end with the gentrification of Bangkok's formerly neglected Chinatown.

Err
Full-flavoured Thai street eats in a charming – and mercifully air-conditioned – setting. (p75)

Muay Thai Lab
Bright new training centre/museum dedicated to Thailand's unofficial national sport. (p77)

Sugar Ray
Taste Thai-style mixology at this fun, closet-sized boozer. (p149)

Studio Lam
Travel back in time at this retro-themed new bar with an emphasis on domestic tunes. (p150)

Bangkok Bold
The latest incarnation of a previously lauded Thai cookery school. (p90)

Parking Toys' Watt
The latest (and much more accessible) branch of a suburban live-music legend. (p152)

Ceresia
New venue serving serious coffee drinks, including some using Thai beans. (p137)

Hotel Indigo
Eccentric new hotel that takes its design cues from the surrounding neighbourhood's history and culture. (p197)

Khua Kling Pak Sod
House-bound restaurant serving the spicy cuisine of Thailand's southern provinces. (p163)

Yim Huai Khwang Hostel
An inviting new hostel that provides an excuse to stay outside of the city centre. (p191)

Beat Hotel
Fun, new art-themed hotel delightfully distant from the tourist track. (p204)

For more recommendations and reviews, see **lonelyplanet. com/thailand/bangkok**

Need to Know

For more information, see Survival Guide (p235)

Currency
Thai baht (B)

Language
Thai

Visas
Most nationalities can receive a 30-day visa exemption on arrival at international airports or a 15-day visa at land borders; a 60-day tourist visa is available through Thai consulates.

Money
ATMs widespread; 150B foreign-account fee. Upmarket places accept Visa and MasterCard.

Mobile Phones
GSM and 4G networks available through inexpensive prepaid SIM cards.

Time
Asia/Bangkok (GMT/UTC +7 hours)

Tourist Information
Tourism Authority of Thailand (TAT; ☎call centre 1672; www.tourismthailand.org) National tourism department.

Bangkok Information Center (☎02 225 7612-4; www.bangkoktourist.com; 17/1 Th Phra Athit; ⊙9am-7pm Mon-Fri, to 5pm Sat & Sun; ☀Phra Athit/Banglamphu Pier) City-specific; staffed booths throughout city.

Daily Costs

Budget:
Less than 1500B
➡ Dorm bed/basic guesthouse room 230–800B

➡ Street-stall meals 150–300B

➡ One or two of the big-hitter sights 500–600B

➡ Getting around on public transport 20–100B

Midrange:
1500B to 3000B
➡ Flashpacker guesthouse or midrange hotel room 800–1500B

➡ Street and restaurant meals 500–1000B

➡ Most, if not all, of the big sights 500–1000B

➡ Getting around with public transport and occasional taxis 100–300B

Top End:
More than 3000B
➡ Boutique hotel room 3000B

➡ Fine dining 1500–3000B

➡ Private tours from 1000B

➡ Getting around in taxis 300–800B

Advance Planning
Three months before Book a room at a smaller boutique hotel, especially if visiting during December/January.

One month before Make reservations at nahm (p135); if you plan to stay in Thailand longer than 30 days, apply for a visa at the Thai embassy or consulate in your home country.

One week before Book lessons at a Thai cooking school.

Useful Websites
Lonely Planet (www.lonelyplanet.com/thailand/bangkok) Destination information, hotel bookings, traveller forum and more.

BK (www.bk.asia-city.com) Online version of Bangkok's best listings magazine.

Bangkok 101 (www.bangkok101.com) Tourist-friendly listings mag.

Bangkok Post (www.bangkokpost.com) English-language daily.

WHEN TO GO

Late December to early January is Bangkok's coolest time and its peak tourist season. Go in November or February for (relatively) fewer people.

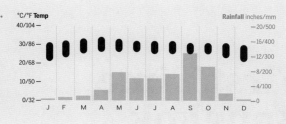

Arriving in Bangkok

Suvarnabhumi International Airport The Airport Rail Link runs from Phaya Thai station to Suvarnabhumi (45B, 30 minutes, from 6am to midnight). Metered taxis run 24 hours and cost 200B to 300B plus a 50B airport surcharge and optional expressway tolls.

Don Mueang International Airport There are two bus lines from Bangkok's de facto budget airport: bus A1 makes stops at BTS Mo Chit (30B, frequent from 7.30am to 11.30pm), while bus A2 makes stops at BTS Mo Chit and BTS Victory Monument (30B, every 30 minutes from 7.30am to 11.30pm). Metered taxis from Don Mueang also charge a 50B airport surcharge, and trips to town start at 200B.

For much more on **arrival** see p236

Getting Around

➡ **BTS** The elevated Skytrain runs from 5.15am to midnight. Tickets 10B to 52B.

➡ **MRT** The metro runs from 6am to midnight. Tickets 16B to 42B.

➡ **Taxi** Outside of rush hours, Bangkok taxis are a great bargain. Flag fall 35B.

➡ **Chao Phraya Express Boat** Runs from 6am to 8pm, charging from 10B to 40B.

➡ **Klorng boat** Bangkok's canal boats run from 5.30am to 7.15pm most days. Tickets from 9B to 19B.

➡ **Bus** Cheap but a slow and confusing way to get around Bangkok. Tickets 5B to 30B.

For much more on **getting around** see p238

Sleeping

Travellers are spoilt for accommodation options in Bangkok, with the added benefit that much of what's available is excellent value. If you're on a budget, dorm beds can be had for as little as 230B, while cheap rooms start at about 500B. There's a wide choice of midrange hotels and an astonishing number of top-end places. Be sure to book ahead if you're arriving during peak tourist season (from approximately November to February) and are keen on the smaller, boutique-type hotel.

Websites

➡ **Travelfish** (www.travelfish. org) Independent reviews of budget and midrange places, with lots of reader feedback.

➡ **Agoda** (www.agoda.com/ city/bangkok-th.html) Asia-based hotel-booking site that offers a lowest-price guarantee.

➡ **Lonely Planet** (www. lonelyplanet.com/thailand/ bangkok/hotels) Find reviews and make bookings.

For much more on **sleeping** see p187

HOW LONG TO STAY FOR?

Bangkok is a major stopover point for long-haul flights (and connecting flights to the islands), with many visitors spending a couple of days here before moving on. If you're keen to see more than the top temples and the insides of Bangkok's shopping malls, spend at least four days here. This way, you'll also be able to eat at some of the best restaurants, check out a few rooftop bars, spend a morning at Chatuchak Weekend Market and squeeze in a cooking class, with time to spare for a famous Thai massage (or two).

First Time Bangkok

For more information, see Survival Guide (p235)

Checklist

➡ Make sure your passport is valid for at least six months past your arrival date.

➡ Confirm your airline's baggage restrictions.

➡ For visits longer than 30 days, apply for a tourist visa at a Thai embassy or consulate in your home country.

➡ Inform your bank and/or debit-/credit-card company that you'll be travelling.

➡ Arrange for appropriate travel insurance.

What to Pack

➡ Phrasebook

➡ Power converter

➡ GSM mobile phone and charger

➡ Lightweight clothes

➡ Hat and sunglasses

➡ Comfortable sandals

➡ Sunscreen (available but expensive in Bangkok)

➡ Earplugs

Top Tips for Your Trip

➡ Learn a few Thai phrases (see p248) and always smile.

➡ Don't try to cover too much ground in a day; Bangkok's heat and traffic will ensure that doing so is more of an ordeal than a holiday.

➡ Ignore any taxi driver who refuses to use the meter.

➡ The BTS (Skytrain) is one of the fastest and most convenient ways to get around 'new' Bangkok; the Chao Phraya Express Boat is a slow but steady way to get to the older parts of town.

➡ Keep your cool when bargaining or if in an altercation with a local.

What to Wear

Light, loose-fitting clothes are generally the most comfortable in Bangkok's tropical, urban heat. Shorts are usually acceptable and comfortable, but when you visit temples, wear clothes that cover to your elbows and knees. Likewise, sandals are cool and easily removed at temples, but bring at least one non-shorts-and-sandals outfit if you plan on clubbing, fine dining or visiting any of the city's nicer rooftop bars.

Be Forewarned

Bangkok is generally a safe city, but there are a few things to be aware of.

➡ In recent years, Bangkok has been the site of political protests that have occasionally turned violent; check your embassy's advisory travel warnings before leaving.

➡ Criticising the Thai monarchy in any way is a very serious social faux pas that carries potentially incriminating repercussions; don't do it.

➡ Avoid the common scams: one-day gem sales, suspiciously low transport prices, dodgy tailors.

➡ Bangkok's streets are extremely dangerous, and its drivers rarely yield to pedestrians. Look in both directions before crossing any street (or pavement) and yield to anything with more metal than you.

➡ Most of Bangkok's street-food vendors close shop on Monday.

➡ Bangkok's rainy season is from May to October, when daily downpours – and occasional flooding – are the norm.

➡ Smoking is banned indoors at bars and restaurants.

Money

Debit and credit cards are accepted at department stores, mall-bound retail outlets and at midrange to top-end eating and drinking establishments, but most places in Bangkok continue to deal only in cash.

ATMs are ubiquitous in Bangkok but there is a 150B foreign-transaction fee in addition to whatever fees your bank back home charges. To keep ATM withdraws to a minimum, take out as much cash as you feel comfortable carrying. Most ATMs allow you to withdraw a maximum of 20,000B per day.

Bargaining

If there is no posted price on an item, then bargaining is acceptable. Ask for the price, follow up by asking for a discount, offer a counter and accept what is offered in return. Always smile, and don't start bargaining if you're not interested in buying.

Tipping

At high-end establishments, a 10% service charge is added to the bill. Elsewhere, tipping is not standard nor expected in Bangkok, but it is appreciated. If there is a small bit of change from a restaurant bill or metered taxi fare, it is common to leave it as a tip.

DAVID BUFFINGTON / GETTY IMAGES ©

Túk-túk (p239)

Etiquette

Bangkokians are generally very understanding and hospitable, but there are some important taboos and social conventions to be aware of.

➡ **Monarchy** Never make any disparaging remarks about any member of Thailand's royal family. Treat objects depicting the king (like money) with respect.

➡ **Temples** Wear clothing that covers to your knees and elbows. Remove your shoes when you enter a temple building. Sit with your feet tucked behind you to avoid pointing the bottom of your feet at Buddha images. Women should never touch a monk or a monk's belongings; step out of a monk's way on footpaths and don't sit next to a monk on public transport.

➡ **Save Face** Never get into an argument with a Thai. It is better to smile through any social friction.

Language

Bangkok is well stocked with English speakers, though market vendors and bus and taxi drivers are less competent, so it helps to know some Thai basics.

Thailand has its own script. Street signs are always transliterated into English, but there is no universally accepted system so spellings vary widely. Not all letters are pronounced as they appear (eg 'Ph' is an aspirated 'p' not an 'f').

Top Itineraries

Day One

Ko Ratanakosin & Thonburi (p58)

 Get up as early as you can and take the Chao Phraya Express Boat north to Chang Pier to explore one of Ko Ratanakosin's museums such as the **Museum of Siam**, as well as one of its must-see temples, like **Wat Pho**.

> **Lunch** Plunge into Bangkok-style street food at Pa Aew (p75).

Riverside, Silom & Lumphini (p125)

Refresh with a spa treatment at **Health Land** or soothe those overworked legs with a traditional Thai massage at **Ruen-Nuad Massage Studio**. After freshening up, get a new perspective on Bangkok with rooftop cocktails at **Moon Bar**.

> **Dinner** nahm (p135) serves arguably the best Thai food in Bangkok.

Riverside, Silom & Lumphini (p125)

If you've still got it in you, get dancing at **Tapas Room**, or head over to **Telephone Pub** or any of the other bars in Bangkok's lively gaybourhood. For a night that doesn't end until the sun comes up, bang on the door at **Wong's Place**.

Day Two

Siam Square, Pratunam, Phloen Chit & Ratchathewi (p108)

Take the BTS (Skytrain) to National Stadium and start your day with a visit to the popular and worthwhile museum that is **Jim Thompson House**. Follow this by exploring nearby **Baan Khrua** or by making a wish at the **Erawan Shrine**.

> **Lunch** The MBK Food Island (p115) is an ideal introduction to Thai food.

Siam Square, Pratunam, Phloen Chit & Ratchathewi (p108)

Walk, or let the BTS escort you, through Bangkok's ultramodern commercial district, stopping off at linked shopping centres including **MBK Center**, **Siam Paragon** and **Siam Square**. Make time for a sweet snack at **Gourmet Paradise** or an afternoon cuppa at the **Erawan Tea Room**.

> **Dinner** Try Thai food with a modern twist at Sra Bua (p115).

Greater Bangkok (p156)

If it's Tuesday, Friday or Saturday, consider catching a Thai-boxing match at **Lumpinee Boxing Stadium**, or make a point of schlepping over to eastern Bangkok's RCA/Royal City Ave to check out fun clubs such as **Route 66** or **Onyx**.

CHALERMKIAT SEEDOKMAI / GETTY IMAGES ©

Democracy Monument (p81)

Day Three

Ko Ratanakosin & Thonburi (p58)

 Take the Chao Phraya Express Boat to Chang Pier and set off on a **long-tail boat tour** of Thonburi's canals. Alternatively, combine canals and the culinary arts with a visit to **Amita Thai Cooking Class**.

 Lunch Take advantage of the air-con and spicy eats at Err (p75).

Banglamphu (p78)

 Spend the afternoon shopping at the **Th Khao San Market** and visiting the surrounding sights such as the **Golden Mount** and **Wat Suthat**. Or, if you've got energy to spare, book an afternoon or night bike tour of the area with **Velo Thailand** or **Grasshopper Adventures**.

Dinner Take a temporary break from Thai food at Nasir Al-Masri (p147).

Sukhumvit (p142)

End the night with a Thai-themed cocktail at a cosy local such as **WTF** or **Badmotel**, or a streetside Singha at **Cheap Charlie's**. If it's still too early for you to turn in, extend the night with a visit to clubs **Grease** or **Arena 10**.

Day Four

Greater Bangkok (p156)

If it's a weekend, take the BTS north for a half-day of shopping at the **Chatuchak Weekend Market**. Otherwise, consider a half-day excursion outside the city to the provincial-feeling **Nonthaburi Market**, the artificial island of **Ko Kret** or the recreated ruins at **Ancient City**.

 Lunch Chatuchak Weekend Market (p158) has cheap and tasty food stalls.

Chinatown (p99)

Recover from the market in the relative cool of the late afternoon before taking the MRT (metro) to Chinatown to visit the home of the Golden Buddha, **Wat Traimit**, and the Chinese-style **Wat Mangkon Kamalawat**. Consider popping over to **Phahurat** to sample that neighbourhood's South Asian feel, or if you're there after dark, the flower market at **Pak Khlong Talat**.

Dinner Follow our walking tour (p104) of Chinatown's best street eats.

Banglamphu (p78)

Make the brief taxi ride to Banglamphu and begin the evening with drinks at **Madame Musur**, followed by a rowdy live-music show at **Brick Bar** or dancing at **The Club**. If bedtime is irrelevant, head for the *shishas* (water pipes) and dance floor of **The Bank**.

If You Like...

Temples

Wat Phra Kaew The grandaddy of Thai temples – not to mention the home of a certain Emerald Buddha. (p60)

Wat Pho If you haven't seen the ginormous reclining Buddha here, you haven't seen Bangkok. (p65)

Wat Suthat One of Thailand's biggest Buddhas and equally impressive floor-to-ceiling temple murals await visitors here. (p80)

Wat Arun Predating Bangkok, this temple – known as Temple of Dawn – makes the best of a unique riverside location. (p69)

Wat Mangkon Kamalawat The epitome of the hectic, smoky, noisy Chinese-style Buddhist temple. (p103)

Sri Mariamman Temple Bangkok's main Hindu temple practically leaps from the street, taking all comers. (p128)

Museums

National Museum An occasionally dusty but wholly worthwhile survey of Thai history. (p70)

Museum of Siam A lively summary of the Thai people and their culture. (p70)

Bangkokian Museum A preserved house that's a time warp back to the Bangkok of the early-to-middle 20th century. (p127)

SYLVAIN SONNET / GETTY IMAGES ©

Detail of Wat Suthat (p80)

Siriraj Medical Museum Not for the faint of heart: a queasy look at the more graphic side of death. (p70)

Architecture

Riverside Architecture Ramble Follow this walking tour, which takes in some of Bangkok's most notable secular structures. (p129)

Jim Thompson House Beautiful former home that brings together Thailand's past and present. (p110)

Ban Kamthieng A perfectly preserved northern-style Thai home – right in the middle of modern Bangkok. (p144)

Ancient City See models of Thailand's most famous structures without having to leave the greater Bangkok area. (p161)

Eating Like a Local

Likhit Kai Yang Where locals fuel up before the big *moo·ay tai* (Thai boxing; also spelt *muay thai*) match. (p97)

MBK Food Island Do the local thing by forgetting about ambience and focusing on the food at this mall-based food court. (p115)

A Taste of Chinatown Take our food-based walking tour and you'll see why Thais are willing to cross town for a bowl of noodles. (p104)

Pa Aew An open-air curry stall that excels in the flavours of Bangkok and Central Thailand. (p75)

Boats

Chao Phraya Express Boat The slow but steady – not to mention scenic – way to get around Bangkok. (p239)

Long-tail boat tour of Thonburi canals Race through the narrow, wooden-house-lined canals of Thonburi, James Bond–style. (p76)

Chaophraya Cruise Dinner on the deck of a cruise ship is an admittedly cheesy, yet obligatory, Bangkok experience. (p134)

Royal Barges National Museum A riverside museum that's home to some of the most ornate boats in the world. (p71)

Hipster Haunts

Never Ending Summer The Thai restaurant that's almost too cool to eat at. (p131)

Another Story One-of-a-kind merch from Thailand and elsewhere. (p153)

Grease Nightclub where celebs and wannabes mix and bump. (p151)

Studio Lam Bangkok circa 1972 is the new cool at this music-themed bar. (p150)

Talat Rot Fai Witness every Thai youth subculture at this open-air market. (p161)

Urban Exploration

Talat Noi Blaze your own path in this web-like riverside neighbourhood. (p102)

Sampeng Lane Explore the narrow lanes that spread from

For more top Bangkok spots, see the following:

➡ Eating (p26)
➡ Drinking & Nightlife (p35)
➡ LGBT Bangkok (p39)
➡ Entertainment (p41)
➡ Shopping (p45)
➡ Sports & Activities (p50)

this market alley in the heart of Bangkok's Chinatown. (p105)

Amulet Market One of Bangkok's most bizarre markets is also a great destination for aimless wandering. (p70)

Church of Santa Cruz Get lost in the winding, elevated lanes surrounding this Thonburi church. (p103)

Art

Jim Thompson House Antique Thai-style house crammed with beautiful works of art from across Southeast Asia. (p110)

100 Tonson Gallery Housed in a villa, 100 Tonson is regarded as one of Bangkok's top commercial galleries. (p113)

Bangkok Art & Culture Centre Contemporary art meets commerce in the centre of Bangkok. (p111)

Tang Gallery Private gallery featuring the work of contemporary Thai and Chinese artists. (p128)

Kathmandu Photo Gallery Period-style shophouse gallery dedicated to local and international photography. (p128)

Month by Month

January

The weather is relatively cool in Bangkok, and the number of foreign tourists remains quite high.

✸ Chinese New Year

Some time from late January to late February, Bangkok's large Thai-Chinese population celebrates the lunar new year, called *drùd jeen* in Thai, with a week full of house cleaning, lion dances and fireworks. The most impressive festivities, not surprisingly, take place in Chinatown.

February

With relatively comfortable (although increasingly warm) temperatures and few tourists, February is a clever time to visit Bangkok.

☆ Kite-Flying Season

During the windy season, from the middle of February to early April, colourful kites battle it out over the skies of Sanam Luang and Lumphini Park.

✸ Makha Bucha

Makha Bucha is held on the full moon of the third lunar month (late February to early March) to commemorate the Buddha preaching to 1250 monks who came to hear him 'without prior summons'. It culminates with a candlelit walk around the main chapel at every *wát*.

April

This is the height of Bangkok's hot season, so it should come as no surprise that the Thais have devised a festival that revolves around splashing water on each other.

✸ Songkran

Songkran is the Thai New Year, and although it has origins in a religious prac- tice of 'bathing' Buddha images, today's celebrations resemble a city-wide water- fight. The most intense bat- tles are fought on Th Khao San – don't carry anything you don't want to get wet.

May

May and June mean the beginning of the rainy season in most parts of Thailand, and some of the festivals during these months have origins in this significant occasion.

✸ Royal Ploughing Ceremony

To kick off the official rice-planting season in early May, the crown prince presides over this ancient Brahman ritual held at San- am Luang. It culminates in sacred white oxen plough- ing the earth and priests declaring it a good or bad year for farmers.

✸ Wai Kru Muay Thai Ceremony

A celebration of Thailand's unofficial national sport of *moo·ay tai* (Thai boxing; also spelt *muay thai*), held at Wat Mahathat, in Ayu- thaya. The one-day event includes demonstrations and a competition; call Ayuthaya's TAT office for exact dates and schedule of events.

🍴 Visakha Bucha

Visakha Bucha, on the full moon of the sixth lunar month (May or June), is considered the date of the Buddha's birth, enlightenment and *parinibbana* (passing away). Activities are centred on the local wát (temple), with candle-lit processions, chanting and sermonising.

July

Thailand's rainy season is well under way during this time. The most significant event of the season is a Buddhist holiday ushering in the rains.

🍴 Asanha Bucha & Khao Phansa

Held on the full moon of the eighth lunar month (July or August), Asanha Bucha commemorates the Buddha's first post-enlightenment sermon. The following day, young men traditionally enter the monkhood and monks sequester themselves in a monastery for three months (known as Khao Phansa).

September

September is the wettest month in and around Bangkok, and tourist numbers are correspondingly low.

🍴 Vegetarian Festival

During the first nine days of the ninth lunar month (September or October), this Chinese-Buddhist festival, called *têt·sà·gahn gin jair,* sees streetside vendors serving meatless meals to help cleanse the body. Most of the action is in Chinatown (p103): look for the yellow banners and white clothes.

November

The rain's (mostly) stopped, the weather's (relatively) cool, the crowds are low and the festivals are plentiful: November is one of the best months to visit Bangkok.

🍴 Loi Krathong

On the night of the full moon of the 12th lunar month, *grà·tong* (boats made of a section of banana trunk) are floated on Mae Nam Chao Phraya. The ceremony is both an offering to the water spirits and a symbolic cleansing of bad luck.

◉ Wat Saket Fair

The grandest of Bangkok's temple fairs *(ngahn wát)* is held at Wat Saket and the Golden Mount (p83) around Loi Krathong. The temple grounds turn into a colourful, noisy fair selling flowers, incense, bells, saffron cloth and tonnes of Thai food.

☆ Concert in the Park

Free concerts from the Bangkok Symphony Orchestra (www.bangkoksymphony.org) are performed Sunday evenings (from 5.30pm to 7.30pm) between late November and mid-February at Lumphini Park.

December

The coolest month of the year sees a handful of outdoor festivals and events. Tourist numbers are at their peak, but this is arguably the most pleasant month to visit the Thai capital.

🍴 King's Birthday/ Father's Day

Celebrating King Bhumibol's birthday (5 December), the city is festooned with lights and large portraits of the king. In the afternoon, Sanam Luang is packed for a fireworks display that segues appropriately into a noisy concert with popular Thai musicians.

☆ Ayutthaya World Heritage & Red Cross Fair

A series of cultural performances and evening sound-and-light shows among the ruins of the World Heritage site in the former Thai capital, Ayuthaya; held in mid-December.

LUNAR CALENDAR

Many Thai festivals follow the lunar calendar (a complex system based on astrology) and therefore change dates annually relative to the Gregorian calendar. Contact local tourist offices for exact festival dates.

With Kids

There aren't a whole lot of attractions in Bangkok designed to appeal specifically to little ones, but there's no lack of locals willing to provide attention. This means kids are welcome almost anywhere and you'll rarely experience the sort of eye-rolling annoyance often seen in the West.

Handling snakes at Dusit Zoo (p97)

Parks & Playgrounds

Lumphini Park

Central Bangkok's biggest park (p130) is a trusty ally in the cool hours of the morning and afternoon for kite flying (in season – February to April), swan-boat rentals and fish feeding, as well as stretching of the legs and lungs. Nearby, kids can view lethal snakes becoming reluctant altruists at the antivenin-producing Queen Saovabha Memorial Institute (p130), aka the Snake Farm.

Animals

In addition to the animals, Dusit Zoo (p97) has shady grounds, plus a lake in the centre with paddle boats for hire and a small children's playground.

It's not exactly a zoo, but kids can join the novice monks and Thai children at Thewet Pier as they throw food (bought on the pier) to thousands of flapping fish.

Play Centres & Amusement Parks

For kid-specific play centres, consider Funarium (p155), central Bangkok's largest, or the impressive KidZania (p124). Alternatively, Siam Park City (p161), Safari World (p161) or Dream World (p161) are all vast amusement parks found north of the city.

Rainy-Day Fun

If you're visiting during the rainy season (approximately from June to October), the brief-but-daily downpours will inevitably complicate things, so you'll need a few indoor options in your back pocket.

Megamalls

MBK Center (p246) and Siam Paragon (p120) both have bowling alleys to keep the older ones occupied. The latter also has an IMAX theatre and Siam Ocean World (p112), a basement-level aquarium. For those particularly hot days, CentralWorld (p122) has an ice rink. All of these malls and most others in Bangkok have amusement centres with video games, small rides and playgrounds (they're often located near the food courts).

Bangkok Doll Factory & Museum

This somewhat hard-to-find museum (p113) houses a colourful selection of traditional Thai dolls, both new and antique.

Kid-Friendly Museums

Children's Discovery Museum

This recently renovated kid-themed museum (p161) has interactive displays ranging in topic from construction to culture.

Museum of Siam

Although not specifically targeted towards children, the Museum of Siam (p70) has lots of interactive exhibits that will appeal to kids.

Madame Tussauds

Siam Discovery has a branch of this famous wax museum (p122).

Ancient City (Muang Boran)

Outside of town, this open-air museum (p161) recreates Thailand's most famous monuments. They're linked by bicycle paths and were practically built for being climbed on.

Practicalities

Many hotels offer family deals, adjoining rooms and (in midrange and top-end hotels) cots, so enquire specifically. Car seats, on the other hand, are almost impossible to find, and even if you bring your own most taxis have no seatbelt in the back. Taxi drivers generally won't temper their speed because you're travelling with a child, so don't hesitate to tell them to *cháh cháh* ('slow down').

For moving by foot, slings are often more useful than prams, as Bangkok's pavements are infamously uneven.

Infants

Nappies (diapers), international brands of milk formula and other infant requirements are widely available. For something

PLAN YOUR TRIP WITH KIDS

more specific, you'll find Central Chidlom (p123) is as well stocked as anywhere on earth (there's an entire floor devoted to kids). In general, Thai women don't breastfeed in public, though in department stores they'll often find a changing room.

Eating

Dining with children in Thailand, particularly with infants, is a liberating experience, as Thai people are so fond of kids. Take it for granted that your babies will be fawned over, played with – and even carried around – by restaurant waitstaff. Consider this a much-deserved break, not to mention a bit of free cultural exposure.

For the widest choice of food, child-friendly surroundings and noise levels that will drown out even the loudest child, you may find the food courts of Bangkok's many megamalls to be the most comfortable family dining options. High-chairs are rare outside expensive restaurants.

Because much of Thai food is so spicy, there is an entire art devoted to ordering 'safe' dishes for children, and the vast majority of Thai kitchens are more than willing to oblige. Many a child in Thailand has grown up on a diet of little more than *gaang jèut*, a bland, Chinese-influenced soup containing ground pork, soft tofu and a handful of noodles, or variations on *kôw pàt*, fried rice. Other mild options include *kôw man gài*, Hainanese chicken rice, and *jóhk*, rice gruel. For something bland, big hotels usually sell their baked goods for half price after 6pm.

Street food stall

Eating

*Nowhere else is the Thai reverence for food more evident than in Bangkok.
To the outsider, the life of a Bangkokian appears to be a string of meals
and snacks punctuated by the odd stab at work, not the other way around.
If you can adjust your mental clock to this schedule, your visit will be a
delicious one indeed.*

Bà·mèe (wheat-and-egg noodles with barbecued pork)

The Flavours of Bangkok

The people of central Thailand are fond of sweet, savoury, herbal flavours, and many dishes include freshwater fish, pork, coconut milk and palm sugar – common ingredients in the central Thai plains. Because of the region's proximity to the Gulf of Thailand, central Thai eateries, particularly those in Bangkok, also serve a wide variety of seafood. A classic central Thai dish worth seeking out is *yam ʰblah dùk foo*, fried shredded catfish, chilli and peanuts served with a sweet/tart mango dressing.

Another significant influence on the city's kitchens has come from the Bangkok-based royal court, which has been producing sophisticated and refined takes on central Thai dishes for nearly 300 years. Although originally only available within the palace walls, so-called 'royal' Thai dishes such as *máh hór*, an appetiser combining mandarin, orange or pineapple and a sweet/savoury/peppery topping that includes pork, chicken, peanuts, sugar, peppercorns and coriander root, can be found in a few restaurants across the city.

Immigrants from southern China have been influencing Thai cuisine for centuries, and it was most likely Chinese labourers and vendors who introduced the wok and several varieties of noodle dishes to Thailand. They have also influenced Bangkok's cuisine in other ways: beef is not widely eaten in Bangkok due to a Chinese-Buddhist teaching that forbids eating 'large' animals. Perhaps the most common Thai-Chinese dish in Bangkok is *bà·mèe*, wheat-and-egg noodles typically served with slices of barbecued pork.

Muslims are thought to have first visited Thailand during the late 14th century. Along with the Quran, they brought with them a meat- and dried-spice-based cuisine from their homelands in India and the Middle East. Nearly 700 years later, the

NEED TO KNOW

Price Ranges

Prices are for the cost of a meal (a main dish and a drink), as indicated in eating reviews.

$	less than 150B
$$	150B to 350B
$$$	more than 350B

Opening Hours

Restaurants serving Thai food are generally open from 10am to 8pm or 9pm. Foreign-cuisine restaurants tend to keep only lunch and dinner hours (ie 11am to 2pm and 6pm to 10pm).

Bangkok has passed a citywide ordinance banning street vendors from setting up shop on Mondays.

Reservations

If you have a lot of friends in tow or will be attending a formal restaurant (including hotel restaurants), reservations are recommended. Bookings are also recommended for Sunday brunches and dinner cruises. Otherwise, you shouldn't have a problem scoring a table at the vast majority of restaurants in Bangkok.

Tipping

You shouldn't be surprised to learn that tipping is not obligatory in Thailand. Some people leave roughly 10% at any sit-down restaurant where someone fills their glass every time they take a sip; others don't. Most upmarket restaurants will apply a 10% service charge to the bill.

Other Resources

Keep up with the ever-changing food scene in Bangkok by following the Restaurants section of BK (www.bk.asia-city.com) or Bangkok 101 (www.bangkok101).

Goods for sale at Or Tor Kor Market (p162)

DAVID THOMPSON – CHEF & AUTHOR

We sat down with David Thompson, Michelin-starred chef, best-selling author and head chef behind **nahm** (p135), to talk about eating in Bangkok.

What are some of your favourite Bangkok-style dishes? I like some of the dishes in Chinatown, whether it be the oyster place I adore (Nai Mong Hoi Thod, see p106), or whether it be noodles with fish dumplings or with roast duck; *ɓoo pàt pǒng gàrìi* (crab fried with curry powder), when done well, is bloody delicious and accessible. And *pàt tai* – well, you can't really escape from the cliché, however delicious it might be.

Your favourite neighbourhood to eat in? It depends on what I'm looking for. Chinatown, for smoked duck or noodles. But if you want to eat Thai food, you need to go to the markets. Bangkok still has some remnants of the city or villages that it was. For Muslim food you can go down near the Mandarin Oriental, or for Portuguese cakes, you can go to the Church of Santa Cruz (p103).

Your favourite restaurant? It changes all the time. I like Krua Apsorn (p84). It's local. It's good. It's unreformed. It's not too precious. They cook for Thais, they feed Thais and it is Thai.

Your favourite Bangkok market? Of course, Or Tor Kor Market (p162). Even though it's sanitised, its soul has not been expunged from it as it has modernised. There's some great stuff there.

Can you offer some eating advice for a first-time visitor? Just bloody well eat it – don't think about it – just eat it. It's so unlikely you'll get sick, but you will kick yourself for not actually just diving in. Go to places that look busiest, because they're busy for a reason. And a bit of food poisoning, well that adds local colour, doesn't it?

THE FLAVOURS OF BANGKOK

Pongtawat 'Ian' Chalermkittichai is a native of Bangkok, a former host of *Iron Chef: Thailand* and other TV cookery programs, an author, chef/owner of Issaya Siamese Club (p135) and, perhaps most significantly, the inspiration for two flavours of Lay's potato chips.

What are the flavours of Bangkok food? Central Thai food is complex; it doesn't just have one level of flavour. It doesn't rely on ingredients that have very intense flavours. It's rich; curries in the central Thai region have coconut milk. And you can get any ingredients here: we're close to the sea so you can get seafood, and there's also freshwater fish and food from where the sea and rivers meet.

What are some classic Bangkok-style dishes? Curries served over rice; wok-fried dishes and Thai-Chinese; lots of noodles, such as *pàt tai* or boat noodles. Some people still make royal Thai dishes, but these are really rare.

What are some good stalls and restaurants for Bangkok-style food? I like the boat noodles near Pratunam Pier; Jay Fai (p87) does a great crab omelette; Krua Apsorn (p84) does a good green curry with chicken, and a good fried *pàk kràchèt* (water mimosa; a type of vegetable).

What part of Bangkok is a good introduction to local food? Th Thong Lor has some good choices. There's a sticky-rice vendor who's been there for 30 years, a good oyster-omelette vendor, good braised duck noodles, and good restaurants such as Soul Food Mahanakorn (p148).

A good Bangkok market? I like to take people to **Wong Wian Yai Market** (p175). People call it the Lao Market because there's lots of stuff from the countryside, lots of herbs, and things like frogs, and some good seafood. There's also a lot of cooked food, as well as Thai-style snacks and sweets.

impact of this culinary commerce can still be felt in Bangkok. While some Islamic world–influenced dishes such as *roh·đee*, a fried bread similar to the Indian paratha, have changed little, if at all, others such as *gaang mát·sà·màn*, known sometimes as 'Muslim curry', are a unique blend of Thai and Indian/Middle Eastern cooking styles and ingredients.

Bangkok's Dining Scene

During the last couple of decades, Thai food has become internationally famous, and Bangkok is, not surprisingly, the best place in the world to eat it. From roadside stalls to restaurants with Michelin stars in their eyes, the whole spectrum of Thai food is available here. Bangkok is home to its own unique cuisine, and because of its position as a cultural and literal crossroads, just about every regional Thai cuisine is available in the city as well. And more recent immigration to the city has resulted in a contemporary dining scene with options ranging from Korean to French, and touching on just about everything in between. If you're new to Thai cuisine, check out our crash course on Thai food (p225) before digging in.

Where to Eat & Drink

Prepared food is available just about everywhere in Bangkok, and it shouldn't come as a surprise that the locals do much of their eating outside the home. In this regard, as a visitor, you'll fit right in.

Open-air markets and food stalls are among the most popular dining spots for Thais. In the mornings, stalls selling coffee and Chinese-style doughnuts spring up along busy commuter corridors. At lunchtime, diners might grab a plastic chair at yet another stall for a simple stir-fry, or pick up a foam box of noodles to scarf down at the office. In Bangkok's suburbs, night markets often spring up in the middle of town with a cluster of food vendors, metal tables and chairs, and some shopping as an after-dinner mint.

For impromptu drinking and snacking, Bangkok also has an overabundance of modern cafes – including branches of several international chains. Most serve passable takes on Western-style coffee drinks, cakes and sweets.

There are, of course, restaurants *(ráhn ah·hăhn)* in Bangkok. Lunchtime is the right time to point and eat at the *ráhn kôw gaang* (rice and curry shops), which sell a

Food Spotter's Guide

Spanning four distinct regions, influences from China to the Middle East, a multitude of ingredients and a reputation for spice, Thai food can be more than a bit overwhelming. In Bangkok, geography, the influence of the royal palace and the country's main minorities – Chinese and Muslims – have all served to shape the local cuisine. To point you in the direction of the good stuff, we've put together a shortlist of must-eat Bangkok dishes.

1. Kôw man gài
Chicken rice, originally from the Chinese island of Hainan, is now found in just about every corner of Bangkok.

2. Pàt tai
Thin rice noodles fried with egg, tofu and shrimp, and seasoned with fish sauce, tamarind and dried chilli, have emerged as the poster boy for Thai food – and justifiably so.

3. Yam
This family of Thai 'salads' combines meat or seafood with a tart and spicy dressing and fresh herbs.

4. Kà·nŏm bêu·ang
The old-school version of these taco-like snacks comes in two varieties: sweet and savoury.

5. Gaang sôm
Central Thailand's famous 'sour soup' often includes freshwater fish, vegetables and/or herbs, and a thick, tart broth.

6. Đôm yam
The 'sour Thai soup' moniker featured on many English-language menus is a feeble description of this mouth-puckeringly tart and intensely spicy herbal broth.

7. Gaang kěe·o wăhn
Known outside of Thailand as green curry, this intersection of a piquant, herbal spice paste and rich coconut milk is singlehandedly emblematic of Thai cuisine's unique flavours and ingredients.

8. Mèe gròrp
Crispy noodles made the traditional way, with a sweet/sour flavour (a former palace recipe), are a dying breed.

9. Kôw mòk
The Thai version of biriani couples golden rice and tender chicken with a sweet-and-sour dip and a savoury broth.

10. Gŏoay dĕeo reua
Known as boat noodles because they were previously served from canals in central Thailand, these intense pork- or beef-based bowls are among the most full-flavoured of all Thai noodle dishes.

AUSTIN BUSH / GETTY IMAGES ©

AUSTIN BUSH / GETTY IMAGES ©

COFFEE LOVER / GETTY IMAGES ©

AUSTIN BUSH / GETTY IMAGES ©

ALEXANDRALAW1977 / GETTY IMAGES ©

AUSTIN BUSH / GETTY IMAGES ©

AUSTIN BUSH / GETTY IMAGES ©

THAI NOODLES 101

In Thailand, noodles are ubiquitous, cheap and tasty. But they're also extremely varied and somewhat complicated to order. So with this in mind, we've provided a crash course in Thai noodles.

The Noodles

You'll find four main kinds of noodle in Thailand. When ordering, it's generally necessary to specify which noodle you want. It's also possible to order some types of noodle dishes minus the noodles, with a bowl of rice instead; this is called *gǎo lǎo*.

Bà·mèe Made from wheat flour and egg, this noodle is yellowish in colour and sold only in fresh bundles.

Kà·nǒm jeen This noodle is produced by pushing a rice-based dough through a sieve into boiling water, much the way some types of Italian pasta are made.

Sên gǒo·ay đěe·o The most common type of noodle in Thailand is made from rice flour mixed with water to form a paste, which is steamed to form wide, flat sheets, then sliced into various widths.

Wún·sên An almost clear noodle made from mung-bean starch and water, this noodle features occasionally in noodle soups, but is usually the central ingredient in *yam wún sên*, a hot and tangy salad made with lime juice, *prík kêe nǒo* (tiny chillies), shrimp, ground pork and seasoning.

The Dishes

Some Thai noodle dishes can be ordered *hâang*, meaning 'dry', in which the noodles are served with just enough broth to keep them moist.

Bà·mèe These eponymous Chinese-style noodles are typically served with barbecued pork slices, greens and, if you like, wontons.

Gǒo·ay jáp Rice noodles and pork offal served in a fragrant, peppery broth; a dish popular among the Thai-Chinese.

Gǒo·ay đěe·o kaang A Thai-Muslim dish of rice noodles served with a curry broth, often including garnishes such as peanuts and hard-boiled egg.

Gǒo·ay đěe·o lôok chín This dish combines rice noodles in a generally clear broth with pork- or fish-based (or less commonly, beef or chicken) balls; one of the most common types of noodles across the country.

Gǒo·ay đěe·o reu·a Known as boat noodles because they were previously served from the canals of central Thailand, these intense pork- or beef-based bowls are among the most full-flavoured of noodle dishes.

Kà·nǒm jeen This dish, named after its noodle, combines thin rice threads and a typically mild, curry-like broth, served with a self-selection of fresh and pickled vegetables and herbs.

Kôw soy Associated with northern Thailand is this dish that combines wheat-and-egg noodles with a fragrant, rich, curry-based broth.

Yen đah foh A crimson broth with meat balls, blood cubes and crispy greens, this dish is probably the most intimidating but popular noodle dish in Bangkok.

The Seasoning

Thai noodle dishes are often served slightly underseasoned. In these cases, you season your own bowl, typically using some or all of four condiments: *prík nám sôm* (sliced mild chillies in vinegar), *nám ɓlah* (fish sauce), *prík ɓòn* (dried red chilli, flaked or ground to a near powder) and *nám·đahn* (plain white sugar). These condiments offer three ways to make the soup hotter – hot and sour, hot and salty, and just plain hot – and one to make it sweet.

The typical eater will add a teaspoonful of each one of these to the noodle soup, except for the sugar, which in sweet-tooth Bangkok usually rates a full tablespoon. Until you're used to these strong seasonings, we recommend adding them a small bit at a time, tasting the soup along the way to make sure you don't go overboard.

selection of pre-made dishes. The more generic *ráhn ah·hǎhn đahm sàng* (made-to-order restaurants) can often be recognised by a display of raw ingredients – Chinese kale, tomatoes, chopped pork, fresh or dried fish, noodles, eggplant, spring onions – and offer a standard repertoire of Thai and Chinese-Thai dishes. As the name implies, the cooks will attempt to prepare any dish you can name – a potentially difficult operation if you can't speak Thai.

The most common type of restaurant in Bangkok – and arguably the most delicious – is the open-fronted shophouse restaurant. The cooks at these places have most likely been serving the same dish, or a limited repertoire of dishes, for several decades, and really know what they're doing. The food may cost slightly more than on the street, but the setting is usually more comfortable and hygienic, not to mention the fact that you're eating a piece of history. While such restaurants rarely have English-language menus, you can usually point to a picture or dish. If that fails, turn to the language chapter (p248) and practise your Thai.

Bangkok is of course also home to dozens of upmarket restaurants. For the most part, those serving Thai cuisine have adjusted their recipes to suit foreign palates – for more authentic food you're much better off eating at the cheaper shophouse-style restaurants. On the other hand, upmarket and hotel restaurants are probably the best places in Bangkok for authentic Western-style food. If these are outside your price range, you'll be happy to know that there's also a huge spread of midrange foreign restaurants in today's Bangkok; many of them are quite good.

Cooking Courses

Bangkok has a number of great cooking courses that are geared towards visitors wanting to recreate the cuisine at home. For details on what to expect in a typical course, see p52. Recommended cookery schools are listed on p53.

Food Markets

If you take pleasure in seeing food in its raw form, Bangkok is home to dozens of traditional-style wet markets, ranging from the grungy to the flashy; they can also be a good place to eat.

Eating by Neighbourhood

→ **Banglamphu** Classic old-school Bangkok-style eateries. (p84)

→ **Thewet & Dusit** Breezy, riverfront dining. (p97)

→ **Chinatown** Thai-Chinese street eats. (p105)

→ **Siam Square, Pratunam, Phloen Chit & Ratchathewi** Mall-based food courts and domestic and international franchises. (p114)

→ **Riverside, Silom & Lumphini** The full spectrum of Thai food, from cut-rate lunchtime food courts to decadent hotel restaurants. (p130)

→ **Sukhumvit** This seemingly never-ending street has an outpost of just about every global cuisine. (p144)

→ **Greater Bangkok** Head to the 'burbs for vibrant markets and restaurants serving regional Thai cuisine. (p163)

PLAN YOUR TRIP EATING

JOHN BORTHWICK / GETTY IMAGES ©

Amita Thai Cooking Class (p77)

Lonely Planet's Top Choices

nahm (p135) Upmarket Thai that's worth every baht.

Eat Me (p132) The best of contemporary, eclectic dining.

Krua Apsorn (p84) Full-flavoured central Thai fare in a homely setting.

Jay Fai (p87) Decades-old shophouse serving flash-fried masterpieces.

MBK Food Island (p115) Cheap, cheerful and tasty: Bangkok's best food court.

Best by Budget

$

Nai Mong Hoi Thod (p106) Long-standing hole-in-the-wall serving delicious fried oysters and mussels.

Thip Samai (p84) The city's most legendary venue for *pàt tai*.

Nuer Koo (p114) Sublime beef noodles at this, the street stall in a mall.

$$

Likhit Kai Yang (p97) Generations of Thai boxing fans can't be wrong about this temple to northeastern Thai.

Kai Thort Jay Kee (p134) Decadent fried chicken with a dedicated fan base.

Samsara (p106) Playful, tasty Thai fusion at the edge of Mae Nam Chao Phraya.

$$$

Bo.lan (p146) Ancient Thai recipes, prepared meticulously.

Little Beast (p146) Flavourful, fun, American-influenced fine dining.

Benjarong (p133) Fine-dining Thai with ingenious international twists.

Best for Bangkok-Style Food

Khun Yah Cuisine (p105) Travel back to the flavours of Bangkok's past.

Sam-Ang Kulap (p117) Go-to place for the city's famous 'boat noodles'.

Pa Aew (p75) Simple street stall touting Bangkok's sophisticated tastes.

Best Street Stalls

Nay Hong (p105) A delicious introduction to Chinatown-style street eats – if you can find it.

Thanon Phadungdao Seafood Stalls (p106) These stalls are so 'street' you risk getting bumped by a car.

Foontalop (p159) Open-air dining in the middle of Chatuchak Weekend Market.

Best for Regional Thai Cuisine

Dao Tai (p75) The best of a knot of simple restaurants specialising in southern Thai cuisine.

Khua Kling Pak Sod (p163) Full-flavoured southern Thai dishes in a semi-formal setting.

Jay So (p131) Unfettered northeastern Thai served in a streetside shack.

Best Foreign-Cuisine Restaurants

Jidori-Ya Kenzou (p148) Chicken skewers grilled over coals with a precision that could only be Japanese.

Din Tai Fung (p114) Lauded Taiwanese chain that is the place to go for *xiao long bao*, Chinese 'soup' dumplings.

Gokfayuen (p144) An authentic Hong Kong noodle shop – in Bangkok.

Best for Dessert

Puritan (p163) Excellent cakes in a whimsical setting.

Old Siam Plaza (p106) A candy-land of traditional Thai sweets.

Ann's Sweet (p86) Shophouse cafe that does some of the best Western-style desserts in town.

Best Food Markets

Or Tor Kor Market (p162) The Saks Fifth Avenue of Bangkok markets.

Nonthaburi Market (p161) Travel upcountry – and back in time – at this provincial market.

Talat Mai (p102) Hectic alleyway excelling in Chinese edibles.

Sky Bar (p136)

Drinking & Nightlife

Shame on you if you think Bangkok's only nightlife options include the word 'go-go'. As in any big international city, the drinking and partying scene in Bangkok ranges from trashy to classy, and touches on just about everything in between.

The Scene

Bangkok is a party animal – even when on a tight leash. Way back in 2001, the Thaksin administration started enforcing closing times and curtailing other excesses that had previously made the city's nightlife famous. Since his 2006 ousting, the laws had been increasingly circumvented or inconsistently enforced. Yet post the 2014 coup, there are indications that Bangkok is seeing something of a return to 2001-era strictly enforced operating hours and zoning laws.

Bars

Bangkok's watering holes cover the spectrum from English-style pubs where you can comfortably sit with a pint and the paper to chic dens where the fair and beautiful go to be seen, not imbibe. Perhaps most famously, Bangkok is also one of the few big cities in the world where nobody seems to mind if you slap a bar on top of a skyscraper (although it's worth noting that most rooftop bars enforce a dress code – no shorts or sandals). But many visitors associate Bangkok with the

NEED TO KNOW

Opening Hours

Officially, Bangkok's bars and clubs are supposed to close by midnight, a rule that's been enforced lately. A complicated zoning system sees venues in designated 'entertainment areas', including RCA/Royal City Ave, Th Silom and parts of Th Sukhumvit, open until 1am or 2am, but even these 'later' licences are subject to police whimsy.

Smoking

Smoking has been outlawed at all indoor (and some quasi-outdoor) entertainment places since 2008.

Dress Code

Most rooftop bars enforce a dress code – no shorts or sandals. This is also the case with many of Bangkok's dance clubs.

ID

The drinking age in Thailand is 20, although it's only usually dance clubs that ask for ID.

Wine Whinge

Imported wine is subject to a litany of taxes, making Thailand among the most expensive places in the world to drink wine. A bottle typically costs 400% of its price back home, up to 600% in upmarket restaurants. Even domestic wines are subject to many of the same taxes, making them only marginally cheaper.

Other Resources

To keep crowds interested, clubs host weekly theme parties and visiting DJs that ebb and flow in popularity. To find out what's on, check out Dudesweet (www.dudesweet.org) and Paradise Bangkok (www.facebook.com/paradisebangkok), organisers of hugely popular monthly parties, or local listings such as BK (www.bk.asia-city.com), Bangkok 101 (www.bangkok101.com), the *Bangkok Post's* Friday supplement, *Guru*, or Siam2nite (www.siam2nite.com).

kind of bars that don't have an address – found just about everywhere in the city. Think streetside seating, plastic chairs, car exhaust, and tasty dishes absent-mindedly nibbled between toasts.

Bangkok bars don't have cover charges, but they do generally enforce closing time at midnight, and sometimes earlier if they suspect trouble from the cops.

If you want to drink your way through Bangkok's best nightlife zone, take our Banglamphu pub crawl (p88).

Nightclubs

Bangkok's club scene is a fickle beast, and venues that were pulling in thousands a night just last year might be a vague memory today. Clubs here tend to heave on certain nights – Fridays and Saturdays, during a visit from a foreign DJ, or for a night dedicated to the music flavour of the month – then hibernate every other night.

What used to be a rotating cast of hot spots has slowed to a few standards on the sois off Th Sukhumvit, Th Silom, Th Ratchadaphisek and RCA/Royal City Ave – the city's designated 'entertainment zones' – which qualify for the 2am closing time (though at the time of research, some of the bigger places were stretching this to 3am). Most joints don't begin filling up until midnight. Cover charges can run as high as 600B and usually include a drink or two. At the bigger places, you'll need ID to prove you're legal (20 years old); they'll card even the grey-haired.

If you find 2am too early to call it a night, don't worry – Thais have found curiously creative methods of flouting closing times. Speakeasies have sprung up all over the city, so follow the crowds – few people will actually be heading home. Some places just remove the tables and let people drink on the floor (somehow this is an exemption), while other places serve beer in teapots.

For live music, traditional performances and Bangkok's infamous 'adult' entertainment, see our Entertainment chapter (p41).

Drinks

Bangkok is renowned for its food and nightlife, but markedly less so for its beverages. Yet drinks are the glue that fuse these elements, and without them, that cabaret show would be markedly less entertaining.

BEER

People in Bangkok generally drink a lot. And a lot of the time, that means beer. Yet until recently, there was very little variety in the domestic beer scene.

Advertised with such slogans as *'bràa·têht row, bee·a row'* ('our land, our beer'), the Singha label is considered the quintessen-

To the surprise of many foreigners, most Thais drink their beer with ice. Before you rule out this supposed blasphemy, there are a few reasons why the Thais actually prefer beer on the rocks. Thailand's domestic beer does not possess the most sophisticated bouquet in the world and is best drunk as cold as possible. The weather in Thailand is often extremely hot, so it makes sense to maintain your beer at maximum chill. And lastly, domestic brews are generally quite high in alcohol and the ice helps to dilute this, preventing dehydration and a Beer Chang hangover the next day. Taking these theories to the extreme, some places serve *bee·a wún,* or 'jelly beer' – beer that has been semi-frozen until it reaches a deliciously slushy and refreshing consistency.

SPIRITS

Thai rice whisky has a sharp, sweet taste – not unlike rum – with an alcohol content of 35%. The most famous brand for many years was Mekong (pronounced *mâa kŏng*), but today there are domestic brands meant to appeal to the can't-afford-Johnnie-Walker-yet set, including Blue Eagle, 100 Pipers and Spey Royal, each with a 40% alcohol content. Also popular is Sang Som, a domestic rum. In Thailand, booze typically comes in 750mL bottles called *glom,* or in 375mL flask-shaped bottles called *baan.*

Thais normally buy whisky by the bottle and drink it with ice, plenty of soda water and a splash of Coke. If you don't finish your bottle, simply tell your waiter, who will write your name and the date on the bottle and keep it for your next visit.

Moon Bar (p136)

tial Thai beer by *fa·ràng* (Westerners) and locals alike. Pronounced *sĭng* and boasting 6% alcohol, this pilsner claims about half the domestic market. Singha's biggest rival, Beer Chang, pumps the alcohol content up to 7%. Boon Rawd (the maker of Singha) responded with its own cheaper brand, Leo. Sporting a black-and-red leopard label, Leo costs only slightly more than Beer Chang but is similarly high in alcohol. Other Thai-brewed beers, all at the lower end of the price spectrum, include Cheers and Beer Thai. Also popular are foreign brands brewed under licence in Thailand such as Asahi, Heineken, Kirin and San Miguel. The very first trickle of domestic microbrews was appearing at the time of research, an indication that more variation in Thai beer brands is likely in the coming years.

Conversely, the selection of imported microbrews is astounding, with bottled and draught beers and ciders from across the world available in Bangkok. The city is now home to several pubs that specialise in imported beers, so if you're missing your local brew, it's entirely possible that you will be able to find it in Bangkok.

Drinking & Nightlife by Neighbourhood

➡ **Ko Ratanakosin & Thonburi** Romantic riverside drinking. (p77)

➡ **Banglamphu** Rowdy Th Khao San is one of the city's best areas for a night out. (p87)

➡ **Siam Square, Pratunam, Phloen Chit & Ratchathewi** Bangkok's most central zone is home to a scant handful of bars. (p117)

➡ **Riverside, Silom & Lumphini** Bangkok's gaybourhood has fun bars and dance clubs for all comers. (p135)

➡ **Sukhumvit** Home to Bangkok's most sophisticated bars and clubs. (p149)

➡ **Greater Bangkok** Suburban RCA/Royal City Ave is the city's best clubbing strip; good live-music venues dot other regions. (p164)

Lonely Planet's Top Choices

WTF (p149) A sophisticated yet friendly local boozer.

Hippie de Bar (p87) Fun, meandering, retro-themed bar in the middle of Th Khao San.

Moon Bar (p136) Casual ambience and stunning views make this our fave of Bangkok's original rooftop bars.

DJ Station (p138) One of the most legendary gay dance clubs in Bangkok – and Asia.

Route 66 (p165) Long-standing megaclub that still manages to pull thousands.

Bangkok's Best Nightclubs

DJ Station (p138) Gay clubs in Bangkok don't get better than this.

Route 66 (p165) Join the throngs at this long-standing megaclub.

Grease (p151) Party complex that at the time of research was wearing the crown as the king of Bangkok's nightclubs.

The Club (p87) Dance with a virtual UN of partiers at this Th Khao San–based disco.

Nung-Len (p151) For a loud, lushy, Thai-style night out on the town.

Best Cocktails

Sugar Ray (p149) Some of Bangkok's wackiest – and tastiest – cocktails.

J. Boroski Mixology (p150) Leave it to the creative barkeeps here to concoct your drink on the spot.

Tep Bar (p107) Cocktails with unique Thai touches.

Best Bars with Food

Tuba (p149) Full-flavoured bar snacks that span Isan (north-eastern Thailand) to Italy.

Madame Musur (p87) Singha almost tastes good when coupled with the northern-Thai-style dishes here.

Badmotel (p149) Quirky twists on Thai and international dishes.

Best Rooftop Bars

Moon Bar (p136) One of the originals that remains among Bangkok's best.

River Vibe (p107) Budget-guesthouse prices, million-dollar views.

Cloud 47 (p136) Hyper-urban scenery reminiscent of *Blade Runner*.

Roof (p77) Breathtaking views of Wat Arun from this riverside rooftopper.

Park Society (p136) Gaze down at Lumphini Park from your 29th floor perch.

Sky Bar (p136) Go on, order a 'hangovertini'.

Best Late-Night Bars & Clubs

Wong's Place (p137) Open from midnight until the last punter crawls out.

The Bank (p87) Puff on a *shisha* or dance into the wee hours on Th Khao San.

Narz (p152) With three vast zones to keep clubbers raving 'til dawn.

Levels (p152) When most Soi 11 bars begin to close, this club heats up.

Best Bars for Chilling Out

Hippie de Bar (p87) Kick back with locals at this retro Th Khao San spot.

Rolling Bar (p89) Escape the hubbub at this quiet canalside boozer.

Walden (p150) Known for its Japanese-style 'highballs' and US craft beers.

Tuba (p149) Quirky local watering hole with moreish chicken wings to boot.

Shades of Retro (p151) Vintage vibe, cool local tunes and free popcorn.

LGBT Bangkok

Bangkok has a notoriously pink vibe to it, from kinky male-underwear shops mushrooming on street corners to lesbian-only get-togethers. As a homosexual you could eat, shop and play here for days without ever leaving the comfort of gay-friendly venues. Unlike elsewhere in Southeast Asia, homosexuality is not criminalised in Thailand and the general attitude remains extremely laissez-faire.

Gay Men

Gay people are out and ubiquitous in Bangkok. Yet gay male (and lesbian) couples, like straight couples, do not show affection in public, unless they are purposefully flouting social mores.

Lesbians

Although it would be a stretch to claim that Bangkok's lesbian scene is as vibrant as its male gay scene, lesbians have become more visible in recent years. It's worth noting that, perhaps because Thailand is still a relatively conservative place, lesbians in Bangkok generally adhere to rather strict gender roles. Overtly 'butch' lesbians, called *tom* (from 'tomboy'), typically have short hair, bind their breasts and wear men's clothing. Femme lesbians refer to themselves as *dêe* (from 'lady'). Visiting lesbians who don't fit into one of these categories may be met with confusion.

Transgender People

Bangkok is famous for its open and visible transgender population – known locally as *gà·teu·i* (also spelt *kàthoey*). Some are cross-dressers, while others have had sex reassignment surgery – Thailand is one of the leading countries for this procedure. Foreigners seem to be especially fascinated by Thai transwomen as they often appear very feminine, and *gà·teu·i* cabarets aimed at tourists are popular. For more information, see our interview with a transgender activist on p113.

Issues

Beneath the party vibe, serious issues remain for Bangkok's vast and visible population of LGBT people. After the government's initial success slowing the progression of HIV among the general population, there are new signs of an epidemic among young gay men. Transgender people are often treated as outcasts, same-sex couples enjoy no legal rights and lesbians have the added burden of negotiating a patriarchal society. In short, Bangkok's LGBT community may party as they please, sleep with whomever they want or even change their sex, but they do so without the protection, respect and rights enjoyed by heterosexuals – particularly heterosexual men.

LGBT by Neighbourhood

➡ **Riverside, Silom & Lumphini** Lower Th Silom is Bangkok's unofficial gaybourhood. (p138)

➡ **Greater Bangkok** RCA/Royal City Ave and Th Ratchadaphisek are home to suburban Bangkok's gay scenes. (p164)

NEED TO KNOW

Websites

➜ Bangkok Lesbian (www.bangkoklesbian. com) is the city's premier website for ladies who love ladies.

➜ BK (www.bk.asia-city. com) and Siam2nite (www.siam2nite.com) are good sources for LGBT events in Bangkok.

➜ Trasher (www.face book.com/trasher bangkok) are noted pop parodists; they also organise gay-friendly parties, so check the website to see if one's on when you're in town.

Pride

Bangkok's former pride festival appears to be on permanent hiatus, but a good alternative is the annual party, coinciding with Songkran, put on by gCircuit (www.gcircuit.com).

Lonely Planet's Top Choices

DJ Station (p138) One of the most iconic gay nightclubs in Asia.

Telephone Pub (p138) Long-standing bar right in the middle of Bangkok's pinkest zone.

Best Gay Nightclubs

DJ Station (p138) Bangkok's most popular gay club for good reason.

G Bangkok (p138) Where to go after all the other Silom bars have closed.

Castro (p165) The only gay destination on the nightlife strip known as RCA.

Fake Club The Next Gen (p164) Suburban megaclub in handsome new digs.

Best LGBT Bars

Telephone Pub (p138) An old favourite in Bangkok's pinkest zone.

Balcony (p138) Streetside watering hole for local and visiting gays.

Bearbie (p138) The entirety of Bangkok's bear scene.

Maggie Choo's (p136) Sunday is gay day at this otherwise hetero boozer.

Best Cabaret & Drag Shows

Playhouse Magical Cabaret (p118) Unapologetically camp drag shows.

Mambo Cabaret (p165) Long-standing Bangkok cabaret legend.

Calypso Bangkok (p137) The cabaret show in Asiatique market.

AUSTIN BUSH / GETTY IMAGES ©

Telephone Pub (p138)

Saxophone Pub & Restaurant (p118)

 # Entertainment

Although Bangkok often seems to cater to the inner philistine in all of us, the city is home to a diverse but low-key art scene. Add to this dance performances, live music, some of the world's best-value cinemas and, yes, the infamous go-go bars, and you have a city whose entertainment scene spans from – in local parlance – lo-so (low society) to hi-so (high society).

Live Music

As Thailand's media capital, Bangkok is the centre of the Thai music industry, packaging and selling pop, crooners, *lôok tûng* (Thai-style country music) and the recent phenomenon of indie bands. Music is a part of almost every Thai social gathering; the matriarchs and patriarchs like dinner with an easy-listening soundtrack – typically a Filipino band and a synthesiser. Patrons pass their request (on a napkin) up to the stage. An indigenous rock style, *pleng pêu·a chee·wít* ('songs for life'), makes appearances at a dying breed of country-and-western bars decorated with buffalo horns and pictures of Native Americans. Several dedicated bars throughout the city feature blues and rock bands, but are relatively scant on live indie-scene performances. Up-and-coming garage bands occasionally pop up at free concerts where the kids hang out, often at Siam Sq. For more subdued tastes, Bangkok also attracts grade-A jazz musicians to several hotel bars. See p221 for more on the ins and outs of the Thai music scene.

NEED TO KNOW

Opening Hours

Live-music venues generally close by 1am. A complicated zoning system sees venues open until 2am in designated 'entertainment areas', including RCA/Royal City Ave, Th Silom and parts of Th Sukhumvit, but even these 'later' licences are subject to police whimsy.

Bars in the various red-light districts are open until 2am.

Reservations

Reservations are recommended for prominent theatre events. Tickets can often be purchased through Thai Ticket Major (www.thaiticketmajor.com).

Bars and clubs with live music are allowed to stay open until 1am, but this is subject to police discretion. The drinking age is 20 years old.

Traditional Theatre & Dance

The stage in Thailand typically hosts a kŏhn performance, one of the six traditional dramatic forms. Acted only by men, kŏhn drama is based upon stories of the Ramakian, Thailand's version of India's epic Ramayana, and was traditionally staged only for royal audiences.

The less formal lá-kon dances, of which there are many dying subgenres, usually involve costumed dancers (of both sexes) performing elements of the Ramakian and traditional folk tales. If you hear the din of drums and percussion from a temple or shrine, follow the sound to see traditional lá-kon gâa bon (shrine dancing). At Lak Meuang (p73) and the Erawan Shrine (p111), worshippers commission costumed troupes to perform dance movements that are similar to classical lá-kon, but not as refined.

Another option for viewing Thai classical dance is at a dinner theatre. Most dinner theatres in Bangkok are heavily promoted through hotels to an ever-changing clientele, so standards are poor to fair.

See p223 for further information about traditional Thai dance.

Gà·teu·i Cabaret

Over the last decade, watching Thai transpeople (gà·teu·i; also spelt kàthoey) perform choreographed stage shows featuring Broadway high kicks and lip-synched pop tunes has become a 'must-do' fixture on the Bangkok tourist circuit. Popular venues include Calypso Bangkok (p137), Mambo Cabaret (p165) and Playhouse Theater Cabaret (p118).

Cinemas

Hollywood movies are released in Bangkok's theatres in a relatively timely fashion. But as home-grown cinema grows bigger, more and more Thai films, often subtitled in English, fill the roster. Foreign films are sometimes altered by Thailand's film censors before distribution; this usually involves obscuring nude sequences.

The shopping-centre cinemas have plush VIP options. Despite the heat and humidity on the streets, keep in mind that Bangkok's movie theatres pump in air-conditioning with such vigour that taking a jumper is an absolute necessity. Ticket prices range from 120B to 220B for regular seats, and more than 1000B for VIP seats.

Bangkok also hosts a handful of small annual film festivals, including the World Film Festival of Bangkok (www.worldfilm bkk.com) in November.

See p223 for more on Thai film.

Moo·ay tai (Thai Boxing)

Quintessentially Thai, almost anything goes in moo·ay tai (also spelt muay thai), the martial art more commonly known elsewhere as Thai boxing or kickboxing. If you don't mind the violence, a Thai-boxing match is well worth attending for the pure spectacle: the wild musical accompaniment, the ceremonial beginning of each match and the frenzied betting.

The best of the best fight at Bangkok's two boxing stadiums. Built on royal land at the end of WWII, the Art Deco–style Ratchadamnoen Stadium (p98) is the original and has a relatively formal atmosphere. The other main stage, Lumpinee Boxing Stadium (p164), has recently moved from its eponymous 'hood to a new modern home north of Bangkok.

Admission fees vary according to seating. Ringside seats (from 2000B) are the most expensive and will be filled with subdued VIPs; tourists usually opt for the 2nd-class seats (from 1500B); diehard *moo·ay tai* fans bet and cheer from 3rd class (1000B). If you're thinking these prices sound a bit steep for your average fight fan (taxi drivers are big fans and they make about 600B a day), then you're right – foreigners pay several times what the Thais do. We recommend the 2nd- or 3rd-class seats. The 2nd-class area is filled with numbers-runners who take bets from fans in rowdy 3rd class, which is fenced off from the rest of the stadium. Akin to a stock-exchange pit, hand signals communicate bets, and odds fly between the areas. Most fans in 3rd class follow the match (or their bets) too closely to sit down, and we've seen stress levels rise to near-boiling point. It's all very entertaining.

Most programs have eight to 10 fights of five rounds each. English-speaking 'staff' outside the stadium, who practically tackle you upon arrival, will hand you a fight roster and steer you to the foreigners' ticket windows; they can also be helpful in telling you which fights are the best match-ups (some say that welterweights, between 61.2kg and 66.7kg, are the best). To avoid supporting scalpers, purchase your tickets from the ticket window, not from a person outside the stadium.

See the boxed text on p96 for more on the history of *moo·ay tai*; for the inside scoop on the fighters, and upcoming programs, see www.muaythai2000.com.

Go-Go Bars

Although technically illegal, prostitution is fully 'out' in Bangkok, and the influence of organised crime and lucrative kickbacks mean that it will be a long while before the existing laws are ever enforced. Yet despite the image presented by much of the West-ern media, the underlying atmosphere of Bangkok's red-light districts is not one of illicitness and exploitation (although these do inevitably exist), but rather an aura of tackiness and boredom.

Patpong (p138) earned notoriety during the 1980s for its wild sex shows, involving everything from ping-pong balls and razors to midgets on motorbikes. Today it is more of a circus for curious spectators than sexual deviants. Soi Cowboy (p153) and Nana Entertainment Plaza (p153) are the real scenes of sex for hire. Not all of the sex business is geared towards Westerners: Th Thaniya, off Th Silom, is filled with massage parlours for Japanese expats and visitors, while the immense massage parlours outside of central Bangkok service almost exclusively Thai customers.

See the Sex Industry in Thailand chapter (p231) for a discussion of the issues related to prostitution.

Entertainment by Neighbourhood

➡ **Ko Ratanakosin & Thonburi** The area to visit for traditional Thai performances, both scheduled and impromptu. (p77)

➡ **Banglamphu** Home to some of the city's best live-music venues. (p89)

➡ **Thewet & Dusit** This is where you'll find the city's oldest *moo·ay tai* stadium. (p98)

➡ **Siam Square, Pratunam, Phloen Chit & Ratchathewi** Bangkok's best cinemas. (p118)

➡ **Riverside, Silom & Lumphini** Traditional Thai dinner theatre. (p137)

➡ **Sukhumvit** Offers a bit of everything, from live jazz to go-go. (p152)

➡ **Greater Bangkok** Bangkok's 'burbs are where you'll find some of the city's best live-music venues and its other premier *moo·ay tai* stadium. (p164)

Lonely Planet's Top Choices

Brick Bar (p89) Live-music den that's famous among locals, for whom dancing on the tables in practically obligatory.

Ratchadamnoen Stadium (p98) The country's premier venue for Thai boxing.

Living Room (p152) As the name implies, live jazz in a comfortable setting.

Parking Toys (p164) Far from the city centre is this eclectic shed, one of Bangkok's best venues for live music.

Best for Thai-Style Live Music

Lam Sing (p153) Over-the-top glam cave for Thai-style country music.

Tawandang German Brewery (p135) Giant beer hall with even bigger stage shows.

Raintree (p119) Earthy, suburban pub that's a bastion of contemporary Thai folk music.

Best for Western-Style Live Music

Ad Here the 13th (p89) Tiny blues bar in the backpacker district.

Titanium (p153) Nightly performances by Unicorn, an all-girl band that's bound to get you bouncing.

Saxophone Pub & Restaurant (p118) One of Bangkok's most legendary live-music venues.

Best for Traditional Performance

National Theatre (p77) State-sanctioned destination for traditional Thai performance.

Sala Chalermkrung (p107) Traditional Thai drama with contemporary twists.

Sala Rim Naam (p138) Classy venue for Thai-performance-themed dinner theatre.

Best Cinemas

Paragon Cineplex (p118) The epitome of state-of-the-art cinema.

House (p165) The city's only real art-house theatre.

Scala (p118) Fantastical old-school cinema.

Best for Moo·ay Tai (Thai Boxing)

Ratchadamnoen Stadium (p98) Bangkok's oldest and most venerable venue for *moo·ay tai* matches.

Lumpinee Boxing Stadium (p164) The city's other main boxing stage is now in new digs north of town.

Shopping

Prime your credit card and shine your baht, as shopping is serious business in Bangkok. Hardly a street corner in this city is free from a vendor, hawker or impromptu stall, and it doesn't stop there: Bangkok is also home to one of the world's largest outdoor markets, not to mention some of Southeast Asia's largest malls.

Markets & Malls

Although the tourist brochures tend to tout the upmarket malls, Bangkok still lags slightly behind Singapore and Hong Kong in this arena, and the open-air markets are where the best deals and most original items are to be found.

Antiques

Real Thai antiques are rare and costly and reserved primarily for serious collectors. Everything else is designed to look old and most shopkeepers are happy to admit it. Reputable antique dealers will issue an authentication certificate. Contact the **Office of the National Museum** (Map p265; ☑02 224 1370, 02 224 7493; National Museum, 4 Th Na Phra That; ⊙9am-4pm Tue-Fri; ⊠Chang Pier, Maharaj Pier, Phra Chan Tai Pier) to obtain the required licence for exporting religious images and fragments, either antique or reproductions.

It's worth noting that trading in bona fide antiquities might not be either ethical or, in your country, legal. For more on this issue and the campaign to preserve Southeast Asia's cultural heritage, see Heritage Watch (www.heritagewatchinternational.org).

Gems & Jewellery

Countless tourists are sucked into the prolific and well-rehearsed gem scam, in which they are taken to a store by a helpful stranger and tricked into buying bulk gems that can supposedly be resold in their home country for 100% profit. The expert con artists (part of a well-organised cartel) seem trustworthy and convince tourists that they need a citizen of the country to circumvent tricky customs regulations. Unsurprisingly, the gem world doesn't work like that, and what most tourists end up with are worthless pieces of glass. By the time you sort all this out, the store has closed and changed names, and the police can do little to help.

Tailor-Made Clothes

Many tourists arrive in Bangkok with the notion of getting clothes custom-tailored at a bargain price. While this is possible, there are a few things to be aware of. Prices are almost always lower than what you'd pay at home, but common scams such as commission-hungry túk-túk (pronounced *dúk dúk*) drivers, shoddy workmanship and inferior fabrics make bespoke tailoring in Bangkok a potentially disappointing investment.

The golden rule of custom tailoring is that you get what you pay for. If you sign up for a suit, two pants, two shirts and a tie, with a silk sarong thrown in, for just US$199 (a very popular offer in Bangkok), chances are it will look and fit like a sub-US$200 wardrobe. Although an offer may seem great on the surface, the price may fluctuate significantly depending on the fabric you choose. Supplying your own fabric won't necessarily reduce the price by much, but it should ensure you get exactly the look you're after.

Have a good idea of what you want before walking into a shop. If it's a suit you're after, should it be single- or double-breasted? How

NEED TO KNOW

Opening Hours

Most family-run shops are open from 10am to 7pm daily. Malls are open from approximately 10am to 10pm. Street markets are either daytime (from 9am to 5pm) or night-time (from 7pm to midnight). Note that city ordinance forbids streetside vendors from cluttering the pavements on Mondays, but they are present every other day.

Scams

Thais are generally so friendly and laid-back that some visitors are lulled into a false sense of security, forgetting that Bangkok is a big city with the usual untrustworthy characters. While your personal safety is rarely at risk in Thailand, you may be unwittingly charmed out of the contents of your wallet or fall prey to a scam.

Bargaining

At Bangkok's markets and at a handful of its malls, you'll have to bargain for most, if not all, items. In general, if you see a price tag, it means that the price is fixed and bargaining isn't an option.

Counterfeits

Bangkok is ground zero for the production and sale of counterfeit goods. Although they may seem cheap, keep in mind that counterfeit goods are almost always shoddy.

Shopping Guide

Bangkok's intense urban tangle sometimes makes orientation a challenge, and it can be difficult to find some shops and markets. Nancy Chandler's Map of Bangkok (www.nancychandler.net) tracks all sorts of small, out-of-the-way shopping venues and markets, and dissects the innards of the Chatuchak Weekend Market (p158). The colourful map is sold in bookshops throughout the city.

many buttons? What style of trousers? Of course, if you have no idea, the tailor will be more than happy to advise. Alternatively, bring a favourite garment from home and have it copied.

Set aside a week to get clothes tailored. Shirts and trousers can often be turned around in 48 hours or less with only one fitting, but no matter what a tailor may tell you, it takes at least one and often more than two fittings to create a good suit. Most reliable tailors will ask for two to five sittings. Any tailor who can sew your order in less than 24 hours should be treated with caution.

The strip of Th Sukhumvit between BTS stops at Nana and Asok is home to tonnes of tailors – both reputable and otherwise. Some of the former:

Raja's Fashions (Map p282; ☎02 253 8379; www.rajasfashions.com; 160/1 Th Sukhumvit; 🕐10.30am-8pm Mon-Sat; [S]Nana exit 4) With his photographic memory for names, Bobby will make you feel as important as the long list of ambassadors, foreign politicians and officers he's fitted over his family's decades in the business.

Rajawongse (Map p282; ☎02 255 3714; www.dress-for-success.com; 130 Th Sukhumvit; 🕐10.30am-8pm Mon-Sat; [S]Nana exit 2) Another legendary and long-standing Bangkok tailor; Jesse and Victor's creations are particularly renowned among American visitors and residents.

Ricky's Fashion House (Map p282; ☎02 254 6887; www.rickysfashionhouse.com; 73/5 Th Sukhumvit; 🕐11am-10pm Mon-Sat & 1-5.30pm Sun; [S]Nana exit 1) Ricky gets positive reviews from locals and resident foreigners alike for his more casual styles of custom-made trousers and shirts.

Nickermann's (Map p282; ☎02 252 6682; www.nickermanns.net; basement, Landmark Hotel, 138 Th Sukhumvit; 🕐10am-8.30pm Mon-Sat, noon-6pm Sun; [S]Nana exit 2) Corporate women rave about Nickermann's tailor-made power suits. Formal ball gowns are another area of expertise.

Counterfeits

One of the most ubiquitous aspects of shopping in Bangkok, and a drawcard for many visitors, is fake merchandise. Counterfeit clothes, watches and bags line sections of Th Sukhumvit and Th Silom, while there are entire malls dedicated to copied DVDs, music CDs and software. Fake IDs are available up and down Th Khao San, and there are even fake Lonely Planet guides, old editions of which are made over with a new cover and 'publication date' to be resold (often before the new editions have even been written!). Fakes are so prominent

AN INSIDER'S TIPS ON SHOPPING IN BANGKOK

Nima Chandler of Nancy Chandler Graphics (www.nancychandler.net), whose colourful maps are some of the best guides to shopping in Bangkok, shares her Bangkok shopping secrets:

Your favourite Bangkok Market? Chatuchak (p158) remains my top recommendation. It has everything you're looking for plus everything you didn't know you were looking for. There's always surprises, lots of little new designers surprising people with new things. But I also like Bangkok's smaller markets such as the relocated **Talat Rot Fai** (p161), now on Srinakharin Soi 51 behind Seacon Square, which sees crowds descend on weekend nights for vintage flea-market finds.

Your favourite Bangkok mall? MBK (p246) is a treasure trove for most travellers. There's clothing that fits foreigners on the 6th floor – if you can find it – souvenirs on the 3rd floor, and lots of mobile phone accessories. I've had visiting friends who ate there every day because it has three food courts with lots of variety.

Where's a good place to go for Thai handicrafts? The ThaiCraft Fairs (p154), which are held in the Sukhumvit area. ThaiCraft is a social enterprise that promotes traditional Thai arts and crafts. The products are fair trade, and help village artisans take a craft and create things that appeal to an international market. I've bought welded, colourful elephants that make great decor; they have lots of traditional basket weaving, in more colours and shapes than Chatuchak; and the textiles are unique and come from across the country. It's a fair-type atmosphere and people come from across the country to take part.

A good place for quirky souvenirs? Propaganda (p122) makes you giggle. They have things like an emergency wedding ring in a pop-out card – I've used it before – a wine glass with spiders attached, and mugs with the brand's anatomically correct mascot.

Where's a good place to go for Thai fashion? The mecca is the 3rd-floor Siam Center (p120), which has been reborn as an 'ideopolis'. There are several Thai brands, and each boutique is required to be a flagship, which means they have unique designs exclusive to Siam Center, and they release their new collections there before anywhere else.

Where's a good place in Bangkok for antiques? There's a network of people who deal antiques from home by appointment, but unless you know what you're looking for, I'd suggest River City (p139), which has all the top antique dealers, and both real and repro-duction antiques.

Any insider tips for approaching Chatuchak Weekend Market? Take the Skytrain (BTS) to Mo Chit – it's faster than the subway or a taxi – then the subway (MRT) one stop to Kamphaeng Phet station. This will take you directly to the more interesting sec-tions of the market. If you see something and you love it, buy it; some items you won't ever find again. And do try to make it Section 7, which is like an art gallery. The vendors sell small souvenirs in addition to the big pieces, and it's nice to support the community of independent artists.

in Bangkok that there's even a **Museum of Counterfeit Goods** (☎02 653 5546; www. tilleke.com/firm/community/museum; Tilleke & Gibbins, 26th fl, Supalai Grand Tower, 1011 Th Phra Ram III; ⏰2pm Mon & 10am Thu, by appointment only; MKhlong Toei exit 1 & taxi) FREE, where all the counterfeit booty that has been col-lected by the law firm Tilleke & Gibbins over the years is on display.

The brashness with which fake goods are peddled in Bangkok gives the impression that black-market goods are fair game, which is and isn't true. Technically, knock-offs are illegal, and periodic crackdowns by the Thai police have led to the closure of shops and the arrest of vendors. The shops typically open again after a few months, however, and the purchasers of fake merchandise are rarely the target of such crackdowns.

The tenacity of Bangkok's counterfeit goods trade is largely due to the fact that tourists aren't the only ones buying the stuff. A poll conducted by Bangkok Univer-sity's research centre found that 80% of the

1104 people polled in Bangkok admitted to having purchased counterfeit goods (only 48% said they felt guilty for having bought fakes).

It's worth pointing out that some companies, including even a few luxury brands, argue that counterfeit goods can be regarded as a net positive. They claim that a preponderance of fake items inspires brand awareness and fosters a demand for 'real' luxury items while also acting as a useful gauge of what's hot. But the argument against fake goods points out that the industry supports organised crime and potentially exploitative and abusive labour conditions, circumvents taxes and takes jobs away from legitimate companies.

If the legal or moral repercussions aren't enough to convince you, keep in mind that in general, with fake stuff, you're getting exactly what you pay for. Consider yourself lucky if, after arriving home, the Von Dutch badge on your new hat hasn't peeled off within a week, and if your 'Rolex' is still ticking after the first rain.

Bargaining

Many of your purchases in Bangkok will involve an ancient skill that has long been abandoned in the West: bargaining. Contrary to what you'll see on a daily basis on Th Khao San, bargaining (in Thai, *gahn dòr rah·kah*) is not a terse exchange of numbers and animosity. Rather, bargaining Thai-style is a generally friendly transaction where two people try to agree on a price that is fair to both of them.

The first rule to bargaining is to have a general idea of the price. Ask around at a few vendors to get a rough notion. When you're ready to buy, it's generally a good strategy to start at 50% of the asking price and work up from there. If you're buying several of an item, you have much more leverage to request and receive a lower price. If the seller immediately agrees to your first price you're probably paying too much, but it's bad form to bargain further at this point. In general, keeping a friendly, flexible demeanour throughout the transaction will almost always work in your favour. And remember: only begin bargaining if you're really planning on buying the item. Most importantly, there's simply no point in getting angry or upset over a few baht – the locals, who inevitably have less money than you, never do this.

Tax Refunds

A 7% Value Added Tax (VAT) applies to most purchases in Thailand, but if you spend enough and get the paperwork, the kindly Revenue Department will refund it at the airport when you leave. To qualify to receive a refund, you must not be a Thai citizen, part of an airline air crew or have spent more than 180 days in Thailand during the previous year. Your purchase must have been made at an approved store; look for the blue-and-white VAT Refund sticker. Minimum purchases must add up to 2000B per store in a single day and to at least 5000B total for the whole trip. Before you leave the store, get a VAT Refund form and tax invoice. Most major malls in Bangkok will direct you to a dedicated VAT Refund desk, which will organise the appropriate paperwork (it takes about five minutes). Note that you won't get a refund on VAT paid in hotels or restaurants.

At the airport, your purchases must be declared at the customs desk in the departure hall, which will give you the appropriate stamp; you can then check them in. Smaller items (such as watches and jewellery) should be carried on your person, as they will need to be reinspected once you've passed immigration. You actually get your money at a VAT Refund Tourist Office; at Suvarnabhumi International Airport these are located on Level 4 in both the east and west wings. For how-to info, go to www.rd.go.th/vrt/engindex.html.

Shopping by Neighbourhood

➡ **Ko Ratanakosin & Thonburi** Shopping here is limited to the amulet vendors (p70) and traditional Thai medicine shops that line Th Maha Rat.

➡ **Banglamphu** Home to a couple of souvenir shops, not to mention the streetside wares of Th Khao San. (p89)

➡ **Chinatown** Street markets with a flea-market feel. (p102)

➡ **Siam Square, Pratunam, Phloen Chit & Ratchathewi** Malls, malls and more malls. (p120)

➡ **Riverside, Silom & Lumphini** The place to go for antiques and art. (p139)

➡ **Sukhumvit** Upmarket malls and touristy street markets. (p153)

➡ **Greater Bangkok** Bangkok's best fresh and open-air markets lie a fair hike outside the city centre. (p158)

Lonely Planet's Top Choices

Chatuchak Weekend Market (p158) One of the world's largest markets and a must-do Bangkok experience.

MBK Center (p246) The Thai market in a mall.

Th Khao San Market (p89) Handicrafts, souvenirs and backpacker essentials.

Siam Square (p120) Ground zero for Thai teen fashion in Bangkok.

Best Malls

MBK Center (p246) A Thai market-style mall.

Siam Square (p120) The place for Thai teen fashion.

Siam Paragon (p120) 'Mall' doesn't quite capture the essence of this immense, commerce-themed urban park.

CentralWorld (p122) One of the biggest malls in Southeast Asia: come for the shopping, stay for the ice rink.

Terminal 21 (p154) Wacky airport-themed mall equipped for both shopping and selfies.

Best for Clothes

Siam Center (p120) The place to check into the Thai fashion scene.

Baiyoke Garment Center (p120) More T-shirts than you've ever seen in one location, ever.

Platinum Fashion Mall (p122) Seemingly endless stalls of cheap togs.

Best for Handicrafts

Heritage Craft (p90) Small yet classy showroom of beautiful wares.

ThaiCraft Fair (p154) Twice-monthly fair with unique items from across the country.

Sop Moei Arts (p154) Handsome handmade cloths and baskets from northern Thailand.

Best Markets

Chatuchak Weekend Market (p158) Bangkok's biggest and best market for absolutely everything.

Pak Khlong Talat (p102) The capital's famous flower market; come late at night and don't forget your camera.

Talat Mai (p102) This frenetic fresh market is a slice of China in Bangkok.

Thanon Khao San Market (p89) For all your backpacking 'essentials'.

Nonthaburi Market (p161) An authentic upcountry market only minutes from Bangkok.

Best for One-of-a-Kind Souvenirs

Shop @ TCDC (p153) Forward-thinking and fun Thai souvenirs and housewares.

Muay Thai Lab (p77) Grab a Thai-boxing-themed souvenir for the warrior in your life.

ZudRangMa Records (p153) Pick up some vinyl or an exotic compilation at the headquarters of this eponymous music label.

Best Tailors

Raja's Fashions (p46) A Bangkok tailoring staple.

Rajawongse (p46) Go-to venue for quality bespoke threads.

July (p139) Tailor to Thailand's royalty.

Best for Antiques

River City (p139) The mall dedicated to beautiful ancient stuff.

House of Chao (p139) Shophouse full of one-of-a-kind aged items.

Talat Rot Fai (p161) The kitschier side of the antique trade.

Sports & Activities

Seen all the big sights? Eaten enough pàt tai *for a lifetime? When you're done taking it all in, consider some of Bangkok's more active pursuits. Massage and spa visits are justifiably a huge draw, but the city is also home to some great guided tours and courses, the latter in subjects ranging from Thai cookery to meditation.*

Jogging

Lumphini Park (p130) and Benjakiti Park (p144) host early-morning and late-evening runners. For something more social, one of Bangkok's longest-running sports groups is the Hash House Harriers (www.bangkokhhh.com), which puts on weekly runs.

Cycling

A bike path circles Benjakiti Park (p144), and cycling is allowed in Lumphini Park (p130) between 10am and 3pm. Cyclists also have their own hash, with the Bangkok Hash House Bikers (www.bangkokbikehash.org) meeting one Sunday a month for a 40km to 50km mountain-bike ride and post-ride refreshments. For more on cycling, see p52.

Gyms

Bangkok has plenty of gyms, ranging in style from long-running, open-air affairs in spaces such as Lumphini Park to ultramodern megagyms complete with high-tech equipment. Most large hotels have gyms and swimming pools, as do a growing number of small hotels.

Yoga & Pilates

Yoga studios – and enormous accompanying billboards of smiling gurus – have popped up faster than mushrooms at a Full Moon Party. Expect to pay about 500B for a one-off class.

Golf

Bangkok's outer suburbs are well stocked with golf courses, with green fees ranging from 250B to 5000B, plus the customary 200B tip for caddies. The website Thai Golfer (www.thaigolfer.com) rates every course in Thailand (click through to 'Course Reviews').

Spas & Massage

According to the teachings of traditional Thai healing, the use of herbs and massage should be part of a regular health-and-beauty regimen, not just an excuse for pampering. In other words, you need no excuse to get a massage in Bangkok, and it's just as well, because the city could mount a strong claim to being the massage capital of the world. Exactly what type of massage you're after is another question. Variations range from shopfront traditional Thai massage to an indulgent 'spa experience' with service and style. And even within the enormous spa category there are many options: there's plenty of pampering going around but some spas now focus more on the medical than the sensory, while plush resort-style spas offer a menu of appealing beauty treatments.

The most common variety is traditional Thai massage *(nôo·at păan boh·rahn)*. Although it sounds relaxing, at times it can seem more closely related to Thai boxing than to shiatsu. Thai massage is based on yogic techniques for general health, which involve pulling, stretching, bending and manipulating pressure points. If done well, a traditional massage will leave you sore but revitalised. Full-body massages usually include camphor-scented balms or herbal compresses. Note that 'oil massage' is sometimes taken as code for 'sexy massage'. A foot massage is arguably (and it's a strong argument) the best way to treat the leg-weariness of sightseeing.

Depending on the neighbourhood, prices for massages in small parlours are 200B to 350B for a foot massage and 300B to 600B for a full-body massage. Spa experiences start at about 1000B and climb like a Bangkok skyscraper.

Tours
GUIDED TOURS

If you're not travelling with a group but would like a guide, recommended outfits include **Tour with Tong** (☑081 835 0240; www.tourwithtong.com; tours from 1000B), whose team of guides conducts tours in and around Bangkok, and **Thai Private Tour Guide** (☑082 799 1099; www.thaitourguide.com; tours from 2000B), whose guides have garnered heaps of positive feedback.

WALKING/SPECIALITY TOURS

Although the pollution and heat are significant obstacles, Bangkok is a fascinating city to explore on foot. If you'd rather do it with an expert guide, **Bangkok Private Tours** (www.bangkokprivatetours.com; tours from US$150) and Co van Kessel Bangkok Tours (p141) conduct themed walking tours of the city. Foodies will appreciate the offerings at **Bangkok Food Tours** (☑095 943 9222; www.bangkokfoodtours.com; tours from 1150B) or **Chili Paste Tours** (☑085 143 6779, 094 552 2361; www.foodtoursbangkok.com; tours from 1800B), both of which offer half-day culinary tours of Bangkok's older neighbourhoods.

BICYCLE TOURS

You might be wondering who the hell would want to get on a bike and subject themselves to the traffic jams and sauna-like conditions of Bangkok's streets. But the fact that they sound so unlikely is part of what makes these trips so cool. The other part is that you discover a side of the city that's virtually off-limits to four-wheeled transport. Routes include unusual circuits around Chinatown and Ko Ratanakosin, but the pick are journeys across the river to Thonburi and, in particular, to the Phrapradaeng Peninsula. Better known as Bang Kachao, this exquisite expanse of mangrove,

NEED TO KNOW
Bookings

Long-term courses like language or meditation ideally should be booked a month or so in advance. Shorter courses, including cookery courses and most guided tours, can be arranged a few days in advance. Massage and spa treatments can often be booked on the same day.

Websites

For reviews of even more spas, head to the 'Bangkok's Best Spas' page at Bangkok.com (www.bangkok.com/spa-reviews).

banana and coconut plantations lies just a stone's throw from the frantic city centre, on the opposite side of Mae Nam Chao Phraya. You cycle to the river, take a boat to Bang Kachao and then follow elevated concrete paths that zigzag through the growth to a local village for lunch. Several companies run regular, well-received tours starting at about 1000B for a half-day.

RIVER & CANAL TRIPS

The cheapest and most obvious way to commute between riverside attractions is on the commuter boats run by Chao Phraya Express Boat (p239). The terminus for most northbound boats is Nonthaburi Pier, while for most southbound boats it's Sathon Pier (also called Central Pier), near the Saphan Taksin BTS station (although some boats run as far south as Wat Ratchasingkhon).

For a more personal view, consider chartering a long-tail boat along the city's canals; see p76 for details on exploring Thonburi's canals by chartered boat. Alternatively, Pandan Tour (p76) offers 'small-boat', full-day private tours of Bangkok's canals. Or try one of the dinner cruises on Mae Nam Chao Phraya (see p134).

Courses
MEDITATION

Although most of the time Bangkok seems like the most un-Buddhist place on earth, there are a few places where foreigners can practise Theravada Buddhist meditation. Some, like Center Meditation Wat Mahadhatu (p77), allow drop-ins on a daily basis, while others, such as House of Dhamma (p166), require advance notice. See p219 for background information on Buddhism.

THE RISE OF CYCLING

Over the past few years, cycling has exploded in popularity in Bangkok. Bike sales are booming, the 23km bicycle track that circles Suvarnabhumi International Airport was being upgraded at the time of research, and a Bangkok cycling event in mid-2015 drew nearly 40,000 participants. And there's a new, green, protected, bike-only lane that runs along parts of Banglamphu and Ko Ratanakosin. The track is part of Pun Pun (www.punpunbike share.com), an initiative that includes 50 bicycle hire stations across town and a clearly marked (although not always protected) bike path. To borrow a bike, you'll first need to register online (http://pcc.punpunbikeshare.com/member). You then pick up a smartcard at one of eight staffed stations. The card costs 320B, and includes 100B of credit; bikes are free for the first 15 minutes, then cost approximately 10B per subsequent hour.

A growing number of people in Bangkok are also turning to bikes for commuting. We spoke to Canadian expat Greg Jorgensen, who rides his bicycle to and from work.

Why commute via bicycle? It's cheaper, it takes about the same amount of time, and I get some exercise. I get sweaty, but probably less than when I used to walk. I wear a bike shirt and when I get to work, stop in the bathroom, clean up, apply deodorant and change my shirt. I've asked a very honest co-worker, and he said that I don't stink!

Is riding a bike in Bangkok safe? I would never say that riding a bike in Bangkok is safe. But if you take the right precautions, it's manageable. You have to be patient. And you need to understand how traffic works here so you can anticipate what's going to happen.

Any insider tips for riding in Bangkok? Don't wear headphones; you need to be aware of what's going on around you. Some people wear a mask, but I don't feel it's necessary. And be aware that you're competing with motorcycles for road. If you get a flat, you can just pay a túk-túk to take you and your bike to where you want to go.

For recreational cycling, where do you like to go? Bangkok has some really amazing landscapes within half an hour. The trick is figuring out how to get there. Bangkok also has hundreds of kilometres of tiny roads, often along canals, but riding there requires a lot of planning. My favourite rides are west to Phutthamonthon, or north of the city to Ko Kret.

THAI BOXING

Training in *moo·ay tai* (also spelt *muay thai*) for foreigners has increased in popularity in the last decade and many camps all over the country are tailoring their programs for English-speaking fighters of both sexes. Food and accommodation can often be provided for an extra charge. The website Muay Thai Camps (www.muaythai campsthailand.com) contains information on Thailand's various training centres.

COOKING

A visit to a Thai cooking school has become a must-do for many Bangkok itineraries; for some visitors it's a highlight of their trip. Courses range in price and value, but a typical half-day course should include a basic introduction to Thai ingredients and flavours and a hands-on chance to prepare and cook several dishes. Nearly all lessons include printed recipes and end with a communal lunch consisting of your handiwork.

THAI LANGUAGE

Although their courses generally involve a pretty serious time commitment, several schools in Bangkok specialise in teaching Thai to foreigners, including Union Language School (p124) and AAA (p124).

THAI MASSAGE

Few places in Bangkok offer English-language instruction in Thai-style massage; the exceptions include Chetawan Traditional Massage School (p77) and Phussapa Thai Massage School (p154).

Sports & Activities by Neighbourhood

➡ **Ko Ratanakosin & Thonburi** Canal- and river-based boat tours, and Thai massage. (p77)

➡ **Banglamphu** Bike tours. (p89)

➡ **Siam Square, Pratunam, Phloen Chit & Ratchathewi** Spas, yoga and language courses. (p124)

➡ **Riverside, Silom & Lumphini** Some of Bangkok's best cooking schools and spas. (p141)

➡ **Sukhumvit** The city's greatest variety of good-quality massage and spas. (p154)

➡ **Greater Bangkok** Bangkok's most serious Thai boxing schools are in the suburbs. (p166)

Lonely Planet's Top Choices

Amita Thai Cooking Class (p77) Thai cooking course led by charming hosts in a beautiful, home-based location.

Oriental Spa (p141) Riverside spa that sets the standard for luxury and pampering.

Health Land (p141) Quite possibly one of the best-value massage studios in the world.

Co van Kessel Bangkok Tours (p141) Tours of Bangkok that span foot, bicycle and boat.

Best Spas

Spa 1930 (p124) Cosy spa located in an atmospheric antique house.

Thann Sanctuary (p124) Chic, mall-bound spa employing the eponymous brand's fragrant herbal products.

Divana Massage & Spa (p155) Semi-concealed, classy spa.

Lavana (p155) Specialises in traditional Thai healing using herbal compresses.

Rakuten (p155) Japanese-themed but offers good Thai-style massage.

Best Bicycle Tours

Grasshopper Adventures (p90) Lauded bike tours of Bangkok's lesser-known corners.

ABC Amazing Bangkok Cyclists (p155) Guided excursions in Bangkok's back alleys.

Velo Thailand (p90) Two-wheeled day and night tours of Bangkok.

Best for Meditation

Center Meditation Wat Mahadhatu (p77) Offers informal daily meditation classes.

House of Dhamma (p166) Meditation classes, workshops and retreats.

Best for Thai-Style Massage

Ruen-Nuad Massage Studio (p141) Charming, reputable massage studio.

Asia Herb Association (p155) Massage with an emphasis on Thai-style herbal compresses.

Coran (p155) Serious Thai massage in a homely-feeling villa.

Best for Moo·ay Tai (Thai Boxing)

MuayThai Institute (p166) Serious tuition in Thailand's national sport.

Fairtex Muay Thai (p166) Respected training centre for Thai boxing.

Muay Thai Lab (p77) Shiny new training centre dedicated to *moo·ay tai*.

Best Thai Cookery Schools

Helping Hands (p154) Cooking school that also offers a unique Bangkok experience.

Silom Thai Cooking School (p141) Fun, good-value courses in Thai cookery.

Bangkok Bold Cooking Studio (p90) Chic new venue for tuition in Thai cuisine.

Explore Bangkok

BANGKOK'S TOP SIGHTS

Neighbourhoods at a Glance

❶ Ko Ratanakosin & Thonburi p58

The artificial island of Ko Ratanakosin is Bangkok's birthplace, and the Buddhist temples and royal palaces here comprise some of the city's most important and most visited sights. By contrast, Thonburi, located across Mae Nam Chao Phraya (Chao Phraya River),

is a seemingly forgotten yet visit-worthy zone of sleepy residential districts connected by *klorng* (canals; also spelt *khlong*).

❷ Banglamphu p78

Leafy lanes, antique shophouses, buzzing wet markets and golden temples convene in Banglamphu – easily the city's most quintessentially 'Bangkok' neighbourhood. It's a quaint postcard picture of the city that

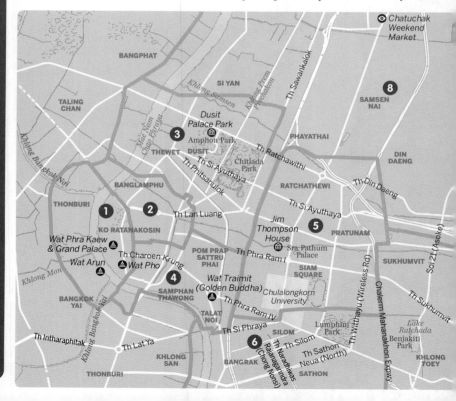

used to be – that is, until you stumble upon Th Khao San, arguably the world's most famous backpacker enclave.

❸ Thewet & Dusit p91

With its wide boulevards, manicured parks, imposing palaces and statues dedicated to former kings, Dusit has a knack for making you second-guess what city you're in. The reality check comes in neighbouring Thewet, where its soggy riverside setting, busy wet market and relentless traffic are classic Bangkok.

❹ Chinatown p99

Although many generations removed from the motherland, Bangkok's Chinatown could be a bosom buddy of any Chinese city. The streets are crammed with bird's-nest restaurants, gaudy gold and jade shops, and flashing neon signs in Chinese characters.

It's Bangkok's most hectic neighbourhood, where half the fun is getting completely lost.

❺ Siam Square, Pratunam, Phloen Chit & Ratchathewi p108

Multistorey malls, outdoor shopping precincts and never-ending markets leave no doubt that Siam Square, Pratunam and Phloen Chit combine to form Bangkok's commercial district. The BTS (Skytrain) interchange at Siam has also made this area the centre of modern Bangkok, while only a few blocks away, scruffy Ratchathewi has a lot more in common with provincial Thai cities.

❻ Riverside, Silom & Lumphini p125

Although you may not see it behind the office blocks, high-rise condos and hotels, Mae Nam Chao Phraya forms a watery backdrop to these linked neighbourhoods. History is still palpable in the riverside area's crumbling architecture, while heading inland, Silom, Bangkok's de facto financial district, is frenetic and modern, and Th Sathon is the much more subdued embassy zone.

❼ Sukhumvit p142

Japanese enclaves, burger restaurants, Middle Eastern nightlife zones, tacky 'sexpat' haunts: it's all here along Th Sukhumvit, Bangkok's unofficial international district. Where temples and suburban rice fields used to be, today you'll also find shopping centres, nightlife and a host of other amenities that cater to middle-class Thais and resident foreigners.

❽ Greater Bangkok p156

Once ringed by rice fields, modern Bangkok has since expanded in every possible direction with few concessions to agriculture or charm. The sights may be relatively few and far between, but the upside is that Bangkok's 'burbs are a good place to get a taste of provincial Thailand if you don't have the time to go upcountry.

Ko Ratanakosin & Thonburi

Neighbourhood Top Five

1 Trying to stop your jaw from dropping to the floor upon encountering the enormous reclining Buddha at **Wat Pho** (p65) for the first time.

2 Basking in the glow of the Emerald Buddha at **Wat Phra Kaew** (p60).

3 Getting up close with the iconic riverside temple known as **Wat Arun** (p69).

4 Getting lost in the weirdness of commerce that is the **Amulet Market** (p70).

5 Learning about the origins of Thai culture at the **Museum of Siam** (p70).

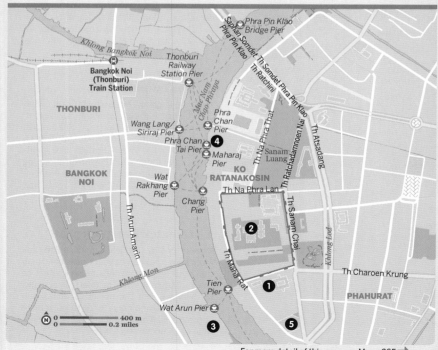

For more detail of this area see Map p265 ➡

Explore: Ko Ratanakosin & Thonburi

The birthplace of Bangkok, the artificial island of Ko Ratanakosin is where it all started more than 200 years ago. The remnants of this history are today Bangkok's biggest sights. The big-hitters, Wat Phra Kaew and the Grand Palace, and Wat Pho, are a short walk from the Chao Phraya Express Boat piers at Chang Pier, Maharaj Pier and Tien Pier, and are within walking distance of each other, although the hot sun may make doing this a more demanding task than it appears. Alternatively, túk-túk (pronounced *đúk đúk*) are a dime a dozen around here. If you're planning on visiting several sights, arrive early in the morning for the cooler weather and to avoid the crowds. Evening is best for photography, particularly if you're hoping for the classic sunset shot of Wat Arun.

Across the river, neighbouring Thonburi has significantly less to offer in terms of sights, but is great for those who fancy urban exploration. The area is accessible via the 3B river-crossing ferries at Chang Pier and Tien Pier.

Local Life

→**Cross the River** Ko Ratanakosin is probably Bangkok's most touristy neighbourhood, but hop on any of the 3B river-crossing ferries and you'll be whisked to Thonburi, where regular Thai life carries on uninterrupted.

→**Dance Floor** Lak Meuang (p73) receives daily supplications from Thai worshippers, some of whom commission classical Thai dancers to perform *lá·kon gâa bon* (shrine dancing) as thanks for granted wishes.

→**Life Aquatic** Thonburi is home to several *klorng* (canals; also spelt *khlong*) that once were responsible for Bangkok's former nickname, 'Venice of the East'.

→**Traditional Healing** Along Th Maha Rat, dozens of shophouses feature family-run herbal medicine and traditional massage shops.

Getting There & Away

→**River boat** To Ko Ratanakosin: Tien Pier, Chang Pier, Maharaj Pier and Phra Chan Tai Pier. To Thonburi: Wang Lang/Siriraj Pier, Thonburi Railway Station Pier and Phra Pin Klao Bridge Pier. Several cross-river ferries also connect to Bangkok piers.

→**BTS** To Thonburi: Krung Thonburi and Wongwian Yai. To Ko Ratanakosin: National Stadium or Phaya Thai and taxi.

→**Bus** To Ko Ratanakosin: air-con 503, 508 and 511; ordinary 3, 25, 39, 47 and 53. To Thonburi: air-con 507 and 509; ordinary 21, 42 and 82.

→**Taxi** Best taken outside of rush hours.

Lonely Planet's Top Tip

Anyone standing outside any of the big sights in Ko Ratanakosin who claims that the sight is closed is either a gem tout or con artist – ignore them and proceed inside.

 Best Places to Eat

➡ Pa Aew (p75)
➡ Ming Lee (p75)
➡ Err (p75)
➡ Khunkung (p76)

For reviews, see p75. ➡

 Best Temples

➡ Wat Phra Kaew (p60)
➡ Wat Pho (p65)
➡ Wat Arun (p69)

For reviews, see p60. ➡

 Best Museums

➡ Museum of Siam (p70)
➡ National Museum (p70)
➡ Siriraj Medical Museum (p70)

For reviews, see p70. ➡

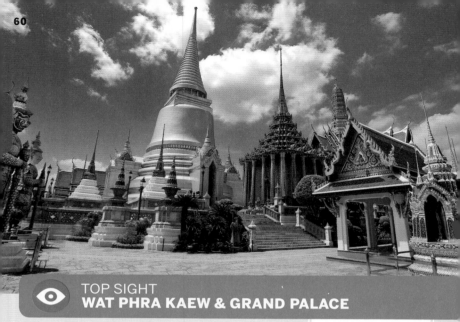

⊙ TOP SIGHT
WAT PHRA KAEW & GRAND PALACE

Wat Phra Kaew (Temple of the Emerald Buddha) gleams and glitters with so much colour and glory that its earthly foundations seem barely able to resist the celestial pull. Architecturally fantastic, the temple complex is also the spiritual core of Thai Buddhism and the monarchy, symbolically united in what is the country's most holy image, the Emerald Buddha. Attached to the temple complex is the former royal residence, once a sealed city of intricate ritual and social stratification, although most of it is off-limits to visitors.

The ground was consecrated in 1782, the first year of Bangkok rule, and is today Bangkok's biggest tourist attraction and a pilgrimage destination for devout Buddhists and nationalists. The 94.5-hectare grounds encompass more than 100 buildings that represent 200 years of royal history and architectural experimentation. Most of the architecture, royal or sacred, can be classified as Ratanakosin (old-Bangkok style).

Guides can be hired at the ticket kiosk; ignore anyone outside. An audio guide can be rented for 200B for two hours. Wat Phra Kaew and the Grand Palace are best reached either by a short walk south from Banglamphu, via Sanam Luang, or by Chao Phraya Express Boat to Chang Pier or Maharaj Pier. From the Siam Sq area (in front of the MBK Center, Th Phra Ram I), take bus 47.

DON'T MISS...

➡ Emerald Buddha
➡ *Ramakian* murals
➡ Grand Palace structures

PRACTICALITIES

➡ วัดพระแก้ว, พระบรมมหาราชวัง
➡ Map p265 C5
➡ Th Na Phra Lan
➡ admission 500B
➡ ⊙8.30am-3.30pm
➡ 🚢Chang Pier, Maharaj Pier, Phra Chan Tai Pier

Wat Phra Kaew

Ramakian Murals

Outside the main *bòht* (ordination hall) is a stone statue of the Chinese goddess of mercy, Kuan Im; nearby are two cow figures, representing the birth year of Rama I (King

Phraphutthayotfa Chulalok; r 1782–1809). In the 2km-long cloister that defines the perimeter of the complex are 178 murals depicting the *Ramakian* (the Thai version of the Indian *Ramayana* epic) in its entirety, beginning at the north gate and moving clockwise around the compound.

The story begins with the hero, Rama (the green-faced character), and his bride, Sita (the beautiful, shirtless maiden). The young couple are banished to the forest, along with Rama's brother. In this pastoral setting, the evil king Ravana (the character with many arms and faces) disguises himself as a hermit in order to kidnap Sita.

Rama joins forces with Hanuman, the monkey king (logically depicted as the white monkey), to attack Ravana and rescue Sita. Although Rama has the pedigree, Hanuman is the unsung hero. He is loyal, fierce and clever. En route to the final fairytale ending, great battles and schemes of trickery ensue until Ravana is finally killed. After withstanding a loyalty test of fire, Sita and Rama are triumphantly reunited.

If the temple grounds seem overrun by tourists, the mural area is usually mercifully quiet and shady.

Emerald Buddha

Upon entering Wat Phra Kaew you'll meet the *yaksha,* brawny guardian giants from the *Ramakian.* Beyond them is a courtyard where the central *bòht* houses the Emerald Buddha. The spectacular ornamentation inside and out does an excellent job of distracting first-time visitors from paying their respects to the image. Here's why: the Emerald Buddha is only 66cm tall and sits so high above worshippers in the main temple building that the gilded shrine is more striking than the small figure it cradles. No one knows exactly where it comes from or who sculpted it, but it first appeared on record in 15th-century Chiang Rai (in northern Thailand). Stylistically it seems to belong to Thai artistic periods of the 13th to 14th centuries.

Because of its royal status, the Emerald Buddha is ceremoniously draped in monastic robes. There are now three royal robes (for the hot, rainy and cool seasons), which are still solemnly changed at the beginning of each season. This duty was traditionally performed by the king, though in recent years the crown prince has presided over the ceremony.

Photography inside the *bòht* is not permitted.

Grand Palace

Adjoining Wat Phra Kaew is the Grand Palace (Phra Borom Maharatchawang), a former royal residence that is today only used on ceremonial occasions.

DRESS CODE

At Wat Phra Kaew and in the Grand Palace grounds, dress rules are strictly enforced. If you're wearing shorts or a sleeveless shirt you will not be allowed into the temple grounds – this applies to both men and women. If you're showing a bit too much calf or ankle, expect to be shown into a dressing room and issued with a sarong (rental is free, but you must provide a 200B deposit). Officially, sandals and flip-flops are not permitted, though the guards are less zealous in enforcing this rule.

Despite the name, the Emerald Buddha is actually carved from a single piece of nephrite (a type of jade).

TICKETS

Enter Wat Phra Kaew and the Grand Palace complex through the clearly marked third gate from the river pier. Tickets are purchased inside the complex; anyone telling you it's closed is a gem tout or con artist. Remember to keep your ticket: it also allows same-day entry to Dusit Palace Park (p93).

Wat Phra Kaew & Grand Palace

EXPLORE BANGKOK'S PREMIER MONUMENTS TO RELIGION AND REGENCY

The first area tourists enter is the Buddhist temple compound generally referred to as Wat Phra Kaew. A covered walkway surrounds the area, the inner walls of which are decorated with the **murals of the *Ramakian* ❶** and **❷**. Originally painted during the reign of Rama I (r 1782–1809), the murals, which depict the Hindu epic the *Ramayana*, span 178 panels that describe the struggles of Rama to rescue his kidnapped wife, Sita.

After taking in the story, pass through one of the gateways guarded by *yaksha* ❸ to the inner compound. The most important structure here is the ***bòht*, or ordination hall ❹**, which houses the **Emerald Buddha ❺**.

ALINA_ZIENEA / GETTY IMAGES ©

Kinaree
These graceful half-swan, half-women creatures from Hindu-Buddhist mythology stand outside Prasat Phra Thep Bidon.

Prasat Phra Thep Bidon

Borombhiman Hall

Amarindra Hall

Phra Si Ratana

The Murals of the *Ramakian*
These wall paintings, which begin at the eastern side of Wat Phra Kaew, often depict scenes more reminiscent of 19th-century Thailand than of ancient India.

ANTONIO D'ALBORE / GETTY IMAGES ©

Hanuman
Rows of these mischievous monkey deities from Hindu mythology appear to support the lower levels of two small *chedi* near Prasat Phra Thep Bidon.

Head east to the so-called Upper Terrace, an elevated area home to the **spires of the three primary** *chedi* **6**. The middle structure, Phra Mondop, is used to house Buddhist manuscripts. This area is also home to several of Wat Phra Kaew's noteworthy mythical beings, including beckoning *kinaree* **7** and several grimacing **Hanuman** **8**.

Proceed through the western gate to the compound known as the Grand Palace. Few of the buildings here are open to the public. The most noteworthy structure is **Chakri Mahaprasat** **9**. Built in 1882, the exterior of the hall is a unique blend of Western and traditional Thai architecture.

The Three Spires
The elaborate seven-tiered roof of Phra Mondop, the Khmer-style peak of Prasat Phra Thep Bidon, and the gilded Phra Si Ratana *chedi* are the tallest structures in the compound.

THANT ZAW WAI / GETTY IMAGES ©

Emerald Buddha
Despite the name, this diminutive statue (it's only 66cm tall) is actually carved from nephrite, a type of jade.

ALEXEY STIOP / GETTY IMAGES ©

The Death of Thotsakan
The panels progress clockwise, culminating at the western edge of the compound with the death of Thotsakan, Sita's kidnapper, and his elaborate funeral procession.

Chakri Mahaprasat
This structure is sometimes referred to as *fa·ràng sài chá·dah* (Westerner in a Thai crown) because each wing is topped by a *mon·dòp*: a spire representing a Thai adaptation of a Hindu shrine.

DESIGN PICS / GETTY IMAGES ©

Dusit Hall

9

ZZVET / GETTY IMAGES ©

Yaksha
Each entrance to the Wat Phra Kaew compound is watched over by a pair of vigilant and enormous *yaksha*, ogres or giants from Hindu mythology.

Bòht
(Ordination Hall)
This structure is an early example of the Ratanakosin school of architecture, which combines traditional stylistic holdovers from Ayuthaya along with more modern touches from China and the West.

THE TRAVELS OF THE EMERALD BUDDHA

Some time in the 15th century, the Emerald Buddha is said to have been covered with plaster and gold leaf and placed in Chiang Rai's own Wat Phra Kaew. Many valuable Buddha images were masked in this way to deter potential thieves and marauders during unstable times. Often the true identity of the image was forgotten over the years until a 'divine accident' exposed its precious core. The Emerald Buddha experienced such a divine revelation while it was being transported to a new location. In a fall, the plaster covering broke off, revealing the brilliant green inside. But while this was seen as a divine revelation, the return of the Phra Kaew would prove anything but peaceful for the people of Siam and Laos.

During territorial clashes with Laos, the Emerald Buddha was seized and taken to Vientiane in the mid-16th century. Some 200 years later, after the fall of Ayuthaya and the ascension of the Bangkok-based kingdom, the Thai army marched up to Vientiane, razed the city and hauled off the Emerald Buddha. It was enshrined in the then capital, Thonburi, before the general who led the sacking of Vientiane assumed the throne and had it moved to its current location.

Visitors can survey a portion of the Grand Palace grounds, but are allowed to enter only one of the remaining palace buildings.

At the eastern end, **Borombhiman Hall** is a French-inspired structure that served as a residence for Rama VI (King Vajiravudh; r 1910–25). Today it can only be viewed through its iron gates. But in April 1981 General San Chitpatima used it as the headquarters for an attempted coup. **Amarindra Hall** (open from Monday to Friday) to the west, was originally a hall of justice but is used (very rarely indeed) for coronation ceremonies. Visitors can generally enter this building, which holds a golden, boat-shaped throne that looks considerably more ornate than comfortable.

The largest of the palace buildings is the triple-winged **Chakri Mahaprasat** (Grand Palace Hall). Completed in 1882 following a plan by British architects, the exterior shows a peculiar blend of Italian Renaissance and Thai architecture. It is believed the original plan called for the palace to be topped with a dome, but Rama V (King Chulalongkorn; r 1868–1910) was persuaded to go for a Thai-style roof instead. The tallest of the *mon·dòp* (the layered, heavily ornamented spire), in the centre, contains the ashes of Chakri kings; the flanking *mon·dòp* enshrine the ashes of the many Chakri princes who failed to inherit the throne.

The last building to the west is the Ratanakosin-style **Dusit Hall**, which initially served as a venue for royal audiences and, later, as a royal funerary hall.

Until Rama VI decided one wife was enough for any man, even a king, Thai kings housed their huge harems in the inner palace area (not open to the public), which was guarded by combat-trained female sentries. The intrigue and rituals that occurred within the walls of this cloistered community live on in the fictionalised epic *Four Reigns*, by Kukrit Pramoj, which follows a young girl named Phloi growing up within the Royal City.

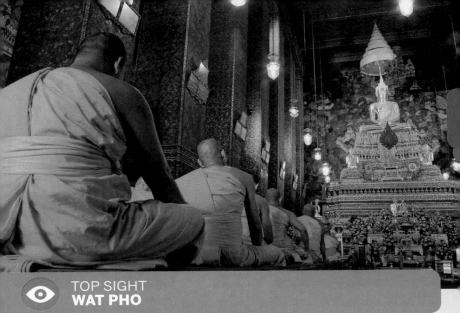

TOP SIGHT
WAT PHO

Of all Bangkok's temples, Wat Pho is arguably the one most worth visiting, for both its remarkable Reclining Buddha image and its sprawling, stupa-studded grounds. The temple compound boasts a long list of credits: the oldest and largest *wát* in Bangkok; the longest Reclining Buddha and the largest collection of Buddha images in Thailand; and the country's first public education institution.

For all that, Wat Pho sees (slightly) fewer visitors than neighbouring Wat Phra Kaew and feels (somewhat) less commercial.

Narrow Th Chetuphon divides the grounds in two, and it's well worth entering Wat Pho from either this quiet lane or Th Sanam Chai to avoid the touts and tour groups of the main entrance on Th Thai Wang.

DON'T MISS...

- ➡ Reclining Buddha
- ➡ Granite statues
- ➡ Massage pavilions

PRACTICALITIES

- ➡ วัดโพธิ์/วัดพระเชตุพน, Wat Phra Chetuphon
- ➡ Map p265, D5
- ➡ Th Sanam Chai
- ➡ admission 100B
- ➡ ⏰8.30am-6.30pm
- ➡ 🚢Tien Pier

Reclining Buddha

In the northwest corner of the site you'll find Wat Pho's main attraction, the enormous Reclining Buddha. The figure was originally commissioned by Rama III (King Phranangklao; r 1824–51), and illustrates the passing of the Buddha into nirvana. It is made of plaster around a brick core and finished in gold leaf, which gives it a serene luminescence that keeps you looking, and looking again, from different angles.

Phra Ubosot

Phra Ubosot, the compound's main ordination hall *(bòht)*, is constructed in Ayuthaya style and is strikingly more subdued than Wat Phra Kaew's. A temple has stood on this site since the 16th century, but in 1781 Rama I ordered the original Wat Photharam to be completely rebuilt as part of his new capital. Rama I's remains are interred in the base of the presiding Buddha figure in Phra Ubosot. The images on display in the four *wí-hǎhn* (sanctuaries) surrounding Phra Ubosot are worth investigation. Particularly beautiful are

Wat Pho

A WALK THROUGH THE BIG BUDDHAS OF WAT PHO

The logical starting place is the main *wi·hăhn* (sanctuary), home to Wat Pho's centrepiece, the immense **Reclining Buddha ❶**. Apart from its huge size, note the **mother-of-pearl inlays ❷** on the soles of the statue's feet. The interior walls of the *wi·hăhn* are covered with murals depicting previous lives of the Buddha, and along the south side of the structure are 108 bronze monk bowls; for 20B you can buy 108 coins, each of which is dropped in a bowl for good luck.

Exit the *wi·hăhn* and head east via the two **stone giants ❸** who guard the gateway to the rest of the compound. Directly south of these are the four towering **royal *chedi* ❹**.

Continue east, passing through two consecutive **galleries of Buddha**

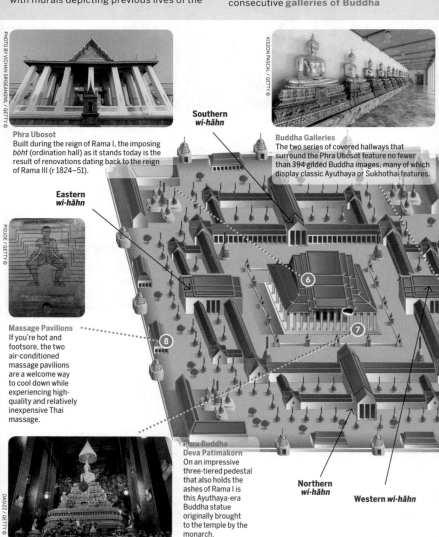

Phra Ubosot
Built during the reign of Rama I, the imposing *bòht* (ordination hall) as it stands today is the result of renovations dating back to the reign of Rama III (r 1824–51).

Southern *wi·hăhn*

Buddha Galleries
The two series of covered hallways that surround the Phra Ubosot feature no fewer than 394 gilded Buddha images, many of which display classic Ayuthaya or Sukhothai features.

Eastern *wi·hăhn*

Massage Pavilions
If you're hot and footsore, the two air-conditioned massage pavilions are a welcome way to cool down while experiencing high-quality and relatively inexpensive Thai massage.

Phra Buddha Deva Patimakorn
On an impressive three-tiered pedestal that also holds the ashes of Rama I is this Ayuthaya-era Buddha statue originally brought to the temple by the monarch.

Northern *wi·hăhn*

Western *wi·hăhn*

PHOTO BY VICHAN SRISEANGNIL / GETTY ©

KISZON PASCAL / GETTY ©

PIDJOE / GETTY ©

OASISZZ / GETTY ©

statues **5** linking four *wí·hǎhn*, two of which contain notable Sukhothai-era Buddha statues; these comprise the exterior of **Phra Ubosot 6**, the immense ordination hall that is Wat Pho's second-most noteworthy structure. The base of the building is surrounded by bas-relief inscriptions, and inside is the notable Buddha statue, **Phra Buddha Deva Patimakorn 7**.

Wat Pho is often referred to as Thailand's first university, a tradition that continues today in an associated traditional Thai medicine school and, at the compound's eastern extent, two **massage pavilions 8**.

Interspersed throughout the eastern half of the compound are several additional minor *chedi* and rock gardens.

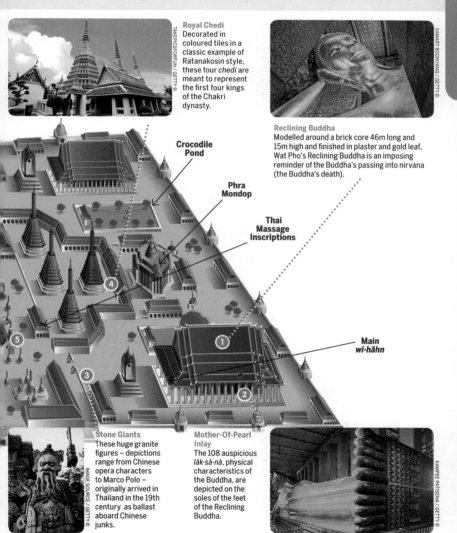

Royal Chedi
Decorated in coloured tiles in a classic example of Ratanakosin style, these four *chedi* are meant to represent the first four kings of the Chakri dynasty.

Reclining Buddha
Modelled around a brick core 46m long and 15m high and finished in plaster and gold leaf, Wat Pho's Reclining Buddha is an imposing reminder of the Buddha's passing into nirvana (the Buddha's death).

Crocodile Pond

Phra Mondop

Thai Massage Inscriptions

Main *wí·hǎhn*

Stone Giants
These huge granite figures – depictions range from Chinese opera characters to Marco Polo – originally arrived in Thailand in the 19th century as ballast aboard Chinese junks.

Mother-Of-Pearl Inlay
The 108 auspicious *lák·sà·nà*, physical characteristics of the Buddha, are depicted on the soles of the feet of the Reclining Buddha.

WAT PHO'S GRANITE STATUES

Aside from monks and sightseers, Wat Pho is filled with an altogether stiffer crowd: dozens of giants and figurines carved from granite. The rock giants first arrived in Thailand as ballast aboard Chinese junks and were put to work in Wat Pho (and other wát, including Wat Suthat), guarding the entrances of temple gates and courtyards. Look closely and you'll see an array of Chinese characters. The giants with bulging eyes and Chinese opera costumes were inspired by warrior noblemen and are called Lan Than. The figure in a straw hat is a farmer, forever interrupted during his day's work cultivating the fields. And can you recognise the guy in the fedora-like hat with a trimmed beard and moustache? Marco Polo, of course, who introduced such European styles to the Chinese court.

What other holy site in the world includes massage? The air-conditioned massage pavilions near Wat Pho's east gate provide a unique opportunity to combine relaxation with sightseeing.

the Phra Chinnarat and Phra Chinnasri Buddhas in the western and southern chapels, both rescued from Sukhothai by relatives of Rama I. Encircling Phra Ubosot is a low marble wall with 152 bas-reliefs depicting scenes from the *Ramakian*. You'll recognise some of these figures when you exit the temple past the hawkers with mass-produced rubbings for sale: these are made from cement casts based on Wat Pho's reliefs.

Royal Chedi

On the western side of the grounds is a collection of four towering tiled *chedi* (stupa) commemorating the first four Chakri kings. The surrounding wall was built on the orders of Rama IV (King Mongkut; r 1851–68), who for reasons we can only speculate about decided he didn't want any future kings joining the memorial. Note the square bell shape with distinct corners, a signature of Ratanakosin style. Among the compound's additional 91 smaller *chedi* are clusters that contain the ashes of lesser royal descendants.

Massage Pavilions

A small pavilion west of Phra Ubosot has Unesco-awarded inscriptions detailing the tenets of traditional Thai massage. These and other similar inscriptions led Wat Pho to be regarded as Thailand's first university. Today it maintains that tradition as the national headquarters for the teaching and preservation of traditional Thai medicine, including Thai massage. The famous school has two **massage pavilions** (Map p265; Thai massage per hr 420B; ⊙9am-6pm) located within the temple area and additional rooms within the training facility (p77) outside the temple.

Gardens

Small Chinese-style rock gardens and hill islands interrupt the compound's numerous tiled courtyards providing shade, greenery and quirky decorations depicting daily life. Keep an eye out for the distinctive rockery festooned with figures of the hermit Khao Mor – who is credited with inventing yoga – in various healing positions. According to the tradition, a few good arm stretches should cure idleness.

TOP SIGHT
WAT ARUN

The missile-shaped temple that rises from Mae Nam Chao Phraya's banks is known as Temple of Dawn, and was named after the Indian god of dawn, Aruna. It was here that, after the destruction of Ayuthaya, King Taksin stumbled upon a small local shrine and interpreted the discovery as such an auspicious sign that this should be the site of the new capital of Siam.

King Taksin built a palace beside the shrine, which is now part of Navy Headquarters, as well as a royal temple that housed the Emerald Buddha for 15 years until Taksin was assassinated and the capital moved across the royal river to Bangkok.

At the time of research, the spire of Wat Arun was closed until 2016 due to renovation. Visitors can enter the compound, but cannot, as in previous years, climb the tower.

The Spire
Today, the central feature of Wat Arun is the 82m-high Khmer-style *brahng* (spire), constructed during the first half of the 19th century by Rama II (King Phraphutthaloetla Naphalai; r 1809–24). From the river it is not apparent that this corn-cob-shaped steeple is adorned with colourful floral murals made of glazed porcelain, a common temple ornamentation in the early Ratanakosin period, when Chinese ships calling at Bangkok used porcelain as ballast.

DON'T MISS...

➡ A close-up look at the tile-coated Khmer-style *brahng* (spire)

➡ Buddhist murals inside the main *bòht*

➡ Exploring the surrounding neighbourhood

➡ A sunset cocktail and photo op at Roof or Amorosa

PRACTICALITIES

➡ วัดอรุณฯ

➡ Map p265, B6

➡ www.watarun.net

➡ off Th Arun Amarin

➡ admission 50B

➡ ⊙8am-6pm

➡ ⊠cross-river ferry from Tien Pier

Buddhist Murals
Worth a look is the interior of the *bòht*. The main Buddha image is said to have been designed by Rama II himself, whose ashes are interred beneath. The murals date to the reign of Rama V. Particularly impressive is one depicting Prince Siddhartha (the Buddha) encountering examples of birth, old age, sickness and death outside his palace walls, an experience that led him to abandon the worldly life.

Exploring the Neighbourhood
Wat Arun is directly across from Wat Pho, on the Thonburi side of the river. A lot of people visit the *wát* on long-tail boat tours, but it's easier and more rewarding to just jump on the 3B cross-river ferry from Tien Pier. For our money, visiting Wat Arun in the late afternoon is best, with the sun shining from the west lighting up the *brahng* and the river behind it. If you come earlier, consider taking a stroll away from the river on Th Wang Doem, a quiet tiled street of wooden shophouses.

Sunset Cocktails
Sunset views of the temple compound can be caught from across the river at the private piers off Th Maha Rat – although be forewarned that locals may ask for a 20B 'fee'. Other great viewpoints include Roof (p77) or Amorosa (p77), rooftop bars located directly across from the temple.

◉ SIGHTS

WAT PHRA KAEW &
GRAND PALACE BUDDHIST TEMPLE
See p60.

WAT PHO BUDDHIST TEMPLE
See p65.

WAT ARUN BUDDHIST TEMPLE
See p69.

AMULET MARKET MARKET
Map p265 (ตลาดพระเครื่องวัดมหาธาตุ; Th Maha Rat; ⊘7am-5pm; 🚢Chang Pier, Maharaj Pier, Phra Chan Pier) This arcane and fascinating market claims both the footpaths along Th Maha Rat and Th Phra Chan, as well as a dense network of covered market stalls that run south from Phra Chan Pier; the easiest entry point is clearly marked Trok Maha That. The trade is based around small talismans that are carefully prized by collectors, monks, taxi drivers and people in dangerous professions.

Potential buyers, often already sporting many amulets, can be seen bargaining and flipping through magazines dedicated to the amulets, some of which command astronomical prices. It's a great place to just wander and watch men (because there are rarely women) looking through magnifying glasses at the tiny amulets, seeking hidden meaning and, if they're lucky, hidden value.

MUSEUM OF SIAM MUSEUM
Map p265 (สถาบันพิพิธภัณฑ์การเรียนรู้แห่งชาติ; www.museumsiam.org; Th Maha Rat; admission 300B; ⊘10am-6pm Tue-Sun; ♿; 🚢Tien Pier) This fun museum employs a variety of media to explore the origins of the Thai people and their culture. Housed in a European-style 19th-century building that was once the Ministry of Commerce, the exhibits are presented in a contemporary, engaging and interactive fashion not typically found in Thailand's museums. They are also refreshingly balanced and entertaining, with galleries dealing with a range of questions about the origins of the nation and its people.

Each room has an informative narrated video started by a sensory detector, keeping waiting to a minimum. An Ayuthaya-era battle game, a room full of traditional Thai toys and a street vending cart where you can be photographed pretending to whip up a pan of *pàt tai* (fried noodles) will help keep kids interested for at least an hour,

adults for longer. Check out the attached shop for some innovative gift ideas.

NATIONAL MUSEUM MUSEUM
Map p265 (พิพิธภัณฑสถานแห่งชาติ; 4 Th Na Phra That; admission 200B; ⊘9am-4pm Wed-Sun; 🚢Chang Pier, Maharaj Pier, Phra Chan Tai Pier) Often touted as Southeast Asia's biggest museum, Thailand's National Museum is home to an impressive, albeit occasionally dusty, collection of items, best appreciated on one of the museum's twice-weekly guided **tours** (free with museum admission; ⊘9.30am Wed & Thu).

Most of the museum's structures were built in 1782 as the palace of Rama I's viceroy, Prince Wang Na. Rama V turned it into a museum in 1874, and today there are three permanent exhibitions spread out over several buildings. At the time of research some of the exhibition halls were being renovated.

The **history wing** has made impressive bounds towards contemporary curatorial aesthetics with a succinct chronology of prehistoric, Sukhothai-, Ayuthaya- and Bangkok-era events and figures. Gems include King Ramkamhaeng's inscribed stone pillar, said to be the oldest record of Thai writing (although this has been contested); King Taksin's throne; the Rama V section; and the screening of a movie about Rama VII, *The Magic Ring*.

The **decorative arts and ethnology exhibit** covers seemingly every possible handicraft; traditional musical instruments, ceramics, clothing and textiles, woodcarving, regalia and weaponry. The **archaeology and art history wing** has exhibits ranging from prehistoric to the Bangkok period.

In addition to the main exhibition halls, the **Bhuddhaisawan (Phutthaisawan) Chapel** includes some well-preserved murals and one of the country's most revered Buddha images, Phra Phuttha Sihing. Legend claims the image came from Sri Lanka, but art historians attribute it to the 13th-century Sukhothai period.

SIRIRAJ MEDICAL MUSEUM MUSEUM
Map p265 (พิพิธภัณฑ์นิติเวชศาสตร์สงกรานต์นิยมเสน; 2nd fl, Adulyadejvikrom Bldg, Siriraj Hospital; admission 200B; ⊘10am-4pm Wed-Mon; 🚢Wang Lang/Siriraj Pier, Thonburi Railway Station Pier) Various appendages, murder weapons and crime-scene evidence, including a bloodied T-shirt from a victim stabbed to death with a dildo, are on display at these linked mu-

seums – collectively dubbed the Museum of Death – dedicated to anatomy, pathology and forensic science.

The easiest way to reach the museum is by taking the river-crossing ferry from Chang Pier to Wang Lang/Siriraj Pier in Thonburi. At the exit to the pier, turn right (north) to enter Siriraj Hospital and follow the green Museum signs.

Although the intent is ostensibly to educate rather than nauseate, exhibits such as the preserved body of Si Ouey, a serial killer who murdered – and then ate – more than 30 children in the 1950s before being executed, often do the latter. (For decades Si Ouey has functioned as a Thai bogeyman, his name used to scare misbehaving children into submission: 'Behave yourself or Si Ouey will come for you!')

If you're still with us at this point, you'll probably also enjoy the adjacent **Parasite Museum**.

NATIONAL GALLERY
ART GALLERY

Map p265 (พิพิธภัณฑสถานแห่งชาติหอศิลป์/หอศิลป์เจ้าฟ้า; www.facebook.com/TheNationalGalleryBangkok; 4 Th Chao Fa; admission 200B; ⊗9am-4pm Wed-Sun; ⊠Chang Pier, Maharaj Pier, Phra Chan Tai Pier) Housed in a building that was the Royal Mint during the reign of Rama V, the National Gallery's permanent exhibition is admittedly a rather dusty and dated affair. Secular art is a relatively new concept in Thailand and most of the country's best examples of fine art reside in the temples for which they were created – much as historic Western art is often found in European cathedrals. As such, most of the permanent collection here documents Thailand's homage to modern styles.

More interesting are the rotating exhibits held in the spacious rear galleries; take a look at the Facebook page or the posters out front to see what's on.

ROYAL BARGES NATIONAL MUSEUM
MUSEUM

Map p265 (พิพิธภัณฑสถานแห่งชาติ เรือพระราชพิธี/เรือพระที่นั่ง; Khlong Bangkok Noi or 80/1 Th Arun Amarin; admission 100B, camera 100B; ⊗9am-5pm; ⊠Phra Pin Klao Bridge Pier) The royal barges are slender, fantastically ornamented vessels used in ceremonial processions. The tradition dates back to the Ayuthaya era, when travel (for commoners and royals) was by boat. When not in use, the barges are on display at this Thonburi museum.

The most convenient way to get here is by motorcycle taxi from Phra Pin Klao Pier (ask the driver to go to *reu·a prá têe nâng*). The museum is also an optional stop on long-tail boat trips through Thonburi's canals.

Suphannahong, the king's personal barge, is the most important of the six boats on display here. Made from a single piece of timber, it's said to be the largest dugout in the world. The name means Golden Swan, and a huge swan head has been carved into the bow. Lesser barges feature bows that are carved into other Hindu-Buddhist mythological shapes such as the *naga* (mythical sea serpent) and *garuda* (Vishnu's bird mount).

Historic photos help envision the grand processions in which the largest of the barges would require a rowing crew of 50 men, plus seven umbrella bearers, two helmsmen and two navigators, as well as a flagsman,

KO RATANAKOSIN & THONBURI SIGHTS

ⓘ BANGKOK STREET SMARTS

Keep the following in mind to survive the traffic and avoid joining the list of tourists sucked in by Bangkok's numerous scam artists:

➡ Ignore 'helpful', often well-dressed, English-speaking locals who tell you that tourist attractions and public transport are closed for a holiday or cleaning; it's the beginning of a con, most likely a gem scam.

➡ Skip the offer of a 50B túk-túk ride unless you have the time and willpower to resist a heavy sales pitch in a tailor's or gem shop. Regardless of what you might hear, good jewellery, gems and tailor shops aren't found through a túk-túk driver.

➡ Don't expect any pedestrian rights; put a Bangkokian between you and any oncoming traffic, and yield to anything with more metal than you.

➡ Walk away from the tourist strip to hail a taxi that will actually use the meter. Tell the driver 'meter'. If the driver refuses to put the meter on, get out.

🏃 Neighbourhood Walk
Ko Ratanakosin Stroll

START CHANG PIER
END WAT ARUN
LENGTH 4KM; THREE TO FIVE HOURS

The bulk of Bangkok's 'must-see' destinations are in the former royal district, Ko Ratanakosin. Start early to beat the heat and get in before the hordes have descended. Remember to dress modestly in order to gain entry to the temples and ignore any strangers who approach you offering advice on sightseeing or shopping.

Start at Chang Pier and follow Th Na Phra Lan east, with a quick diversion to ❶ **Silpakorn University** (p74), Thailand's premier fine-arts university. If you haven't already been, continue east to the main gate into ❷ **Wat Phra Kaew & Grand Palace** (p60), two of Bangkok's most famous attractions.

Return to Th Maha Rat and proceed north, through an enclave of herbal apothecaries and sidewalk amulet sellers. Immediately after passing the cat-laden newsstand (you'll know it when you smell it), turn left into ❸ **Trok Tha Wang**, a narrow alleyway holding a hidden classic Bangkok neighbourhood. Returning to Th Maha Rat, continue moving north; on your right is ❹ **Wat Mahathat**, one of Thailand's most respected Buddhist universities.

Across the street, turn left into narrow Trok Maha That to discover the cramped ❺ **Amulet Market** (p70). As you continue north alongside the river, food vendors appear. The emergence of white-and-black uniforms is a clue that you are approaching ❻ **Thammasat University** (p74), known for its law and political science departments.

Exiting at Phra Chan Pier, cross Th Maha Rat and continue east until you reach ❼ **Sanam Luang** (p73), the 'Royal Field'. Cross the field and continue south along Th Ratchadamnoen Nai until you reach the home of Bangkok's city spirit, ❽ **Lak Meuang** (p73). After paying your respects, head south along Th Sanam Chai and turn right onto Th Thai Wang, which will lead you to the entrance of ❾ **Wat Pho** (p65), home of the giant reclining Buddha.

If you've still got the energy, head to adjacent Tien Pier to catch the cross-river ferry to ❿ **Wat Arun** (p69).

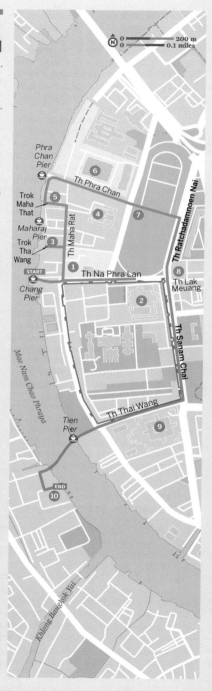

rhythm keeper and chanter. Today, the royal barge procession is an infrequent occurrence, most recently performed in 2012 in honour of the king's 85th birthday.

LAK MEUANG   MONUMENT

Map p265 (ศาลหลักเมือง; cnr Th Sanam Chai & Th Lak Meuang; ⏰6.30am-6.30pm; ⛴Chang Pier, Maharaj Pier, Phra Chan Tai Pier) Serving as the spiritual keystone of Bangkok, Lak Meuang is a phallus-shaped wooden pillar erected by Rama I during the foundation of the city in 1782. Part of an animistic tradition, the city pillar embodies the city's guardian spirit (Phra Sayam Thewathirat) and also lends a practical purpose as a marker of a town's crossroads and measuring point for distances between towns.

If you're lucky, lá·kon gâa bon (a commissioned dance) may be in progress. Brilliantly costumed dancers measure out subtle movements as gratitude to the guardian spirit for granting a worshipper's wish.

SANAM LUANG   PARK

Map p265 (สนามหลวง; bounded by Th Na Phra That, Th Ratchadamnoen Nai & Th Na Phra Lan; ⏰dawn-dusk; ⛴Chang Pier, Maharaj Pier, Phra Chan Tai Pier) On a hot day, Sanam Luang (Royal Field) is far from charming: a shadeless expanse of dying grass and concrete pavement ringed by flocks of pigeons and homeless people. Yet despite its shabby appearance, it has been at the centre of royal ceremony since Bangkok was founded.

Large funeral pyres are constructed here during elaborate, but infrequent, royal cremations, and explain the field's alternate name, Thung Phra Men (Cremation Ground). The most recent cremation was a six-day, 300-million-baht ceremony for King Bhumibol Adulyadej's sister, Princess Galyani Vadhana, in November, 2009; it took 11 months to prepare. Sanam Luang also draws the masses in December for the King's Birthday (5 December), Constitution Day (10 December) and New Year.

Less dramatic events staged here include the annual Royal Ploughing Ceremony, in which the king (or more recently, the crown prince) officially initiates the rice-growing season, an appropriate location given that Sanam Luang was used to grow rice for almost 100 years after the royals moved into Ko Ratanakosin. After the rains, the kite-flying season (mid-February to April) sees the air above filled with butterfly-shaped Thai kites. Matches are held between teams flying either a 'male' or 'female' kite in a particular territory; points are won if they can force a competitor into their zone.

TAXI ALTARS: INSURANCE ON THE DASHBOARD

As your taxi races into Bangkok from the airport, your delight at being able to do the 30km trip for less than US$15 might soon be replaced by uneasiness, anxiety and eventually outright fear – 150km/h is fast, you're tailgating the car in front and there's no seatbelt. You can rest assured (or not), however, that your driver will share none of these concerns.

All of this makes the humble taxi trip an instructive introduction to Thai culture. Buddhists believe in karma and thus that their fate is, to a large extent, predestined. Unlike Western ideas, which take a more scientific approach to road safety, many Thais believe factors such as speed, concentration, seatbelts and actual driving skills have no bearing whatsoever on your chances of being in a crash. Put simply, if you die a horrible death on the road, karma says you deserved it. The trouble is that when a passenger gets into a taxi they bring their karma, and any bad spirits the passenger might have, along for the ride. Which could upset the driver's own fate.

To counteract such bad influences most Bangkok taxi drivers turn the dashboard and ceiling into a sort of life-insurance shrine. The ceiling will have a yantra diagram drawn in white powder by a monk as a form of spiritual protection. This will often be accompanied by portraits of notable royals. Below this a red box dangling red tassels, beads and amulets hangs from the rear-vision mirror, while the dashboard is populated by Buddhist and royal statuettes, quite possibly banknotes with the king's image prominent, and more amulets. With luck, the talismans will protect your driver from any bad karma you bring into the cab. Passengers, meanwhile, must simply hope that their driver's number is not up. If you feel like it might be, try saying cháh cháh soothingly – that is, ask your driver to slow down. For a look inside some of Bangkok's 100,000 or so taxis, check out Still Life in Moving Vehicles (www.lifeinmovingvehicle.blogspot.com).

WORTH A DETOUR

ARTIST'S HOUSE

Sort of a gallery, kind of a coffeeshop, seemingly a cultural centre... It's hard to pin down **Artist's House** (บ้านศิลปิน; www.facebook.com/Baansilapin; Khlong Bang Luang; ◷9am-6pm; Ⓢ Wongwian Yai exit 2) FREE, an old wooden house on Khlong Bang Luang, in Thonburi. There's food available on weekends, as well as a free traditional Thai puppet show scheduled at 2pm, but the best excuse to come is simply to soak up the old-world canalside vibe.

Artist's House can be reached on canal boat tours of Thonburi, or on land via Soi 3, Th Charansanitwong; cross the canal at the bridge by the 7-Eleven, turn left and it's about 100m down.

SILPAKORN UNIVERSITY
UNIVERSITY

Map p265 (มหาวิทยาลัยศิลปากร; www.su.ac.th; 31 Th Na Phra Lan; ⛴Chang Pier, Maharaj Pier, Phra Chan Tai Pier) Thailand's universities aren't usually repositories for interesting architecture, but Silpakorn (pronounced *sǐn lá bà gorn*), the country's premier art school, breaks the mould. The classical buildings form the charming nucleus of what was an early Thai aristocratic enclave, and the traditional artistic temperament still survives.

The building immediately facing the Th Na Phra Lan gate was once part of a palace and now houses the **Silpakorn University Art Centre** (Map p265; www.facebook.com/ArtCentre.SilpakornUniversity; 31 Th Na Phra Lan; ◷9am-7pm Mon-Fri, to 4pm Sat; ⛴Chang Pier, Maharaj Pier) FREE. To the right of the building is a shady sculpture garden displaying the work of Corrado Feroci (also known as Silpa Bhirasri), the Italian art professor and sculptor who came to Thailand at royal request in the 1920s and later established the university (which is named after him), sculpted parts of the Democracy Monument and, much to his own annoyance, the Victory Monument.

THAMMASAT UNIVERSITY
UNIVERSITY

Map p265 (มหาวิทยาลัยธรรมศาสตร์; www.tu.ac.th; 2 Th Phra Chan; ⛴Chang Pier, Maharaj Pier, Phra Chan Tai Pier) Much of the drama that followed Thailand's transition from monarchy to democracy has unfolded on this quiet riverside campus. Thammasat University was established in 1934, two years after the bloodless coup that deposed the absolute monarchy. Its remit was to instruct students in law and political economy, considered to be the intellectual necessities for an educated democracy.

The university was founded by Dr Pridi Phanomyong, whose statue stands in Pridi Court at the centre of the campus.

Pridi was the leader of the civilian People's Party that successfully advocated a constitutional monarchy during the 1920s and '30s. He went on to serve in various ministries, organised the Seri Thai movement (a Thai resistance campaign against the Japanese during WWII) and was ultimately forced into exile when the postwar government was seized by a military dictatorship in 1947.

Pridi was unable to counter the dismantling of democratic reforms, but the university he established continued his crusade. Thammasat was the hotbed of pro-democracy activism during the student uprising era of the 1970s. On 14 October 1973, an estimated 10,000 protesters convened on the parade grounds beside the university's Memorial Building demanding the government reinstate the constitution. From the university the protest grew and moved to the Democracy Monument, where the military and police opened fire on the crowd, killing 77 and wounding 857. The massacre prompted the king to revoke his support of the military rulers and for a brief period a civilian government was reinstated. On 6 October 1976, Thammasat itself was the scene of a bloody massacre, when at least 46 students were shot dead while rallying against the return from exile of former dictator Field Marshal Thanom Kittikachorn. Near the southern entrance to the university is the Bodhi Court, where a sign beneath the Bodhi tree explains more about the democracy movement that germinated at Thammasat.

SARANROM ROYAL GARDEN
PARK

Map p265 (สวนสราญรมย์; bounded by Th Ratchini, Th Charoen Krung & Th Sanam Chai; ◷5am-9pm; ⛴Tien Pier) Easily mistaken for a European public garden, this Victorian-era green space was originally designed as a royal residence in the time of Rama IV. After Rama VII (King Prajadhipok; r 1925–35) abdicated in 1935, the palace served as the headquarters of the People's Party, the political organisation that orchestrated the handover of the government. The open space remained and in 1960 was opened to the public.

Today a wander through the garden reveals a Victorian gazebo, paths lined with frangipani and a moat around a marble monument built in honour of one of Rama V's favourite wives, Queen Sunantha, who died in a boating accident in 1880. The queen was on her way to Bang Pa-In Summer Palace in Ayuthaya when her boat began to sink. The custom at the time was that commoners were forbidden to touch royalty, which prevented her attendants from saving her from drowning.

✕ EATING

In stark contrast to the rest of Bangkok, there aren't many restaurants or stalls in Ko Ratanakosin, and those that are here predominately serve Thai cuisine. For something more international, consider heading to Banglamphu, a short taxi ride away.

PA AEW   CENTRAL THAI **$**

Map p265 (Th Maha Rat, no roman-script sign; mains 20-60B; ⊙10am-5pm Tue-Sat; ⚓Tien Pier) Pull up a plastic stool for some rich, seafood-heavy, Bangkok-style fare. It's a bare-bones, open-air curry stall, but for taste, Pa Aew is one of our favourite places to eat in this part of town.

There's no English-language sign; look for the exposed trays of food directly in front of the Krung Thai Bank near the corner with Soi Pratu Nokyung.

MING LEE   CHINESE-THAI **$**

Map p265 (28-30 Th Na Phra Lan, no roman-script sign; mains 70-100B; ⊙11.30am-6pm; ⚓Chang Pier, Maharaj Pier, Phra Chan Tai Pier) Hidden in plain sight across from Wat Phra Kaew is this decades-old shophouse restaurant. The menu spans Western-Chinese dishes (stewed tongue, for example) and Thai standards (such as the impossibly tart and garlicky 'beef spicy salad'). Often closed before 6pm, Ming Lee is best approached as a post-sightseeing lunch option.

There's no English-language sign here; look for the last shophouse before Silpakorn University.

WANG LANG MARKET   THAI **$**

Map p265 (Trok Wang Lang; mains 30-80B; ⊙10am-3pm Mon-Fri; ⚓Wang Lang/Siriraj Pier) Running south from Siriraj Hospital is this busy market bringing together takeaway stalls and basic restaurants. Options range from noodles to curries ladled over rice, and come lunch, the area is positively mobbed by the area's office staff.

ERR   THAI **$$**

Map p265 (www.errbkk.com; off Th Maha Rat; dishes 65-360B; ⊙11am-late Tue-Sun; ⚓Tien Pier) Think of all those different smoky, spicy, crispy, meaty bites you've encountered on the street. Now imagine them assembled in one funky, retro-themed locale, and coupled with tasty Thai-themed cocktails and domestic microbrews. If Err (a Thai colloquialism for agreement) seems

---

LOCAL KNOWLEDGE

THONBURI'S SOUTHERN THAI RESTAURANTS

The area around Thonburi's Siriraj Hospital is one of the best places in Bangkok for southern Thai food, the theory being that the cuisine took root here because of the nearby train station that served southern destinations. In particular, between Soi 8 and Soi 13 of Th Wang Lang there is a knot of authentic, southern Thai–style curry shops: **Dao Tai** (508/26 Th Wang Lang, no roman-script sign; mains from 30B; ⊙7am-8.30pm; ⚓Wang Lang/Siriraj Pier), **Ruam Tai** (376/4 Th Wang Lang, no roman-script sign; mains from 30B; ⊙7am-9pm; ⚓Wang Lang/Siriraj Pier) and **Chawang** (375/5-6 Th Wang Lang; mains from 30B; ⊙7am-7pm; ⚓Wang Lang/Siriraj Pier). A menu isn't necessary as all feature bowls and trays of prepared curries, soups, stir-fries and relishes; simply point to whatever looks tastiest. And when eating, don't feel ashamed if you're feeling the heat; even Bangkok Thais tend to find southern Thai cuisine spicy.

to good to be true, we empathise, but insist that it's true.

KHUNKUNG
CENTRAL THAI **$$**

Map p265 (Navy Club; 77 Th Maha Rat; mains 70-450B; ⊙11am-2pm & 6-10pm Mon-Fri, 11am-10pm Sat & Sun; ⚑Chang Pier, Maharaj Pier, Phra Chan Tai Pier) The restaurant of the Royal Navy Association has one of the few coveted riverfront locations along this stretch of Mae Nam Chao Phraya. Locals come for the combination of views and cheap and tasty seafood-based eats – ostensibly not for the cafeteria-like atmosphere. Khunkung is just off the main road; look for the sign on Th Maha Rat that says 'Navy Club'.

SAVOEY
THAI **$$**

Map p265 (www.savoey.co.th; 1st fl, Maharaj Pier, Th Maha Rat; mains 125-1800B; ⊙10am-10pm; ⚑Maharaj Pier, Chang Pier) A chain with other branches across town, you're not going to find heaps of character here, but you will get consistency, river views, air-con, and a seafood-heavy menu. Come cool evenings, take advantage of the open-air, riverside deck.

SALA RATTANAKOSIN
EATERY & BAR
THAI **$$$**

Map p265 (☎02 622 1388; www.salaresorts.com/rattanakosin; Sala Rattanakosin, 39 Th Maha Rat; mains 240-1100B; ⊙11am-4.30pm & 5.30-11pm; ⚑Tien Pier) Located on an open-air deck next to the river, with Wat Arun virtually towering overhead, the Sala Rattanakosin hotel's signature restaurant has nailed the location. The food – largely central and northern Thai dishes with occasional Western twists – doesn't necessarily live up to the scenery, but for upscale-ish dining in this corner of town it's really the only option.

WORTH A DETOUR

EXPLORING THONBURI'S CANALS

Bangkok was formerly known as the Venice of the East, as the city used to be crisscrossed by an advanced network of *klorng* (also spelt *khlong*), artificial canals that inhabitants used both for transport and to ship goods. Today, cars and motorcycles have superseded boats, and the majority of Bangkok's canals have been filled in and covered by roads, or are fetid and drying up. Yet a peek into the watery Bangkok of yesteryear can still be had west of Mae Nam Chao Phraya, in Thonburi.

Thonburi's network of canals and river tributaries still carries a motley fleet of watercraft, from paddle canoes to rice barges. Homes, trading houses and temples are built on stilts with front doors opening out to the water. According to residents, these waterways protect them from the seasonal flooding that plagues the capital. **Khlong Bangkok Noi** is lined with greenery and historic temples; smaller **Khlong Mon** is largely residential. **Khlong Bangkok Yai** was in fact the original course of the river until a canal was built to expedite transits. Today, long-tail boats that ply these and other Thonburi canals are available for charter at Chang Pier and Tien Pier, both on Ko Ratanakosin. Prices at these piers are slightly higher than elsewhere and allow little room for negotiation, but you stand the least chance of being conned or hit up for tips and other unexpected fees.

Trips generally traverse Khlong Bangkok Noi and Khlong Mon, taking in the Royal Barges National Museum, Wat Arun and a riverside temple with fish feeding. Longer trips diverge into Khlong Bangkok Yai, and can include a visit to an orchid farm. On weekends, you have the option of visiting the **Taling Chan Floating Market** (p180). However, it's worth pointing out that to actually disembark and explore any of these sights, the most common tour of one hour (1000B, up to six people) is simply not enough time; you'll most likely need 1½ or two hours (1300/1500B). Most operators have set tour routes, but if you have a specific destination in mind, you can request it. Tours are generally conducted from 8am to 5pm.

If you'd prefer something longer or more personalised, **Pandan Tour** (☎02 689 1232, 087 109 8873; www.thaicanaltour.com; tours from 2295B) conducts a variety of mostly full-day tours. And a budget alternative is to take the one-way-only **commuter long-tail boat** (Map p265; Chang Pier, off Th Maha Rat; 25B; ⊙4.30am-7.30pm; ⚑Chang Pier) from Chang Pier to Bang Yai, at the distant northern end of Khlong Bangkok Noi, although foreigners are sometimes discouraged from doing so.

DRINKING & NIGHTLIFE

As with restaurants, bars are a rare sight in Ko Ratanakosin. Fortunately, the nightlife of Banglamphu is only a short taxi ride away.

ROOF   BAR
Map p265 (www.salaresorts.com/rattanakosin; 5th fl, Sala Rattanakosin, 39 Th Maha Rat; ⊗5pm-midnight Mon-Thu, to 1am Fri-Sun; ⓢTien Pier) The open-air bar on top of the Sala Rattanakosin hotel has upped the stakes for sunset views of Wat Arun – if you can see the temple at all through the wall of selfie-snapping tourists. Arrive early for a good seat.

AMOROSA   BAR
Map p265 (www.arunresidence.com; rooftop, Arun Residence, 36-38 Soi Pratu Nokyung; ⊗5pm-midnight Mon-Thu, to 1am Fri-Sun; ⓢTien Pier) Perched above the Arun Residence, Amorosa takes advantage of a location directly above the river and opposite Wat Arun. The cocktails aren't going to blow you away, but watching boats ply their way along the royal river as Wat Arun glows is a beautiful reminder that you're not home any more.

☆ ENTERTAINMENT

NATIONAL THEATRE   THEATRE
Map p265 (☎02 224 1342; 2 Th Ratchini; tickets 60-100B; ⓢChang Pier, Maharaj Pier, Phra Chan Tai Pier) The National Theatre holds performances of *khŏn* (masked dance-drama based on stories from the *Ramakian*) at 2pm on the first and second Sundays of the month from January to September, and *lá·kon* (Thai dance-dramas) at 2pm on the first and second Sundays of the month from October to December. Tickets go on sale an hour before performances begin.

🏃 SPORTS & ACTIVITIES

★ AMITA THAI COOKING CLASS   COOKING COURSE
(☎02 466 8966; www.amitathaicooking.com; 162/17 Soi 14, Th Wutthakat, Thonburi; 3000B; ⊗lessons 9.30am-1pm Thu-Tue; ⓢklorng boat from Maharaj Pier) One of Bangkok's most charming cooking schools is held in this canalside house in Thonburi. Taught by the delightfully enthusiastic Piyawadi 'Tam' Jantrupon, a course includes a romp through the garden and instruction in four dishes. The fee covers transport, which takes the form of a boat ride from Maharaj Pier.

CENTER MEDITATION WAT MAHADHATU   MEDITATION
Map p265 (☎02 223 3813, 02 222 6011; Section 5, Wat Mahathat, Th Maha Rat; donations accepted; ⊗lessons 7am, 1pm & 6pm; ⓢChang Pier, Maharaj Pier, Phra Chan Tai Pier) Located within Wat Mahathat, this small centre offers informal daily meditation classes. Taught by English-speaking Prasuputh Chainikom (Kosalo), classes last three hours. Longer periods of study, which include accommodation and food, can be arranged, but students are expected to follow a strict regimen of conduct.

MUAY THAI LAB   MARTIAL ARTS
Map p265 (☎02 024 1326; www.muaythailab.net; 2nd fl, Maharaj Pier, Th Maha Rat; lessons from 990B; ⊗11am-8pm; ⓢMaharaj Pier, Chang Pier, Phra Chan Tai Pier) Muay Thai Lab is a new, impressive one-stop centre for everything related to Thai boxing. Start in the lobby, which has free displays on the history and culture of Thai boxing and a small shop stocked with both souvenirs and gear, before heading to the open-air rooftop gym, which looks over Mae Nam Chao Phraya.

Drop-ins are encouraged to join the introductory lessons, which take place from 11am to 3pm daily; the fee includes clothing and equipment, access to a locker and showers, and a towel.

CHETAWAN TRADITIONAL MASSAGE SCHOOL   MASSAGE
Map p265 (☎02 622 3551; www.watpomassage.com; 392/32-33 Soi Phen Phat; lessons from 2500B, Thai massage per hour 420B; ⊗lessons 9am-4pm, massage 9am-6pm; ⓢTien Pier) Associated with the nearby temple of the same name, this institute offers basic and advanced courses in traditional massage. Basic courses offer 30 hours spread over five days and cover either general massage or foot massage. The advanced course spans 60 hours, requires the basic course as a prerequisite, and covers therapeutic and healing massage. Thai massage is also available for non-students.

The school is outside the temple compound in a restored Bangkok shophouse in unmarked Soi Phen Phat.

Banglamphu

Neighbourhood Top Five

1 Visiting **Th Khao San** (p85): more than just backpackers with dreadlocks in fisherman pants, it is a unique cultural melting pot with something for (almost) everyone.

2 Taking in the panoramic views of old Bangkok from **Golden Mount** (p83).

3 Tasting classic Bangkok-style nosh at old-school restaurants such as **Krua Apsorn** (p84).

4 Dancing on the tables with Thai hipsters at **Brick Bar** (p89).

5 Sitting and gazing at the huge Buddha and sky-high murals in **Wat Suthat** (p80).

For more detail of this area see Map p268

Explore: Banglamphu

Antique shophouses, classic restaurants, ancient temples: Banglamphu is old Bangkok encapsulated in one leafy, breezy district. If you've come for the sights, arrive early, while the heat is still tolerable and the touts few. It's worth sticking around Banglamphu for lunch, as this is when the majority of the area's street stalls and shophouse restaurants are operating. Come evening, young locals flood the area in search of a cheap meal and a cold Chang, giving the area an entirely different vibe. There are enough restaurants and bars here that there's no need to consider another destination for the night.

Despite being one of Bangkok's best areas for accommodation, sights, eating and nightlife, Banglamphu is not very well linked up with the rest of the city by public transport networks. During the day, a good strategy is to approach the area via the river ferry at Phra Athit/Banglamphu Pier – most of the sights are within walking distance. At night, most of the action is centered on and around Th Khao San, which can be accessed via taxi from the BTS stop at National Stadium or the MRT stop at Hua Lamphong.

Local Life

→**Local Cuisine** Bangkok's most traditional district is not surprisingly one of the best places to try authentic central Thai- and Bangkok-style food.

→**Streetside Shopping** Goods available in this district range from backpacker staples along Th Khao San to delicious Thai curry pastes and high-quality handicrafts in the more traditional areas nearby.

→**Pop & Lock** Most evenings the wide expanse in front of Bangkok's City Hall becomes a place for youngsters who meet to practise their break-dancing moves.

→**Les Champs Élysées de Bangkok** The royal boulevard of Th Ratchadamnoen Klang serves to link the Grand Palace in Ko Ratanakosin with newer palaces in Dusit, and is suitably adorned with billboard-sized pictures of Thai royalty.

→**Lucky Number** Because the national lottery office has its office nearby, both sides of Th Ratchadamnoen Klang east of the Democracy Monument (p81) are often clogged with vendors selling lottery tickets.

Getting There & Away

→**River boat** Phra Athit/Banglamphu Pier.
→**Taxi** From the BTS stops at National Stadium or Phaya Thai, or from the MRT stop at Hua Lamphong.
→**Klorng boat** Phanfa Leelard Pier.
→**Bus** Air-con 44, 79, 503 and 511; ordinary 2, 15, 49, 59, 60, 69 and 70.

Lonely Planet's Top Tip

Boats – both the Chao Phraya Express and *klorng* boats – are a steady, if slow, way to reach Banglamphu, but remember that most only run until about 7pm.

 Best Places to Eat

→ Krua Apsorn (p84)
→ Jay Fai (p87)
→ Shoshana (p85)
→ Thip Samai (p84)

For reviews, see p84.

Best Drinking & Entertainment

→ Hippie de Bar (p87)
→ Brick Bar (p89)
→ Madame Musur (p87)
→ Phra Nakorn Bar & Gallery (p87)

For reviews, see p87.

Best Places to Shop

→ Thanon Khao San Market (p89)
→ Heritage Craft (p90)
→ Nittaya Thai Curry (p90)

For reviews, see p89.

◉ SIGHTS

BAN BAAT   NEIGHBOURHOOD

Map p268 (บ้านบาตร, Monk's Bowl Village; off Soi Ban Bat; ⊙9am-5pm; 🚤klorng boat to Phanfa Leelard Pier) FREE The residents of Ban Baat inhabit the only remaining village of three established in Bangkok by Rama I (King Phraphutthayotfa; r 1782–1809) to produce *bàht,* the distinctive bowls used by monks to receive morning food donations. Tourists – not temples – are among the customers these days, and a bowl purchase is usually rewarded with a demonstration of how the bowls are made.

To find the village – today reduced to a single alleyway – from Th Bamrung Meuang, turn down Soi Ban Bat, then take the first right.

As cheaper factory-made bowls are now the norm, the artisanal tradition has shrunk to one extended family. You can observe the process of hammering the bowls together from eight separate pieces of steel, said to represent Buddhism's eightfold path. The joints are then fused with melted copper wire, and the bowl is beaten, polished and coated with several layers of black lacquer.

WAT RATCHANATDARAM   BUDDHIST TEMPLE

Map p268 (วัดราชนัดดาราม; Th Mahachai; ⊙8am-5pm; 🚤klorng boat to Phanfa Leelard Pier) FREE This temple was built for Rama III (King Phranangklao; r 1824-51) in the 1840s, and its design is said to derive from metal temples built in India and Sri Lanka more than 2000 years ago.

At the back of the compound, behind the formal gardens, is a well-known market selling *prá krêu·ang* (Buddhist amulets) in all sizes, shapes and styles.

The temple is most stunning at night when the 37 spires – representing the 37 virtues that lead to enlightenment – of the all-metal **Loha Prasat** (Metal Palace) are lit up like a medieval birthday cake. The interior is relatively unadorned by Thai temple standards, but the hallways and square edges contribute to a symmetry reminiscent of the much earlier temples at Angkor, in Cambodia.

SAO CHING-CHA   MONUMENT

Map p268 (เสาชิงช้า, Giant Swing; Th Bamrung Meuang; ⊙24hr; 🚤klorng boat to Phanfa Leelard Pier) FREE This spindly red arch – a symbol of Bangkok – formerly hosted a Brahman festival in honour of Shiva, in which par-

---

◉ TOP SIGHT
WAT SUTHAT

The main attraction at this temple compound is Thailand's biggest *wí·hǎhn* (sanctuary) and the imperious yet serene 8m-high **Phra Si Sakayamuni** that resides within. The Buddha image is Thailand's largest surviving Sukhothai-period bronze, cast in the former capital in the 14th century. The ashes of Rama VIII (King Ananda Mahidol; r 1935–46) are contained in the base of the image.

Colourful, if now somewhat faded, *Jataka* (murals depicting scenes from the Buddha's life) cover every wall and pillar. The deep-relief wooden doors are also impressive and were carved by artisans including Rama II (King Phraphutthaloetla Naphalai; r 1809–24) himself.

Behind the *wí·hǎhn,* the *bòht* (ordination hall) is the largest of its kind in the country. To add to its list of 'largests', Wat Suthat holds the rank of Rachavoramahavihan, the highest royal temple grade. It maintains a special place in the national religion because of its association with the Brahman priests who perform important ceremonies, such as the Royal Ploughing Ceremony in May. These priests also perform religious rites at two Hindu shrines near the *wát:* **Dhevasathan** (เทวสถาน (โบสถ์พราหมณ์); Map p268; Th Din So); and the smaller **Vishnu Shrine** (Map p268; Th Unakan).

DON'T MISS...

➡ Phra Si Sakayamuni
➡ Temple murals

PRACTICALITIES

➡ วัดสุทัศน์
➡ Map p268, E7
➡ Th Bamrung Meuang
➡ admission 20B
➡ ⊙8.30am-9pm
➡ 🚤klorng boat to Phanfa Leelard Pier

ticipants would swing in ever higher arcs in an effort to reach a bag of gold suspended from a 15m-high bamboo pole. Whoever grabbed the gold could keep it, but that was no mean feat, and deaths were as common as successes. A black-and-white photo illustrating the risky rite can be seen at the ticket counter at adjacent Wat Suthat.

The Brahmans once enjoyed a mystical position within the royal court, primarily in the coronation rituals. But after the 1932 revolution the Brahmans' waning power was effectively terminated and the festival, including the swinging, was discontinued during the reign of Rama VII (King Prajadhipok; r 1925–35).

In 2007, the Giant Swing was replaced with the current model, which was made from six giant teak logs from Phrae, in northern Thailand. The previous version is kept at the National Museum.

PHRA SUMEN FORT & SANTI CHAI
PRAKAN PARK   NOTABLE BUILDING, PARK
Map p268 (ป้อมพระสุเมรุ, สวนสันติชัยปราการ; Th Phra Athit; ⊘5am-9pm; ⛴Phra Athit/Banglamphu Pier) FREE Formerly the site of a sugar factory, today Santi Chai Prakan Park is a tiny patch of greenery with a great river view and lots of evening action, including comical communal aerobics classes. The riverside pathway heading southwards makes for a serene promenade.

The park's most prominent landmark is the blindingly white Phra Sumen Fort, which was built in 1783 to defend the city against a river invasion.

Named for the mythical Phra Sumen (Mt Meru) of Hindu-Buddhist cosmology, the octagonal brick-and-stucco bunker was one of 14 city watchtowers that formerly punctuated the old city wall alongside Khlong Rop Krung (now Khlong Banglamphu but still called Khlong Rop Krung on most signs). Apart from Mahakan Fort (p83), this is the only one still standing.

WAT BOWONNIWET   BUDDHIST TEMPLE
Map p268 (วัดบวรนิเวศวิหาร; www.watbowon.org; Th Phra Sumen; ⊘8.30am-5pm; ⛴Phra Athit/Banglamphu Pier) FREE Founded in 1826, Wat Bowonniwet (known colloquially as Wat Bowon) is the national headquarters for the Thammayut monastic sect, a reformed version of Thai Buddhism. The rest of us should visit the temple for the noteworthy murals in its *bòht* (ordination hall), which include Thai depictions of Western life

---

> ### ⓘ THA OR PIER?
> *Tâh,* often transliterated as *tha,* is the Thai word for 'pier', which explains why some of the signs for the Chao Phraya Express Boat stops say Tha XXX instead of XXX Pier.

(possibly copied from magazine illustrations) during the early 19th century.

Because of its royal status, visitors should be particularly careful to dress properly for admittance to this wát – shorts and sleeveless clothing are not allowed.

Rama IV (King Mongkut; r 1851–68), who set out to be a scholar, not a king, founded the Thammayut sect and began the royal tradition of ordination at this temple. In fact, Mongkut was the abbot of Wat Bowon for several years. Rama IX (King Bhumibol Adulyadej; r 1946–present) and Crown Prince Vajiralongkorn, as well as several other males in the royal family, have been ordained as monks here.

TH BAMRUNG MEUANG
RELIGIOUS SHOPS   AREA
Map p268 (ถนนบำรุงเมือง; Th Bamrung Meuang; ⊘9am-6pm; ⛴klorng boat to Phanfa Leelard Pier) The stretch of Th Bamrung Meuang (one of Bangkok's oldest streets and originally an elephant path leading to the Grand Palace) from Th Mahachai to Th Tanao is lined with shops selling all manner of Buddhist religious paraphernalia. You probably don't need a car-sized Buddha statue or an eerily lifelike effigy of a famous monk, but browsing is fun, and who knows when you might need to do a great deal of Thai-style merit making?

DEMOCRACY MONUMENT   MONUMENT
Map p268 (อนุสาวรีย์ประชาธิปไตย; Th Ratchadamnoen Klang; ⊘24hr; ⛴klorng boat to Phanfa Leelard Pier) FREE The Democracy Monument is the focal point of the grand, European-style boulevard that is Th Ratchadamnoen Klang. As the name suggests, it

---

> ### WHAT'S IN A NAME?
> Banglamphu means 'Place of Lamphu', a reference to the *lam·poo* tree (*Duabanga grandiflora*) that was once prevalent in the area.

A BANGKOK TONGUE-TWISTER

Upon completion of the royal district of Ko Ratanakosin in 1785, at a three-day conse-cration ceremony attended by tens of thousands of Siamese, the capital of Siam was given a new name: 'Krungthep mahanakhon amonratanakosin mahintara ayuthaya mahadilok popnopparat ratchathani burirom udomratchaniwet mahasathan amon-piman avatansathit sakkathattiya witsanukamprasit'. This lexical gymnastic feat translates roughly as: 'Great City of Angels, the Repository of Divine Gems, the Great Land Unconquerable, the Grand and Prominent Realm, the Royal and Delightful Capi-tal City full of Nine Noble Gems, the Highest Royal Dwelling and Grand Palace, the Divine Shelter and Living Place of Reincarnated Spirits'.

Understandably, foreign traders continued to call the capital Bang Makok, which eventually truncated itself to 'Bangkok', the name most commonly known to the out-side world. These days all Thais understand 'Bangkok' but use a shortened version of the official name, Krung Thep (City of Angels). When referring to greater Bangkok, they talk about Krung Thep Mahanakhon (Metropolis of the City of Angels). Expats liv-ing in Bangkok have numerous nicknames for their adopted home, with the Big Mango being the most common.

was erected to commemorate Thailand's momentous transformation from absolute to constitutional monarchy. It was designed by Thai architect Mew Aphaiwong and the relief sculptures were created by Italian Corrado Feroci who, as Silpa Bhirasri, gives his name to Silpakorn University. Feroci combined the square-jawed 'heroes of so-cialism' style popular at the time with Mew Aphaiwong's art deco influences.

There are 75 cannonballs around the base to signify the year BE (Buddhist Era) 2475 (AD 1932); the four wings of the monu-ment stand 24m tall, representing 24 June, the day the constitution was signed; and the central plinth stands 3m high (June was then the third month in the Thai calendar) and supports a chiselled constitution. Each wing has bas-reliefs depicting soldiers, po-lice and civilians who helped usher in the modern Thai state.

During previous periods of military dictatorships, demonstrators have assem-bled here to call for a return to democracy, most notably in 1973 and 1992.

KING PRAJADHIPOK MUSEUM MUSEUM

Map p268 (พิพิธภัณฑ์พระบาทสมเด็จพระปกเกล้า เจ้าอยู่หัว; www.kingprajadhipokmuseum.org; 2 Th Lan Luang; ⊘9am-4pm Tue-Sun; 🚤klorng boat to Phanfa Leelard Pier) FREE This museum assembles old photos and memorabilia to illustrate the rather dramatic life of Rama VII (also known as King Prajadhipok), Thailand's last absolute monarch. The mu-seum occupies a grand neocolonial-style building constructed on the orders of Rama

V for his favourite firm of Bond St mer-chants; it was the only foreign business al-lowed on the royal road linking Bangkok's two palace districts.

The exhibitions reveal that Prajadhipok did not expect to become king, but once on the throne showed considerable diplomacy in dealing with what was, in effect, a revo-lution fomented by a new intellectual class of Thais. The 1st floor deals with the life of Queen Rambhai Barni, while the upper two floors cover the king's own life, revealing, for example, that the army-officer-turned-king spent many of his formative years in Europe where he became fond of British democracy. (Ironically, those plotting his downfall had themselves learned of democ-racy during years of European education.) A coup, carried out while the king and queen were playing golf, ended Thailand's absolute monarchy in 1932. Prajadhipok's reign eventually ended when he abdicated while in England in 1935; he died there in 1941.

OCTOBER 14 MEMORIAL MONUMENT

Map p268 (อนุสรณ์สถาน ๑๔ ตุลา; cnr Th Ratch-adamnoen Klang & Th Tanao; ⊘24hr; 🚤klorng boat to Phanfa Leelard Pier) FREE A peaceful amphitheatre commemorates the civil-ian demonstrators who were killed by the military during a pro-democracy rally on 14 October 1973. Over 200,000 people had as-sembled at the Democracy Monument and along the length of Th Ratchadamnoen to protest against the arrest of political cam-paigners and continuing military dictatorship. Although some in Thailand continue to deny it, photographs confirm that more than 70 demonstrators were killed when the tanks met the crowd.

The complex is an interesting adaptation of Thai temple architecture for a secular and political purpose. A central *chedi* (stupa) is dedicated to the fallen and a gallery of historic photographs lines the interior wall.

RATCHADAMNOEN CONTEMPORARY ART CENTER   ART GALLERY

Map p268 (RCAC; www.facebook.com/Ratcha damnone; Th Ratchadamnoen Klang; ☺10am-7pm Tue-Sun; 🚤klorng boat to Phanfa Leelard Pier) FREE This new, three-storey structure hosts changing exhibitions of mixed-media contemporary domestic art.

MAHAKAN FORT   NOTABLE BUILDING

Map p268 (ป้อมมหากาฬ; Th Ratchadamnoen Klang; ☺24hr; 🚤klorng boat to Phanfa Leelard Pier) FREE The whitewashed Mahakan Fort is one of two surviving citadels that defended the old walled city. The octagonal fort is a picturesque, if brief and hot, stop en route to Golden Mount, but the neighbouring village is more interesting. This small community of wooden houses has been here

for more than 100 years, but since the mid-1990s it has fought the Bangkok municipal government's plan to demolish it and create a 'tourist' park.

The community blocked progress and even proposed the development of another tourist attraction: a *li·gair* (bawdy dance-drama) museum honouring the dance tradition that traces its creation to a school located here in 1897. Some of the homes were eventually demolished, resulting in the park you see today. But behind the fort many others remain (for now). Visitors are welcome. Climb the ramparts (not for children) running away from the fort and walk to the far end, where stairs lead down and into the village.

QUEEN'S GALLERY   ART GALLERY

Map p268 (www.queengallery.org; 101 Th Ratchadamnoen Klang; admission 30B; ☺10am-7pm Thu-Tue; 🚤klorng boat to Phanfa Leelard Pier) This royal-funded museum presents five floors of rotating exhibitions of modern and traditionally influenced art. The building is sleek and contemporary and the artists hail from the upper echelons of the conservative Thai art world. The attached shop is filled with fine-art books and gifts.

TOP SIGHT
GOLDEN MOUNT & WAT SAKET

Before glass and steel towers began growing out of Bangkok's flat riverine plain, the massive **Golden Mount** (ภูเขาทอง) was the only structure to make any significant impression on the horizon. The mount was commissioned by Rama III (King Phranangklao; r 1824–51), who ordered that the earth dug out to create Bangkok's expanding *klorng* (canal) network be piled up to build a 100m-high, 500m-wide *chedi* (stupa). As the hill grew, however, the weight became too much for the soft soil beneath and the project was abandoned until his successor built a small gilded *chedi* on its crest and added trees to stave off erosion. Rama V (King Chulalongkorn; r 1886–1910) later added to the structure and interred a Buddha relic from India in the *chedi.* The concrete walls were added during WWII. At the peak is a breezy 360-degree view of Bangkok's most photogenic side.

Next door, seemingly peaceful **Wat Saket** (วัดสระเกศ; Map p268;) FREE contains murals that are both beautiful and gory; proceed directly to the pillar behind the Buddha statue for explicit depictions of Buddhist hell.

In November there's a festival in the grounds that includes an enchanting candlelight procession up the Golden Mount.

DON'T MISS...

➡ View from summit of Golden Mount

➡ Temple paintings at Wat Saket

PRACTICALITIES

➡ ภูเขาทอง & วัดสระเกศ
➡ Phu Khao Thong
➡ Map p268, H6
➡ Th Boriphat
➡ admission to summit of Golden Mount 10B
➡ ☺7.30am-5.30pm
➡ 🚤klorng boat to Phanfa Leelard Pier

 EATING

Banglamphu is famous for its old-school central-Thai food – the predominant cuisine in this part of town. For something more international, head to Th Khao San, where you'll find a few international fast-food franchises as well as foreign and vegetarian restaurants.

THIP SAMAI
CENTRAL THAI $

Map p268 (313 Th Mahachai; mains 50-250B; ⏰5pm-2am; 🛥klorng boat to Phanfa Leelard Pier) Brace yourself – you should be aware that the fried noodles sold from carts along Th Khao San have little to do with the dish known as *pàt tai*. Luckily, less than a five-minute túk-túk ride away lies Thip Samai, home to some of the most legendary fried noodles in town.

Note that Thip Samai is closed on alternate Wednesdays.

NUTTAPORN
THAI $

Map p268 (94 Th Phraeng Phuthon; mains from 20B; ⏰9am-4pm Mon-Sat; 📷; 🛥Phra Athit/Banglamphu Pier) A crumbling shophouse that for the last 70 years has been churning out some of Bangkok's most famous coconut ice cream – in our opinion, the ideal palate cleanser after a bowl of spicy noodles. Other uniquely domestic flavours include mango, Thai tea, and our favourite, durian.

CHOTE CHITR
CENTRAL THAI $

Map p268 (146 Th Phraeng Phuthon; mains 60-200B; ⏰11am-10pm; 🛥klorng boat to Phanfa Leelard Pier) This third-generation shophouse restaurant boasting just six tables is a Bangkok foodie landmark. The kitchen can be inconsistent and the service is consistently grumpy, but when they're on, dishes like *mèe gròrp* (crispy fried noodles) and

yam tòo·a ploo (wing-bean salad) are in a class of their own.

ROTI-MATABA
THAI, HALAL $

Map p268 (136 Th Phra Athit; dishes 19-115B; ⏰9am-10pm Tue-Sun; 📷; 🛥Phra Athit/Banglamphu Pier) This classic Bangkok eatery may have grown a bit too big for its britches in recent years, but it still serves tasty Islamic world influenced dishes such as roti, *gaang mát·sà·màn* ('Muslim curry'), tart fish curry and *má·tà·bà* (a stuffed Islamic-style pancake). An upstairs air-con dining area and a couple of outdoor tables provide barely enough seating for loyal fans and curious tourists alike.

KIMLENG
THAI $

Map p268 (158-160 Th Tanao; mains 60-150B; ⏰10am-10pm Mon-Sat; 🛥klorng boat to Phanfa Leelard Pier) This tiny family-run restaurant specialises in the dishes and flavours of central Thailand. It's a good place to dip your toes in the local cuisine via an authentic *yam* (Thai-style salad), such as *yam ʼblah dùk foo*, a mixture of catfish deep-fried until crispy and strands of tart, green mango.

★KRUA APSORN
THAI $$

Map p268 (www.kruaapsorn.com; Th Din So; mains 80-400B; ⏰10.30am-8pm Mon-Sat; 🛥klorng boat to Phanfa Leelard Pier) This homely dining room is a favourite of members of the Thai royal family and restaurant critics alike. Just about all of the central and southern Thai dishes are tasty, but regulars never miss the chance to order the decadent 'stir-fried crab with yellow chilli' or the *tortilla Española*–like 'omelet with crab'.

There's another branch on Th Samsen in Thewet & Dusit (p97).

BANGLAMPHU'S VEGETARIAN RESTAURANTS

Due to the strong foreign influence, there's an abundance of vegetarian restaurants in the Banglamphu area. In addition to **Hemlock** (p87), **Shoshana** (p85), **Snack Bar** (p86) and **Ranee's Velo Restaurant** (Map p268; https://www.facebook.com/Ranees-Restaurant-/188135527897042; 15 Trok Mayom; mains 100-300B; ⏰3pm-midnight; 📷; 🛥Phra Athit/Banglamphu Pier), all of which have generous meat-free menus, other vegie dining destinations include **Arawy Vegetarian Food** (Map p268; 152 Th Din So; mains from 30B; ⏰7am-8pm; 📷; 🛥klorng boat to Phanfa Leelard Pier), with heaps of prepared meat-free curries, dips and stir-fries; and **May Kaidee's** (Map p268; www.maykaidee.com; 33 Th Samsen; mains 80-120B; ⏰9am-10pm; 📷; 🛥Phra Athit/Banglamphu Pier), a long-standing restaurant that also houses a vegie Thai cooking school.

SHOSHANA ISRAELI $$

Map p268 (88 Th Chakraphatdi Phong; mains 70–240B; ⊘10am-midnight; 📷; 🚢Phra Athit/ Banglamphu Pier) One of Khao San's longest-running Israeli restaurants, Shoshana resembles your grandparents' living room right down to the tacky wall art and plastic placemats. Feel safe in ordering anything deep-fried – they do an excellent job of it – and don't miss the deliciously garlicky eggplant dip.

WHAT'S SO LONELY ABOUT KHAO SAN ROAD?

Th Khao San, better known as Khao San Rd, is genuinely unlike anywhere else on earth. It's an international clearing house of people either entering the liberated state of travelling in Southeast Asia or returning to the coddling bonds of first-world life, all coming together in a neon-lit melting pot in Banglamphu. Its uniqueness is probably best illustrated by a question: apart from airports, where else could you share space with the citizens of dozens of countries at the same time, people ranging from first-time backpackers scoffing banana pancakes to 75-year-old grandparents ordering G&Ts, and everyone in between, including hippies, hipsters, nerds, glamazons, package tourists, global nomads, people on a week's holiday and those taking a gap year, people of every colour and creed looking at you looking at them looking at everyone else?

Th Khao San (*kâw sǎhn,* meaning 'uncooked rice') is perhaps the most high-profile bastard child of the age of independent travel. Of course, it hasn't always been this way. For its first two centuries or so it was just another unremarkable road in old Bangkok (to see what it was like back in the day, stop into the new **Khaosan Museum** (Map p268; 1st fl, 201 Th Khao San; ⊘9am-9pm; 🚢Phra Athit/Banglamphu Pier; FREE). The first guesthouses appeared in 1982, and as more backpackers arrived throughout the '80s the old wooden homes were converted one by one into low-rent dosshouses. By the time Alex Garland's novel *The Beach* was published in 1997, with its opening scenes set in the seedier side of Khao San, staying here had become a rite of passage for backpackers coming to Southeast Asia.

The publicity from Garland's book, and the movie that followed, pushed Khao San into the mainstream, romanticising the seedy, and stereotyping the backpackers it attracted as unwashed and countercultural ist. It also brought the long-simmering debate about the relative merits of Th Khao San to the top of backpacker conversations across the region. Was it cool to stay on KSR? Was it uncool? Was this 'real travel' or just an international anywhere surviving on the few baht Western backpackers spent before they headed home to start their high-earning careers? Was it really Thailand at all?

Perhaps one of Garland's characters summed it up most memorably when he said: 'You know, Richard, one of these days I'm going to find one of those Lonely Planet writers and I'm going to ask him, what's so fucking lonely about the Khao San Road?'

Today more than ever the answer would have to be: not that much. With the help of all that publicity, Khao San continued to evolve, with bedbug-infested guesthouses replaced by boutique hotels, and downmarket TV bars showing pirated movies transformed into hip design bars peopled by flashpackers in designer threads. But the most interesting change has been in the way Thais see Khao San.

Once written off as home to cheap, dirty *fà·ràng kêe ngók* (stingy foreigners), Banglamphu has become just about the coolest district in Bangkok. Attracted in part by the long-derided independent traveller and their modern ideas, the city's own counterculture kids have moved in and brought with them a tasty selection of small bars, organic cafes and shops. Indeed, Bangkok's indie crowd has proved to be the Thai spice this melting pot always lacked.

Not that Khao San has moved completely away from its backpacker roots. The strip still anticipates every traveller need: meals to soothe homesickness, cafes and bars for swapping travel tales about getting to the Cambodian border, tailors, travel agents, teeth whitening, secondhand books, hair braiding and, of course, the perennial Akha women trying to harass everyone they see into buying wooden frogs. No, it's not very lonely at all...

ANN'S SWEET   CAFE **$$**

Map p268 (www.facebook.com/page.annsweet; 138 Th Phra Athit; mains from 150B; ☺noon-7.30pm Tue-Sun; ☻Phra Athit/Banglamphu Pier) Anshada is a native of Bangkok and a graduate of the Cordon Bleu cooking program. Come to her cosy, shophouse-bound cafe for coffee and some of the most authentic Western-style desserts you'll find in Bangkok.

SNACK BAR   INTERNATIONAL **$$**

Map p268 (80 Soi 2, Th Samsen; mains 120-170B; ☺noon-midnight Tue-Sun; ✎; ☻Phra Athit/Banglamphu Pier) You've conquered the deep-fried scorpion, now wrangle with poutine, deep-fried potatoes topped with cheese curds and gravy. Run by guys from Quebec, Snack Bar is the place to go for this and other French-Canadian specialities, Francophone pop and the latest hockey game (as well as dishes ranging in cuisine from Thai to Lebanese).

ESCAPADE BURGERS & SHAKES   AMERICAN **$$**

Map p268 (112 Th Phra Athit; mains 120-330B; ☺4pm-midnight Tue-Sun; ☻Phra Athit/Banglamphu Pier) Escapade is proof that, when it comes to American food, Thais have moved light years beyond McDonald's. Squeeze into the narrow, bar-like dining room for messy burgers with edgy ingredients such as 'toasted rice mayo', not to mention some pretty decadent milkshakes.

POJ SPA KAR   CENTRAL THAI **$$**

Map p268 (443 Th Tanao; mains 65-200B; ☺12.30-8.30pm; ☻klorng boat to Phanfa Leelard Pier) Pronounced *pôht sà·pah kahn*, this is allegedly the oldest restaurant in Bangkok, and it continues to maintain recipes handed down from a former palace cook. Be sure to order the simple but tasty lemongrass omelette or the deliciously sour-sweet *gaang sôm*, a traditional central Thai soup.

LOCAL KNOWLEDGE

TH PHRA ATHIT'S NOODLE RESTAURANTS

Despite being virtually next door to touristy Th Khao San, Th Phra Athit remains a microcosm of noodle dishes from Bangkok – and beyond. If you're interested in sampling some of Thailand's more obscure noodle dishes, consider one of the following:

Soy (Map p268; 100/2-3 Th Phra Athit, mains 60-100B; ☺7am-5.30pm; ☻Phra Athit/Banglamphu Pier) Long-standing and lauded Soy serves big, hearty bowls of beef noodle soup. Choose between the fall-apart tender braised beef, fresh beef, beef balls, or try them all. There's no English-language sign here; look for the open-fronted shophouse with red plastic chairs.

Khun Daeng (Map p268; Th Phra Athit; mains 45-55B; ☺11am-9.30pm Mon-Sat; ☻Phra Athit/Banglamphu Pier) This popular place does *gŏo·ay jáp yoo·an*, identified on the English-language menu as 'Vietnamese noodle'. Introduced to northeastern Thailand via Vietnamese immigrants, the dish combines peppery pork sausage, a quail egg, thin rice noodles and a garnish of crispy fried shallots in a slightly viscous broth. Khun Daeng has no English-language sign; look for the white and green shopfront.

Somsong Phochana (Map p268; off Th Lamphu, no roman-script sign; mains from 30B; ☺9.30am-4pm; ☻Phra Athit/Banglamphu Pier) This is one of the few places in Bangkok that serves *gŏo·ay dĕe·o sù·kŏh·tai*, Sukhothai-style noodles: slices of barbecued pork and thin rice noodles in a clear pork broth seasoned with a little sugar, supplemented with sliced green beans and garnished with ground peanuts. To find Somsong, enter Th Lamphu, then take the first left, opposite Watsungwej School; the restaurant is on the right.

Pua-Kee (Map p268; Th Phra Athit; mains 50-90B; ☺9am-4pm; ☻Phra Athit/Banglamphu Pier) Come here for the central Thai classic, *gŏo·ay dĕe·o dôm yam* ('rice noodle soup hotspicy with mixed ball' on the menu), fishball noodles pre-seasoned with sugar, lime and dried chilli, and served with a crispy deep-fried wonton. There's no English-language sign here, but it's located next door to the clearly labelled Makalin Clinic.

HEMLOCK THAI $$

Map p268 (56 Th Phra Athit; mains 75–280B;
◷4pm-midnight Mon-Sat; ⚲; 🚢Phra Athit/
Banglamphu Pier) Taking full advantage of
its cosy shophouse location, this perennial
favourite has enough style to feel like a special night out, but doesn't skimp on flavour
or preparation. And unlike at other similar
places, the eclectic menu here reads like an
ancient literary work, reviving old dishes
from aristocratic kitchens across the country, not to mention several meat-free items.

★JAY FAI CENTRAL THAI $$$

Map p268 (327 Th Mahachai; mains 180–1000B;
◷3pm-2am Mon-Sat; 🚢klorng boat to Phanfa
Leelard Pier) You wouldn't think so by looking at her bare-bones dining room, but Jay
Fai is known far and wide for serving Bangkok's most expensive *pàt kêe mow* ('drunk-
ard's noodles'; wide rice noodles fried with
seafood and Thai herbs).

Jay Fai is located in a virtually unmarked
shophouse on Th Mahachai, directly across
from a 7-Eleven.

The *pàt kêe mow* price is justified by the
copious fresh seafood, as well as Jay Fai's
distinct frying style that results in an almost oil-free finished product.

🍷 DRINKING & NIGHTLIFE

HIPPIE DE BAR BAR

Map p268 (www.facebook.com/hippie.debar;
46 Th Khao San; ◷3pm-2am; 🚢Phra Athit/
Banglamphu Pier) Our vote for Banglamphu's
best bar, Hippie boasts a funky retro vibe
and indoor and outdoor seating, all set to
the type of indie/pop soundtrack that you're
unlikely to hear elsewhere in town. Despite
being located on Th Khao San, there are
surprisingly few foreign faces, and it's a
great place to make some new Thai friends.

MADAME MUSUR BAR

Map p268 (41 Soi Ram Buttri; ◷8am-1am; 🚢Phra
Athit/Banglamphu Pier) Saving you the trip
north to Pai, Madame Musur pulls off that
elusive combination of 'northern Thailand
meets *The Beach* meets Th Khao San'. It's a
fun place to chat, drink and people-watch,
and, serving a short menu of northern Thai
dishes (dishes from 100B to 200B), it's also
not a bad place to eat.

BOOZING LOCAL-STYLE

Although Th Khao San remains associated with foreign tourists, in recent
years the general area has also become a popular nightlife destination
for young locals. Check out the live
music pubs along Th Phra Athit or the
low-key bars south of Th Ratchadamnoen Klang for a more local drinking
scene.

PHRA NAKORN BAR & GALLERY BAR

Map p268 (www.facebook.com/Phranakornbar
andgallery; 58/2 Soi Damnoen Klang Tai; ◷6pm-
1am; 🚢klorng boat to Phanfa Leelard Pier) Located an ambivalent arm's length from the
hype of Th Khao San, Phra Nakorn Bar &
Gallery is a home away from hovel for students and arty types, with eclectic decor
and changing gallery exhibits. Our tip:
head directly for the breezy rooftop and
order some of the bar's cheap 'n' tasty Thai
food.

THE CLUB CLUB

Map p268 (www.facebook.com/theclubkhao
sanbkk; 123 Th Khao San; admission 120B Fri
& Sat; ◷9pm-2am; 🚢Phra Athit/Banglamphu
Pier) Located right in the middle of Th
Khao San, this cavernlike dance hall hosts
a good mix of locals and backpackers;
check the Facebook page for upcoming
events and guest DJs.

COMMÉ BAR

Map p268 (100/4-5 Th Phra Athit; ◷6pm-1am;
🚢Phra Athit/Banglamphu Pier) The knot of
vintage motorcycles is your visual cue,
but most likely you'll hear Commé before
you see it. A staple for local hipsters, this
classic Th Phra Athit semi-open-air bar is
the place to go for a loud, boozy, Thai-style
night out.

THE BANK BAR

Map p268 (3rd fl, 44 Th Chakraphatdi Phong;
◷6pm-late; 🚢Phra Athit/Banglamphu Pier)
This vaguely Middle Eastern–themed bar
represents the posh alter ego of Th Khao
San. There's live music, lounges for puff-
ing on *shisha*, and a dark club. And the
bar's elevated setting appears to lend it
some leniency with the city's strict closing
times.

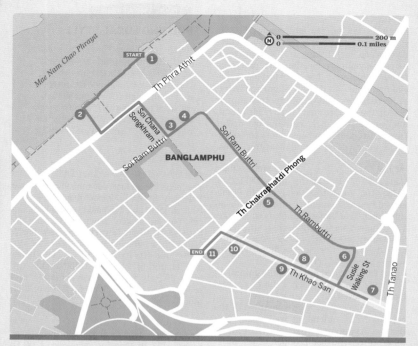

Neighbourhood Walk
Banglamphu Pub Crawl

START SHEEPSHANK
END THE BANK
LENGTH 1.5KM; THREE TO SIX HOURS

You don't need to go far to find a decent bar in Banglamphu, but why limit yourself to one? With this in mind, we've assembled a pub crawl that spans people-watching, river views, live music and late-night shenanigans.

Begin your crawl in sophisticated, air-conditioned comfort at ❶**Sheepshank** (located next door to Phra Athit/Banglamphu Pier), a gastropub with an intriguing menu of bar snacks and classic cocktails. If you still have space for tapas, head west along the riverfront promenade until you reach ❷**Babble & Rum**, the Riva Surya hotel's open-air restaurant-bar.

From Th Phra Athit, enter Soi Chana Songkhram and take a left at Soi Ram Buttri, where you begin phase two of your crawl: people-watching. ❸**Gecko Bar** is a frugal and fun place to gawk at other patrons and passers-by, while a few doors

down, ❹**Madame Musur** (p87) offers the same perks, but with a bit more sophistication and tasty northern-style eats.

It's time to add some music to the mix, so for phase three, cross Th Chakraphatdi Phong and head down Th Rambuttri towards one of the open-air live music bars such as ❺**Barlamphu** (p89) or ❻**Molly Bar** (p89).

At this point, you should be lubricated enough for the main event, so, crossing via Susie Walking St, proceed to Th Khao San. If you need a bathroom or a blast of air-con, make a pit stop at ❼**Mulligans**, a tidy Irish-themed bar in the Buddy Lodge. Otherwise, get a bird's-eye view of the human parade from elevated ❽**Roof Bar & Restaurant**, or ringside at the noisy and buzzy ❾**Center Khao Sarn** (p89).

End the night on a good note by planting yourself at ❿**Hippie de Bar** (p87), one of Banglamphu's best bars. Or if 2am is too early to call it a night, crawl over to ⓫**The Bank** (p87), a rooftop lounge and nightclub that stays open until late.

CENTER KHAO SARN BAR

Map p268 (Th Khao San; ⌚24hr; ⛴Phra Athit/Banglamphu Pier) The open-air terrace here offers ringside seats for the human parade along Th Khao San. The upstairs bar hosts late-night bands.

JHAM JUN BAR

Map p268 (rooftop, Fortville Guesthouse, 9 Th Phra Athit; ⌚6pm-1am; ⛴Phra Athit/Banglamphu Pier) Boasting a rooftop address, a casual, loungey vibe, live music and an emphasis on food, Jham Jun is a characteristically Thai-style drinking spot a short walk from Th Khao San.

ROLLING BAR BAR

Map p268 (Th Prachathipatai; ⌚5pm-midnight; ⛴klorng boat to Phanfa Leelard Pier) An escape from hectic Th Khao San is a good enough excuse to schlep to this quiet canalside boozer. Live music and salty bar snacks are reasons to stay.

ENTERTAINMENT

★BRICK BAR LIVE MUSIC

Map p268 (www.brickbarkhaosan.com; basement, Buddy Lodge, 265 Th Khao San; admission 150B Sat & Sun; ⌚8pm-1.30am; ⛴Phra Athit/Banglamphu Pier) This basement pub, one of our favourite destinations in Bangkok for live music, hosts a nightly revolving cast of bands for an almost exclusively Thai crowd – many of whom will end the night dancing on the tables. Brick Bar can get packed, so be sure to get there early.

AD HERE THE 13TH LIVE MUSIC

Map p268 (www.facebook.com/adhere13thbluesbar; 13 Th Samsen; ⌚6pm-midnight; ⛴Phra Athit/Banglamphu Pier) Located beside Khlong Banglamphu/Khlong Rob Krung, this closet-sized blues bar is everything a neighbourhood joint should be: lots of regulars, cold beer and heart-warming tunes delivered by a masterful house band (starting at 10pm). Everyone knows each other, so don't be shy about mingling.

JAZZ HAPPENS! LIVE MUSIC

Map p268 (www.facebook.com/JazzHappens; 62 Th Phra Athit; ⌚7pm-1am; 📶; ⛴Phra Athit/Banglamphu Pier) Linked with Silpakorn University, Thailand's most famous arts university, Jazz Happens! is a stage for aspiring musical talent. With four acts playing most nights and a huge selection of bar snacks, you'll be thoroughly entertained.

BROWN SUGAR LIVE MUSIC

Map p268 (www.brownsugarbangkok.com; 469 Th Phra Sumen; ⌚5pm-1am Tue-Thu, to 2am Sat & Sun; ⛴klorng boat to Phanfa Leelard Pier, Phra Athit/Banglamphu Pier) This long-standing, live music staple has found a cosy new home in old Bangkok. The live music starts at 8pm most nights.

SHOPPING

★THANON KHAO SAN MARKET SOUVENIRS

Map p268 (Th Khao San; ⌚10am-midnight; ⛴Phra Athit/Banglamphu Pier) The main guesthouse strip in Banglamphu is a day-and-night shopping bazaar peddling all the backpacker 'essentials': foul-mouthed

BANGLAMPHU'S LIVE MUSIC SCENE

Banglamphu is home to Bangkok's greatest concentration of live music bars. The western stretch of Th Phra Athit, in particular, is home to half a dozen back-to-back pint-sized music pubs that offer lots of loud Thai pop, but not a whole lot of breathing room.

For something a bit more approachable, head to Th Khao San's chilled-out next-door neighbour, Th Rambuttri, where there's an abundance of open-air live music restaurant-pubs, including the bluesy **Barlamphu** (Map p268; Th Rambuttri; ⌚noon-1am; ⛴Phra Athit/Banglamphu Pier), or the poppier **Suk Sabai** (Map p268; 96 Th Rambuttri; ⌚24hr; ⛴Phra Athit/Banglamphu Pier) or **Molly Bar** (Map p268; 108 Th Rambuttri; ⌚8pm-1am; ⛴Phra Athit/Banglamphu Pier).

One street over, Th Khao San is home to one of our favourite places in Bangkok for live music, **Brick Bar**. Just around the corner is **The Bank** (p87), which occasionally hosts indie Thai rock bands, while **Ad Here the 13th**, a Bangkok blues stalwart, and **Brown Sugar**, a Bangkok live music legend, are only a couple of blocks away.

T-shirts, bootleg MP3s, hemp clothing, fake student ID cards, knock-off designer wear, selfie sticks, orange juice and of course, those croaking wooden frogs.

HERITAGE CRAFT HANDICRAFTS
Map p268 (35 Th Bamrung Meuang; ⊙11am-6pm Mon-Fri; ⊛klorng boat to Phanfa Leelard Pier) Handicrafts with a conscience: this new boutique is an atmospheric showcase for the quality domestic wares of ThaiCraft (p154), some of which are produced via fair trade practices. Items include silks from Thailand's northeast, baskets from the south and jewellery from the north, and there's also an inviting on-site cafe.

NITTAYA THAI CURRY FOOD & DRINK
Map p268 (136-40 Th Chakraphatdi Phong; ⊙9am-7pm Mon-Sat; ⊛Phra Athit/Banglamphu Pier) Follow your nose: Nittaya is famous throughout Thailand for her pungent but high-quality curry pastes. Pick up a couple of takeaway canisters for prospective dinner parties or peruse the snack and gift sections, where visitors to Bangkok load up on local specialities for friends and family back in the provinces.

LOFTY BAMBOO HANDICRAFTS
Map p268 (1st fl, Buddy Hotel, 265 Th Khao San; ⊙10.30am-8pm; ⊛Phra Athit/Banglamphu Pier) No time to make it to northern Thailand? No problem. At this new shop you can get the type of colourful, hill-tribe-inspired clothes, cloth items and other handicrafts you'd find at the markets in Chiang Mai and Chiang Rai. And best of all, a purchase supports economic self-sufficiency in upcountry villages.

TAEKEE TAEKON HANDICRAFTS
Map p268 (118 Th Phra Athit; ⊙9am-6pm Mon-Sat; ⊛Phra Athit/Banglamphu Pier) This atmospheric shop has a decent selection of Thai textiles from the country's main silk-producing areas, especially northern Thailand, as well as interesting postcards not widely available elsewhere.

THAI NAKON HANDICRAFTS
Map p268 (79 Th Prachathipatai; ⊙10am-6pm Mon-Sat; ⊛klorng boat to Phanfa Leelard Pier) This family-owned enterprise has been in business for 70 years and often fills commissions from the royal family for nielloware and silver ornaments. Silver cases and clutches, ceremonial bowls and tea

sets are also among the offerings. Ask to go behind the showroom to witness the aged artisans at work.

SPORTS & ACTIVITIES

BANGKOK BOLD COOKING STUDIO COOKING COURSE
Map p268 (☎098 829 4310; www.bangkokbold. com; 503 Th Phra Sumen; courses 2000B; ⊙lessons 9am-1pm & 2-5pm; ⊛klorng boat to Phanfa Leelard Pier) The newest venture by a team that previously ran a popular cooking school on Th Khao San, Bold offers two daily courses of instruction in three Thai dishes, with lessons taught in a chic shophouse setting.

VELO THAILAND BICYCLE TOUR
Map p268 (☎02 628 8628, 089 201 7782; www. velothailand.com; 29 Soi 4, Th Samsen; tours from 1100B; ⊙10am-7pm; ⊛Phra Athit/Banglamphu Pier) Velo is a small and personal bike-tour outfit based out of Banglamphu. Day and night tours to Thonburi and further afield are on offer.

BAAN CHAO YOGA YOGA
Map p268 (☎062 007 4796; ASTV Bldg, Th Phra Athit; courses 300B; ⊙lessons 5.15pm & 6.30pm Mon-Fri, 10.30am Sat; ⊛Phra Athit/Banglamphu Pier) A new yoga studio with daily hour-long sessions and English-language instruction, located a brief walk from Th Khao San. Walk-ins are encouraged.

SOR VORAPIN GYM MARTIAL ARTS
Map p268 (☎02 282 3551; www.thaiboxings.com; 13 Th Kasab; ⊙lessons 7.30-9.30am & 3-5pm; ⊛Phra Athit/Banglamphu Pier) Conveniently located steps from Th Khao San, this gym offers training in Thai boxing (500/9000B per session/month) for foreign students of both genders.

GRASSHOPPER ADVENTURES BICYCLE TOUR
Map p268 (☎02 280 0832; www.grasshopper adventures.com; 57 Th Ratchadamnoen Klang; half-/full-day tours from 1100/1600B; ⊙8.30am-6.30pm; ⊛klorng boat to Phanfa Leelard Pier) This lauded outfit runs a variety of unique bicycle tours in and around Bangkok, including a night tour and a tour of the city's green zones.

Thewet & Dusit

Neighbourhood Top Five

1 Witnessing Victorian sense and Thai sensibilities merge in the former royal enclave of **Dusit Palace Park** (p93).

2 Seeing Thai boxing – the sport that makes Steven Seagal look as soft as a pillow – at **Ratchadamnoen Stadium** (p98).

3 Enjoying the breezy, tasty riverside dining at restaurants such as **Khinlom Chom Sa-Phan** (p98).

4 Wondering what country you're in while wandering among the Carrara marble, European-style frescos and red carpet of **Wat Benchamabophit** (p95).

5 Sampling homestyle Thai food good enough for royalty at **Krua Apsorn** (p97).

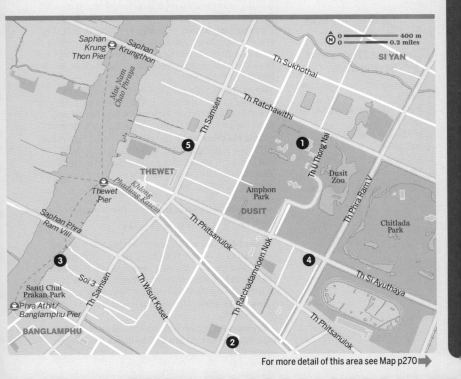

For more detail of this area see Map p270 ➡

Lonely Planet's Top Tip

If you're keen to see a Thai boxing match at Ratchadamnoen Stadium, go on a Thursday night, when aficionados say the best-matched bouts are on.

Best Places to Eat

➡ Likhit Kai Yang (p97)

➡ Krua Apsorn (p97)

➡ Nang Loeng Market (p97)

For reviews, see p97. ➡

Best Drinking & Entertainment

➡ Post Bar (p98)

➡ Ratchadamnoen Stadium (p98)

➡ Khinlom Chom Sa-Phan (p98)

For reviews, see p98. ➡

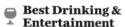

Best Historical Structures

➡ Vimanmek Teak Mansion (p93)

➡ Wat Benchamabophit (p95)

➡ Abhisek Dusit Throne Hall (p94)

➡ Ananta Samakhom Throne Hall (p95)

For reviews, see p93. ➡

Explore: Thewet & Dusit

Thewet, particularly the area near Th Samsen, has the hectic, buzzy feel often associated with Bangkok: relentless traffic, throngs of civil servants and school kids, and a soggy market. The adjacent river is the only respite from the action, and it also functions as a good point from which to approach the area, as most sights and restaurants are a short walk from the river ferry pier. Plan to visit this area at lunch or dinner time to best take advantage of the riverside restaurants.

Dusit, on the other hand, is possibly Bangkok's most orderly district, home to the kind of tree-lined avenues and regal monuments you'd expect to find in Paris. Set aside a few hours – ideally in the cool morning – to visit the area's gems: Dusit Palace Park and Wat Benchamabophit.

In theory, the two districts are within walking distance of each other, although this is made difficult by the harsh Bangkok sun. Dusit's sights are relatively far apart and are best approached by taxi or túk-túk (pronounced *đúk đúk*).

Local Life

➡ **Local Hero** Visit the Rama V Memorial (p96) on any Tuesday (the day of his birth) to witness worshippers making offerings. An even larger celebration is on 23 October, the anniversary of the former monarch's death.

➡ **Boxing Day Dinner** Planning to watch Thai boxing at Ratchadamnoen Stadium (p98)? Do as the locals do: grab a plate of *gài yâhng* (grilled chicken) beforehand from the restaurants surrounding the stadium, such as Likhit Kai Yang (p97).

➡ **Royal Digs** Chitlada Palace (p97) is the official residence of the royal family. The compound is generally closed to the public, and you're not likely to see any royals, but it's worth taking a peek through the gates.

➡ **Time Machine** Nang Loeng Market (p97) provides a glimpse into Bangkok's yesteryear. Particularly emblematic is the market area's wooden movie theatre, allegedly the city's oldest and slated to be renovated in time for its 2018 centenary.

Getting There & Away

➡ **River boat** One way to approach the Thewet and Dusit areas is via the river ferry stop at Thewet Pier. From here it's a brief walk through shady walkways to the riverside restaurants, or a short túk-túk or taxi ride to Dusit Palace Park and other attractions.

➡ **Bus** Air-con 505, 510 and 510; ordinary 3, 16, 18, 32, 53, 70 and 72.

➡ **Skytrain** An option best attempted outside of rush hours is to take the BTS to Phaya Thai before continuing by taxi.

INGOLF POMPE / LOOK-FOTO / GETTY IMAGES ©

TOP SIGHT
DUSIT PALACE PARK

Following his first European tour in 1897, Rama V (King Chulalongkorn; r 1868–1910) returned with visions of European castles and set about transforming these styles into a uniquely Thai expression, today's Dusit Palace Park. The royal palace, throne hall and minor palaces for extended family were all moved here from Ko Ratanakosin, and were supplemented with beaux-arts institutions and Victorian manor houses.

Today, the current king has yet another home (in Hua Hin) and this complex now holds a house museum and other cultural collections. All of this, and the expansive gardens, make Dusit Palace Park a worthwhile escape from the chaos of modern Bangkok.

Vimanmek Teak Mansion

Arguably the highlight of Dusit Palace Park is this structure, said to be the world's largest golden-teak mansion, allegedly built with nary a single nail. The mansion was originally constructed on Ko Si Chang in 1868 as a retreat for Rama V; the king had it moved to its present site in 1901. For the following few years it served as Rama V's primary residence, with the 81 rooms accommodating his enormous extended family. The interior of the mansion contains various personal effects of the king and a treasure trove of early Ratanakosin-era and European art objects and antiques.

Compulsory English-language tours of the building start every 30 minutes and last around an hour, though it's a matter of luck as to whether your guide will actually speak comprehensible English or not.

DON'T MISS...

- Vimanmek Teak Mansion
- Abhisek Dusit Throne Hall
- Royal Thai Elephant Museum
- Ancient Cloth Museum

PRACTICALITIES

- วังสวนดุสิต
- Map p270, C2
- bounded by Th Ratchawithi, Th U Thong Nai & Th Nakhon Ratchasima
- admission to all Dusit Palace Park sights adult/child 100/20B, or free with Grand Palace ticket
- 🕐9.30am-4pm Tue-Sun
- ⛴Thewet Pier, [S]Phaya Thai exit 2 & taxi

VERSAILLES OF BANGKOK

In 1897, Rama V became the first Thai monarch to visit Europe, a trip that seemingly had a profound impact on the king. Upon returning to Siam, he soon set about building a new royal district comprised of relocated Thai structures and spacious, grand, Western-style buildings surrounded by expansive gardens (Suan Dusit means 'Celestial Gardens') – a significant contrast to the increasingly crowded walled district of Ko Ratanakosin. Having chosen a rural-feeling spot within walking distance of the Grand Palace – the king was allegedly a fan of the new-fangled trend of bicycling – Rama V hired a team of German and Italian architects and imported materials such as Carrara marble for the construction of his new European-style home.

COVER UP!

Because Dusit Palace Park is royal property, visitors should wear long pants (no capri pants) or long skirts and sleeved shirts.

Abhisek Dusit Throne Hall

Visions of Moorish palaces and Victorian mansions must have still been spinning around in King Rama V's head when he commissioned this intricate building of porticoes and fretwork fused with a distinctive Thai character. Built as the throne hall for the palace in 1904, it opens onto a big stretch of lawn and flowerbeds, just like any important European building. Inside, the heavy ornamentation of the white main room is quite extraordinary, especially if you've been visiting a lot of overwhelmingly gold temples or traditional wooden buildings. Look up to just beneath the ceiling to see the line of brightly coloured stained-glass panels in Moorish patterns. The hall displays regional handiwork crafted by members of the Promotion of Supplementary Occupations & Related Techniques (Support) foundation, a charity organisation sponsored by Queen Sirikit.

Royal Thai Elephant Museum

Near the Th U Thong Nai entrance, two large stables that once housed three white elephants – animals whose auspicious albinism automatically make them crown property – are now the Royal Thai Elephant Museum. One of the structures contains artefacts and photos outlining the importance of elephants in Thai history and explaining their various rankings according to physical characteristics. The second stable holds a life-sized model of the king's first white elephant. Draped in royal vestments, the statue is more or less treated as a shrine by the visiting Thai public.

Ancient Cloth Museum

This museum contains a beautiful – and informative – assemblage of traditional silks and cottons from across the Tai-speaking world, although at the time of research it was closed indefinitely for renovations.

HM King Bhumibol Photography Exhibitions

Near the Th Ratchawithi entrance, two residence halls display the HM King Bhumibol Photography Exhibitions, a collection of photographs and paintings by the present monarch, a man rarely pictured without a Canon SLR slung around his neck. Among the photos of his wife and children are pictures of the king playing clarinet with Benny Goodman and Louis Armstrong in 1960.

SIGHTS

DUSIT PALACE PARK MUSEUM, HISTORIC SITE

See p93.

WAT BENCHAMABOPHIT BUDDHIST TEMPLE

Map p270 (วัดเบญจมบพิตร (วัดเบญจะฯ); cnr Th Si Ayuthaya & Th Phra Ram V; admission 20B; ⏲8am-6pm; ⛴Thewet Pier, [S]Phaya Thai exit 3 & taxi) You might recognise this temple from the back of the 5B coin. Made of white marble imported from Italy, the distinctive *bòht* (ordination hall) of Wat Ben, as it's colloquially known, was built in the late 19th century under Rama V. The base of the central Buddha image, a copy of Phitsanulok's revered Phra Phuttha Chinnarat, contains his ashes.

The structure is a unique example of modern Thai temple architecture, as is the interior design, which melds Thai features with European influences: the red carpets, the gold-on-white motifs painted repetitively on the walls, the walls painted like stained-glass windows and the royal blue wall behind the central Buddha image are strongly reminiscent of a European palace. It's not all that surprising when you consider how enamoured Rama V was with Europe – just walk across the street to Dusit Palace Park for further evidence.

The courtyard behind the *bòht* has 53 Buddha images (33 originals and 20 copies) representing every *mudra* (gesture) and style from Thai history, making this the ideal place to compare Buddhist iconography. If religious imagery isn't your thing, this temple still offers a pleasant stroll beside landscaped canals filled with blooming lotus and Chinese-style footbridges.

ANANTA SAMAKHOM THRONE HALL MUSEUM

Map p270 (พระที่นั่งอนันตสมาคม; www.artsofthekingdom.com; Th U Thong Nai; admission 150B; ⏲10am-5pm Tue-Sun; ⛴Thewet Pier, [S]Phaya Thai exit 3 & taxi) The domed neoclassical building behind the Rama V Memorial was originally built as a royal reception hall during the reign of Rama V, but wasn't completed until 1915, five years after his death. Today the building houses an exhibit called *Arts of the Kingdom,* which, like the nearby Abhisek Dusit Throne Hall, displays the products of Queen Sirikit's Support foundation.

The hall was designed as a place to host – and impress – foreign dignitaries, and on occasion it still serves this purpose, most notably during celebrations of King Bhumibol Adulyadej's 60th year on the throne, when royals from around the world converged here in full regalia (you may encounter a much-published picture of this meeting while in Bangkok). The first meeting of the Thai parliament was held in the building before being moved to a facility nearby.

THE ORIGINAL WHITE ELEPHANTS

Think 'white elephant' and something like Howard Hughes' *Spruce Goose* comes to mind. But why is it that this and other supposedly valuable but hugely expensive and basically useless items are known as white elephants? The answer lies in the sacred status given to albino elephants by the kings of Thailand, Cambodia, Laos and Myanmar.

The tradition derives from the story in which the Buddha's mother is said to have dreamt of a white elephant presenting her with a lotus flower – a symbol of purity and wisdom – just before she gave birth. Extrapolating from this, a monarch possessing a white elephant was regarded as a just and benign ruler. Across the region any genuinely albino elephant automatically became crown property; the physical characteristics used to identify and rank white elephants are outlined in the **Royal Thai Elephant Museum** (p94). Laws prevented sacred white elephants from working, so despite being highly regarded, they were of no practical value and cost a fortune to keep.

In contemporary Thailand, the white elephant has retained its sacred status – indeed, the animal was prominently featured on the flag of Siam from 1855 to 1916 – and the current king possesses 11 of them, more than any previous monarch. The elephants were previously kept at Chitlada Palace in Bangkok, but now reside at three different locations upcountry.

RAMA V MEMORIAL   MONUMENT
Map p270 (พระบรมรูปทรงม้า; Th U Thong Nai;
⬛Thewet Pier, ⬛Phaya Thai exit 3 & taxi) The
bronze figure on horseback is Rama V
(King Chulalongkorn; r 1868–1910), the
monarch widely credited with steering the
country into the modern age and for pre-
serving Thailand's independence from European colonialism. He is also considered
a champion of the common person for his

THAI BOXING

More formally known as Phahuyut (from the Pali-Sanskrit *bhahu* or 'arm' and *yodha*
or 'combat'), Thailand's ancient martial art of *moo·ay tai* (or muay Thai) is one of the
kingdom's most striking national icons. Overflowing with colour and ceremony as well
as exhilarating moments of clenched-teeth action, the best matches serve up a blend
of such skill and tenacity that one is tempted to view the spectacle as emblematic
of Thailand's centuries-old devotion to independence in a region where most other
countries fell under the European colonial yoke.

Many martial-arts aficionados agree that *moo·ay tai* is the most efficient, effective and generally unbeatable form of ring-centred, hand-to-hand combat practised
today. According to legend, it has been for a while. After the Siamese were defeated at
Ayuthaya in 1767, several expert *moo·ay boh·rahn* (from which *moo·ay tai* is derived)
fighters were among the prisoners hauled off to Burma. A few years later a festival was
held; one of the Thai fighters, Nai Khanom Tom, was ordered to take on prominent Burmese boxers for the entertainment of the king and to determine which martial art was
most effective. He promptly dispatched nine opponents in a row and, as legend has it,
was offered money or beautiful women as a reward; he promptly took two new wives.
Today a *moo·ay tai* festival in Ayuthaya is named after Nai Khanom Tom.

In the early days of the sport, combatants' fists were wrapped in thick horse-
hide for maximum impact with minimum knuckle damage; tree bark and seashells
were used to protect the groin from lethal kicks. But the high incidence of death and
physical injury led the Thai government to ban *moo·ay tai* in the 1920s; in the 1930s
the sport was revived under a modern set of regulations. Bouts were limited to five
three-minute rounds separated by two-minute breaks. Contestants had to wear
international-style gloves and trunks, and their feet were taped – to this day no shoes
are worn. In spite of all these concessions to safety, today all surfaces of the body
remain fair targets, and any part of the body except the head may be used to strike
an opponent. Common blows include high kicks to the neck, elbow thrusts to the face
and head, knee hooks to the ribs and low kicks to the calf. Punching is considered the
weakest of all blows, and kicking merely a way to 'soften up' one's opponent; knee and
elbow strikes are decisive in most matches.

Unlike some martial disciplines, such as kung fu or *qi gong, moo·ay tai* doesn't
entertain the idea that martial-arts techniques can be passed only from master to
disciple in secret. Thus the *moo·ay tai* knowledge base hasn't fossilised – in fact, it
remains ever open to innovation, refinement and revision. Thai champion Dieselnoi,
for example, created a new approach to knee strikes that was so difficult to defend
that he retired at 23 because no one dared to fight him anymore.

Another famous *moo·ay tai* champion is Parinya Kiatbusaba, aka Nong Thoom, a
gà·teu·i (transgendered person) from Chiang Mai who arrived for weigh-ins wearing
lipstick and rouge. After a 1998 triumph at Lumphini, Parinya used the prize money to
pay for sex-change surgery; in 2003, the movie *Beautiful Boxer* was made about her life.

While Bangkok has long attracted foreign fighters, it wasn't until 1999 that French
fighter Mourad Sari became the first non-Thai fighter to take home a weight-class
championship belt from a Bangkok stadium. Several Thai *nák moo·ay* (fighters) have
gone on to triumph in world championships in international-style boxing. Khaosai
Galaxy, one of the greatest Asian boxers of all time, successfully defended his World
Boxing Association super-flyweight world title 19 times before retiring in 1991.

abolition of slavery and corvée (the requirement that every citizen be available for state labour when called on).

Rama V's accomplishments are so revered, especially by Thailand's middle class, that his statue attracts worshippers (particularly on Tuesdays, the day of his birth), who make offerings of candles, flowers (predominately pink roses) and bottles of whisky. The statue is also the site of a huge celebration on 23 October, the anniversary of the monarch's death.

DUSIT ZOO   ZOO

Map p270 (สวนสัตว์ดุสิต (เขาดิน); www.dusit zoo.org; Th Ratchawithi; adult/child 150/70B; ⊙8am-6pm; ⛴Thewet Pier, ⓈPhaya Thai exit 3 & taxi) Originally a private botanic garden for Rama V, Dusit Zoo (Suan Sat Dusit or *kŏw din*) was opened in 1938 and is now one of the premier zoological facilities in Southeast Asia. Squeezed into the 19 hectares are more than 300 mammals, 200 reptiles and 800 birds, including relatively rare indigenous species. The shady grounds feature trees labelled in English, plus a lake in the centre with paddle boats for rent.

CHITLADA PALACE   NOTABLE BUILDING

Map p270 (พระราชวังจิตรลดา; cnr Th Ratchawithi & Th Phra Ram V; ⛴Thewet Pier, ⓈPhaya Thai exit 3 & taxi) Formerly the current royal family's official residence (at time of writing the king was in hospital), Chitlada Palace is also a royally funded agriculture centre demonstrating the reigning king's commitment to the progress of the country's major industry.

The palace is not open to the general public and it's pretty difficult to see much from the outside, but you can spot rice paddies and animal pastures – smack in the middle of Bangkok – through the perimeter fence.

NATIONAL LIBRARY   LIBRARY

Map p270 (Th Samsen; ⊙9am-6.30pm Mon-Fri, to 5pm Sat & Sun; ⛴Thewet Pier) **FREE** The country's largest repository of books has few foreign-language resources, but its strength is in its astrological books and star charts; the collection also holds recordings by the king, sacred palm-leaf writings and ancient maps.

✖ EATING

Thewet's workaday vibe and Dusit's nearly restaurant-free avenues mean that Thai is virtually the only option in this part of town. For a bit more culinary diversity, head to adjacent Banglamphu.

NANG LOENG MARKET   THAI $

Map p270 (btwn Soi 8-10, Th Nakhon Sawan; mains 30-80B; ⊙10am-2pm Mon-Fri; ⛴Thewet Pier, ⓈPhaya Thai exit 3 & taxi) Dating back to 1899, this atmospheric fresh market offers a charming glimpse of old Bangkok – not to mention a great place to grab a bite. Nang Loeng is renowned for its Thai sweets, and at lunchtime it's also an excellent place to fill up on central-Thai-style curries or some Chinese-influenced noodles.

THAMNA   VEGETARIAN $

Map p270 (175 Th Samsen; mains 90-190B; ⊙11am-3pm & 5-9pm Mon-Sat; ✐; ⛴Thewet Pier) This self-professed 'hometaurant' specialises in fusiony vegetarian dishes that will make even the meat-eaters smile.

★LIKHIT KAI YANG   NORTHEASTERN THAI $$

Map p270 (off Th Ratchadamnoen Nok, no roman-script sign; mains 50-280B; ⊙9am-9pm; ⛴Thewet Pier, ⓈPhaya Thai exit 3 & taxi) Located just behind Ratchadamnoen Stadium (avoid the grotty branch directly adjacent to the stadium), this decades-old restaurant is where locals come for a northeastern-Thai-style meal before a Thai boxing match. The friendly English-speaking owner will steer you through the ordering process, but don't miss the deliciously herbal, eponymous 'charcoal roasted chicken'.

The restaurant has no English-language sign; look for the huge yellow banner.

★KRUA APSORN   THAI $$

Map p270 (www.kruaapsorn.com; 503-505 Th Samsen; mains 80-400B; ⊙10.30am-7.30pm Mon-Fri, to 6pm Sat; ⛴Thewet Pier) This is the original branch of this homely, award-winning and royally patronised restaurant. Expect a clientele of fussy families and big-haired, middle-aged ladies, and a cuisine revolving around full-flavoured, largely seafood- and vegetable-heavy central and southern Thai dishes. If you have dinner in mind, be sure to note the early closing times.

THEWET & DUSIT EATING

LOCAL KNOWLEDGE

THEWET'S RIVERSIDE RESTAURANTS

Dinner beside Mae Nam Chao Phraya, where the breezes are cool and aquariums serve as your menu, is a local tradition and a classic Bangkok experience. And while Thewet and Dusit may lack in culinary diversity, they excel in riverfront views. So to narrow your choices, here's the scoop on the areas' riverside restaurants:

Khinlom Chom Sa-Phan (Map p270; ☎02 628 8382; www.khinlomchomsaphan.com; 11/6 Soi 3, Th Samsen; mains 95-2500B; ⏲11.30am-midnight; ⛴Thewet Pier) Locals crowd this covered deck just about every night for seafood and live music; as such, you'll need to book ahead for the best tables. It's probably the best all-around riversider.

Steve Café & Cuisine (Map p270; www.stevecafeandcuisine.com; 68 Soi 21, Th Si Ayuthaya; mains 160-390B; ⏲11.30am-2.30pm Mon-Fri, 11.30am-11pm Sat & Sun; ⛴Tha Thewet) Despite the cheesy name, Steve is the most sophisticated of the area's riverside restaurants. The menu spans a diverse selection of Thai dishes, and service is friendly and efficient, even when the place is mobbed. To get here, enter Th Si Ayuthaya and walk through Wat Thevaratkunchong until you reach the river; locals will point the way.

Kaloang Home Kitchen (Map p270; Th Si Ayuthaya; mains 80-300B; ⏲10am-10pm; ⛴Tha Thewet) Don't be alarmed by the peeling paint and dilapidated deck at this charmingly unrefined riverside staple – the return customers at Kaloang Home Kitchen certainly aren't. To reach the restaurant, follow the final windy stretch of Th Si Ayuthaya all the way to the river.

In Love (Map p270; Th Krung Kasem; mains 80-280B; ⏲11.30am-midnight; ⛴Thewet Pier) The budget option for a riverside night out, In Love charms with its great views of Saphan Phra Ram VIII and approachable prices.

SEVEN SPOONS INTERNATIONAL **$$$**

Map p270 (☎02 629 9214, 084 539 1819; 22-24 Th Chakraphatdi Phong; mains 160-780B; ⏲11am-3pm & 6pm-1am Tue-Sat, 6pm-1am Sun; ⛴Thewet Pier, [S]Phaya Thai exit 3 & taxi) With its interior of dark woods and smooth concrete, and a menu featuring influences ranging from Montreal to Morocco, Seven Spoons is a bit of a surprise - one simply doesn't expect a place this modern and cosmopolitan in such an antiquated corner of Bangkok. There are lots of vegetarian options and a decent cocktail list, too.

DRINKING & NIGHTLIFE

There's very little – almost nothing, really – in terms of nightlife in this part of town. Luckily, Banglamphu and Th Khao San are a brief walk or taxi ride away. Alternatively, the area's riverside restaurants also function as open-air bars.

POST BAR BAR

Map p270 (161 Th Samsen; ⏲7pm-1am; ⛴Thewet Pier) If 'Chinese pawn shop' can be considered a legitimate design theme, Post Bar has nailed it. The walls of this narrow, shophouse-bound bar are decked with retro Thai kitsch, the soundtrack is appropriately classic rock, and the clientele overwhelmingly Thai.

ENTERTAINMENT

RATCHADAMNOEN STADIUM SPECTATOR SPORT

Map p270 (off Th Ratchadamnoen Nok; tickets 3rd-class/2nd-class/ringside 1000/1500/2000B; ⛴Thewet Pier, [S]Phaya Thai exit 3 & taxi) Ratchadamnoen Stadium, Bangkok's oldest and most venerable venue for *moo·ay tai* (Thai boxing; also spelt *muay thai*), hosts matches on Monday, Wednesday and Thursday from 6.30pm to around 11pm, and Sunday at 3pm and 6.30pm. Be sure to buy tickets from the official ticket counter, not from the touts and scalpers who hang around outside the entrance.

Chinatown

Neighbourhood Top Five

1 Dining alfresco at decades-old street-food stalls such as **Nay Hong** (p105).

2 Witnessing 5.5 tonnes of solid gold Buddha at **Wat Traimit** (p101).

3 Checking out the oil-stained machine shops, hidden Chinese temples and twisting lanes of **Talat Noi** (p102).

4 Watching chaos and commerce battle it out in **Talat Mai** (p102), China-town's frenetic, photogenic fresh-food market.

5 Enjoying Bollywood-style markets and Indian food in **Phahurat** (p103).

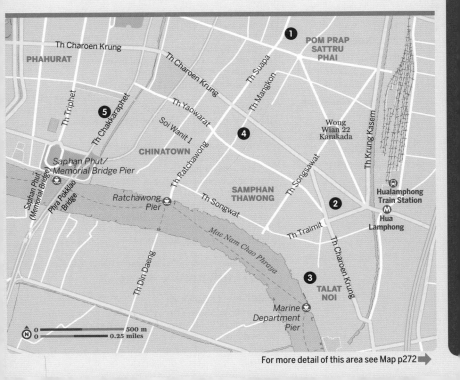

For more detail of this area see Map p272

CHINATOWN

Lonely Planet's Top Tip

Bangkok's street stalls and family-run restaurants operate frustratingly inconsistent business hours. So if you're heading to Chinatown with the intent of eating at a specific stall, it's always a good idea to have a Plan B. And remember, most of Bangkok's street-food vendors close up shop on Monday, so don't plan on eating in Chinatown on this day.

 Best Places to Eat

➡ Nay Hong (p105)

➡ Samsara (p106)

➡ Th Phadungdao Seafood Stalls (p106)

➡ Royal India (p106)

For reviews, see p105.➡

 Best Markets

➡ Talat Mai (p102)

➡ Pak Khlong Talat (p102)

➡ Sampeng Lane (p105)

For reviews, see p102.➡

 Best Temples & Churches

➡ Wat Traimit (p101)

➡ Wat Mangkon Kamalawat (p103)

➡ Church of Santa Cruz (p103)

➡ Holy Rosary Church (p105)

For reviews, see p101.➡

Explore: Chinatown

Chinatown embodies everything that's hectic, noisy and polluted about Bangkok, but that's what makes it such a fascinating area to explore. The area's big sights – Wat Traimit (Golden Buddha) and the street markets – are worth hitting, but be sure to set aside enough time to do some map-free wandering among the neon-lit gold shops, hidden temples, crumbling shopfronts and pencil-thin alleys, especially the tiny winding lanes that extend from Soi Wanit 1 (aka Sampeng Lane).

For ages, Chinatown was home to Bangkok's most infamous traffic jams, but the arrival of the MRT (Metro) in 2005 finally made the area a sane place to visit. Still, the station is about a kilometre from many sights, so you'll have to take a longish walk or a short taxi ride. An alternative is to take the Chao Phraya Express Boat to the stop at Ratchawong Pier, from where it's a brief walk to most restaurants and a bit further to most sights.

The whole district is buzzing from dawn until after dusk, but Chinatown is at its best during these two times. There aren't many interesting lunch options in the area, so eat between 7pm and 9pm instead.

Local Life

➡ **Street Food** Although Chinatown can appear dominated by restaurants serving shark-fin and bird's-nest soup, the true Chinatown meal is what's usually prepared by the street vendors lining Th Yaowarat after dark. Locals come from all over Bangkok to eat at Chinatown's stalls, and so should you.

➡ **Markets** The Phahurat (p103) and Chinatown districts have interconnected markets selling fabrics, clothes and household wares, as well as wholesale shops for every imaginable bulk item and a few places selling gems and jewellery.

➡ **Prayers** In many of Chinatown's temples, you'll see locals shaking cans of thin sticks called *see-am see*. When a stick falls to the floor, look at its number and find the corresponding paper that gives a no-nonsense appraisal of your future in Thai, Chinese and English.

➡ **Nightlife** Or should we say, lack thereof. Other than a few new bars on Soi Nana, there's little in the realm of non-dodgy nightlife in Chinatown. Instead, eat here, then head to nearby Banglamphu or Silom for drinks.

Getting There & Away

➡ **MRT** Hua Lamphong.

➡ **River boat** Marine Department Pier, Ratchawong Pier, Saphan Phut/Memorial Bridge Pier and Pak Klong Taladd Pier.

➡ **Bus** Air-con 507 and 508; ordinary 1, 4, 25, 33, 37, 49 and 53.

TOP SIGHT
WAT TRAIMIT (GOLDEN BUDDHA)

Wat Traimit, also known as the Temple of the Golden Buddha, is home to the world's largest gold statue, a gleaming, 3m-tall, 5.5-tonne Buddha with a mysterious past and a current value of nearly US$200 million in gold alone. Sculpted in the graceful Sukhothai style, the image is thought to date from around the late 15th century. But if it is possible for a Buddha to lead a double life, then this piece has most certainly done so.

Possibly sometime in the 17th century, at what is thought to have been a time of great danger to the Siamese kingdom – presumably prior to an invasion from Burma – the Buddha was rendered with a plaster exterior in an attempt to disguise it from the looting hordes. And it worked. After various assaults, the Burmese hauled off vast quantities of Thai treasure, but this most valuable of all Buddha images – indeed, the most valuable in all of Buddhism – remained as shabby-looking and anonymous as intended. It was moved first to Bangkok and later to Wat Traimit, the only temple in the Chinatown area modest enough to take such a world-weary Buddha. And thus it remained, beneath a tin roof, until the mid-1950s, when the temple had collected enough money to build a proper shelter for the image. During the move the Buddha was dropped from a crane, an act of such ill fortune that the workers are said to have downed tools and run. When the abbot inspected the Buddha the following day he found the plaster had cracked and, after centuries of anonymity, the golden Buddha's true identity was finally revealed.

The image remained seated in its modest pavilion until 2009, benevolently smiling down upon a seemingly endless procession of tour groups, which seem to have scared off most of the genuine worshippers. But Wat Traimit's days of poverty are long gone. A new marble hall has been built with a combination of Chinese-style balustrades and a steep, golden Thai-style roof. Surrounding it is a narrow strip of grass watered via mist fountains.

The 2nd floor of the structure is home to the **Phra Buddha Maha Suwanna Patimakorn Exhibition** (Map p271; admission 100B; ☺8am-4pm Tue-Sun), which has exhibits on how the statue was made, discovered and came to arrive at its current home, while the 3rd floor is home to the **Yaowarat Chinatown Heritage Center** (Map p271; admission 100B; ☺8am-4pm Tue-Sun), a small but engaging museum with multimedia exhibits on the history of Bangkok's Chinatown and its residents.

DON'T MISS...

➡ The Golden Buddha
➡ Phra Buddha Maha Suwanna Patimakorn Exhibition
➡ Yaowarat Chinatown Heritage Center

PRACTICALITIES

➡ วัดไตรมิตร, Temple of the Golden Buddha
➡ Map p272, E3
➡ Th Mittaphap Thai-China
➡ admission 40B
➡ ☺8am-5pm
➡ ⛴Ratchawong Pier, Ⓜ Hua Lamphong exit 1

⊙ SIGHTS

**WAT TRAIMIT
(GOLDEN BUDDHA)**   BUDDHIST TEMPLE
See p101.

TALAT NOI   NEIGHBOURHOOD
Map p271 (ตลาดน้อย; off Th Charoen Krung;
⊘7am-7pm; 🚢Marine Department Pier) This
microcosm of soi life is named after a small
(nóy) market *(dà·làht)* that sets up between
Soi 22 and Soi 20, off Th Charoen Krung.
Wandering here you'll find streamlike soi
turning in on themselves, weaving through
noodle shops, grease-stained machine
shops and people's living rooms.

SAN JAO SIEN KHONG   CHINESE TEMPLE
Map p271 (ศาลเจ้าเซียนโค้ง; off Soi Charoen Phanit; ⊘6am-6pm; 🚢Marine Department Pier)
FREE This is one of the city's oldest Chinese
shrines, and is guarded by a playful rooftop terracotta dragon; it's also one of the
best places to come during the yearly Vegetarian Festival. It's below the River View
Guesthouse.

TALAT MAI   MARKET
Map p271 (ตลาดใหม่; Soi Yaowarat 6/Charoen
Krung 16; ⊘6am-6pm; 🚢Ratchawong Pier, Ⓜ Hua
Lamphong exit 1 & taxi) With nearly two centuries of commerce under its belt, New Market is no longer an entirely accurate name
for this strip of commerce. Regardless, this
is Bangkok's, if not Thailand's, most Chinese market, and the dried goods, seasonings, spices and sauces will be familiar to
anyone who's ever spent time in China. The
hectic atmosphere (be on guard for motorcycles squeezing between shoppers) and
exotic sights and smells culminate in something of a surreal sensory experience.

While much of the market centres on
cooking ingredients, the section north of
Th Charoen Krung (equivalent to Soi 21,
Th Charoen Krung) is known for selling
incense, paper effigies and ceremonial
sweets – the essential elements of a traditional Chinese funeral.

PAK KHLONG TALAT   MARKET
Map p271 (ปากคลองตลาด, Flower Market; Th
Chakkaraphet; ⊘24hr; 🚢Pak Klong Taladd Pier,
Saphan Phut/Memorial Bridge Pier) This sprawl-

LOCAL KNOWLEDGE

CHINATOWN'S STREETS OF COMMERCE

Chinatown is the neighbourhood version of a megastore divided up into categories of
commerce, with streets as aisles; here's your in-store guide:

Th Charoen Krung (🚢Ratchawong Pier, Ⓜ Hua Lamphong exit 1 & taxi) Starting on the
western end of the street, near the intersection of Th Mahachai, is a collection of old
record stores. **Talat Khlong Ong Ang** (Map p272; ⊘9am-5pm) consumes the next
block, selling all sorts of used and new electronic gadgets. **Nakhon Khasem** (Map
p272; ⊘9am-5pm) is the reformed thieves' market where restaurant owners and vendors come to stock up on kitchenwares. Further east, near Th Mahachak, is **Talat
Khlong Thom** (Map p272; ⊘9am-5pm), a hardware centre. West of Th Ratchawong is
everything you'd need to give a Chinese funeral.

Th Yaowarat A hundred years ago this was a poultry farm; now it's gold street, the
biggest trading centre of the precious metal in the country. Along Th Yaowarat, gold is
sold by the *bàht* (a unit of weight equivalent to 15g) from neon-lit storefronts that look
more like shrines than shops. Near the intersection of Th Ratchawong, stores shift to
Chinese and Singaporean tourists' tastes: dried fruit and nuts, chintzy talismans and
accoutrements for Chinese festivals. The area also retains a few Chinese apothecaries, smelling of wood bark and ancient secrets.

Th Mittraphan (Map p272; ⊘9am-5pm; 🚢Ratchawong Pier, Ⓜ Hua Lamphong exit 2) Sign-
makers can be found along this street, which branches off Wong Wian 22 Karakada;
Thai and roman letters are typically cut out by a hand-guided lathe placed prominently beside the pavement.

Th Santiphap (Map p272; ⊘9am-5pm; 🚢Ratchawong Pier, Ⓜ Hua Lamphong exit 2) Car
parts and other automotive gear.

Still haven't found what you're looking for? Try **Sampeng Lane** (p105) or **Talat Mai**.

CHINATOWN VEGETARIAN FESTIVAL

During the annual Vegetarian Festival in September/October, Bangkok's Chinatown becomes a virtual orgy of nonmeat cuisine. The festivities centre on Chinatown's main street, Th Yaowarat, and the **Talat Noi** area, but food shops and stalls all over the city post yellow flags to announce their meat-free status.

Celebrating alongside the ethnic Chinese are Thais who look forward to the special dishes that appear during the festival period. Most restaurants put their normal menus on hold and instead prepare soy-based substitutes for standard Thai dishes like *dôm yam* (Thai-style spicy/sour soup) and *gaang kĕe·o wăhn* (green curry). Even Thai regional cuisines are sold (without the meat, of course). Yellow Hokkien-style noodles often make an appearance in the special festival dishes, usually in stir-frys along with meaty mushrooms and big hunks of vegetables.

Along with abstinence from meat, the 10-day festival is celebrated with special visits to the temple, often requiring worshippers to dress in white.

ing wholesale flower market has become a tourist attraction in its own right. The endless piles of orchids, rows of roses and stacks of button carnations are a sight to be seen. The best time to come is late at night, when the goods arrive from upcountry. During the day, Pak Khlong Talat is one of the city's largest wholesale vegetable markets.

PHAHURAT   NEIGHBOURHOOD

Map p271 (พาหุรัด; Th Chakkaraphet; ⊙9am-5pm; ⛴Saphan Phut/Memorial Bridge Pier, Pak Klong Taladd Pier) Heaps of South Asian traders set up shop in Bangkok's small but bustling Little India, where everything from Bollywood movies to bindis is sold. It's a great area to just wander through, stopping for masala chai and a Punjabi sweet as you go.

The bulk of the action unfolds along unmarked Soi ATM, which runs alongside the large India Emporium shopping centre.

The emphasis is on cloth – from boisterously coloured textiles and traditional Thai dance costumes, to machine-made Thai textiles and children's clothes.

WAT MANGKON KAMALAWAT   BUDDHIST TEMPLE

Map p271 (วัดมังกรกมลาวาส; cnr Th Charoen Krung & Th Mangkon; ⊙6am-6pm; ⛴Ratchawong Pier, Ⓜ Hua Lamphong exit 1 & taxi) FREE Clouds of incense and the sounds of chanting form the backdrop at this Chinese-style Mahayana Buddhist temple. Surrounding the temple are vendors selling food for the gods – steamed lotus-shaped dumplings and oranges – which are donated to the temple in exchange for merit. Dating back to 1871, it's the largest and most important religious structure in the area, and during the annual

Vegetarian Festival, religious and culinary activities are particularly active here.

CORRECTIONS MUSEUM   MUSEUM

Map p271 (พิพิธภัณฑ์ราชทัณฑ์; Rommaneenart Park, 436 Th Mahachai; ⊙9am-4pm Mon-Fri; ⛴Saphan Phut/Memorial Bridge Pier, Pak Klong Taladd Pier, Ⓜ Hua Lamphong exit 1 & taxi) FREE Learn about the painful world of Thai-style punishment at what's left of this former jail, where life-sized models re-enact a variety of horrendous executions and punishments.

SOY SAUCE FACTORY   GALLERY

Map p271 (www.facebook.com/soysaucefactory; Soi 24, Th Charoen Krung; ⊙10am-7pm Tue-Sun; Ⓜ Hua Lamphong exit 1) A former soy sauce factory-turned-gallery (or event space, or bar, or photo studio...) Whatever it is, check the Facebook page to see what's currently on at this artsy, open-ended gathering place, indicative of the kind of changes currently underfoot in Bangkok's Chinatown.

CHURCH OF SANTA CRUZ   CHURCH

Map p271 (โบสถ์สังตาครูส; Soi Kuti Jiin; ⊙7am-noon Sat & Sun; ⛴river-crossing ferry from Atsadang Pier) FREE Centuries before Sukhumvit became Bangkok's international district, the Portuguese claimed *fa·ràng* (Western) supremacy on a riverside plot of land given to them by King Taksin in appreciation for their support after the fall of Ayuthaya. Located on this concession, the Church of Santa Cruz dates to 1913.

Very little activity occurs on the grounds, but small, fascinating streets break off from the main courtyard into the area known as Kuti Jiin, the local name for the church. On Soi Kuti Jiin 3, a few houses continue to sell Portuguese-inspired cakes and sweets.

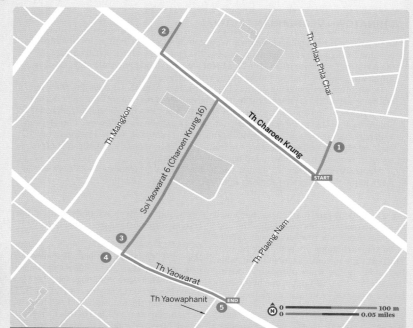

CHINATOWN

🏃 Neighbourhood Walk
A Taste of Chinatown

START CNR TH PLAENG NAM &
TH CHAROEN KRUNG
END CNR TH YAOWAPHANIT &
TH YAOWARAT
LENGTH 1KM; TWO TO THREE HOURS

Street food rules in Chinatown, making the area ideal for a culinary adventure. Although many vendors stay open late, the more popular stalls tend to sell out quickly, so the best time to feast in this area is from 7pm to 9pm. Don't try this walk on a Monday, when most of the city's street vendors stay at home. Bringing a friend (or three) and sharing is a good way to ensure that you can try as many dishes as possible.

Start your walk at the intersection of Th Plaeng Nam and Th Charoen Krung. Head north along Th Phlap Phla Chai, staying on the right-hand side for about 50m, until you reach ❶ **Nai Mong Hoi Thod** (p106), a shophouse restaurant renowned for its delicious *or sòo·an* (oysters fried with egg and a sticky batter).

Backtrack to Th Charoen Krung and turn right. Upon reaching Th Mangkon make a right; on your left-hand side you'll see ❷ **Jek Pui**, a table-less stall famous for its Chinese-style Thai curries.

Cross Th Charoen Krung again, turn left, and continue east until you reach Soi Yaowarat 6/Charoen Krung 16, also known as Talat Mai, the area's most famous strip of commerce. At the end of the alley you'll see a gentleman making ❸ **gŏo·ay đĕe·o kôo·a gài**, rice noodles fried with chicken, egg and garlic oil.

Upon emerging at Th Yaowarat, cross over to the busy market area directly across the street. The first vendor on the right, ❹ **Nay Lek Uan**, sells *gŏo·ay jáp nám săi*, an intensely peppery broth containing noodles and pork offal.

Returning back to Th Yaowarat, turn right and continue until the next intersection. On the corner of Th Yaowaphanit and Th Yaowarat you'll see ❺ **Mangkorn Khao**, a stall selling *bà·mèe* (Chinese-style wheat noodles) and barbecued pork.

SAMPENG LANE
MARKET

Map p271 (สำเพ็ง; Soi Wanit 1; ☺8am-6pm; 🚢Ratchawong Pier, Ⓜ Hua Lamphong exit 1 & taxi) Soi Wanit 1 – colloquially known as Sampeng Lane – is a narrow artery running parallel to Th Yaowarat and bisecting the commercial areas of Chinatown and Phahurat. The Chinatown portion of Sampeng Lane is lined with wholesale shops of hair accessories, pens, stickers, household wares and knick-knacks. Near Th Chakrawat, gem and jewellery shops abound. Weekends are horribly crowded, and it takes a gymnast's flexibility to squeeze past the pushcarts, motorcycles and other roadblocks.

SAPHAN PHUT NIGHT BAZAAR
MARKET

Map p271 (ตลาดนัดสะพานพุทธ; Th Saphan Phut; ☺8pm-midnight Tue-Sun; 🚢Saphan Phut/Memorial Bridge Pier, Pak Klong Taladd Pier) On the Bangkok side of Tha Saphan Phut, this night market has bucketloads of cheap clothes, late-night snacking and a lot of people-watching. As Chatuchak Weekend Market (p158) becomes more design-orientated, Saphan Phut has begun filling the closets of fashion-forward, baht-challenged teenagers.

HOLY ROSARY CHURCH
CHURCH

Map p271 (วัดแม่พระลูกประคำ กาลหว่าร์; cnr Th Yotha & Soi Charoen Phanit; ☺Thai-language mass 7.30pm Mon-Sat, 8am, 10am & 7.30pm Sun; 🚢Marine Department Pier) FREE Portuguese seafarers were among the first Europeans to establish diplomatic ties with Siam, and their influence in the kingdom was rewarded with prime riverside real estate. When a Portuguese contingent moved across the river to the present-day Talat Noi area (p102) of Chinatown in 1787, they were given this piece of land, and built the Holy Rosary Church, known in Thai as Wat Kalawan, from the Portuguese 'Calvario'.

Over the years the Portuguese community dispersed and the church fell into disrepair. However, Vietnamese and Cambodian Catholics displaced by the Indochina wars adopted it, and together with Chinese speakers now constitute much of the parish. Of note are the splendid Romanesque stained-glass windows, gilded ceilings and a Christ statue that is carried through the streets during Easter celebrations.

HUALAMPHONG
TRAIN STATION
HISTORIC BUILDING

Map p271 (สถานีรถไฟหัวลำโพง; off Th Phra Ram IV; Ⓜ Hua Lamphong exit 2) At the southeastern edge of Chinatown, Bangkok's main train station was built by Dutch architects and engineers between 1910 and 1916.

It was designed in a neoclassical style by Italian architect-and-engineer combination Mario Tamagno and Annibale Rigotti, who were working at the same time on the grand Ananta Samakhom Throne Hall (p95) at Dusit. It also embraces other influences, such as the patterned, two-toned skylights that exemplify nascent De Stijl Dutch modernism – it is through these that it is known as an early example of the shift towards Thai art deco. Look for the vaulted iron roof and neoclassical portico, which were a state-of-the-art engineering feat.

GURDWARA SIRI GURU
SINGH SABHA
SIKH TEMPLE

Map p271 (พระศาสนสถานคุรุดวารา; off Th Chakkaraphet; ☺9am-5pm; 🚢Saphan Phut/Memorial Bridge Pier, Pak Klong Taladd Pier) FREE This gold-domed Sikh temple's large hall, somewhat reminiscent of a mosque interior, is devoted to the worship of the *Guru Granth Sahib*, the 17th-century Sikh holy book, which is itself considered the last of the religion's 10 great gurus.

Prasada (blessed food offered to Hindu or Sikh temple attendees) is distributed among devotees every morning around 9am, and if you arrive on a Sikh festival day you can partake in the *langar* (communal Sikh meal) served in the temple. If you do visit this shrine, be sure to climb to the top for panoramic views of Chinatown.

✖️ EATING

NAY HONG
CHINESE-THAI $

Map p271 (off Th Yukol 2, no roman-script sign; mains 35-50B; ☺4-10pm; 🚢Ratchawong Pier, Ⓜ Hua Lamphong exit 1 & taxi) The reward for locating this hole-in-the-wall is one of the best fried noodle dishes in Bangkok: *gŏo·ay đĕe·o kôo·a gài*, flat rice noodles fried with garlic oil, chicken and egg.

To find it, proceed north from the corner of Th Suapa and Th Luang, then turn right into the first side-street; it's at the end of the narrow alleyway.

KHUN YAH CUISINE
CENTRAL THAI $

Map p271 (off Th Mittaphap Thai-China, no roman-script sign; mains from 40B; ☺6am-1.30pm Mon-Fri; 🚢Ratchawong Pier, Ⓜ Hua Lamphong exit 1) Khun Yah specialises in the full-flavoured curries, relishes, stir-fries and noodle dishes of central Thailand. But be sure to get here early; by noon, many dishes are already sold out. It's located just east of the Golden Buddha, in the same compound.

NAI MONG HOI THOD
CHINESE-THAI $

Map p271 (539 Th Phlap Phla Chai; mains 50-70B; ◷5-10pm Tue-Sun; 🚤Ratchawong Pier, Ⓜ Hua Lamphong exit 1 & taxi) A shophouse restaurant renowned for its delicious *or sòo·an* (mussels or oysters fried with egg and a sticky batter) and a decent crab fried rice.

OLD SIAM PLAZA
SWEETS $

Map p271 (cnr Th Phahurat & Th Triphet; mains 30-90B; ◷10am-7pm; 🚤Saphan Phut/Memorial Bridge Pier, Pak Klong Taladd Pier) The ground floor of this shopping centre is a candyland of traditional Thai sweets and snacks, most made right before your eyes.

SAMSARA
JAPANESE, THAI $$

Map p271 (Soi Khang Wat Pathum Khongkha; mains 110-320B; ◷4pm-midnight Tue-Thu, to 1am Fri-Sun; 🗷; 🚤Ratchawong Pier, Ⓜ Hua Lamphong exit 1 & taxi) Combining Japanese and Thai dishes, Belgian beers and an artfully ramshackle atmosphere, Samsara is Chinatown's most eclectic place to eat. It's also very tasty, and the riverside breezes and views simply add to the package. It's at the end of Soi Khang Wat Pathum Khongkha, just west of the temple of the same name.

THANON PHADUNGDAO SEAFOOD STALLS
THAI $$

Map p271 (cnr Th Phadungdao & Th Yaowarat; mains 100-600B; ◷4pm-midnight Tue-Sun; 🚤Ratchawong Pier, Ⓜ Hua Lamphong exit 1 & taxi) After sunset, these two opposing open-air restaurants – each of which claims to be the original – become a culinary train wreck of outdoor barbecues, screaming staff, iced seafood trays and messy sidewalk seating. The vast majority of diners are foreign tourists, but this has little impact on the cheerful setting, the fun experience and the cheap bill.

ROYAL INDIA
INDIAN $$

Map p271 (392/1 Th Chakkaraphet; mains 70-350B; ◷10am-10pm; 🗷; 🚤Saphan Phut/Memorial Bridge Pier, Pak Klong Taladd Pier) Yes, we're aware that this hole-in-the-wall has been in every edition of this guide, but it's still the most reliable place to eat in Bangkok's Little India. Try any of the delicious breads or rich curries, and don't forget to finish with a homemade Punjabi sweet.

HOON KUANG
CHINESE-THAI $$

Map p271 (381 Th Yaowarat; mains 90-240B; ◷11am-7.45pm Mon-Sat; 🚤Ratchawong Pier, Ⓜ Hua Lamphong exit 1 & taxi) Serving the food of Chinatown's streets in air-con comfort is this low-key, long-standing staple. Don't miss the 'prawn curry flat rice noodle', a unique mash-up of two Chinese-Thai dishes – crab in curry powder and flash-fried noodles – that

---

LOCAL KNOWLEDGE

BIRD'S-NEST & SHARK-FIN SOUP

Most of the ostentatious, neon-signed shops you'll see along Th Yaowarat, Chinatown's main drag, do business in gold, but a few deal in two other more obscure, but similarly valued commodities: bird's nests and shark fins.

The bird's nests don't consist of twigs or grass, but rather are the hardened saliva of a type of swiftlet. Pried from the walls of island-bound caves in southern Thailand, the nests are rehydrated and cleaned of impurities before being combined with broth and served as a soup. Despite consisting of jellylike, tasteless strands (the soup is often supplemented with honey and egg to provide it with some flavour), the dish is considered a delicacy by the Chinese, who also believe it benefits the skin. Depending on the colour and purity of the bird's nest, a bowl of the soup can cost as much as 2000B or more. The nests can be harvested sustainably, but over-exploitation does occur.

Many of the same restaurants that sell bird's-nest soup also serve shark-fin soup. Yet another Chinese delicacy that is believed to have healing properties, shark-fin soup has become highly stigmatised in recent years, as many animal welfare experts have pointed out that the fins are gathered via a process that is unsustainable and cruel – the sharks are often caught and stripped of their fins, then dumped in the water to die. Compared to other countries in the region, including even China, Thailand has done little to discourage the consumption of shark-fin soup, and the dish remains a popular item in Bangkok's Chinatown and at Thai-Chinese banquets.

SOI NANA'S DRINKING SCENE

No, not that Nana (p153); at this emerging strip of shophouse-based bar/galleries you'll get custom cocktails, art installations and cute cafes, not go-go dancing. To see a neighbourhood that seems to be at the cusp of gentrification, pop into one of these:

Tep Bar (Map p271; www.facebook.com/Tepbar; 69-71 Soi Nana; ⊘5pm-midnight Tue-Sun; ⓂHua Lamphong exit 1) We certainly never expected to find a bar this sophisticated – yet this fun – in Chinatown. Tep does it with a Thai-tinged, contemporary interior, tasty signature cocktails, Thai drinking snacks, and come Friday to Sunday, raucous live Thai music performances.

Teens of Thailand (Map p271; 76 Soi Nana; ⊘7pm-midnight Tue-Sun; ⓂHua Lamphong exit 1) Probably the edgiest of the new bars in Soi Nana; squeeze through the tiny wooden door of this refurbished shophouse to emerge at an artsy warehouse-like interior, with hipster bar-keeps serving creative gin-based drinks.

El Chiringuito (Map p271; ☑086 340 4791; www.facebook.com/elchiringuitobangkok; 221 Soi Nana; ⊘6pm-midnight Thu-Sun; ⓂHua Lamphong exit 1) Come to this retro-feeling bar for sangria, Spanish gin and bar snacks, or the revolving art exhibitions. Opening hours can be sporadic, so call or check the Facebook page before heading out.

23 Bar & Gallery (Map p271; 92 Soi Nana; ⊘7pm-midnight Tue-Sun; ⓂHua Lamphong exit 1) Low-key is an understatement when describing the vibe of this new bar/gallery. Sit on a crate and nurse a Singha while eyeing the latest exhibition and bumping to a soundtrack that's more fun than most.

Nahim (Map p271; www.facebook.com/nahimcafe.handncraft; 78-80 Soi Nana; ⊘10am-9pm Thu-Tue; 🛜; ⓂHua Lamphong exit 1) A hyper-cute cafe with a good selection of coffee and tea drinks and cartoon llamas stamped on baked goods and on the wall.

will make you wonder why they were ever served apart.

HUA SENG HONG　　　　CHINESE $$
Map p271 (371-373 Th Yaowarat; mains 50-1200B; ⊘9am-1am; 🚤Ratchawong Pier, ⓂHua Lamphong exit 1 & taxi) Hua Seng Hong's varied menu, which includes dim sum, braised goose feet and noodles, makes it a handy destination for anybody craving Chinese.

DRINKING & ENTERTAINMENT

RIVER VIBE　　　　　　　BAR
Map p271 (8th fl, River View Guesthouse, off Soi Charoen Phanit; ⊘7.30-11pm; 🚤Marine Department Pier, ⓂHua Lamphong exit 1 & taxi) Can't afford the overpriced cocktails at Bangkok's upmarket rooftop bars? The excellent river views from the top of this guesthouse will hardly feel like a compromise. We urge getting dinner elsewhere, though.

SOULBAR　　　　　　　LIVE MUSIC
Map p271 (www.facebook.com/livesoulbarbangkok; 945 Th Charoen Krung; ⊘8.30am-12.30am; 🚤Marine Department Pier, ⓂHua Lamphong exit 1 & taxi) This recently converted shophouse plays host to live blues, jazz and soul from 9pm Tuesday to Saturday.

RED ROSE　　　　　　　LIVE MUSIC
Map p271 (2nd fl, Shanghai Mansion, 479-481 Th Yaowarat; ⊘6-11pm; 🚤Ratchawong Pier, ⓂHua Lamphong exit 1 & taxi) One of the only non-karaoke-based places of entertainment on Chinatown's main drag is this cosy lounge in the Shanghai Mansion hotel. Come for smooth acoustic jazz (nightly from 7.30pm to 9pm) and affordable cocktails.

SALA CHALERMKRUNG　　　　THEATRE
Map p271 (☑02 222 0434; www.salachalermkrung.com; 66 Th Charoen Krung; tickets 800-1200B; ⊘shows 7.30pm Thu & Fri; 🚤Saphan Phut/Memorial Bridge Pier, ⓂHua Lamphong exit 1 & taxi) This art deco Bangkok landmark, a former cinema dating to 1933, is one of the few remaining places *kŏhn* can be witnessed. The traditional Thai dance-drama is enhanced here by laser graphics, high-tech audio and English subtitles. Concerts and other events are also held here; check the website for details.

Siam Square, Pratunam, Phloen Chit & Ratchathewi

Neighbourhood Top Five

❶ Visiting **Jim Thompson House** (p110), the teak mansion that put Thai style on the map – before its ex-spy owner disappeared off that map.

❷ Shopping at the malls, department stores and shops that surround Siam Square, such as **MBK Center** (p120).

❸ Exploring **Baan Khrua** (p112), the canal-side Muslim village where Jim Thompson first encountered Thai silk.

❹ Making a wish at the crossroads of commerce and faith that is the **Erawan Shrine** (p111).

❺ Enjoying the luxury of what must be one of the world's best-value cinemas, **Paragon Cineplex** (p118).

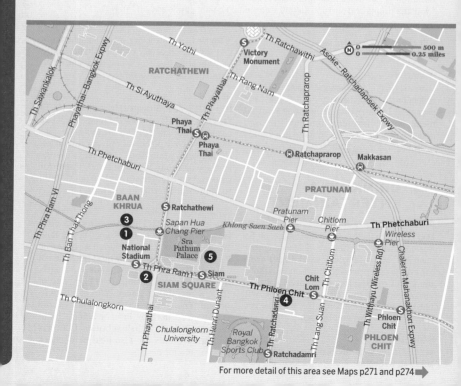

For more detail of this area see Maps p271 and p274 ➡

Explore: Siam Square, Pratunam, Phloen Chit & Ratchathewi

Siam Sq, Pratunam and Phloen Chit combine to form the de facto geographical and commercial centre of modern Bangkok. Huge malls, towering hotels, international fast-food chains and open-air shopping centres dominate this area, and if you're serious about shopping, set aside the better part of a day to burn your baht here. Try to arrive around 11am, when the crowds are minimal. Likewise, try to avoid Sundays when half of Bangkok seems to flock to the area's air-conditioned malls. Siam Sq is most easily accessed via the BTS (Skytrain), and if you're going to hit all the area's malls, it makes sense to start at National Stadium and work your way east, taking advantage of the bridges, mall corridors and elevated walkways that link the various shopping centres.

Ratchathewi has less to offer; the attractions in this area can be covered in a couple hours, and most are within walking distance of the BTS stop at Victory Monument.

Local Life

➡ **Mall-hopping** On weekends a significant part of Bangkok's population is drawn to this area's malls to socialise in stylish settings and air-con comfort.

➡ **Air-conditioned dining** A mall-based food court may not seem like the most authentic place to eat *pàt tai* (fried noodles), but several of Bangkok's most famous restaurants and stalls maintain branches at the various Siam Sq area malls.

➡ **Wholesale retail** For local penny-pinchers and visiting wholesalers, the ultimate destination is Pratunam district, where a seemingly never-ending clothing bazaar stocks both locally made and cheap import items.

➡ **Keeping it real** For a view of Bangkok without the malls, fashionistas and tourists, take the BTS north to the Victory Monument in Ratchathewi district, where you'll find ordinary Thais doing ordinary Thai things.

Getting There & Away

➡ **BTS** To Siam Sq, Pratunam and Phloen Chit: Siam, National Stadium, Chit Lom, Phloen Chit and Ratchadamri. To Ratchathewi: Ratchathewi, Phaya Thai and Victory Monument.

➡ **Klorng boat** To Siam Sq, Pratunam and Phloen Chit: Sapan Hua Chang Pier, Pratunam Pier and Wireless Pier. To Ratchathewi: Pratunam Pier.

➡ **Bus** To Siam Sq, Pratunam and Phloen Chit: air-con 141, 183, 204, 501, 508 and 547; ordinary 15, 16, 25, 47 and 73. To Ratchathewi: air-con 503, 513 and 536; ordinary 29, 36, 54, 59 and 112.

Lonely Planet's Top Tip

They may lack street cred, but the mall-based food courts that abound in this part of town are among the most user-friendly introductions to Thai food in Bangkok. They're generally clean and convenient, and also have the benefit of using English-language menus, so ordering is a snap.

✕ Best Places to Eat

➡ MBK Food Island (p115)
➡ Nuer Koo (p114)
➡ Din Tai Fung (p114)
➡ Sam-Ang Kulap (p117)

For reviews, see p114. ➡

⊖ Best Drinking & Entertainment

➡ Hyde & Seek (p117)
➡ Red Sky (p117)
➡ Saxophone Pub & Restaurant (p118)

For reviews, see p117. ➡

⌂ Best Places to Shop

➡ MBK Center (p120)
➡ Siam Square (p120)
➡ Siam Center (p120)
➡ Siam Paragon (p120)
➡ Baiyoke Garment Center (p120)

For reviews, see p120. ➡

SIAM SQUARE, PRATUNAM, PHLOEN CHIT & RATCHATHEWI

TOP SIGHT
JIM THOMPSON HOUSE

In 1959, 12 years after he single-handedly turned Thai silk into a hugely successful export business, American Jim Thompson bought a piece of land next to Khlong Saen Saeb and built himself a house. It wasn't, however, any old house. Thompson's love of all things Thai saw him buy six traditional wooden homes and reconstruct them in his garden.

Although he met a mysterious end in 1967, today Thompson's house remains, both as a museum to these unique structures and as a tribute to the man.

DON'T MISS...

- Thompson's art and antique collection
- A walk in the jungle-like garden
- Jim Thompson Art Center

PRACTICALITIES

- Map p274, A2
- www.jimthompsonhouse.com
- 6 Soi Kasem San 2, Th Phra Ram I
- adult/student 150/100B
- ⏲9am-6pm, compulsory tours every 20min
- ⛴klorng boat to Sapan Hua Chang Pier, [S]National Stadium exit 1

The Man

Born in Delaware, USA, in 1906, Jim Thompson served in a forerunner of the CIA in Thailand during WWII. When in 1947 he spotted some silk in a market and was told it was woven in Baan Khrua, he found the only place in Bangkok where silk was still woven by hand.

Thompson's Thai silk eventually attracted the interest of fashion houses in New York, Milan, London and Paris, and he gradually built a worldwide clientele for a craft that had, just a few years before, been in danger of dying out.

By 1967 Thai silk had annual sales of almost US$1.5 million. In March that year Thompson went missing while out for an afternoon walk in the Cameron Highlands of western Malaysia; his business success, spy background and the fact that his sister was also murdered in the same year made it an international mystery. Thompson has never been heard from since, but the conspiracy theories have never stopped. Was it communist spies? Business rivals? A man-eating tiger? Although the mystery has never been solved, evidence revealed by American journalist Joshua Kurlantzick in his profile of Thompson, *The Ideal Man,* suggests that the vocal anti-American stance Thompson took later in his life may have made him a potential target of suppression by the CIA.

The House

Traditional Thai homes were multipurpose affairs, with little space for luxuries like separate living and sleeping rooms. Thompson adapted his six buildings, joining some, to create a larger home in which each room had a more familiar Western function. One room became an air-conditioned study, another a bedroom and the one nearest the *klorng* (canal; also spelt *khlong*) his dining room. Another departure from tradition is the way Thompson arranged each wall with its exterior side facing the house's interior, thus exposing the wall's bracing system.

Thompson's small but splendid Asian art collection is also on display in the main house; photography is not allowed inside any of the buildings. After the tour, be sure to poke around the house's jungle-like gardens, which include ponds filled with exotic fish. The compound also includes the excellent **Jim Thompson Art Center** (⏲9am-8pm), a cafe and a shop flogging Jim Thompson–branded goods.

Beware of well-dressed touts in the soi near the Jim Thompson House who will tell you it is closed and then try to haul you off on a dodgy buying spree.

SIGHTS

Siam Square, Pratunam & Phloen Chit

JIM THOMPSON HOUSE HISTORIC BUILDING
See p110.

ERAWAN SHRINE MONUMENT
Map p274 (ศาลพระพรหม; cnr Th Ratchadamri & Th Phloen Chit; ⌚6am-11pm; [S]Chit Lom exit 8) [FREE] The Erawan Shrine was originally built in 1956 as something of a last-ditch effort to end a string of misfortunes that occurred during the construction of a hotel, at that time known as the Erawan Hotel.

After several incidents ranging from injured construction workers to the sinking of a ship carrying marble for the hotel, a Brahmin priest was consulted. Since the hotel was to be named after the elephant escort of Indra in Hindu mythology, the priest determined that Erawan required a passenger, and suggested it be that of Lord Brahma. A statue was built and, lo and behold, the misfortunes miraculously ended.

Although the original Erawan Hotel was demolished in 1987, the shrine still exists, and today remains an important place of pilgrimage for Thais, particularly those in need of some material assistance. Those making a wish from the statue should ideally come between 7am and 8am, or 7pm and 8pm, and should offer a specific list of items that includes candles, incense, sugar cane or bananas, all of which are almost exclusively given in multiples of seven. Particularly popular are teak elephants, with money from the sale of these items donated to a charity run by the current hotel, the Grand Hyatt Erawan. And as the tourist brochures depict, it is also possible to charter a classical Thai dance, often done as a way of giving thanks if a wish is granted.

A bomb exploded near the shrine in August 2015, killing 20 and slightly damaging the shrine. It was repaired and reopened just two days later. For more on the turbulent history of the shrine, see p116.

BANGKOK ART & CULTURE CENTRE ART GALLERY
Map p274 (BACC; www.bacc.or.th; cnr Th Phayathai & Th Phra Ram I; ⌚10am-9pm Tue-Sat; [S]National Stadium exit 3) [FREE] This large,

TOP SIGHT
SUAN PAKKAD PALACE MUSEUM

Everyone loves the Jim Thompson House, but few have even heard of Suan Pakkad Palace Museum (Lettuce Farm Palace), another noteworthy traditional Thai house-museum. Once the residence of Princess Chumbon of Nakhon Sawan (and before that a lettuce farm – hence the name), the museum is a collection of eight traditional wooden Thai houses linked by elevated walkways containing varied displays of art, antiques and furnishings. The landscaped grounds are a peaceful oasis complete with ducks, swans and a semi-enclosed, Japanese-style garden.

The diminutive **Lacquer Pavilion** at the back of the complex dates from the Ayuthaya period (the building originally sat in a monastery compound on the banks of Mae Nam Chao Phraya, just south of Ayuthaya) and features gold-leaf *Jataka* and *Ramayana* murals as well as scenes from daily Ayuthaya life. Larger residential structures at the front of the complex contain displays of Khmer, Hindu and Buddhist art, Ban Chiang ceramics and a collection of historic **Buddhas**, including a beautiful late U Thong–style image. Amid the noise and confusion of Bangkok, the gardens offer a tranquil retreat.

DON'T MISS...

- Lacquer Pavilion
- Buddha statue collection

PRACTICALITIES

- วังสวนผักกาด
- Map p271, A3
- Th Si Ayuthaya
- admission 100B
- ⌚9am-4pm
- [S]Phaya Thai exit 4

WORTH A DETOUR

BAAN KHRUA

The canal-side neighbourhood of **Baan Khrua** (บ้านครัว; Map p274; klorng boat to Sapan Hua Chang Pier, Ratchathewi exit 1, National Stadium exit 1) dates back to the turbulent years at the end of the 18th century, when Cham Muslims from Cambodia and Vietnam fought on the side of the new Thai king and were rewarded with this plot of land east of the new capital. The immigrants brought their silk-weaving traditions with them, and the community grew when the residents built Khlong Saen Saeb to better connect them to the river.

The 1950s and '60s were boom years for Baan Khrua after Jim Thompson hired the weavers and began exporting their silks across the globe. The last 50 years, however, haven't been so great. Silk production was moved elsewhere following Thompson's disappearance, and the community spent 15 years successfully fighting to stop a freeway being built right through the area. Through all this, many Muslims moved out of the neighbourhood; today it is estimated that only about 30% of the population is Muslim, the rest primarily immigrants from northeast Thailand.

Today's Baan Khrua consists of old, tightly packed homes threaded by tiny paths barely wide enough for two people to pass. There's a mosque, and two family-run outfits, **Phamai Baan Krua** (Map p274; www.phamaibaankrua.com; Soi 9, Soi Phaya Nak; 8.30am-5pm; klorng boat to Sapan Hua Chang Pier, Ratchathewi exit 1, National Stadium exit 1) and **Aood Bankrua Thai Silk** (Map p274; 02 215 9864; Soi 9, Soi Phaya Nak; 9am-8pm; klorng boat to Sapan Hua Chang Pier, Ratchathewi exit 1, National Stadium exit 1), which continue to be involved in every step of silk cloth production, from the dyeing of threads to weaving the cloth by hand on old wood looms. Of the two, Phamai Baan Krua claims to be the original. Run by English- and German-speaking Niphon Manuthas, the company continues to produce the type of high-quality handwoven silk that originally attracted Jim Thompson, although at much cheaper prices than that sold across the *klorng*.

Baan Khrua is an easy stop after visiting the Jim Thompson House; simply cross the bridge over the canal at the end of Soi Kasem San 3. Alternatively, from the BTS stop at Ratchathewi, enter Soi Phaya Nak, take the third left (the soi that leads to Da-Ru-Fa-Lah Mosque), following it to the canal; turn right and look for the signs.

modern building in the centre of Bangkok has become one of the more significant players in the city's contemporary arts scene. As well as its three floors and 3000 sq metres of gallery space, the centre also contains shops, private galleries, cafes and an art library. Visit the website to see what exhibitions are on when you're in town.

LINGAM SHRINE
MONUMENT

Map p274 (ศาลเจ้าแม่ทับทิม; Swissôtel Nai Lert Park, Th Witthayu/Wireless Rd; 24hr; klorng boat to Wireless Pier, Phloen Chit exit 1) FREE Every village-neighbourhood has a local shrine, either a sacred banyan tree tied up with coloured scarves or a spirit house. But it isn't every day you see a phallus garden like this lingam shrine, tucked back behind the staff quarters of the Swissôtel Nai Lert Park.

When facing the entrance of the hotel, follow the small concrete pathway to the right, which winds down into the building

beside the car park. The shrine is at the end of the building next to the *klorng*.

Clusters of carved stone and wooden shafts surround a spirit house and shrine built by millionaire businessman Nai Loet to honour Jao Mae Thap Thim, a female deity thought to reside in the old banyan tree on the site. Someone who made an offering shortly after the shrine was built had a baby, and the shrine has received a steady stream of worshippers – mostly young women seeking fertility – ever since.

SIAM OCEAN WORLD
AQUARIUM

Map p274 (สยามโอเชี่ยนเวิร์ล; www.siamocean world.com; basement, Siam Paragon, 991/1 Th Phra Ram I; adult/child from 990/790B; 10am-9pm; Siam exits 3 & 5) More than 400 species of fish, crustaceans and even penguins populate this vast underground facility. Diving with sharks (for a fee) is an option if you have your diving licence, and there are shark and penguin feedings, although note that animal-welfare groups suggest interaction with animals held in captivity creates stress for these creatures.

JAMJUREE ART GALLERY ART GALLERY

Map p274 (Jamjuree Bldg, Chulalongkorn University, Th Phayathai; ⏰10am-7pm Mon-Fri, noon-6pm Sat & Sun; [S]Siam exit 2 & taxi) [FREE] This gallery, part of Chulalongkorn University's Faculty of Arts, emphasises modern spiritual themes and brilliantly coloured abstracts from emerging student artists.

100 TONSON GALLERY ART GALLERY

Map p274 (www.100tonsongallery.com; 100 Th Ton Son; ⏰11am-7pm Thu-Sun; [S]Chit Lom exit 4) [FREE] Housed in a spacious residential villa, and generally regarded as one of the city's top commercial galleries, 100 Tonson hosts a variety of contemporary exhibitions of all genres by local and international artists.

Ratchathewi

BANGKOK DOLL FACTORY & MUSEUM MUSEUM

Map p271 (พิพิธภัณฑ์ตุ๊กตาบางกอกดอลล์; ☎02 245 3008; www.bangkokdolls.com; 85 Soi Ratchataphan/Mo Leng; ⏰10am-4.30pm Mon-Sat; [S]Phaya Thai exit 3 & taxi) [FREE] This workshop was founded by Khunying Tongkorn Chandavimol in 1956 after she completed a doll-making course while living in Japan. Her dolls draw on Thai mythology and historical periods. Today her personal collection includes 400 dolls from around the world, plus important pieces from her own workshop, where you can watch the figures being crafted by hand.

The museum is rather tricky to find; take a taxi from BTS Phaya Thai and get the driver to call the museum for directions.

BAIYOKE II TOWER NOTABLE BUILDING

Map p271 (ตึกใบหยก ๒; 22 Th Ratchaprarop; admission 300B; ⏰9am-11pm; ⛴klorng boat to Pratunam Pier) Cheesiness and altitude run in equal parts at Baiyoke Tower II, Bangkok's tallest building (to be usurped by a 'super tower' slated to be finished in 2016). Ascend through a corridor decked with aliens and planets (and the *Star Wars* theme song) to emerge at the 84th-floor, open-air revolving platform that looks over a city whose concrete sprawl can appear never-ending.

VICTORY MONUMENT MONUMENT

Map p271 (อนุสาวรีย์ชัย; cnr Th Ratchawithi & Th Phayathai; ⏰24hr; [S]Victory Monument exit 2) This obelisk monument was built by the then military government in 1941 to commemorate a 1940 campaign against the French in Laos. Today the monument is primarily a landmark for observing the social universe of local university students and countless commuters. It's worth exploring the neighbourhood around Victory Monument, which is reminiscent of provincial Thai towns, if not exactly hicksville. It's also something of a transport hub, with minivans to Ko Samet, Kanchanaburi and Ayuthaya stopping here, and there's a useful BTS stop.

LOCAL KNOWLEDGE

PREMPREEDA PRAMOJ NA AYUTTHAYA – TRANSWOMAN ACTIVIST

We talked with LGBT researcher and activist Prempreeda Pramoj Na Ayutthaya about transgendered people in Thailand.

Why does Thailand appear to have so many transgender people? It's a cultural heritage based on a very old concept of gender that can even be found in ancient palm leaf manuscripts.

The Thai word 'ladyboy' is sometimes used in English to refer to transgender people. How do you prefer to be called? I prefer (the Thai word) *gà·teu·i* (also spelt *kàthoey)* because it goes back to an indigenous Thai belief that sex isn't binary. The words 'ladyboy' and 'shemale' are often used to sell sex and can stigmatise transgender people.

To outsiders, Thailand appears very open to homosexuals and transgender people – is this really the case? In everyday life, transgender people can live freely, but on a policy level we still face many difficulties.

What do you hope to achieve as an activist? I'm working to change the laws and policies so homosexuals and transgender people can feel more comfortable in Thailand.

EATING

Siam Square, Pratunam & Phloen Chit

NUER KOO CHINESE-THAI $

Map p274 (4th fl, Siam Paragon, 991/1 Th Phra Ram I; mains 85-970B; ⏰11.30am-9.15pm; [S]Siam exits 3 & 5) Is this the future of the noodle stall? Mall-bound Nuer Koo does a luxe version of the formerly humble bowl of beef noodles. Choose your cut of beef (including Kobe beef from Japan), enjoy the rich broth and cool air-con, and quickly forget about the good old days.

SOMTAM NORTHEASTERN THAI $

Map p274 (392/14 Soi 5, Siam Sq; mains 75-120B; ⏰10.45am-9.30pm; [S]Siam exit 4) It can't compete with the street stalls for flavour and authenticity, but if you need to be seen, particularly while in air-con and trendy surroundings, this is a good place to sample northeastern Thai specialities. Expect a line at dinner.

SANGUAN SRI CENTRAL THAI $

Map p274 (59/1 Th Witthayu/Wireless Rd, no roman-script sign; mains 70-200B; ⏰10am-3pm Mon-Sat; [S]Phloen Chit exit 5) The English-language menu is limited at this old-school Thai eatery, but simply pointing to the delicious dishes being consumed around you is almost certainly a wiser ordering strategy.

There's no English-language sign here; look for the bunker-like concrete structure.

FOOD PLUS THAI $

Map p274 (btwn Soi 5 & Soi 6, Siam Sq; mains 30-70B; ⏰9am-3pm Tue-Sun; [S]Siam exit 2) This claustrophobic alleyway is bursting with the wares of several *ráhn kôw gaang* (rice and curry stalls). Everything is made ahead of time, so simply point to what looks tasty. You'll be hard-pressed to spend more than 100B, and the flavours are unanimously authentic and delicious.

KOKO THAI $

Map p274 (262/2 Soi 3, Siam Sq; mains 75-250B; ⏰11am-9pm; ✍; [S]Siam exit 2) Ideal for omnivores and vegetarians alike, this casual cafe-like restaurant offers a lengthy vegie menu, not to mention a short but solid repertoire of meat-based Thai dishes, such as a Penang curry served with tender pork, or fish deep-fried and served with Thai herbs.

DIN TAI FUNG CHINESE $$

Map p274 (7th fl, CentralWorld, Th Ratchadamri; dishes 65-315B; ⏰11am-10pm; ✍; [S]Chit Lom exit 9 to Sky Walk, Siam exit 6 to Sky Walk) Most come to this lauded Taiwanese chain for the *xiao long bao,* broth-filled 'soup' dumplings. And so should you. But the other northern-Chinese-style dishes are just as good, and justify exploring the more remote regions of the menu.

LA MONITA MEXICAN $$

Map p274 (www.lamonita.com; 888/26 Mahatun Plaza, Th Phloen Chit; mains 120-550B; ⏰11.30am-10pm; ✍; [S]Phloen Chit exit 2) Admittedly, the menu here is more Texas than Tijuana, but of all the places that have attempted Mexican in Bangkok over the years, we reckon La Monita has done the best job. Come for an inviting, pleasant atmosphere and a repertoire of hearty dishes such as *queso fundido* (a skillet of melted cheese) and burritos.

CRYSTAL JADE LA MIAN XIAO LONG BAO CHINESE $$

Map p274 (basement, Erawan Bangkok, 494 Th Phloen Chit; mains 110-1050B; ⏰11am-10pm; ✍; [S]Chit Lom exit 8) The tongue-twistingly long name of this excellent Singaporean chain refers to the restaurant's signature *la mian* (wheat noodles) and the famous Shanghainese *xiao long bao.* If you order the hand-pulled noodles (which you should do), allow the staff to cut them with kitchen shears, otherwise you'll end up with evidence of your meal on your shirt.

COCA SUKI CHINESE, THAI $$

Map p274 (416/3-8 Th Henri Dunant; mains 98-788B; ⏰11am-11pm; ✍; [S]Siam exit 6) Immensely popular with Thai families, *sù·gêe* takes the form of a bubbling hotpot of broth and the raw ingredients to dip therein. Coca is one of the oldest purveyors of the dish, and this branch reflects the brand's efforts to appear more modern. Insider tip for fans of spice: be sure to request the tangy *tom yam* broth.

ERAWAN TEA ROOM THAI $$

Map p274 (2nd fl, Erawan Bangkok, 494 Th Phloen Chit; mains 180-540B; ⏰10am-10pm; ✍; [S]Chit Lom exit 8) The oversized chairs, panoramic windows and variety of hot drinks make this one of Bangkok's best places to catch up with the newspaper. The lengthy menu of Thai standards will likely encourage you to linger a bit longer, and the selection of jams and teas to take away allows you to recreate the experience at home.

GINZA SUSHI-ICHI JAPANESE $$$

Map p274 (☎02 250 0014; www.ginza-sushiichi.jp/english/shop/bangkok.html; ground fl, Erawan Bangkok, 494 Th Phloen Chit; set lunch 1300-4000B, set dinner 4000-10,000B; ⏲noon-2.30pm Tue-Sun, 6-11pm Tue-Sat, to 10pm Sun; [S]Chit Lom exit 8) This closet-sized restaurant – the Bangkok branch of a Tokyo-based recipient of a Michelin star – is arguably the city's premier place for sushi. The set menus depend on what was purchased at Tokyo's Tsukiji Market the previous day, which means that Ginza Sushi-Ichi does not open immediately following public holidays in Japan; check the website calendar for details.

SRA BUA THAI $$$

Map p274 (☎02 162 9000; www.kempinski.com/en/bangkok/siam-hotel/dining; ground fl, Siam Kempinski Hotel, 991/9 off Th Phra Ram I; mains 650-890B, set meals 1350-2700B; ⏲noon-3pm & 6-10.30pm; [S]Siam exits 3 & 5) Helmed by a Thai and a Dane whose Copenhagen restaurant, Kiin Kiin, snagged a Michelin star, Sra Bua takes a correspondingly international approach to Thai food. Putting local ingredients through the wringer of molecular gastronomy, the couple have created unconventional Thai dishes such as 'warm lobster with frozen curry pearls'. Reservations recommended.

BANGKOK'S BEST FOOD COURTS

The Siam Square area is home to some of Bangkok's biggest malls, which means that it's also home to more than its share of mall-based food courts. They're a great way to dip your toe in the sea of Thai food as they're generally cheap, clean, air-conditioned and have English-language menus. At most, paying is done by exchanging cash for vouchers or a temporary credit card at one of several counters; your change is refunded at the same desk. Tuck in at the following:

MBK Food Island (Map p274; 6th fl, MBK Center, cnr Th Phra Ram I & Th Phayathai; mains 35-150B; ⏲10am-10pm; ✍; [S]National Stadium exit 4) Undergoing a renovation at the time of research, the grandaddy of the genre is set to continue its offer of dozens of vendors selling Thai-Chinese, regional Thai and international dishes.

Gourmet Paradise (Map p274; ground fl, Siam Paragon, 991/1 Th Phra Ram I; mains 35-500B; ⏲10am-10pm; ✍; [S]Siam exits 3 & 5) The perpetually busy Gourmet Paradise unites international fast-food chains, domestic restaurants and food-court-style stalls, with a particular emphasis on the sweet stuff.

Food Republic (Map p274; 4th fl, Siam Center, cnr Th Phra Ram I & Th Phayathai; mains 30-200B; ⏲10am-10pm; ✍; [S]Siam exit 1) The city's most handsome food court has a good mix of Thai and international (mostly Asian) outlets in an open, modern-feeling locale. We particularly fancied the Thai-Muslim dishes at the stall called 'Curry Rice'.

Food Loft (Map p274; www.centralfoodloft.com; 6th fl, Central Chidlom, 1027 Th Phloen Chit; mains 65-950B; ⏲10am-10pm; ✍; [S]Chit Lom exit 5) This department-store-bound food court pioneered the concept of the upmarket food court, and mock-ups of the Indian, Italian, Japanese and other international cuisines aid in the decision-making process.

Eathai (Map p274; www.facebook.com/EathaibyCentral; basement, Central Embassy, 1031 Th Phloen Chit; mains 60-360B; ⏲10am-10pm; ✍; [S]Phloen Chit exit 5) This expansive new food court spans Thai – and only Thai – dishes from just about every corner of the country, including those from several famous Bangkok restaurants and stalls.

FoodPark (Map p274; 4th fl, Big C, 97/11 Th Ratchadamri; mains 30-90B; ⏲9am-9pm; [S]Chit Lom exit 9 to Sky Walk) The selections here may not inspire you to move here, but they are abundant and cheap, and are representative of the kind of 'fast food' Thais enjoy eating.

WATER LIBRARY BRASSERIE

FRENCH, INTERNATIONAL **$$$**

Map p274 (☏02 160 5893; www.waterlibrary.com; 5th fl, Central Embassy, 1031 Th Phloen Chit; mains 240-1390B; ☺10am-10pm Sun-Thu, to midnight Fri & Sat; ⓢPhloen Chit exit 5) The Eiffel Tower–themed dining room of this successful local chain is a slightly cheesy indication of the move to French-influenced bistro fare. But the food is serious, taking the form of decadent twists on humble faves, such as a *croque monsieur* stuffed with prosciutto instead of ham.

TOUGH TIMES AT THE ERAWAN SHRINE

One of the more clichéd tourist images of Bangkok is that of elaborately dressed classical Thai dancers performing at the Hindu shrine in front of the Grand Hyatt Erawan Hotel. Although not a fabrication, as with many things in Thailand, there is great deal hidden behind the serene facade.

After 50 years of largely benign existence, the Erawan Shrine became a point of focus when just after midnight on 21 March, 2006, 27-year-old Thanakorn Pakdeepol, a man with a history of mental illness and depression, destroyed the highly revered, gilded plaster image of Brahma with a hammer. Thanakorn was almost immediately attacked and beaten to death by two Thai rubbish collectors in the vicinity. Although the government ordered a swift restoration of the statue, the incident became a galvanising omen for the protest movement opposing then Prime Minister Thaksin Shinawatra, which was in full swing at the time. At a rally the following day, protest leader Sondhi Limthongkul suggested that the prime minister had masterminded the image's destruction in order to replace the deity with a 'dark force'. Rumours spreading through the capital claimed that Thaksin had hired Cambodian shamans to put spells on Thanakorn so that he would perform the unspeakable deed. In response, Thanakorn's father was quoted as saying that Sondhi was 'the biggest liar I have ever seen.' Thaksin, when asked to comment on Sondhi's accusations, simply replied, 'That's insane.' A new statue, which incorporated pieces of the previous one, was installed a month later, and Thaksin has remained in exile since 2008.

In 2010, the Ratchaprasong Intersection, where the shrine is located, became the main gathering point for anti-government Red Shirt protesters, who occupied the area for several months. Images of the predominately lower class, rural protesters camped out in front of Ratchaprasong's luxury shopfronts became a media staple. When the Red Shirts were forcibly cleared out by the military on 19 May, five people were killed and fleeing protesters set fire to the nearby CentralWorld mall.

CentralWorld was renovated in 2012, but a year later Ratchaprasong Intersection yet again became a major protest site, this time occupied by opponents of Thaksin's sister, then Prime Minister Yingluck Shinawatra. The protests were known colloquially as Shutdown Bangkok (complete with protest merchandise featuring the computer shutdown button icon), and this time media images of the largely middle- and upper-class urban protesters in front of chic malls drew comparisons rather than contrasts. On 20 May, 2014, the Thai Army declared martial law and took over the government in a coup d'état, leading the protesters to disperse.

Yet undoubtedly the most significant event in the shrine's history came on the evening of 17 August, 2015, when a bomb planted in the Erawan Shrine compound exploded, killing 20 and injuring more than 120 people, an apparent act of terrorism that Prime Minister Prayut Chan-o-cha described as the 'worst incident that has ever happened' in Thailand. At the time of research, two suspects had been arrested, although their motives remain unclear.

Why so much turmoil associated with a shrine that most believe to have positive powers? Some feel that the Erawan Shrine sits on land that carries long-standing, and potentially conflicting supernatural powers. Others feel that the area is currently spiritually overcrowded, as other nearby structures also have their own, potentially competing, Hindu shrines. What's certain is that in Thailand, politics, faith, fortune and tragedy are often linked.

GAGGAN INDIAN $$$

Map p274 (☎02 652 1700; www.eatatgaggan.com; 68/1 Th Lang Suan; set menu 2500-4000B; ⏲6-11pm; ✍; [S]Ratchadamri exit 2) The white, refurbished villa that houses Gaggan seems more appropriate for an English-themed tea house than a restaurant serving self-proclaimed 'progressive Indian cuisine', but Gaggan is all about incongruity. The set menus here span up to 10 courses, ranging from the daring (a ball of raita) to the traditional (some excellent tandoori), with bright flavours and unexpected but satisfying twists as a unifying thread.

🍴 Ratchathewi

SAM-ANG KULAP CENTRAL THAI $

Map p271 (Soi 18, Th Ratchawithi, no roman-script sign; dishes from 30B; ⏲8am-5pm; [S]Victory Monument exit 3) The area surrounding the Victory Monument is home to heaps of simple restaurants selling spicy, rich 'boat noodles' – so-called because they used to be sold directly from boats that plied central Thailand's rivers and canals. Our pick of the lot is allegedly the first, the now land-based Sam-Ang Kulap, located just over the canal at the northern end of Soi 18, Th Ratchawhithi.

TIDA ESARN NORTHEASTERN THAI $

Map p271 (1/2-5 Th Rang Nam; mains 40-300B; ⏲10.30am-10.30pm; [S]Victory Monument exit 2) Tida Esarn sells country-style Thai food in a decidedly urban setting. Appropriately, foreigners provide the bulk of the restaurant's customers, but the kitchen still insists on serving full-flavoured Isan-style dishes such as *súp nòr mái*, a tart salad of shredded bamboo.

PATHÉ THAI, INTERNATIONAL $$

Map p271 (www.patherestaurant.com; 507 Th Ratchawithi; mains 94-275B; ⏲7am-midnight; [S]Victory Monument exit 4) The modern Thai equivalent of a 1950s-era American diner, this popular place combines solid Thai food, a fun atmosphere and a jukebox playing scratched records. The menu is equally eclectic, and combines Thai and Western dishes and ingredients; be sure to save room for the deep-fried ice cream. It's also a good place to simply relax with a cold beer.

🍷 DRINKING & ENTERTAINMENT

🍷 Siam Square, Pratunam & Phloen Chit

HYDE & SEEK BAR

Map p274 (www.hydeandseek.com; ground fl, Athenee Residence, 65/1 Soi Ruam Rudi; ⏲11am-1am; [S]Phloen Chit exit 4) The tasty and comforting English-inspired bar snacks and meals here have earned Hyde & Seek the right to call itself a gastropub. But we reckon the real reasons to come are one of Bangkok's best-stocked liquor cabinets and some of the city's tastiest and most sophisticated cocktails.

RED SKY BAR

Map p274 (www.centarahotelsresorts.com/redsky; 55th fl, Centara Grand, CentralWorld, Th Ratchadamri; ⏲6pm-1am; [S]Chit Lom exit 9 to Sky Walk, Siam exit 6 to Sky Walk) Perched on the 55th floor of a skyscraper smack-dab in the modern centre of Bangkok, Red Sky is one of Bangkok's most stunning rooftop bars.

CO-CO WALK BAR

Map p274 (87/70 Th Phayathai; ⏲5pm-midnight; [S]Ratchathewi exit 2) This covered compound is a loud, messy smorgasbord of pubs, bars and live music popular with Thai university students on a night out. We'd list a few specific bars here, but they'd most likely all have changed names by the time you read this – it's just that kinda place.

ROOF BAR

Map p274 (www.siamatsiam.com/dining/roof; 25th fl, Siam@Siam, 865 Th Phra Ram I; ⏲6pm-12.30am; [S]National Stadium exit 1) In addition to views of central Bangkok from 25 floors up, the Roof offers a dedicated personal martini sommelier and an extensive wine and champagne list. Party House One, on the ground floor of the same building, offers live music most nights.

FOREIGN CORRESPONDENTS' CLUB OF THAILAND BAR, RESTAURANT

Map p274 (FCCT; www.fccthai.com; Penthouse, Maneeya Center, 518/5 Th Phloen Chit; ⏲noon-2.30pm & 6pm-midnight Mon-Fri; [S]Chit Lom exit 2) A bar-restaurant, not to mention a bona fide gathering place for the city's hacks and

LOCAL KNOWLEDGE

SIAM SQUARE'S SILVER SCREENS

Each Bangkok mall has its own cinema, but few can rival **Paragon Cineplex** (Map p274; ☎02 129 4635; www.paragoncineplex.com; 5th fl, Siam Paragon, 991/1 Th Phra Ram I; [S]Siam exits 3 & 5). In addition to 16 screens, more than 3000 seats and Thailand's largest IMAX screen, the options here include: the Blue Ribbon Screen, a cinema with a maximum of 72 seats, where you're plied with pillows, blankets, complimentary snacks and drinks, and of course, a 15-minute massage; and Enigma, where in addition to a sofa-like love seat designed for couples, you'll be served cocktails and food (as well as blankets and a massage).

If you're looking for something with less glitz and a bit more character, consider the old-school stand-alone cinemas just across the street, such as **Scala** (Map p274; ☎02 251 2861; Soi 1, Siam Sq; [S]Siam exit 2) and **Lido** (Map p274; ☎02 252 6498; www.apexsiamsquare.com; btwn Soi 2 & Soi 3, Siam Sq; [S]Siam exit 2).

photogs, the FCCT also hosts art exhibitions ranging in genre from photojournalism to contemporary painting (and there's live jazz on Friday nights). Check the website to see what's on when you're in town.

MIXX — CLUB

Map p274 (www.mixx-discotheque.com/bangkok; basement, InterContinental Hotel, 973 Th Phloen Chit; admission 300B; ⏰10pm-2am; [S]Chit Lom exit 7) As the name suggests, Mixx draws a relatively wide swath of Bangkok's partiers, from newly arrived backpackers to hardened working girls, making it the least dodgy of the city's late-night discos.

DIPLOMAT BAR — LIVE MUSIC

Map p274 (ground fl, Conrad Hotel, 87 Th Witthayu/Wireless Rd; ⏰7pm-1am Mon-Thu, to 2am Fri & Sat; [S]Phloen Chit exit 5) Named for its location in the middle of the embassy district, this is one of the few hotel lounges that locals make a point of visiting. Choose from an expansive list of innovative martinis, and sip to live jazz, played gracefully at conversation level. The live music starts at 8pm from Monday to Thursday, and at 8.30pm on Friday and Saturday.

🍷 Ratchathewi

SKY TRAIN JAZZ CLUB — BAR

Map p271 (cnr Th Rang Nam & Th Phayathai; ⏰5pm-2am; [S]Victory Monument exit 2) An evening at this comically misnamed bar is more like chilling on the rooftop of your stoner buddy's flat than any jazz club we've ever been to. But there are indeed views of the BTS, jazz on occasion and a scrappy speakeasy atmosphere.

To find it, look for the sign and proceed up the graffiti-strewn stairway until you reach the roof.

WINE PUB — BAR

Map p271 (www.winepubbangkok.com; 1st fl, Pullman Bangkok King Power, 8/2 Th Rang Nam; ⏰6.30pm-2am; [S]Victory Monument exit 2) If the upmarket but chilled setting and spinning DJ aren't compelling enough reasons to venture from your Sukhumvit comfort zone, consider that this is probably the least expensive place in town to drink wine. Check the website for revolving nibbles promotions that span everything from imported cheeses and cold cuts to tapas.

SAXOPHONE PUB & RESTAURANT — LIVE MUSIC

Map p271 (www.saxophonepub.com; 3/8 Th Phayathai; ⏰7.30pm-1.30am; [S]Victory Monument exit 2) After nearly 30 years, Saxophone remains Bangkok's premier live-music venue – a dark, intimate space where you can pull up a chair just a few metres away from the band and see their every bead of sweat. If you prefer some mystique around your musicians, watch the blues, jazz, reggae or rock from the balcony.

PLAYHOUSE MAGICAL CABARET — CABARET

Map p274 (☎02 215 0571; www.playhousethailand.com; 5 Ratchadapisek Rd, Chompol Sub-District, Chatuchak; adult/child 1200/600B; ⏰show times 7pm & 8.20pm; [S]Ratchathewi exit 1) Watching *gà·teu·i* (transgender people; also spelt *kàthoey*) perform show tunes has, not surprisingly, become the latest must-do fixture on the Bangkok tourist circuit. Playhouse caters to the trend, with choreographed stage shows featuring Broadway high kicks and lip-synched pop performances.

RAINTREE LIVE MUSIC

Map p271 (Soi Ruam Chit; ⌚6pm-1am Mon-Sat; [S]Victory Monument exit 2) This rustic pub is one of the few remaining places in town to hear 'songs for life', Thai folk music with roots in the political movements of the 1960s and '70s. Tasty bar snacks also make it a clever place to have a bite to eat.

MOTORCYCLE MADNESS

It's Friday rush hour in Bangkok and traffic is bumper-to-bumper as far as the eye can see. You need to be somewhere – fast. Assuming you don't have a police escort, the only way out is to hop on the back of a fearless motorcycle taxi, known as a *motorsai*. Hang on tight as your orange-vested driver weaves past belching trucks, zips down tiny back-alleys and, when all else fails, treats the pavement as a bike lane. Even the niftiest túk-túk (pronounced *đúk đúk*) struggles to keep up with a *motorsai*.

Motorsai are an essential lubricant for Bangkok's congested streets, with an estimated 200,000 on the road. They gather at street corners in ranks known as *win*. As well as transporting people and goods, they double as messengers for private companies. Since they can drive down narrow soi, *motorsai* are often the only form of public transport in parts of the city, providing the last leg of bus and train commutes. This is particularly true when there's no Skytrain or subway line.

Not all *motorsai* journeys are mad dashes across town. Plenty of people use them to putter up and down their soi, to run local errands and visit friends. But their finest hours come when traffic is so backed up that a regular taxi or bus just won't do – there's something exhilarating about passing a $50,000 BMW caught in a snarl-up.

Yet while nearly everyone relies on them, *motorsai* have a mixed reputation. Bangkokians swap hair-raising stories of drunken or reckless drivers who should be behind bars. Most parents shudder at the idea that their daughter might bring one home (nearly all are male). Then there's the underworld aspect: *motorsai* ranks are typically run by moonlighting cops or soldiers, a shady practice that former Prime Minister Thaksin Shinawatra tried to stamp out in 2003. He didn't quite succeed, but he won the loyalty of drivers who were fed up with paying their bosses for protection. Most drivers originally come from northeastern Thailand, where Thaksin's brand of economic populism made him a political rock star.

This loyalty to Thaksin, who lost power in 2006, is why *motorsai* drivers were so active in the Red Shirt protests that convulsed Bangkok in 2009 and 2010. As well as joining mass demonstrations, drivers used their bikes to transport supplies into protest camps, bring Red Shirt guards to the front lines and to keep tabs on troop movements. Journalists also relied on nimble *motorsai* to get them in and out of danger zones, particularly when the army moved in in May 2010.

Since then, some drivers have tried to steer a more neutral path through Thailand's colour-coded politics. They prefer to be seen as orange shirts, not Red Shirts (or Yellow Shirts). Their orange vests can be valuable property. Although each numbered vest is supposed to stay with its registered owner, drivers trade or sell them, fetching prices of up to 150,000B on busy corners or in posh neighbourhoods. An average *motorsai* earns 400B to 500B a day. That isn't far off the salary of an office worker, but the hours are longer and the work more hazardous. Drivers must also pay for petrol and maintain their own motorcycle.

Motorsai first became popular in the 1980s as the city spread rapidly outwards and commuters found themselves stranded far from public transport. The peculiar layout of Bangkok – narrow soi, big roads, lots of dead ends – meant that motorcycles had the edge. Like so much of Bangkok's workings, it was an ad hoc response to a failure of central urban planning. Bangkok may be the world's least planned yet most liveable city – and its *motorsai* drivers are the unsung heroes who help make it that way.

Simon Montlake, Asia-based journalist

ROCK PUB LIVE MUSIC

Map p274 (www.therockpub-bangkok.com; 93/26-28 Th Phayathai; ⌚9.30pm-2am; [S]Ratchathewi exit 2) With posters of Iron Maiden as interior design, and black jeans and long hair as the dress code, this long-standing, cave-like, live-music bar is Thailand's unofficial Embassy of Heavy Metal.

SHOPPING

★MBK CENTER SHOPPING CENTRE

Map p274 (www.mbk-center.com; cnr Th Phra Ram I & Th Phayathai; ⌚10am-10pm; [S]National Stadium exit 4) This colossal shopping mall underwent an extensive renovation in 2015 and is set to retain its role as one of Bangkok's top attractions. On any given weekend half of Bangkok's residents (and most of its tourists) can be found here combing through a seemingly inexhaustible range of small stalls and shops that span a whopping eight floors.

MBK is one of the better places to stock up on camera gear (ground floor and 5th floor), and the expansive food court (6th floor) is one of the best in town.

It is also Bangkok's cheapest place to buy mobile phones and accessories (4th floor). Indeed, the 4th floor resembles something of a digital produce market. A confusing maze of stalls sell all the components to send you into the land of cellular: a new phone, a new number and a SIM card. Even if you'd rather keep yourself out of reach, do a walk-through to observe the chaos and the mania over phone numbers. Computer print-outs displaying all the available numbers for sale turn the phone numbers game into a commodities market. The luckier the phone number, the higher the price; the equivalent of thousands of dollars have been paid for numbers composed mostly of nines, considered lucky in honour of the current king, Rama IX (King Bhumibol Adulyadej; r 1946–), and because the Thai word for 'nine' is similar to the word for 'progress'.

LIVING LARGE

At home you may be considered average or even petite, but, based on the Thai measuring stick, you're an extra large, clearly marked on the tag as 'LL' or, worse still, 'XL'. If that batters the body image, then skip the street markets, where you'll bust the seams from the waist up – if you can squirm that far into the openings. If you're larger than a US size 10 or an Australian size 14, you strike out altogether. Men will find that they exceed Thai clothes in length and shoulder width, as well as shoe sizes. For formal wear, many expats turn to custom orders through tailors (see p46 for recommended tailors). For ready-to-wear, many of the vendors at Pratunam Market and several stalls on the 6th floor of MBK Center stock the larger sizes.

★SIAM SQUARE SHOPPING CENTRE

Map p274 (Th Phra Ram I; ⌚11am-9pm; [S]Siam exits 2, 4 & 6) This open-air shopping zone is ground zero for teenage culture in Bangkok. Pop music blares out of tinny speakers, and gangs of hipsters in various costumes ricochet between fast-food restaurants and closet-sized boutiques. It's a great place to pick up labels and designs you're guaranteed not to find anywhere else, though most outfits require a barely there waistline.

SIAM CENTER SHOPPING CENTRE

Map p274 (www.siamcenter.co.th; Th Phra Ram I; ⌚10am-9pm; [S]Siam exit 1) Siam Center, Thailand's first shopping centre, was built in 1976 but, since a recent nip and tuck, hardly shows its age. Its 3rd floor is one of the best locations to check out established local labels such as Flynow III, Senada Theory and Tango.

SIAM PARAGON SHOPPING CENTRE

Map p274 (www.siamparagon.co.th; 991/1 Th Phra Ram I; ⌚10am-10pm; [S]Siam exits 3 & 5) As much air-conditioned urban park as it is a shopping centre, in addition to shops Siam Paragon is home to Siam Ocean World (p112), Paragon Cineplex (p118) and Gourmet Paradise (p115), a huge basement-level food court. On the 3rd floor you'll find Kinokuniya, Thailand's largest English-language bookstore.

BAIYOKE GARMENT CENTER CLOTHING

Map p274 (cnr Th Phetchaburi & Th Ratchaprarop; ⌚10am-10pm; ⛴klorng boat to Pratunam Pier, [S]Ratchathewi exit 4) This rabbit warren of stalls is the undisputed epicentre of Bangkok's garment district. The vendors spill from the covered market area to dozens of nearby shops selling similarly cheap

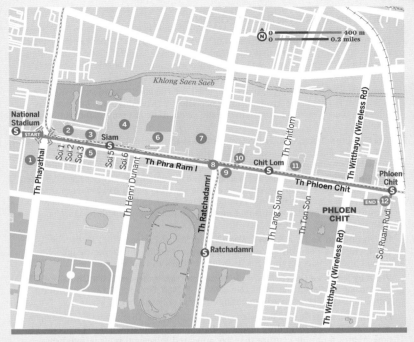

🏃 Neighbourhood Walk
Siam Square Shopping Spree

START MBK CENTER
END HYDE & SEEK
LENGTH 3KM; TWO TO FOUR HOURS

This walk cuts across the heart of Bangkok's most commercial district via elevated walkways, escalators and air-conditioned malls. Start no earlier than 11am, when most shopping centres open.

Begin at **1 MBK Center** (p120), where you can pick up some new sneakers or fuel up for the rest of the walk at the mall's 6th-floor food court.

From MBK, it's possible to continue, more or less, without touching street level again. Following the elevated walkway to **2 Siam Discovery** (p122), continue to **3 Siam Center** (p120) and **4 Siam Paragon** (p120) via linking walkways. Have a sweet snack at Siam Paragon's basement-level food court, or if you're missing the heat and exhaust fumes, detour across Th Phra Ram 1 to the teen-themed shops and restaurants of **5 Siam Square** (p120).

From Siam BTS station, continue east along the elevated walkway known as Sky Walk. After a couple of minutes, on your left you'll see **6 Wat Pathum Wanaram**, an incongruously located Buddhist temple. Turn left on the bridge that connects with **7 CentralWorld** (p122), or continue straight ahead until you reach busy **8 Ratchaprasong Intersection**, the area seized by Red Shirt protesters in 2010 and again in 2013–2014. The intersection is also home to the **9 Erawan Shrine** (p111). Just beyond the junction is **10 Narai Phand** (p123), a government-sponsored handicraft emporium.

If there's anything you've forgotten, you can most likely pick it up at your last stop, **11 Central Chidlom** (p123), a seven-storey department store. Otherwise, end your walk, simultaneously checking your credit-card balance and sipping one of Bangkok's best mixed drinks, at **12 Hyde & Seek** (p117).

LOCAL BRANDS WORTH SUPPORTING

Doi Tung (Map p274; www.doitung.org; 4th fl, Siam Discovery, cnr Th Phra Ram I & Th Phayathai; ⏰10am-9pm; [S]Siam exit 1) Beautiful hand-woven carpets, rustic ceramics and domestic coffee beans are some of the items available at this royally sponsored enterprise.

Tango (Map p274; www.tangothailand.com; 3rd fl, Siam Center, Th Phra Ram 1; ⏰10am-9pm; [S]Siam exit 1) This home-grown brand specialises in leather goods, but you may not even recognise the medium under the layers of bright embroidery and chunky jewels.

The Selected (Map p274; www.facebook.com/theselected; 3rd fl, Siam Center, Th Phra Ram I; ⏰10am-9pm; [S]Siam exit 1) A carefully curated assemblage of modern, mostly Thai-made housewares, knick-knacks, clothing and accessories for the *Kinfolk* generation.

Thann (Map p274; www.thann.info; ground fl & 2nd fl, CentralWorld, Th Ratchadamri; ⏰10am-10pm; [S]Chit Lom exit 9 to Sky Walk, Siam exit 6 to Sky Walk) Smell good enough to eat with these botanical-based spa products. The soaps, shampoos and lotions are all natural, rooted in Thai traditional medicine, and stylish enough to share space with brand-name beauty.

It's Happened To Be A Closet (Map p274; 1st fl, Siam Paragon, 991/1 Th Phra Ram I; ⏰10am-10pm; [S]Siam exits 3 & 5) Garbled grammar aside, this domestic label has gained a glowing reputation for its bright colours and bold patterns.

Viera by Ragazze (Map p274; www.facebook.com/vierabyragazze; 2nd fl, CentralWorld, Th Ratchadamri; ⏰10am-10pm; [S]Chit Lom exit 9 to Sky Walk, Siam exit 6 to Sky Walk) Handsome, high-quality leather items, ranging from shoes to bags.

Flynow III (Map p274; www.flynowiii.com; 3rd fl, Siam Center, Th Phra Ram I; ⏰10am-9pm; [S]Siam exit 1) A long-standing leader in Bangkok's home-grown fashion scene, Flynow creates feminine couture that has appeared in several international shows.

Propaganda (Map p274; 4th fl, Siam Discovery, cnr Th Phra Ram I & Th Phayathai; ⏰10am-9pm; [S]Siam exit 1) Thai designer Chaiyut Plypetch dreamed up this brand's signature character, the devilish Mr P, who appears in anatomically correct cartoon lamps and other products.

Gin & Milk (Map p274; www.facebook.com/ginandmilkstore; 3rd fl, Siam Center, Th Phra Ram I; ⏰10am-9pm; [S]Siam exit 1) A one-stop shop for domestic menswear, with items ranging from leather shoes to accessories, in looks ranging from traditional to edgy.

T-shirts, bags and other no-brand clothing items.

CENTRALWORLD — SHOPPING CENTRE

Map p274 (www.centralworld.co.th; Th Ratchadamri; ⏰10am-10pm; [S]Chit Lom exit 9 to Sky Walk, Siam exit 6 to Sky Walk) Spanning eight storeys of more than 500 shops and 100 restaurants, CentralWorld is one of Southeast Asia's largest shopping centres. In addition to an ice rink, there's an extra-huge branch of bookstore B2S, and you could spend an hour sniffing around the fragrances at Karmakamet on the 3rd floor.

PLATINUM FASHION MALL — CLOTHING

Map p274 (www.platinumfashionmall.com; Th Phetchaburi; ⏰9am-8pm; ⛴klorng boat to Pratunam Pier, [S]Ratchathewi exit 4) Linked with Bangkok's garment district, which lies just north across Th Phetchaburi, is this five-storey mall stocked with an enormous selection of cheap, no-name couture.

SIAM DISCOVERY — SHOPPING CENTRE

Map p274 (www.siamdiscovery.co.th; cnr Th Phra Ram I & Th Phayathai; ⏰10am-10pm; [S]Siam exit 1) Expect the usual line-up of local and international brands at this centrally located mall, which was closed for renovation at the time of research. It's also home to a branch of **Madame Tussauds** (Map p274; www.madametussauds.com/Bangkok/en; 6th fl, Siam Discovery; adult/child 850/650B; ⏰10am-9pm; [S]Siam exit 1).

NARAI PHAND SOUVENIRS

Map p274 (www.naraiphand.com; ground fl, President Tower, 973 Th Phloen Chit; ⏰10am-8pm; [S]Chit Lom exit 7) Souvenir-quality handicrafts are given fixed prices and are displayed in air-conditioned comfort at this government-run facility. You won't find anything here that you haven't already seen at all of the tourist street markets, but it is a good stop if you're pressed for time or are spooked by haggling.

PINKY TAILORS CLOTHING

Map p274 (www.pinkytailor.com; 888/40 Mahatun Plaza, Th Phloen Chit; ⏰10am-7pm Mon-Sat; [S]Phloen Chit exits 2 & 4) Suit jackets have been Mr Pinky's speciality for 35 years. His custom-made dress shirts, for both men and women, also have dedicated fans. Pinky is located behind the Mahatun Building.

PANTIP PLAZA SHOPPING CENTRE

Map p274 (www.pantipplaza.com; 604 Th Phetchaburi; ⏰10am-9pm; [S]Ratchathewi exit 4) If you can tolerate the crowds and annoying pornography vendors ('DVD sex? DVD sex?'), Pantip, a multistorey computer and electronics warehouse – which was undergoing an extensive renovation at the time of research – might just be your kind of paradise. Technorati will find pirated software and music, gear for hobbyists to enhance their machines, flea-market-style peripherals, and other odds and ends.

MARCO TAILOR CLOTHING

Map p274 (430/33 Soi 7, Siam Sq; ⏰9am-7pm Mon-Fri; [S]Siam exit 2) Dealing solely in men's suits, this long-standing and reliable tailor has a wide selection of banker-sensibility wools. If you're considering getting suited, be sure to set aside time over at least a week for the various fittings.

CENTRAL CHIDLOM SHOPPING CENTRE

Map p274 (www.central.co.th; 1027 Th Phloen Chit; ⏰10am-10pm; [S]Chit Lom exit 5) Generally regarded as the country's best department store for quality and selection, Central has 13 branches across Bangkok in addition to this, the chain's chichi flagship.

BANGKOK'S PLASTIC BAG ADDICTION

Buy a can of beer at any store in Bangkok, and it will be presented to you in a tiny plastic bag – typically accompanied by a plastic straw (a container of yoghurt will be accompanied by a plastic spoon – wrapped in plastic). Do your shopping at any Bangkok supermarket, and you'll find that your groceries have been thematically divided (toiletries must never come in contact with food) into a comical and inconvenient-to-carry number of plastic bags. We once bought a backpack that was wrapped in plastic, which a clerk then inserted into a thick plastic sack. A futile exercise: next time when shopping in Bangkok, make a point of telling your checkout person *mâi sài tǔng* ('no bag, please'), and the response will most likely be a blank stare, followed by the person putting your purchase in a plastic bag, insisting *mâi ɓen rai* ('it's no big deal').

In Thailand, a huge producer of plastic products, bags are a big deal. They're also very cheap, and even street vendors who run razor-thin profit margins can afford to be generous with the plastic. As a result, the country – in particular Bangkok – is seemingly addicted to plastic bags. A survey conducted by the country's Department of Environmental Quality Promotion (DEQP) estimated that the average Thai uses eight plastic bags per day. And like most addictions, it's proving harmful. The DEQP estimates that plastic bags form 20% of the country's rubbish. Bangkok's landfills, which receive nearly 10,000 tonnes of rubbish every day, are already overcrowded, and bags that aren't disposed of properly often obstruct drainage systems, contributing to already problematic flooding.

Over the last decade, retailers, such as 7-Eleven and Tesco Lotus, and municipal and government authorities have kick-started numerous informal initiatives to reduce the distribution of plastic bags. Indeed, a 2015 campaign initiated by the Thai Ministry of Natural Resources and Environment pleaded with Thais to part with their precious plastic bags – one day a month. Yet without the mandate of strict anti-plastic-bag policies seen in countries like Bangladesh, it's likely that Thais will continue to consume as much plastic as ever.

SPORTS & ACTIVITIES

ISSAYA COOKING STUDIO — COOKING COURSE

Map p274 (☎02 160 5636; www.issayastudio.com; Eatthai, Lvl LG, Central Embassy, 1031 Th Phloen Chit; 2000-3000B; ⏲lessons 11am-2pm, 3-6pm & 6-8pm; [S]Phloen Chit exit 5) Started up by home-grown celebrity chef, Pongtawat 'Ian' Chalermkittichai, morning lessons here include instruction in four dishes from his linked restaurant, Issaya Siamese Club (p135), while afternoon and evening lessons focus on desserts and mixology; check the calendar to see what's coming up. Specialised and private lessons can also be arranged.

SPA 1930 — SPA

Map p274 (☎02 254 8606; www.spa1930.com; 42 Th Ton Son; Thai massage from 1000B, spa packages from 3500B; ⏲9.30am-9.30pm; [S]Chit Lom exit 4) Discreet and sophisticated, Spa 1930 rescues relaxers from the contrived spa ambience of New Age music and ingredients you'd rather see at a dinner party. The menu is simple (face, body care and body massage) and the scrubs and massage oils are logical players.

KIDZANIA — PLAY CENTRE

Map p274 (☎02 683 1888; www.bangkok.kidzania.com/en; 5th fl, Siam Paragon, 991/1 Th Phra Ram I; adult 425-500, child 425-1000B; ⏲10am-5pm Mon-Fri, 10.30am-8pm Sat & Sun; [S]Siam exits 3 & 5) Kids can pilot a plane, record an album, make sushi or, er, perform a root canal at this new and impressive learn-and-play centre.

THANN SANCTUARY — SPA

Map p274 (☎02 658 6557; www.thann.info/thann_sanctuary.php; 2nd fl, CentralWorld, Th Ratchadamri; Thai massage from 2000B, spa treatments from 2800B; ⏲10am-9pm; [S]Chit Lom exit 9 to Sky Walk, Siam exit 6 to Sky Walk) This local brand of herbal-based cosmetics has launched a series of mall-based spas – perfect for post-shopping therapy.

SF STRIKE BOWL — BOWLING

Map p274 (7th fl, MBK Center, cnr Th Phra Ram I & Th Phayathai; ⏲10am-1am; [S]National Stadium exit 4) Thai teenagers crowd this psychedelically decorated bowling alley. The cost varies (from 30B), depending on what time you play.

YOGA ELEMENTS STUDIO — YOGA

Map p274 (☎02 655 5671; www.yogaelements.com; 23rd fl, Vanissa Bldg, 29 Th Chitlom; sessions from 520B; [S]Chit Lom exit 5) Run by American Adrian Cox, who trained at Om in New York and who teaches primarily vinyasa and ashtanga, this is the most respected yoga studio in town. The high-rise location helps you rise above it all, too.

PILATES STUDIO — YOGA

Map p274 (☎02 650 7797; www.pilatesbangkok.com; 888/58-59 Mahatun Plaza, Th Phloen Chit; sessions from 550B; ⏲8am-7pm; [S]Phloen Chit exit 2) The first choice for those in Bangkok who are looking for pilates instruction and training.

ABSOLUTE YOGA — YOGA

Map p274 (☎02 252 4400; www.absoluteyogabangkok.com; 4th fl, Amarin Plaza, Th Phloen Chit; lessons from 750B; [S]Chit Lom exit 6) This is the largest of Bangkok's yoga studios, teaching Bikram hot yoga plus a host of other styles.

UNION LANGUAGE SCHOOL — LANGUAGE COURSE

Map p274 (☎02 214 6033; www.unionlanguageschool.com; 7th fl, 328 CCT Office Bldg, Th Phayathai; tuition from 7000B; [S]Ratchathewi exit 1) Generally recognised as having the best and most rigorous Thai language courses (many missionaries study here), Union employs a balance of structure- and communication-oriented methodologies in 80-hour, four-week modules.

AAA — LANGUAGE COURSE

Map p274 (Advance Alliance Academy Thai Language School; ☎02 655 5629; www.aaathai.com; 6th fl, 29 Vanissa Bldg, Th Chitlom; tuition from 7000B; [S]Chit Lom exit 3) Opened by a group of experienced Thai-language teachers from various schools, good-value AAA has a loyal following.

Riverside, Silom & Lumphini

RIVERSIDE | SILOM | LUMPHINI

Neighbourhood Top Five

❶ Dining at **nahm** (p135), quite possibly the best Thai restaurant in the city and – according to the critics – one of the best restaurants in the world.

❷ Soaking up the views at tower-top bars such as **Moon Bar** (p136).

❸ Relaxing Bangkok-style among the exercisers and exercise-observers in **Lumphini Park** (p130), the 'lungs of the city'.

❹ Confronting your fear of snakes at **Queen Saovabha Memorial Institute** (p130).

❺ Ending the day (or starting the night) with a **dinner cruise** (p134) on Mae Nam Chao Phraya.

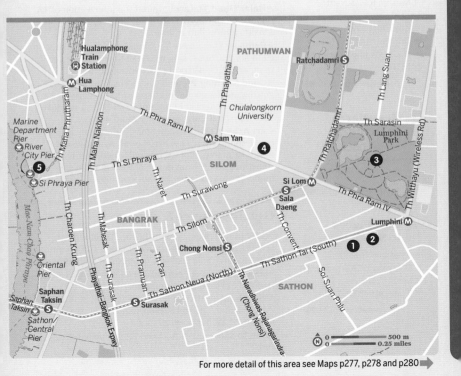

For more detail of this area see Maps p277, p278 and p280 ➡

Lonely Planet's Top Tip

Getting out on Mae Nam Chao Phraya is a great way to escape Bangkok's traffic. So it's fortunate that the city's riverside hotels also have some of the most attractive boats on the river (technically for hotel guests, but that don't check). In most cases these free services run from Sathon/Central Pier to their mother hotel, departing every 10 or 15 minutes. There's no squeeze, no charge, and a uniformed crew will help you on and off.

 Best Places to Eat

➡ nahm (p135)
➡ Eat Me (p132)
➡ Muslim Restaurant (p130)
➡ Kai Thort Jay Kee (p134)
➡ Chennai Kitchen (p131)
➡ Never Ending Summer (p131)

For reviews, see p130. ➡

 Best Places to Drink

➡ Moon Bar (p136)
➡ Smalls (p135)
➡ DJ Station (p138)

For reviews, see p135. ➡

 Best Places to Shop

➡ Asiatique (p139)
➡ Everyday by Karmakamet (p139)
➡ River City (p139)

For reviews, see p139. ➡

Explore: Riverside, Silom & Lumphini

Th Silom, with its towering hotel and office buildings, is Bangkok's de facto financial district, while adjacent Th Sathon is home to many of the city's embassies. Incongruously, lower Th Silom functions as Bangkok's lush gaybourhood. There's a dearth of proper sights in this part of town, so unless you're heading to Lumphini Park – at its best in the early morning – take advantage of the area's street stalls and upmarket restaurants and combine your visit with lunch or dinner. The BTS stop at Sala Daeng and the MRT stop at Si Lom put you at lower Th Silom, perfect jumping-off points for either Lumphini Park or the area's restaurants and sights.

The Riverside area is significantly less flashy, and is great for an aimless wander among old buildings. This stretch of Mae Nam Chao Phraya was formerly Bangkok's international zone, and today retains a particularly Chinese and Muslim feel. Most of the sights in this area can be seen in a morning; the BTS stop at Saphan Taksin is a good starting point.

Local Life

➡ **Halal 'Hood** The area around the intersection of Th Silom and Th Charoen Krung is home to a few Thai-Muslim and Indian restaurants.

➡ **Rainbow Flag** Lower Th Silom, particularly the strip from Soi 2 to Soi 4, is Bangkok's pinkest district, and is popular with both local and visiting gay men.

➡ **Good Morning** Pretend you're Thai-Chinese by getting up at 5am and taking part in the early morning stretching rituals at Lumphini Park. Or you can just show up at a slightly saner hour and watch.

➡ **Art Attack** Those looking for a painting by a contemporary Burmese artist or an Ayuthaya-era Buddhist manuscript cabinet will undoubtedly find something interesting in one of the Th Silom area's numerous art galleries and antique shops.

Getting There & Away

➡ **BTS** To Riverside: Saphan Taksin. To Silom: Sala Daeng (interchange with MRT Si Lom). To Lumphini: Ratchadamri, Sala Daeng, Chong Nonsi and Surasak.

➡ **MRT** To Silom: Si Lom (interchange with BTS Sala Daeng). To Lumphini: Lumphini.

➡ **River boat** To Riverside: River City Pier, Si Phraya Pier, Oriental Pier and Sathon/Central Pier. To Lumphini: Sathon/Central Pier.

➡ **Bus** To Silom: air-con 76 and 77; ordinary 1, 15, 33 and 27.

 SIGHTS

◉ Riverside

OLD CUSTOMS HOUSE HISTORIC BUILDING

Map p280 (กรมศุลกากร; Soi 36, Th Charoen Krung; ⚓Oriental Pier) The country's former Customs House was once the gateway to Thailand, levying taxes on traders moving in and out of the kingdom. It was designed by an Italian architect and built in the 1890s; the front door opened onto its source of income (the river) and the grand facade was ceremonially decorated in columns and transom windows.

Today, with its sagging shutters, peeling yellow paint and laundry flapping on the balconies, the crumbling yet hauntingly beautiful building serves as a residence for members of Bangkok's fire brigade, not to mention a popular destination for wedding photo shoots. And hard-core movie buffs with a keen eye will recognise the Old Customs House from its cameo appearance in Wong Kar Wai's film *In the Mood for Love* (2000).

ASSUMPTION CATHEDRAL CHURCH

Map p280 (อาสนวิหารอัสสัมชัญ; Soi 40/Oriental, Th Charoen Krung; ⊙7am-7pm; ⚓Oriental Pier) **FREE** Marking the ascendancy of the French missionary influence in Bangkok during the reign of Rama II (King Phra-phutthaloetla Naphalai; r 1809–24), this Romanesque church with its rich golden interior dates from 1910, and hosted a Mass by Pope John Paul II in 1984; his statue now stands outside the main door. The schools associated with the cathedral are considered some of the best in Thailand.

SATHORN UNIQUE TOWER BUILDING

(Map p280; Soi 51, Th Charoen Krung; ⚓Sathon/Central Pier, ⚓Saphan Taksin) Known colloquially as the Ghost Tower, as locals believe the plot of land it occupies to be a former cemetery, construction began on Sathorn Unique in 1990. In 1997, with about 75% of the tower completed, the Asian financial crisis reached its peak, funds disappeared, and construction was halted, leaving the tower in its partially finished state ever since. Today, it's both a cringe-worthy reminder of that era and popular destination for urban explorers, though it is officially off-limits to the public due to safety concerns.

RIVERSIDE, SILOM & LUMPHINI SIGHTS

◉ TOP SIGHT
BANGKOKIAN MUSEUM

A collection of three antique structures built during the early 20th century, the Bangkokian Museum illustrates an often-overlooked period of Bangkok's history. The main building was constructed in 1937 as a home for the Surawadee family and, as the signs inform us, was finished by Chinese carpenters on time and for less than the budgeted 2400B (which would barely buy a door handle today). It is filled with beautiful wooden furniture and the detritus of postwar family life, and offers a fascinating window into the period. An adjacent two-storey shophouse contains themed displays of similar items on the ground floor (don't miss the replicated traditional Thai kitchen), while the upper level **Bang Rak Museum** profiles Khet Bang Rak, the district in which the compound is located. The third building, at the back of the block, was built in 1929 as a surgery for a British doctor, though he died soon after arriving in Thailand. A visit takes the form of an informal guided tour in halting English, and photography is encouraged.

DON'T MISS...

➔ Antique wooden buildings
➔ Bang Rak Museum

PRACTICALITIES

➔ พิพิธภัณฑ์ชาวบางกอก
➔ Map p280, D2
➔ 273 Soi 43, Th Charoen Krung
➔ admission by donation
➔ ⊙10am-4pm Wed-Sun
➔ ⚓Si Phraya/River City Pier

Silom

MR KUKRIT PRAMOJ HOUSE
HISTORIC BUILDING

Map p278 (บ้านหม่อมราชวงศ์คึกฤทธิ์ปราโมช; ☎02 286 8185; Soi 7, Th Naradhiwas Rajanagarindra/Chong Nonsi; adult/child 50/20B; 🕒10am-4pm; [S]Chong Nonsi exit 2) Author and statesman Mom Ratchawong Kukrit Pramoj (1911–95) once resided in this charming complex now open to the public. Surrounded by a manicured garden famed for its Thai bonsai trees, the five teak buildings introduce visitors to traditional Thai architecture, arts and to the former resident, who served as prime minister of Thailand in 1974 and '75, wrote more than 150 books (including the highly respected *Four Reigns*) and spent 20 years decorating the house.

The house is occasionally closed for private events, so it's a good idea to call ahead before visiting.

SRI MARIAMMAN TEMPLE
HINDU TEMPLE

Map p278 (วัดพระศรีมหาอุมาเทวี/วัดแขก, Wat Phra Si Maha Umathewi; cnr Th Silom & Th Pan; 🕒6am-8pm; [S]Surasak exit 3) [FREE] Arrestingly flamboyant, this Hindu temple is a wild collision of colours, shapes and deities. It was built in the 1860s by Tamil immigrants and features a 6m facade of intertwined, full-colour Hindu deities. While most of the people working in the temple hail from the Indian subcontinent, you will likely see plenty of Thai and Chinese devotees praying here as well. This is because the Hindu gods figure just as prominently in their individualistic approach to religion.

The official Thai name of the temple is Wat Phra Si Maha Umathewi, but it's often referred to as Wat Khaek – *kàak* being a common expression for people of Indian descent. The literal translation is 'guest', an obvious euphemism for any group of people not particularly wanted as permanent residents; hence most Indian Thais aren't fond of the term.

LOCAL KNOWLEDGE

SILOM'S ART GALLERIES

Upper Th Silom and around is home to some of Bangkok's better art galleries. Located within walking distance of each other, it's possible to stop into all of these listed here in a leisurely afternoon and gain a good overview of the Thai contemporary art scene.

Kathmandu Photo Gallery (Map p278; www.kathmanduphotobkk.com; 87 Th Pan; 🕒11am-7pm Tue-Sun; [S]Surasak exit 3) [FREE] Bangkok's only gallery wholly dedicated to photography is housed in a charmingly restored Sino-Portuguese shophouse. The owner, photographer Manit Sriwanichpoom, wanted Kathmandu to resemble photographers' shops of old, where customers could flip through photographs for sale. Manit's own work is on display on the ground floor, and the small upstairs gallery has changing exhibitions by local and international artists and photographers.

Tang Gallery (Map p278; 5th fl, Silom Galleria, 919/1 Th Silom; 🕒11am-7pm Mon-Sat; [S]Surasak exit 3) [FREE] Bangkok's primary venue for modern artists from China has edged its way to become one of the city's top contemporary galleries. Check the posters in the lobby of Silom Galleria, where it's located, to see what's on.

Number 1 Gallery (Map p278; www.number1gallery.com; 4th fl, Silom Galleria, 919/1 Th Silom; 🕒10am-7pm Mon-Sat; [S]Surasak exit 3) [FREE] This relatively new gallery has established itself by featuring the often attention-grabbing contemporary work of Thai artists such as Vasan Sitthiket, Sutee Kunavichayanont and Thaweesak Srithongdee.

H Gallery (Map p278; www.hgallerybkk.com; 201 Soi 12, Th Sathon Neua/North; 🕒10am-6pm Wed-Sat, by appointment Tue; [S]Chong Nonsi exit 1) [FREE] Housed in a refurbished wooden building, H is generally considered among the city's leading private galleries. It's also regarded as a jumping-off point for Thai artists with international ambitions, such as Jakkai Siributr and Somboon Hormthienthong.

Thavibu Gallery (Map p278; www.thavibu.com; 4th fl, Silom Galleria, 919/1 Th Silom; 🕒11am-6pm Mon-Sat; [S]Surasak exit 3) [FREE] This gallery specialises in contemporary paintings by younger and emerging artists from Thailand, Vietnam and Myanmar.

🏃 Neighbourhood Walk
Riverside
Architecture Ramble

START BTS SAPHAN TAKSIN
END VIVA & AVIV
LENGTH 3KM; TWO TO FOUR HOURS

Bangkok isn't known for its non-religious architecture, but the area that runs parallel to Mae Nam Chao Phraya is home to several noteworthy structures.

Board the BTS, heading towards the river, and get off at Saphan Taksin. Walk north along Th Charoen Krung, passing ancient **1 shophouses** between Th Charoen Wiang and Th Si Wiang. Turn left on Soi 40/ Oriental, home to the **2 Mandarin Oriental** (p200), Bangkok's oldest and most storied hotel. Directly across from the entrance is the classical Venetian-style facade of the **3 East Asiatic Company**, built in 1901. Proceed beneath the overhead walkway linking two buildings to the redbrick **4 Assumption Cathedral** (p127).

Return to Soi 40/Oriental and take the first left. On your right is **5 O.P. Plaza**, built as a department store in 1905. Pass the walls of the French Embassy and turn left. Head towards the river and the **6 Old Customs House** (p127).

Backtrack and turn left beneath the green sign that says Haroon Mosque. You're now in **7 Haroon village**, a Muslim enclave full of sleeping cats, playing kids and gingerbread wooden houses. Wind through Haroon and you'll eventually come to Soi 34, which will lead you back to Th Charoen Krung. Turn left and cross the street opposite the Art Deco **8 General Post Office**. Turn right onto Soi 43 and proceed to the **9 Bangkokian Museum** (p127), home to three antique wooden structures.

Head back to Th Charoen Krung, cross the street and turn right. Turn left on Soi 30. Follow this road past the walls of the **10 Portuguese Embassy**, Bangkok's oldest, to River City – not particularly noteworthy in an architectural sense, but its riverside bar **11 Viva & Aviv** (p135) is a good place to end the walk.

RIVERSIDE, SILOM & LUMPHINI

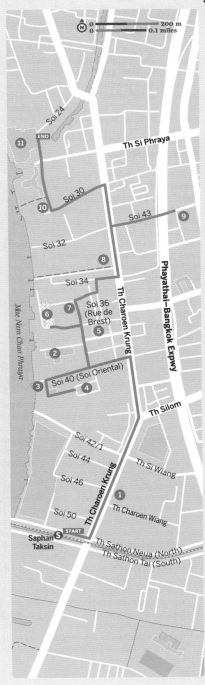

NEILSON HAYS LIBRARY LIBRARY

Map p278 (www.neilsonhayslibrary.com; 195 Th Surawong; admission for non-members 50B; ⏲9.30am-5pm Tue-Sun; [S]Surasak exit 3) The oldest English-language library in Thailand, the Neilson Hays dates back to 1922, and today remains the city's noblest place for a read – with the added benefit of air-con. It has a good selection of children's books and a decent range of titles on Thailand.

👁 Lumphini

QUEEN SAOVABHA MEMORIAL INSTITUTE ZOO

Map p277 (สถานเสาวภา, Snake Farm; cnr Th Phra Ram IV & Th Henri Dunant; adult/child 200/50B; ⏲9.30am-3.30pm Mon-Fri, to 1pm Sat & Sun; 👪; [M]Si Lom exit 1, [S]Sala Daeng exit 3) Thailand's snake farms tend to gravitate towards carnivalesque rather than humanitarian, except at the Queen Saovabha Memorial Institute. Founded in 1923, the snake farm gathers antivenin by milking the snakes' venom, injecting it into horses, and harvesting and purifying the antivenin they produce. The antivenins are then used to treat human victims of snake bites. Regular milkings (11am Monday to Friday) and snake-handling performances (2.30pm Monday to Friday and 11am Saturday and Sunday) are held at the outdoor amphitheatre.

The leafy grounds are home to a few caged snakes, but the bulk of the attractions are found in the Simaseng Building, at the rear of the compound. The ground floor houses several varieties of snakes in glass cages.

🍴 EATING

🍴 Riverside

MUSLIM RESTAURANT THAI, HALAL $

Map p280 (1354-6 Th Charoen Krung; mains 40-140B; ⏲6.30am-5.30pm; ⛴Oriental Pier, [S]Saphan Taksin exit 1) Plant yourself in any random wooden booth of this ancient eatery for a glimpse into what restaurants in Bangkok used to be like. The menu, much like the interior design, doesn't appear to have changed much in the restaurant's 70-year history, and the birianis, curries and samosas remain more Indian-influenced than Thai.

👁 TOP SIGHT LUMPHINI PARK

Named after Buddha's birthplace in Nepal (Lumbini), Lumphini Park is central Bangkok's largest and most popular park. Its 58 hectares are home to an artificial lake surrounded by broad, well-tended lawns, wooded areas, walking paths and startlingly large monitor lizards to complement the shuffling Bangkokians. It's the best outdoor escape from Bangkok without actually leaving town.

The park was originally a royal reserve, but in 1925 Rama VI (King Vajiravudh; r 1910–25) declared it a public space. One of the best times to visit is early morning, when the air is (relatively) fresh and legions of Chinese are practising t'ai chi, doing their best to mimic the aerobics instructor, or doing the half-run half-walk version of jogging that makes a lot of sense in oppressive humidity. There are paddleboats for lovers, playgrounds for the kids and ramshackle weight-lifting areas for stringy old men. Cold drinks are available at the entrances and street-food vendors set up tables outside the park's northwest corner from about 5pm. Late at night the borders of the park are frequented by streetwalking prostitutes, both male and female.

DON'T MISS...

- Enormous monitor lizards
- Early morning t'ai chi and evening aerobics

PRACTICALITIES

- สวนลุมพินี
- Map p277, B1
- bounded by Th Sarasin, Th Phra Ram IV, Th Witthayu/Wireless Rd & Th Ratchadamri
- ⏲4.30am-9pm
- 👪
- [M]Lumphini exit 3, Si Lom exit 1, [S]Sala Daeng exit 3, Ratchadamri exit 2

NEVER ENDING SUMMER · THAI $$

Map p280 (☎02 861 0953; www.facebook.com/
TheNeverEndingSummer; 41/5 Th Charoen Nakhon; mains 140-350B; ☺11am-2pm & 5-11pm
Mon, 11am-11pm Tue-Sun; ☻river-crossing ferry
from River City Pier) The cheesy name doesn't
do justice to this surprisingly sophisticated
Thai restaurant located in a former warehouse by the river. Join Bangkok's beautiful crowd for antiquated Thai dishes such
as cubes of watermelon served with a dry
'dressing' of fish, sugar and deep-fried shallots, or fragrant green curry with pork and
fresh bird's-eye chilli.

INDIAN HUT · INDIAN $$

Map p280 (www.indianhut-bangkok.com; 414-420
Th Surawong; mains 160-380B; ☺11am-11pm;
☑; ☻Oriental Pier) Despite the fast-food
overtones in the name and logo, this long-
standing restaurant is classy and popular
with visiting businesspeople. The emphasis is on northern Indian cuisine, including excellent flatbreads and tandoor-baked
meats, and dishes such as homemade
paneer in a tomato and onion curry.

LE NORMANDIE · FRENCH $$$

Map p280 (☎02 659 9000; www.mandarinori
ental.com/bangkok/fine-dining/le-normandie;
Mandarin Oriental, 48 Soi 40/Oriental, Th Charoen Krung; mains 980-3750B; ☺noon-2.30pm &
7-11pm Mon-Sat, 7-11pm Sun; ☻Oriental Pier or
hotel shuttle boat from Sathon/Central Pier) Although today's Bangkok boasts a plethora
of upmarket choices, Le Normandie has
maintained its niche and is still the only
place to go for a genuinely old-world 'conti-
nental' dining experience. A revolving cast
of Michelin-starred guest chefs and some of
the world's most decadent ingredients keep
up the standard, and appropriately formal
attire (including jacket) is required. Book
ahead, although note that Le Normandie
was closed at the time of research for a
renovation; some of the details above may
have changed by the time it has reopened.

LORD JIM'S · INTERNATIONAL $$$

Map p280 (☎02 659 9000; www.mandarin
oriental.com/bangkok/fine-dining/lord-jims;
Mandarin Oriental Hotel, 48 Soi 40/Oriental, Th
Charoen Krung; buffet 2050-2943B; ☺noon-
2.30pm Mon-Fri, 11.30am-3pm Sat, 11am-3pm
Sun; ☑; ☻Oriental Pier or hotel shuttle boat from
Sathon/Central Pier) Even if you can't afford
to stay at the Oriental, you should save up

for the hotel's decadent riverside buffet.
Dishes such as foie gras are standard, and
weekends, when reservations are recommended, see additional seafood stations.

✖ Silom

CHENNAI KITCHEN · INDIAN $

Map p278 (107/4 Th Pan; mains 70-150B; ☺10am-
3pm & 6-9.30pm; ☑; �$Surasak exit 3) This
thimble-sized mom-and-pop restaurant
puts out some of the best southern Indian
vegetarian food in town. Yard-long *dosai*
(a crispy southern Indian bread) is always
a good choice, but if you're feeling indeci-
sive (or exceptionally famished), go for the
banana-leaf *thali* (set meal) that seems to
incorporate just about everything in the
kitchen.

KALAPAPRUEK · THAI $

Map p278 (27 Th Pramuan; mains 90-330B;
☺8am-6pm Mon-Sat, to 3pm Sun; ☑; �$Surasak
exit 3) This venerable Thai eatery has numerous branches and mall spin-offs around
town, but we still fancy the original branch.
The diverse menu spans Thai specialities
from just about every region, daily specials
and, occasionally, seasonal treats as well.

FOO MUI KEE · CHINESE-THAI $

Map p278 (10-12 Soi 22, Th Silom; mains 60-380B;
☺11am-9pm; �$Surasak exit 3) Foo Mui Kee
has been serving a unique mixture of Thai,
Chinese and European dishes for more
than 80 years. In some offerings, such as
the stewed ox tongue served over rice, the
boundaries between cuisines are not so
distinct, although the bottle of Worcester-
shire sauce on each marble table or wooden
booth gives away the restaurant's Western
leanings.

JAY SO · NORTHEASTERN THAI $

Map p278 (146/1 Soi Phiphat 2; mains 20-80B;
☺11am-4pm Mon-Sat; Ⓜ Si Lom exit 2, �$Sala
Daeng exit 2) Jay So has no menu, but a
mortar and pestle and a huge grill are the
telltale signs of ballistically spicy *sôm·dam*
(green papaya salad), sublime herb-stuffed,
grilled catfish and other northeastern Thai
specialities.

There's no English signage, so look for the
ramshackle, mostly white, Coke-decorated
shack about halfway down Soi Phiphat 2.

KRUA 'AROY-AROY' THAI $

Map p278 (Th Pan; mains 40-100B; ⊕8am-8pm; ⓢSurasak exit 3) Krua 'Aroy-Aroy' (Delicious Kitchen) is the kind of family-run Thai restaurant where nobody seems to notice the cat slumbering on the cash register. Stop by for some of the richest curries around, as well as the interesting daily specials including, on Thursdays, *kôw klúk gà-ʔì* (rice cooked in shrimp paste and served with sweet pork, shredded green mango and other toppings).

SOMTAM CONVENT NORTHEASTERN THAI $

Map p278 ('Hai'; 2/4-5 Th Convent; mains 55-150B; ⊕11am-9pm Mon-Fri, to 5pm Sat; ⓂSi Lom exit 2, ⓢSala Daeng exit 2) Northeastern-style Thai food is usually relegated to less-than-hygienic stalls perched by the side of the road with no menu or English-speaking staff in sight. A less intimidating introduction to the wonders of *lâhp* (a minced meat 'salad'), *sôm·đam* and other Isan delights can be had at this popular, long-standing restaurant.

SOI 10 FOOD CENTRES THAI $

Map p278 (Soi 10, Th Silom; mains 20-60B; ⊕8am-3pm Mon-Fri; ⓂSi Lom exit 2, ⓢSala Daeng exit 1) These two adjacent hangar-like buildings tucked behind Soi 10 are the main lunchtime fuelling stations for the area's office staff. Choices range from southern-style *kôw gaang* (point-and-choose curries ladled over rice) to just about every incarnation of Thai noodle.

TALING PLING THAI $$

Map p278 (Baan Silom, Soi 19, Th Silom; mains 110-275B; ⊕11am-10pm; ✉; ⓢSurasak exit 3) Don't be fooled by the flashy interior; long-standing Taling Pling continues to serve a thick menu of homely, full-flavoured Thai dishes. It's a good starting point for rich, southern and central Thai fare such as *gaang kôo·a* (crabmeat curry with wild betel leaves), with tasty pies and cakes and refreshing drinks rounding out the choices.

DAI MASU JAPANESE $$

Map p278 (www.facebook.com/shichirinizakaya daimasu; 9/3 Soi Than Tawan; dishes 49-300B; ⊕5.30pm-1am; ✆; ⓂSi Lom exit 2, ⓢSala Daeng exit 1) The emphasis at this cosy, retro-themed Japanese restaurant is *yakiniku* (DIY grilled meat). But we also love the tiny, tasty sides ranging from crispy spears of cucumber in a savoury marinade to a slightly bitter salad of paper-thin slices of eggplant.

SUSHI TSUKIJI JAPANESE $$

Map p278 (62/19-20 Th Thaniya; sushi per item 60-700B; ⊕11.30am-2.30pm & 5.30-10.30pm; ⓂSi Lom exit 2, ⓢSala Daeng exit 1) Our pick of the numerous Japanese joints along Th Thaniya is Tsukiji, named after Tokyo's famous seafood market. Dinner at this sleek sushi joint will leave a significant dent in the wallet, so instead come for lunch on a weekday, when Tsukiji does generous sushi sets for a paltry 297B.

PIZZA MASSILIA ITALIAN $$

Map p278 (off Th Sala Daeng; pizzas 250-400B; ⊕11.30am-2pm & 5.30-10pm Tue-Sun; ✆; ⓂSi Lom exit 3, ⓢSala Daeng exit 4) Pizza in a parking lot? An unlikely destination – especially in increasingly image-conscious Bangkok – until you consider that the pies here are wood-fired by an Italian chef, and the tree-shaded parking has heaps of charm.

Look for the marqueed food truck behind the MK Gold restaurant on Th Sala Daeng.

NADIMOS LEBANESE $$

Map p278 (www.nadimos.com; Soi 19, Th Silom; mains 70-400B; ⊕11.30am-11.30pm; ✆; ⓢSurasak exit 3) This white-tableclother does tasty versions of all the Lebanese standards, plus quite a few dishes you'd never expect to see this far from Beirut. Lots of vegetarian options as well.

BONITA CAFE & SOCIAL CLUB VEGETARIAN $$

Map p278 (56/3 Th Pan; mains 160-250B; ⊕11am-10pm Wed-Mon; ✆✉; ⓢSurasak exit 3) Resembling grandma's living room, this homely restaurant serves predominately Western-style vegan and raw dishes.

★EAT ME INTERNATIONAL $$$

Map p278 (✆02 238 0931; www.eatme restaurant.com; Soi Phiphat 2; mains 275-1400B; ⊕3pm-1am; ✆; ⓂSi Lom exit 2, ⓢSala Daeng exit 2) The dishes here, with descriptions like 'charred whitlof and mozzarella salad with preserved lemon and dry aged Cecina beef' may sound all over the map or perhaps somewhat pretentious, but they're actually just plain tasty. A casual-yet-sophisticated atmosphere, excellent cocktails, a handsome wine list, and some of the city's best desserts also make this one of our favourite places in Bangkok to dine.

SILOM'S SWEET SPOTS

Perhaps due to its legacy as Bangkok's former international district, the area around Th Silom has a disproportionately wide selection of sweets, both domestic and imported. Some of the highlights:

Chocolate Buffet (Map p277; www.sukhothai.com; Sukhothai Hotel, 13/3 Th Sathon Tai/South; buffet 900B; ☺2-5pm Fri-Sun; ☑; ⓂLumphini exit 2) For those with an insatiable sweet tooth, the Sukhothai Hotel offers a unique and almost entirely cocoa-based high tea.

Boonsap Thai Desserts (Map p280; www.boonsap.com; 1478 Th Charoen Krung; desserts from 15B; ☺7am-5pm Mon-Sat; ⓢSathon/Central Pier, ⓈSaphan Taksin exit 3) Dating back to the 1940s is this legendary producer of Thai sweets. Couple their sweetened sticky rice with mangoes or coconut custard. There's no English-language sign; look for the white shopfront with the gold letters near Soi 44.

iBerry (Map p278; www.iberryhomemade.com; 2nd fl, Silom Complex, Th Silom; ice cream from 69B; ☺10am-9pm; ☑; ⓂSi Lom exit 3, ⓈSala Daeng exit 4) A domestic chain with correspondingly Thai flavours such as 'guava and salted plum', 'santol sorbet' and, for the daring, durian.

Duc de Praslin (Map p278; www.facebook.com/DucDePraslin; 2nd fl, Silom Complex, Th Silom; chocolates from 28B; ☺10am-10pm; ⓂSi Lom exit 3, ⓈSala Daeng exit 4) A mall-bound cafe featuring domestically made, Belgian-style chocolates. Combine your coffee – or the delicious hot chocolate – with one of the huge variety of bonbons or a bar of chocolate with an exotic pedigree.

Mashoor (Map p278; 38 Th Pan; mains 50-120B; ☺9am-9pm; ☑; ⓈSurasak exit 3) This and a couple of other similar cafes near the Hindu temple do Indian-style sweets.

Eat Me We reckon this restaurant does some of the best desserts in Bangkok; folks are known to have crossed town for the sticky date pudding alone.

RIVERSIDE, SILOM & LUMPHINI EATING

BENJARONG
THAI $$$

Map p278 (☑02 200 9000; www.dusit.com; ground fl, Dusit Thani Hotel, 946 Th Phra Ram IV; set lunch 650-750B, set dinner from 1700B; mains 390-1200B; ☺11am-2.30pm & 6-10pm Mon-Fri, 6-10pm Sat; ⓂSi Lom exit 3, ⓈSala Daeng exit 4) The Dusit Thani's signature Thai restaurant has emerged from a revamp with a sumptuous, decadent dining room and a new captain, the Danish chef Morten Nielsen. Not surprisingly, the dishes blend Western cooking techniques and Thai ingredients, with the occasional foray into other regions of Asia; think tasty twists such as 'crispy sweet pork ribs and salted Sriracha cabbage'.

SENSI
ITALIAN $$$

Map p277 (☑02 117 1618; www.sensibangkok. com; Yak 5, Soi 17, Th Naradhiwas Rajanagarindra/Chong Nonsi; mains 450-1990B; ☺6pm-midnight Mon-Sat; ⓈChong Nonsi exit 2) Sensi is ostensibly an Italian restaurant, but we prefer to view it as one of Bangkok's better examples of contemporary dining. Expect high-quality imported ingredients and modern culinary techniques that complement rath-

er than confuse, served in a sophisticated yet warm setting in a vintage villa.

L'ATELIER DE JOËL ROBUCHON
INTERNATIONAL $$$

Map p278 (☑02 001 0698; www.robuchon-bangkok.com; 5th fl, Mahanakorn Cube, 96 Th Naradhiwas Rajanagarindra/Chong Nonsi; set lunch 950-1850B, set dinner 5000-7500B, mains 450-3200B; ☺11.30am-2.30pm & 6.30-10.30pm; ⓈChong Nonsi exit 3) We'd like to think that you came to Bangkok to eat Thai, but we'd be remiss not to mention this place, one of the biggest openings in the city's recent past. Helmed by the chef who holds more Michelin stars than anyone else, expect modern, French-inspired dishes, beautifully presented and served in a sultry, sophisticated atmosphere, where seating ranges from counter top to private room.

SOMBOON SEAFOOD
CHINESE-THAI $$$

Map p278 (☑02 233 3104; www.somboonseafood.com; cnr Th Surawong & Th Naradhiwas Rajanagarindra/Chong Nonsi; mains 120-900B; ☺4-11.30pm; ⓈChong Nonsi exit 3) Somboon, a hectic seafood hall with a reputation far

MAE NAM CHAO PHRAYA DINNER CRUISES

A dinner cruise along Mae Nam Chao Phraya is touted as an iconic Bangkok experience, and several companies cater to this. Yet it's worth mentioning that, in general, the vibe can be somewhat cheesy, with loud live entertainment and mammoth boats so brightly lit inside you'd never know you were on the water. The food, typically served as a buffet, usually ranges from mediocre to forgettable. But the atmosphere of the river at night, bordered by illuminated temples and skyscrapers, and the cool breeze chasing the heat away, is usually enough to trump all of this.

A good one-stop centre for all your dinner cruise needs is the **River City Boat Tour Check-In Center** (Map p280; www.rivercity.co.th; ground fl, River City, 23 Th Yotha; ⊙10am-10pm; 🚢Si Phraya/River City Pier, or shuttle boat from Sathon/Central Pier), where tickets can be purchased for **Grand Pearl** (Map p280; ☑02 861 0255; www.grandpearlcruise.com; tickets 2000B; ⊙cruise 7.30-9.30pm; 🚢Si Phraya/River City Pier), **Chaophraya Cruise** (Map p280; ☑02 541 5599; www.chaophrayacruise.com; tickets 1700B; ⊙cruise 7-9pm; 🚢Si Phraya/River City Pier), **Wan Fah** (Map p280; ☑02 622 7657; www.wanfah.in.th/eng/dinner; tickets 1300B; ⊙cruise 7-9pm; 🚢Si Phraya/River City Pier), **Chao Phraya Princess** (Map p280; ☑02 860 3700; www.thaicruise.com; tickets 1400B; ⊙cruise 7.50-9.50pm; 🚢Si Phraya/River City Pier) and **White Orchid** (Map p280; ☑02 438 8228; www.thairivercruise.com; tickets 1400B; ⊙cruise 7.20-9.45pm; 🚢Si Phraya/River City Pier). All cruises depart from River City Pier; take a look at the websites to see exactly what's on offer.

For something slightly more upmarket, consider **Manohra Cruises** (☑02 476 0022; www.manohracruises.com; adult 1750-2500B, child 875-1250B; 🚢hotel shuttle boat from Sathon/Central Pier). Operating on a restored teak rice barge, this outfit is markedly classier, and serves what is probably the best food of Bangkok's various dinner cruises. It departs from Anantara Bangkok Riverside Resort & Spa, accessible via hotel shuttle boat from Sathon/Central Pier.

and wide, is known for doing the best curry-powder crab in town. Soy-steamed sea bass *(ƀlah grà·pong nêung see·éw)* is also a speciality and, like all good Thai seafood, should be enjoyed with an immense platter of *kôw pàt ƀoo* (fried rice with crab) and as many friends as you can gather together.

LE DU INTERNATIONAL $$$

Map p278 (☑092 919 9969; www.ledubkk.com; 399/3 Soi 7, Th Silom; mains 300-990B; ⊙6-11pm Mon-Sat; 🖥🍴; 🚇Chong Nonsi exit 2) A play on the Thai word for 'season', Le Du intertwines Thai dishes and Western flavours and cooking techniques with, not surprisingly, an emphasis on fresh, seasonal ingredients. For the full experience, including some inventive desserts, come at dinner for the four- or seven-course tasting menus (990B to 2300B).

INDIGO FRENCH $$$

Map p278 (6 Th Convent; mains 390-1850B; ⊙noon-11pm; 🚇Si Lom exit 2, 🚇Sala Daeng exit 2) Indigo is set in a former schoolhouse, and the charming atmosphere appears to be the main draw here, but the food actually delivers. Think: your neighbourhood French place, if your neighbourhood French place had oysters flown in from Les Halles on a weekly basis, and an interesting cheese selection. It doesn't come cheap, but daily set lunches start at 380B.

🍴 Lumphini

KAI THORT JAY KEE NORTHEASTERN THAI $$

Map p277 (Polo Fried Chicken; 137/1-3 Soi Sanam Khli/Polo; mains 50-350B; ⊙11am-9pm; 🚇Lumphini exit 3) Although the *sôm· đam*, sticky rice and *lâhp* of this former street stall give the impression of a northeastern-Thai-style eatery, the restaurant's namesake deep-fried bird is more southern in origin. Regardless, smothered in a thick layer of crispy deep-fried garlic, it is none other than a truly Bangkok experience.

BAAN THAI $$

Map p277 (☑02 655 8995; www.baanbkk.com; 139/5 Th Witthayu/Wireless Rd; mains 120-450B; ⊙11am-2.30pm & 5.30-10.30pm Wed-Mon; 🚇Lumphini exit 3) *Baan* is Thai for 'home', seemingly a jarring contrast with the slick, modern feel of this new place. But it is in fact a family-run restaurant, and the occasionally obscure dishes with roots in home kitchens, such as the '*baan* signature spicy five-spiced egg soup', reflect this.

★ NAHM   THAI $$$
Map p277 (☑ 02 625 3388; www.comohotels. com/metropolitanbangkok/dining/nahm; ground fl, Metropolitan Hotel, 27 Th Sathon Tai/South; set lunch 550-1500B, set dinner 2300B, dishes 280-750B; ⊙noon-2pm Mon-Fri, 7-10.30pm daily; Ⓜ Lumphini exit 2) Australian chef-author David Thompson is the man behind one of Bangkok's – and if you believe the critics, the world's – best Thai restaurants. Using ancient cookbooks as his inspiration, Thompson has given new life to previously extinct dishes with exotic descriptions such as 'smoked fish curry with prawns, chicken livers, cockles, chillies and black pepper'.

Dinner is best approached via the multicourse set meal, while lunch means *kà·nŏm jeen*, thin rice noodles served with curries.

If you're expecting bland, gentrified Thai food meant for foreigners, prepare to be disappointed. Reservations recommended.

ZANOTTI   ITALIAN $$$
Map p277 (www.zanottigroup.com; 21/2 Th Sala Daeng; mains 190-1600B; ⊙11.30am-2pm & 6-10.30pm; Ⓜ Si Lom exit 3, Ⓢ Sala Daeng exit 4) Zanotti has a well-deserved reputation for serving some of Bangkok's best Italian dishes. But we also fancy the dark woods and framed paintings of the gentlemen's-club-like dining room, not to mention the professional and confident service – the latter a rarity in Bangkok. Come at noon from Monday to Friday for the amazing-value set lunch that starts at only 350B.

ISSAYA SIAMESE CLUB   THAI $$$
Map p277 (☑ 02 672 9040; www.issaya.com; 4 Soi Sri Aksorn; mains 150-580B; ⊙11.30am-

2.30pm & 6-10.30pm; ☑; Ⓜ Khlong Toei exit 1 & taxi) Housed in a charming 1920s-era villa, Issaya is Thai celebrity chef Ian Kittichai's first effort at a domestic outpost serving the food of his homeland. Dishes alternate between somewhat saucy, meaty items and lighter dishes using produce from the restaurant's organic garden.

The restaurant can be a bit tricky to find, and is best approached in a taxi via Soi Ngam Du Phli.

DRINKING & NIGHTLIFE

🍷 Riverside

VIVA & AVIV   BAR
Map p280 (www.vivaaviv.com; ground fl, River City, 23 Th Yotha; ⊙11am-midnight; 🚤 Si Phraya/River City Pier) An enviable riverside location, casual open-air seating and a funky atmosphere make this restaurant-ish bar a contender for one of Bangkok's best sunset cocktail destinations.

🍷 Silom

SMALLS   BAR
Map p278 (186/3 Soi Suan Phlu; ⊙8.30pm-late; Ⓜ Lumphini exit 2 & taxi) The kind of new bar that feels like it's been here forever, Smalls combines a cheekily decadent interior, an inviting rooftop and live music on Thursdays and Fridays. The rather eclectic house cocktails are strong, if sweet, and bar snacks range from rillettes to quesadillas.

NAMSAAH BOTTLING TRUST   BAR
Map p278 (www.namsaah.com; 401 Soi 7, Th Silom; ⊙5pm-2am; Ⓜ Si Lom exit 2, Ⓢ Sala Daeng exit 2) Namsaah is all about twists. From

WORTH A DETOUR

TAWANDANG GERMAN BREWERY
A German beer hall may seem like an odd destination in Bangkok, but the long-standing **Tawandang German Brewery** (www.tawandang.co.th; cnr Th Phra Ram III & Th Naradhiwas Rajanagarindra/Chong Nonsi; ⊙5pm-1am; Ⓢ Chong Nonsi exit 2 & taxi) is a bona fide local institution – not to mention a one-stop venue for a guranateed fun night out. The Thai-German food is tasty (don't miss the 'deep-fried pork knuckle served with spicy sauce', a Thai-German fusion staple), the house-made brews are potable, and the nightly stage shows make singing along a necessity. Music starts at 8.30pm.

its home (a former mansion incongruously painted hot pink and decked out in a dark, clubby vibe), to the cocktails (classics with a tweak or two) and the bar snacks and dishes (think *pàt tai* with foie gras), everything's a little bit off in just the right way.

VOGUE LOUNGE
BAR

Map p278 (5th fl, Mahanakorn Cube, 96 Th Naradhiwas Rajanagarindra/Chong Nonsi; ⏲5pm-late; [S]Chong Nonsi exit 3) At this new venue, an extension of the eponymous magazine, brand placement is thankfully at a minimum. Instead, you get a classy, classic-feeling bar in marble and brass, with an engaging menu of signature drinks and high-end nibbles. Happy hours that extend beyond dark and an outdoor terrace equipped with air-con make Vogue a clever late-night alternative.

THE BAR
BAR

Map p278 (www.whotelbangkok.com/en/thehouseonsathorn; The House on Sathorn, W Bangkok, 106 Th Sathon Neua/North; ⏲noon-midnight; [S]Chong Nonsi exit 1) Located in one of Bangkok's more famous addresses – a registered historical landmark that in previous lives was a mansion, a hotel, and most recently, the Cold War–era Russian Embassy – is this atmospheric bar. The signature drinks are creative and tasty, yet worth it to gain access to the decadent surroundings.

MAGGIE CHOO'S
BAR

Map p278 (www.facebook.com/maggiechoos; basement, Novotel Bangkok Fenix Silom, 320 Th Silom; ⏲7.30pm-2am Sun-Thu, to 3am Fri & Sat; [S]Surasak exit 1) A former bank vault with a Chinatown-opium-den vibe, secret passageways and lounging women in silk dresses. With all this going on, it's easy to forget that Maggie Choo's is actually a bar,

SILOM'S ROOFTOP BARS

In Bangkok, nobody seems to mind if you slap the odd bar on top of a skyscraper. Indeed, the city has become associated with open-air rooftop bars, and the area around Th Sathon and Th Silom is home to some of its best, with locales boasting views that range from riverside to hyper-urban.

Note that nearly all of Bangkok's hotel-based rooftop bars have strictly enforced dress codes barring access to those wearing shorts and/or sandals.

Moon Bar (Map p277; www.banyantree.com/en/web/banyantree/ap-thailand-bangkok/vertigo-and-moon-bar; 61st fl, Banyan Tree Hotel, 21/100 Th Sathon Tai/South; ⏲5pm-1am; [M]Lumphini exit 2) An alarmingly short barrier at this rooftop bar is all that separates patrons from the street, 61 floors down. Located on top of the Banyan Tree Hotel, Moon Bar claims to be among the highest alfresco bars in the world. It's also a great place from which to see the Phrarpadaeng Peninsula (see p166), a vast green area that's colloquially known as Bangkok's green lung.

Cloud 47 (Map p278; https://www.facebook.com/thecloud47; 47th fl, United Center, 323 Th Silom ; ⏲5pm-1am; [M]Si Lom exit 2, [S]Sala Daeng exit 2) If you like a bit of elbow room in your bar/restaurants – say, enough to hold a cricket match – consider this rooftopper. Spread out and enjoy live music and a location in the middle of the city's financial district, where there are impressively tall buildings in just about every direction. The cocktails here are pricey, but the beer – including draught beer and beer 'towers' – is relatively good value.

Park Society (Map p277; 29th fl, Sofitel So, 2 Th Sathon Neua/North; ⏲5pm-2am; [M]Lumphini exit 2) Gazing down at the green expanse of Lumphini Park, abruptly bordered by tall buildings on most sides, you can be excused for thinking that Bangkok almost, kinda, sorta feels like Manhattan. The drink prices at Park Society, 29 floors above the ground, may also remind you of New York City, although there are monthly promotions.

Sky Bar (Map p280; www.lebua.com/sky-bar; 63rd fl, State Tower, 1055 Th Silom; ⏲6pm-1am; ⛴Sathon/Central Pier, [S]Saphan Taksin exit 3) Descend the Hollywood-like staircase to emerge at this bar that juts out over the Bangkok skyline and Mae Nam Chao Phraya. Scenes from *The Hangover Part II* were filmed here, and the 'hangovertini' cocktail is actually quite drinkable. The views, of course, aren't bad either.

although you'll be reminded by the creative and somewhat sweet cocktails, and a crowd that blends selfie-snapping locals and curious tourists.

CRAFT BAR

Map p278 (www.craftbangkok.com; ground fl, Holiday Inn, cnr Th Silom & Th Surasak; ⏲noon-midnight; [S]Surasak exit 3) The microbrew trend that has swept across Sukhumvit has finally reached this part of town. Craft has 20, mostly American, beers on tap and even more bottles in the fridge.

CÉ LA VI CLUB

Map p278 (www.kudeta.com/bangkok; 38th & 39th fl, Sathorn Square Complex, 98 Th Sathon Neua/North; ⏲11am-1am Mon-Thu, to 3am Fri & Sat; [S]Chong Nonsi exit 1) Spanning multiple bars, three restaurants and two clubs, the formerly named Ku Dé Ta remains the biggest thing on Bangkok's club scene – literally and figuratively. Expect an entry fee of 500B after 10pm on Fridays and Saturdays.

HANAKARUTA BAR

Map p278 (www.facebook.com/hanakaruta; Soi 10, Th Sathon Neua/North; ⏲6pm-2am Mon-Sat; [S]Chong Nonsi exit 1) The floor-to-ceiling wall of bottles here is proof of Hanakaruta's dedication to booze. Sake and shochu are specialities, but we love the house-made umeshu (plum wine). There's a menu of bar snacks (from 60B to 680B) that, like the drinks, is served with Japanese efficiency.

VESPER BAR

Map p278 (www.vesperbar.co; 10/15 Th Convent; ⏲noon-2.30pm & 6pm-1am Mon-Fri, 6pm-midnight Sat, noon-2.30pm Sun; [M]Si Lom exit 2, [S]Sala Daeng exit 2) One of the freshest faces on Bangkok's drinking scene is this deceptively classic-feeling bar-restaurant. As the name suggests, the emphasis here is on cocktails, including several revived classics and mixed drinks mellowed by ageing for six weeks in white-oak barrels.

TAPAS ROOM CLUB

Map p278 (114/17-18 Soi 4, Th Silom; admission 100B; ⏲7pm-2am; [M]Si Lom exit 2, [S]Sala Daeng exit 1) Although it sits staunchly at the front of Bangkok's pinkest street, this long-standing two-level disco manages to bring in just about everybody. Come from Thursday to Saturday, when the combination of DJs and live percussion brings the body count to critical level.

🍷 Lumphini

CERESIA CAFE

Map p277 (ground fl, Tisco Tower, 48/2 Th Sathon Neua/North; ⏲8am-6pm Mon-Fri, 9am-6pm Sat; [M]Lumphini exit 2) Finally, a local roastery to rescue us from the caffeinated shackles of you-know-what. And best of all, boasting high-quality exotic and domestic beans, expertly prepared drinks and good pastries, Ceresia is more than just an alternative.

WONG'S PLACE BAR

Map p277 (27/3 Soi Si Bamphen; ⏲9pm-late Tue-Sun; [M]Lumphini exit 1) This dusty den is a time warp into the backpacker world of the early 1980s. The namesake owner died several years ago, but a relative removed the padlock and picked up where Wong left off. It works equally well as a destination or a last resort, but don't bother knocking until midnight, keeping in mind that it stays open until the last person crawls out.

☆ ENTERTAINMENT

BAMBOO BAR LIVE MUSIC

Map p280 (☎02 236 0400; www.mandarinoriental.com/bangkok/fine-dining/the-bamboo-bar; ground fl, Mandarin Oriental, 48 Soi 40/Oriental, Th Charoen Krung; ⏲5pm-1am Sun-Thu, to 2am Fri & Sat; ⛴Oriental Pier or hotel shuttle boat from Sathon/Central Pier) Recently renovated and looking better than ever, the Oriental's Bamboo Bar remains one of the city's premier locales for live jazz. The music starts at 9pm nightly.

THREE SIXTY LIVE MUSIC

Map p280 (☎02 442 2000; 32nd fl, Millennium Hilton, 123 Th Charoen Nakhorn; ⏲5pm-1am; ⛴hotel shuttle boat from Sathon/Central Pier) Feeling frustrated with Bangkok? A set or two of live jazz in this elegant glass-encased perch 32 floors above the city will help you forget some of your troubles, or at the very least, give you a whole new perspective on the city.

CALYPSO BANGKOK CABARET

(☎02 688 1415; www.calypsocabaret.com; Asiatique, Soi 72-76, Th Charoen Krung; adult/child 900/600B; ⏲show times 8.15pm & 9.45pm; ⛴shuttle ferry from Sathon/Central Pier) Located in Asiatique market (p139), Calypso is yet another destination for *gà·teu·i* (transgender; also spelt *kàthoey*) cabaret.

SALA RIM NAAM
THEATRE

Map p280 (📞02 437 3080; www.mandarinoriental.com/bangkok/fine-dining/sala-rim-naam; Mandarin Oriental Hotel, Soi 40/Oriental, Th Charoen Krung; tickets adult/child 1999/1700B; ⏰dinner & show 8.15-9.30pm; ⛴Oriental Pier or hotel shuttle boat from Sathon/Central Pier) The historic Mandarin Oriental hosts dinner theatre in a sumptuous Thai pavilion located across the river in Thonburi. The price is well above the average, reflecting the means of the hotel's client base, but the performance gets positive reviews.

PATPONG
RED-LIGHT DISTRICT

Map p278 (Th Phat Phong & Soi Phat Phong 2; ⏰4pm-2am; Ⓜ Si Lom exit 2, Ⓢ Sala Daeng exit 1) One of the most famous red-light districts in the world, today any 'charm' that

BANGKOK'S GAYBOURHOOD

The side streets off lower Th Silom are so gay that they make San Francisco look like rural Texas. Every night, a pink tractor beam draws gay locals and tourists to the in-your-face sex shows in nearby Duangthawee Plaza, the chilled open-air bars on Soi 4 and the booming clubs in and around Soi 2.

Bars

Soi 4 is a tiny alleyway packed with gay bars, most with strategically positioned seats to best observe the nightly parade.

Telephone Pub (Map p278; www.telephonepub.com; 114/11-13 Soi 4, Th Silom; ⏰6pm-1am; Ⓜ Si Lom exit 2, Ⓢ Sala Daeng exit 1) Telephone is famous for the phones that used to sit on every table, allowing you to ring up that hottie sitting across the room. Its popularity remains even if most of the phones are gone. The clientele is mostly 30-plus white men with their Thai 'friends'.

Balcony (Map p278; www.balconypub.com; 86-88 Soi 4, Th Silom; ⏰5.30pm-2am; 📶; Ⓜ Si Lom exit 2, Ⓢ Sala Daeng exit 1) Located directly across from Telephone, this is yet another long-standing cafe-like pub that features the occasional drag-queen performance.

Bearbie (Map p278; 2nd fl, 82 Soi 4, Th Silom; ⏰8pm-1am Tue-Thu, to 2am Fri-Sun; Ⓜ Si Lom exit 2, Ⓢ Sala Daeng exit 1) A bear bar as perceived through a Thai lens, Bearbie replaces beards and bikers with local 'chubs' and teddy-bear-themed karaoke rooms.

Duangthawee Plaza (Soi Twilight; Map p278; Soi Pratuchai; ⏰7pm-1am; Ⓜ Si Lom exit 2, Ⓢ Sala Daeng exit 3) This strip of male-only go-go bars is the gay equivalent of nearby Th Patpong. Expect tacky sex shows by bored-looking men.

Nightclubs

The area's clubs are located in dead-end Soi 2 and Soi 2/1; if the following are too packed, alternatives are just steps away.

DJ Station (Map p278; www.dj-station.com; 8/6-8 Soi 2, Th Silom; admission from 150B; ⏰10pm-2am; Ⓜ Si Lom exit 2; Ⓢ Sala Daeng exit 1) One of Bangkok's – indeed Asia's – most legendary gay dance clubs, here the crowd is a mix of Thai guppies (gay professionals), money boys and a few Westerners.

G Bangkok (Guys on Display; Map p278; Soi 2/1, Th Silom; admission 300B; ⏰11pm-late; Ⓜ Si Lom exit 2, Ⓢ Sala Daeng exit 1) As the name suggests, Guys on Display is not averse to a little shirtless dancing. Open late, this is where to go after the other clubs have closed.

Saunas

In Bangkok, there's a fine line – often no line at all – between male massage and prostitution. Saunas, on the other hand, don't involve any transaction past the entrance fee.

Babylon (Map p277; www.babylonbangkok.com; 34 Soi Nantha-Mozart; admission 230-350B; ⏰10.30am-10.30pm; Ⓜ Lumphini exit 2) Bangkok's first luxury sauna remains extremely popular with visitors, many from neighbouring Singapore and Hong Kong. B&B-style accommodation is also available.

the area used to possess has been eroded by modern tourism. If you must, be sure to agree to the price of entry and drinks before taking a seat at one of Patpong's 1st-floor 'pussy shows', otherwise you're likely to receive an astronomical bill.

These days, fake Rolexes and Ed Hardy T-shirts are more ubiquitous than flesh in Patpong.

SHOPPING

EVERYDAY BY KARMAKAMET   HANDICRAFTS
Map p278 (Soi Yada; ⊙10am-10pm; MSi Lom exit 2, SSala Daeng exit 1) Part cafe, part showroom for the eponymous brand's vast selection of scented candles, incense, essential oils and other fragrant and non-fragrant items, Karmakamet is the ideal gift stop.

RIVER CITY   ANTIQUES
Map p280 (www.rivercity.co.th; 23 Th Yotha; ⊙10am-10pm; ⊠Si Phraya/River City Pier, or shuttle boat from Sathon/Central Pier) Several upmarket art and antique shops occupy the 3rd and 4th floors of this riverside mall, but, as with many antique stores in Bangkok, the vast majority of pieces appear to come from Myanmar and, to a lesser extent, Cambodia.

A free shuttle boat to River City departs from Sathon/Central Pier every 30 minutes, from 10am to 8pm.

JIM THOMPSON   HANDICRAFTS
Map p278 (www.jimthompson.com; 9 Th Surawong; ⊙9am-9pm; MSi Lom exit 2, SSala Daeng exit 3) The surviving business of the international promoter of Thai silk, the largest Jim Thompson shop sells colourful silk handkerchiefs, place mats, wraps and cushions. The styles and motifs appeal to older, somewhat more conservative tastes.

CHIANG HENG   ACCESSORIES
Map p280 (1466 Th Charoen Krung; ⊙10.30am-7pm; ⊠Sathon/Central Pier, SSaphan Taksin exit 3) In need of a handmade stainless-steel wok or a manually operated coconut-milk strainer? Then we suggest you stop by this third-generation family-run kitchen-supply shop. Even if your cabinets are already stocked, a visit here is a glance into the type of specialised shops that are quickly disappearing from Bangkok. There's no English-language sign; look for the blue doors.

JULY   CLOTHING
Map p278 (☑02 233 0171; www.julytailor.com; 30/6 Th Sala Daeng; ⊙9am-6pm Mon-Sat; MSi Lom exit 2, SSala Daeng exit 4) Tailor to Thailand's royalty and elite, the suits here don't come cheap and the cuts can be somewhat conservative, but the quality is unsurpassed.

HOUSE OF CHAO   ANTIQUES
Map p278 (9/1 Th Decho; ⊙9.30am-7pm; SChong Nonsi exit 3) This three-storey antique shop, appropriately located in an antique shophouse, has everything necessary to deck out your fantasy colonial-era mansion. Particularly interesting are the various weather-worn doors, doorways, gateways and trellises that can be found in the covered area behind the showroom.

TAMNAN MINGMUANG   HANDICRAFTS
Map p278 (2nd fl, Thaniya Plaza, Th Thaniya; ⊙10am-7pm; MSi Lom exit 2, SSala Daeng exit 1) As soon as you step through the doors of this museum-like shop, the earthy smell of dried grass and stained wood rushes to meet you. Rattan, *yahn li·pow* (a fern-like vine) and water hyacinth woven into patterns, and coconut shells carved into delicate bowls, are among the exquisite pieces that will outlast flashier souvenirs available on the streets.

WORTH A DETOUR

ASIATIQUE

One of Bangkok's more popular night markets, **Asiatique** (www.thaiasiatique.com; Soi 72-76, Th Charoen Krung; ⊙4-11pm; ⊠shuttle boat from Sathon/Central Pier), takes the form of warehouses of commerce next to Mae Nam Chao Phraya. Expect clothing, handicrafts, souvenirs and several dining and drinking venues. There's a 60m-high Ferris wheel, and for those curious to see a performance of *gà·teu·i* (transgender; also spelt *kàthoey*) cabaret, there's also a branch of **Calypso Bangkok** (p137).

To get here, take one of the frequent, free shuttle boats from Sathon/Central Pier that run from 4pm to 11.30pm.

THAI HOME INDUSTRIES HANDICRAFTS

Map p280 (35 Soi 40/Oriental, Th Charoen Krung; ⏰9am-6.30pm Mon-Sat; 🚢Oriental Pier) A recent renovation has done away with the dust and clutter of this long-standing shop, housed in a temple-like building. But it's seemingly increased the scope of goods available, which includes attractive woven baskets, cotton farmer shirts, handsome stainless-steel flatware and delicate mother-of-pearl spoons. Much more fun than the typically faceless Bangkok handicraft shop.

PATPONG NIGHT MARKET SOUVENIRS

Map p278 (Th Phat Phong & Soi Phat Phong 2; ⏰6pm-midnight; Ⓜ️Si Lom exit 2, Ⓢ️Sala Daeng exit 1) You'll be faced with the competing distractions of strip-clubbing and shopping

PUSSY GALORE

Super Pussy! Pussy Collection! The neon signs leave little doubt about the dominant industry in Patpong, arguably the world's most infamous strip of go-go bars and clubs running 'exotic' shows. There is enough skin on show in Patpong to make Hugh Hefner blush, and a trip to the upstairs clubs could mean you'll never look at a ping-pong ball or a dart the same way again.

For years opinion on Patpong has been polarised between those people who see it as an exploitative, immoral place that is the very definition of sleaze, and others for whom a trip to Bangkok is about little more than immersing themselves in planet Patpong. But Patpong has become such a caricature of itself that in recent times a third group has emerged: the curious tourist. Whatever your opinion, what you see in Patpong or in any of Bangkok's other high-profile 'adult entertainment' areas depends as much on your personal outlook on life as on the quality of your vision.

Prostitution is technically illegal in Thailand but there are as many as 2 million sex workers, the vast majority of whom – women and men – cater to Thai men. Many come from poorer regional areas, such as Isan in the northeast, while others might be students helping themselves through university. Sociologists suggest Thais often view sex through a less moralistic or romantic filter than Westerners. That doesn't mean Thai wives like their husbands using prostitutes, but it's only recently that the gradual empowerment of women through education and employment has led to a more vigorous questioning of this very widespread practice.

Patpong actually occupies two soi that run between Th Silom and Th Surawong in Bangkok's financial district. The two streets are privately owned by – and named for – the Thai-Chinese Patpongpanich family, who bought the land in the 1940s and initially built Th Phat Phong and shophouses; Soi Phat Phong 2 was laid later. During the Vietnam War the first bars and clubs opened to cater to American soldiers on 'R&R'. The scene and its international reputation grew through the '70s and peaked in the '80s, when official Thai tourism campaigns made the sort of 'sights' available in Patpong a pillar of their marketing.

These days Patpong has mellowed considerably, if not matured. Thanks in part to the popular night market that fills the street after 5pm, it draws so many tourists that it has become a sort of sex theme park. There are still plenty of the stereotypical middle-aged men ogling pole dancers, sitting in dark corners of the so-called 'blowjob bars' and paying 'bar fines' to take girls to hotels that charge by the hour. But you'll also be among other tourists and families who come to see what all the fuss is about.

Most tourists go no further than stolen glances into the ground-floor go-go bars, where women in bikinis drape themselves around stainless-steel poles. Others will be lured to the dimly lit upstairs clubs by men promising sex shows. But it should be said that the so-called 'erotic' shows usually feature bored-looking women performing acts that feel not so much erotic as demeaning to everyone involved. Several of these clubs are also infamous for their scams, usually involving the nonperforming (ie clothed, if just barely) staff descending on wide-eyed tourists like vultures on fresh meat. Before you know it you've bought a dozen drinks, racked up a bill for thousands of baht, followed up with a loud, aggressive argument flanked by menacing-looking bouncers and threats of 'no money, no pussy!'

in this infamous area. And true to the area's illicit leanings, pirated goods (in particular watches) make a prominent appearance even amid a wholesome crowd of families and straight-laced couples. Bargain with determination, as first-quoted prices tend to be astronomically high.

SOI LALAI SAP   CLOTHING

Map p278 (Soi 5, Th Silom; ⊘9am-4pm Mon-Fri; ⓜSi Lom exit 2, ⓢSala Daeng exit 2) The ideal place to buy an authentic Thai secretary's uniform (a frumpy, frilly skirt; a top ideally featuring a cartoon animal; fluffy pink slippers), this 'money-dissolving soi' has mobs of vendors selling insanely cheap clothing, as well as heaps of snacks and housewares.

SPORTS & ACTIVITIES

ORIENTAL SPA   SPA

Map p280 (⌨02 659 9000; www.mandarinorien tal.com/bangkok/luxury-spa; Mandarin Oriental, 48 Soi 40/Oriental, Th Charoen Krung; massage/spa packages from 2900B; ⊘9am-10pm; ⛴Oriental Pier or hotel shuttle boat from Sathon/Central Pier) Regarded as among the premier spas in the world, the Oriental Spa sets the standard for Asian-style spa treatment. Depending on where you flew in from, the jet-lag massage might be a good option, but all treatments require advance booking.

SILOM THAI COOKING SCHOOL   COOKING COURSE

Map p278 (⌨084 726 5669; www.bangkokthai cooking.com; 68 Soi 13, Th Silom; courses 1000B; ⊘lessons 9am-1pm, 1.40-5.30pm & 6-9pm; ⓢChong Nonsi exit 3) Spread over two simple but charming facilities; lessons include a visit to a local market and instruction for six dishes in four hours, making it the best bang for your baht. Hotel pick-up in central Bangkok is available.

BANYAN TREE SPA   SPA

Map p277 (⌨02 679 1052; www.banyantreespa. com; 21st fl, Banyan Tree Hotel, 21/100 Th Sathon Tai/South; massage packages from 3500B, spa packages from 7500B; ⊘9am-10pm; ⓜLumphini exit 2) A combination of highly trained staff and high-tech facilities have provided this hotel spa with a glowing reputation. Come for pampering regimens based on Thai traditions, or unique signature treatments

such as the James Bond–esque 'tranquility hydro mist'.

HEALTH LAND   MASSAGE

Map p278 (⌨02 637 8883; www.healthlandspa. com; 120 Th Sathon Neua/North; 2hr massage 500B; ⊘9am-11pm; ⓢSurasak exit 3) This, the main branch of a long-standing Thai massage mini-empire, offers good-value, no-nonsense massage and spa treatments in a tidy environment.

RUEN-NUAD MASSAGE STUDIO   MASSAGE

Map p278 (⌨02 632 2662; 42 Th Convent; massage per hr 350B; ⊘10am-9pm; ⓜSi Lom exit 2, ⓢSala Daeng exit 2) Set in a refurbished wooden house, this charming place successfully avoids both the tackiness and New Ageness that characterise most Bangkok Thai-massage joints. Prices are relatable, too.

CO VAN KESSEL BANGKOK TOURS   BICYCLE TOUR

Map p280 (⌨02 639 7351; www.covankessel.com; ground fl, River City, 23 Th Yotha; tours from 950B; ⊘6am-7pm; ⛴River City Pier) This originally Dutch-run outfit offers a variety of tours in Chinatown, Thonburi and Bangkok's green zones, many of which also involve boat rides. Tours depart from the company's office in the River City shopping centre.

BLUE ELEPHANT THAI COOKING SCHOOL   COOKING COURSE

Map p278 (⌨02 673 9353; www.blueelephant. com/cooking-school; 233 Th Sathon Tai/South; courses 2800B; ⊘lessons 8.45am-1.30pm & 1.30-5pm Mon-Sat; ⓢSurasak exit 2) Bangkok's most chichi Thai cooking school offers two lessons daily. The morning class squeezes in a visit to a local market, while the afternoon session includes a detailed introduction to Thai ingredients.

ORIENTAL HOTEL THAI COOKING SCHOOL   COOKING COURSE

Map p280 (⌨02 659 9000; www.mandarinorien tal.com/bangkok/hotel/leisure-travel; Mandarin Oriental, 48 Soi 40/Oriental, Th Charoen Krung; lessons 2688-4986B; ⊘lessons 9am-1pm Wed-Mon, also 9am-2pm Sat & Sun & 3.30-7pm Fri; ⛴Oriental Pier or hotel shuttle boat from Sathon/Central Pier) Located across the river in an antique wooden house, the Oriental's cooking classes span a daily revolving menu of four Thai dishes, and in some cases, excursions to a local market. The courses here are less 'hands on' compared to others in Bangkok.

Sukhumvit

Neighbourhood Top Five

1 Spending a night out at **WTF** (p149) or another buzz-worthy bar or nightclub the in-crowd would approve of.

2 Rejuvenating at one of Th Sukhumvit's excellent-value spas, such as **Health Land** (p155).

3 Sampling from Th Sukhumvit's generous spread of international restaurants, such as **Nasir Al-Masri** (p147).

4 Witnessing ancient northern Thailand in contemporary Bangkok at **Ban Kamthieng** (p144).

5 Getting lost in **Khlong Toey Market** (p145), one of the city's largest.

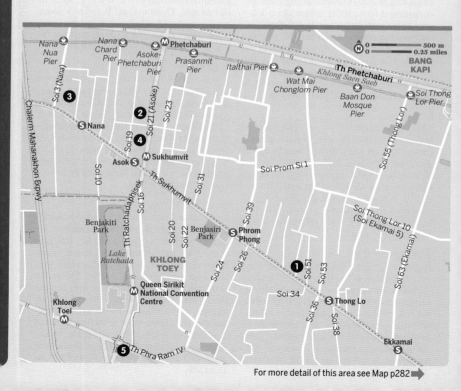

For more detail of this area see Map p282 ➡

Explore: Sukhumvit

You'll probably spend more time on Th Sukhumvit eating, drinking and perhaps sleeping (there's a high concentration of hotels here), rather than sightseeing. Thankfully the BTS (Skytrain) runs along the length of Th Sukhumvit, making it a snap to reach just about anywhere around here. BTS stops are also a convenient way to define the street's various vibes. Lower Sukhumvit, particularly the area around Nana BTS station, is a mix of sexpats and Middle Eastern tourists; street markets and touts make this a frustrating zone to navigate nearly any time of day or night. Middle Sukhumvit, around BTS Asok/MRT Sukhumvit, is dominated by midrange hotels, upmarket condos, international restaurants and businesses meant to appeal to both tourists and resident foreigners. Near BTS Phrom Phong you'll find the well-concealed compounds of wealthy Thai residents and tidy Japanese enclaves, while extending east from BTS Ekkamai, the area feels more provincial and more Thai.

Local Life

➡ **Hi-So hangouts** This is Bangkok's ritziest zone, and is *the* area to observe hi-so (high society) Thais in their natural environment: chatting at a wine bar on Soi 55/Thong Lor or topping up on Fendi bags at Emquartier.

➡ **International dining** Th Sukhumvit's various ethnic enclaves are a logical destination if you've grown tired of Thai food. Known colloquially as Little Arabia, Soi 3/1 is home to several Middle Eastern restaurants, while a handful of Korean restaurants can be found at Soi 12, and several Japanese restaurants are located near BTS Phrom Phong. Not surprisingly, there's relatively little interesting Thai food in the area.

➡ **Clubbing** The streets that extend from Th Sukhumvit are home to many of Bangkok's most popular clubs. Ravers of uni age tend to head to Soi 63/Ekamai; the pampered elite play at Soi 55/Thong Lor; and expats, sexpats and tourists head to the clubs around Soi 11.

Getting There & Away

➡ **BTS** Nana, Asok (interchange with MRT Sukhumvit), Phrom Phong, Thong Lo, Ekkamai, Phra Khanong, On Nut, Bang Chak, Punnawithi, Udom Suk, Bang Na and Bearing.

➡ **MRT** Queen Sirikit National Convention Centre, Sukhumvit (interchange with BTS Asok) and Phetchaburi.

➡ **Klorng boat** Asoke-Phetchaburi Pier, Nana Nua Pier and Nana Chard Pier.

➡ **Bus** Air-con 501, 508, 511 and 513; ordinary 2, 25, 30, 48 and 72.

Lonely Planet's Top Tip

All odd-numbered soi branching off Th Sukhumvit head north, while even numbers run south. Unfortunately, they don't line up sequentially (eg Soi 11 lies directly opposite Soi 8; Soi 39 is opposite Soi 26). Also, some larger soi are better known by alternative names, such as Soi 3/Nana, Soi 21/Asoke, Soi 55/Thong Lor and Soi 63/Ekamai.

Best Places to Eat

➡ Jidori-Ya Kenzou (p148)
➡ Little Beast (p146)
➡ Bo.lan (p146)
➡ Gokfayuen (p144)
➡ Nasir Al-Masri (p147)

For reviews, see p144.

Best Places to Drink

➡ WTF (p149)
➡ Tuba (p149)
➡ Sugar Ray (p149)
➡ Badmotel (p149)

For reviews, see p149.➡

Best Nightclubs

➡ Grease (p151)
➡ Arena 10 (p151)

For reviews, see p149.➡

SUKHUMVIT

SIGHTS

THAILAND CREATIVE & DESIGN CENTER GALLERY

Map p282 (ศูนย์สร้างสรรค์งานออกแบบ, TCDC; ☎02 664 8448; www.tcdc.or.th; 5th fl, Emporium, cnr Th Sukhumvit & Soi 24; 🕐10.30am-9pm Tue-Sun; 📶; [S]Phrom Phong exit 3) A government-backed initiative acting as both a showroom and resource for Thai design. Rotating exhibitions feature profiles of international products and retrospectives of regional handicrafts and creativity. The centre includes a library of design-related books and is a good place to meet young Thai designers; the adjoining cafe has free wi-fi; and the attached shop (p153) has unique souvenirs. At the time of research, it was announced that the TCDC was set to move to a new home.

CHUVIT GARDEN PARK

Map p282 (Th Sukhumvit; 🕐6-10am & 4-8pm; [S]Nana exit 4) [FREE] The eponymous benefactor of this park ran unsuccessfully for Bangkok governor in 2004, and successfully for the Thai parliament in 2005 and 2011. This park was one of his early campaign promises. It's a pretty green patch in a neighbourhood that's lean on trees. Yet the story behind the park is shadier than the plantings. Chuvit Kamolvisit was Bangkok's biggest massage-parlour owner, and was arrested in 2003 for illegally bulldozing, rather than legally evicting, tenants off the land where the park now stands. With all the media attention, he sang like a bird about the police bribes he handed out during his career and became an unlikely activist against police corruption.

BENJAKITI PARK PARK

Map p282 (สวนเบญจกิติ; Th Ratchadaphisek; 🕐5am-8pm; [M]Queen Sirikit National Convention Centre exit 3) This 130-*rai* (20.8-hectare) park is built on what was once a part of the Tobacco Monopoly, a vast, crown-owned expanse of low-rise factories and warehouses. There's an artificial lake that's good for jogging and cycling around its 2km track. **Bikes** can be hired (Map p282; per hr 40B; 🕐8am-7pm).

EATING

GOKFAYUEN CHINESE $

Map p282 (www.facebook.com/wuntunmeen; 161/7 Soi Thong Lor 9; mains 69-139B; 🕐11am-

TOP SIGHT
SIAM SOCIETY & BAN KAMTHIENG

Stepping off cacophonous Soi 21/Asoke and into the Siam Society's Ban Kamthieng is as close to visiting a northern Thai village as you'll come in Bangkok. Ban Kamthieng is a traditional 19th-century home that was located on the banks of Mae Nam Ping in Chiang Mai. Now relocated to Bangkok, the house presents the daily customs and spiritual beliefs of the Lanna tradition. Communicating all the hard facts as well as any sterile museum (with detailed English signage and engaging video installations), Ban Kamthieng also instils in the visitor a palpable sense of place, from the attached rice granary and handmade tools to the wooden loom and woven silks. You can't escape the noise of Bangkok completely, but the houses are refreshingly free of concrete and reflecting glass, and make a brief but interesting break.

Next door are the headquarters of the prestigious Siam Society, publisher of the renowned *Journal of the Siam Society* and a valiant preserver of traditional Thai culture. Those with a serious interest can use the **reference library**, which has the answers to almost any question you might have about Thailand (outside the political sphere, since the society is sponsored by the royal family).

DON'T MISS...

- Ban Kamthieng
- Siam Society's reference library

PRACTICALITIES

- สยามสมาคม & บ้านคำเที่ยง
- Map p282, C3
- www.siam-society.org
- 131 Soi 21/Asoke, Th Sukhumvit
- adult/child 100B/free
- 🕐9am-5pm Tue-Sat
- [M]Sukhumvit exit 1, [S]Asok exit 3 or 6

WORTH A DETOUR

KHLONG TOEY MARKET

This **wholesale market** (ตลาดคลองเตย; Map p282; cnr Th Ratchadaphisek & Th Phra Ram IV; ⏰5-10am; Ⓜ Khlong Toei exit 1), one of the city's largest, is inevitably the origin of many of the meals you'll eat during your stay in Bangkok. Although some corners of the market can't exactly be described as photogenic, you'll still want to bring a camera to capture the cheery fishmongers and stacks of durians. Be sure to get there early, ideally before 10am, when most vendors have already packed up and left.

11.30pm; Ⓢ Thong Lo exit 3 & taxi) This new place has gone to great lengths to recreate classic Hong Kong dishes in Bangkok. Couple your (house-made) wheat-and-egg noodles with roasted pork, steamed vegetables with oyster sauce, or the Hong Kong–style milk tea.

KLANG SOI RESTAURANT THAI $

Map p282 (Soi 49/9 Th Sukhumvit; mains 80-250; ⏰ 11am-2.30pm & 5-10pm Tue-Sun; Ⓢ Phrom Phong exit 3 & taxi) If you had a Thai grandma who lived in the Sukhumvit area, this is where she'd eat. The mimeographed menu spans old-school specialities from central and southern Thailand, as well as a few Western dishes. It's at the end of Soi 49/9, in the Racquet Club complex.

SARAS INDIAN $

Map p282 (www.saras.co.th; Soi 20, Th Sukhumvit; mains 90-200B; ⏰ 9am-10.30pm; ✈; Ⓜ Sukhumvit exit 2, Ⓢ Asok exit 4) Describing your restaurant as a 'fast-food feast' may not be the cleverest PR move we've encountered, but it's a pretty spot-on description of this Indian restaurant. Order at the counter to be rewarded with crispy *dosai* (crispy southern Indian bread), meat-free regional set meals or rich curries (dishes are brought to your table). We wish all fast food could be this satisfying.

BHARANI THAI $

Map p282 (Sansab Boat Noodle; 96/14 Soi 23, Th Sukhumvit; mains 60-250B; ⏰ 11am-10pm; Ⓜ Sukhumvit exit 2, Ⓢ Asok exit 3) This cosy Thai restaurant dabbles in a bit of everything, from ox-tongue stew to rice fried with shrimp paste, but the real reason to come here is for the rich, meaty 'boat noodles' – so called because they used to be sold from boats plying the *klorng* (canals; also spelt *khlong*) of central Thailand.

PIER 21 THAI $

Map p282 (5th fl, Terminal 21, cnr Th Sukhumvit & Soi 21/Asoke; mains 39-200B; ⏰ 10am-10pm;

✈; Ⓜ Sukhumvit exit 3, Ⓢ Asok exit 3) Ascend a seemingly endless series of escalators to arrive at this noisy food court made up of vendors from across the city. The selection is vast (and includes a large vegetarian stall) and the dishes are exceedingly cheap, even by Thai standards.

BOON TONG KIAT
SINGAPORE CHICKEN RICE SINGAPOREAN $

Map p282 (440/5 Soi 55/Thong Lor, Th Sukhumvit; mains 65-300B; ⏰ 10am-10pm; Ⓢ Thong Lo exit 3 & taxi) After taking in the detailed and ambitious chicken rice manifesto written on the walls, order a plate of the restaurant's namesake and witness how a dish can be so simple, yet so delicious. The ideal accompaniment is *rojak* (a spicy-sour fruit 'salad'), referred to here as 'Singapore Som Tam'.

GAME OVER AMERICAN $$

Map p282 (www.gameover.co.th; Liberty Plaza, 1000/39 Soi 55/Thong Lor, Th Sukhumvit; mains 160-340B; ⏰ 11.30am-2.30pm & 5.30-11.30pm Tue-Sun, 5.30-11.30pm Mon; Ⓢ Thong Lo exit 3 & taxi) Indulge your inner teen by playing *Call of Duty* while downing some of Bangkok's best burgers at this new video-game centre and restaurant. For the old at heart there's Scrabble and an impressive selection of imported microbrews.

PIZZA ROMANA PALA ITALIAN $$

Map p282 (Th Sukhumvit; pizza per slice 60-105B, mains 190-240B; ⏰ 11.30am-10pm; ✈; Ⓜ Sukhumvit exit 3, Ⓢ Asok exit 3) Strategically located at the intersection of the BTS and MRT – perfect for that rush-hour snack – this place serves some of Bangkok's best pies. Pizzas are sold by the slice and are made using almost exclusively imported ingredients. Pala also boasts a deli, and in addition to antipasti and simple pasta dishes, you can also pick up a chunk of Pecorino Romano or some salami.

SUKHUMVIT EATING

LOCAL KNOWLEDGE

SUNDAY BRUNCH

Sunday brunch has become a modern Bangkok tradition, particularly among members of the city's expat community, and the hotels along Th Sukhumvit offer some of the city's best – and most diverse – spreads. Here are some of our favourites.

Rang Mahal (Map p282; ☎02 261 7100; www.rembrandtbkk.com/dining/rang-mahal.htm; 26th fl, Rembrandt Hotel, 19 Soi 20, Th Sukhumvit; buffet 850B; ⊙11am-2.30pm Sun; ☑; M Sukhumvit exit 2, S Asok exit 6) Combine views from this restaurant's 26th floor with an all-Indian buffet and a live band, and you have one of the most popular Sunday destinations for Bangkok's South Asian expat community.

Sunday Jazzy Brunch (Map p282; ☎02 649 8888; www.sheratongrandesukhumvit.com/sundayjazzybrunch; 1st fl, Sheraton Grande Sukhumvit, 250 Th Sukhumvit; buffet adult 2500-3700B, child 1250B; ⊙noon-3pm Sun; ☑; M Sukhumvit exit 3, S Asok exit 2) If you require more than just victuals, then consider the Sheraton's Sunday brunch, which unites all the hotel's dining outlets to a live-jazz theme.

Marriott Café (Map p282; ☎02 656 7700; ground fl, JW Marriott, 4 Soi 2, Th Sukhumvit; buffet 2343B; ⊙11am-3pm Sun; ☑; S Nana exit 3) The feast-like Sunday brunch at this American hotel chain is likened to Thanksgiving year-round.

Scandinavian Smorgaas Buffet (Map p282; Stable Lodge, 39 Soi 8, Th Sukhumvit; buffet 583B; ⊙noon-3pm Sat & Sun; ☑; S Nana exit 4) Swap out the usual seafood station for pickled fish, and the roast beef for Swedish meatballs, and you'll get an idea of this unique, excellent-value weekend buffet option.

PRAI RAYA
SOUTHERN THAI $$

Map p282 (Soi 8, Th Sukhumvit; mains 150-600B; ⊙10.30am-10.30pm; S Nana exit 4) This Phuket institution has opened a branch in Bangkok, bringing to the city the southern Thai island's uniquely spicy, occasionally Chinese-influenced cuisine. Although the English-language-menu descriptions may not always make sense, you can't go wrong choosing from the 'Prai Raya's popular dishes' section of the menu.

Prai Raya has no English-language sign; look for the imposing yellow villa.

NEW SRI FAH 33
CHINESE, THAI $$

Map p282 (www.newsrifa33.com; 12/19-21 Soi 33, Th Sukhumvit; mains 80-600B; ⊙11am-2pm & 6pm-midnight; S Phrom Phong exit 5) This former Chinatown shophouse restaurant, originally opened in 1955, has relocated to a tight but classy location in new Bangkok. Just about anything from the Thai-Chinese seafood-heavy menu is bound to satisfy, but we particularly love the 'stir-fried Chinese black olive with pork' and the 'stir-fried water mimosa'.

TAPAS CAFÉ
SPANISH $$

Map p282 (www.tapasiarestaurants.com; 1/25 Soi 11, Th Sukhumvit; dishes 75-800B; ⊙11am-midnight; ☑; S Nana exit 3) Although it's the least expensive of Bangkok's Spanish joints, a visit to this friendly restaurant is in no way a compromise, with tasty tapas, refreshing sangria and a jazzy Latin vibe.

CABBAGES & CONDOMS
THAI $$

Map p282 (www.pda.or.th/restaurant; Soi 12, Th Sukhumvit; mains 120-470B; ⊙11am-11pm; ☑; M Sukhumvit exit 3, S Asok exit 2) ✔ This long-standing garden restaurant is a safe place to gauge the Thai staples. It also stands for a safe cause: instead of after-meal mints, diners receive packaged condoms, and all proceeds go towards the Population & Community Development Association (PDA), a sex education and AIDS prevention organisation.

LITTLE BEAST
INTERNATIONAL $$$

Map p282 (☎02 185 2670; www.facebook.com/littlebeastbar; 44/9-10 Soi Thong Lor 13; mains 300-750B; ⊙5.30pm-1am Tue-Sat, 11am-4pm Sun; 🖥; S Phrom Phong exit 3 & taxi) With influences stemming from modern American cuisine, Little Beast isn't very Bangkok, but it is very good. Expect meaty mains, satisfying salads and some of the best desserts in town (the ice-cream sandwiches alone are worth the visit).

BO.LAN
THAI $$$

Map p282 (☎02 260 2962; www.bolan.co.th; 24 Soi 53, Th Sukhumvit; set meals 980-2680B;

🕒noon-2.30pm & 7-10.30pm Thu-Sun, 11.30am-10.30pm Tue & Wed; 🌿; [S]Thong Lo exit 1) Upmarket Thai is often more garnish than flavour, but Bo.lan has proven to be the exception. Bo and Dylan (Bo.lan is a play on words that also means 'ancient') take a scholarly approach to Thai cuisine, and generous set meals featuring full-flavoured Thai dishes are the results of this tuition (à la carte is not available; meat-free meals are). Reservations recommended.

NASIR AL-MASRI MIDDLE EASTERN **$$$**

Map p282 (4/6 Soi 3/1, Th Sukhumvit; mains 160-370B; 🕒24hr; 🌿; [S]Nana exit 1) One of several Middle Eastern restaurants on Soi 3/1, Nasir Al-Masri is easily recognisable by its floor-to-ceiling stainless steel 'theme'. Middle Eastern food often means meat, meat and more meat, but the menu here also includes several delicious vegie-based *mezze* (small dishes).

QUINCE INTERNATIONAL **$$$**

Map p282 (☎02 662 4478; www.quincebangkok.com; Soi 45, Th Sukhumvit; mains 250-1489B; 🕒11.30am-midnight; 🌿; [S]Phrom Phong exit 3) Back in 2011, Quince made a splash in Bangkok's dining scene with its retro-industrial interior and eclectic, internationally influenced menu. The formula has since been copied ad nauseam, but Quince continues to put out the type of vibrant, full-flavoured dishes, many with palpable Middle Eastern or Spanish influences, that made it stand out in the first place.

APPIA ITALIAN **$$$**

Map p282 (☎02 261 2056; www.appia-bangkok.com; 20/4 Soi 31, Th Sukhumvit; mains 350-980B; 🕒6.30-11pm Tue-Sat, 11.30am-2pm & 6.30-11pm Sun; 🌿; [S]Phrom Phong exit 5) Handmade pastas, slow-roasted meats and a carefully curated and relatively affordable wine list are the selling points of this restaurant serving Roman-style cuisine. Reservations recommended.

MYEONG GA KOREAN **$$$**

Map p282 (ground fl, Sukhumvit Plaza, cnr Soi 12 & Th Sukhumvit; mains 200-950B; 🕒11am-10pm Tue-Sun, 4-10pm Mon; [M]Sukhumvit exit 3,

BANGKOK'S FOOD TRUCKS

In Bangkok, there's no shortage of mobile restaurants. Indeed, the city's wheeled food carts could be regarded as the first food trucks. Thus it's odd (or perhaps it makes perfect sense?) that the trend of actual food trucks has caught on in Bangkok.

Indeed, food trucks are so 'now' that somebody opted to stick one in a mall food court, and in 2015 Bangkok hosted a food-truck festival. Trucks can be found across the city these days, but Th Sukhumvit has the highest density. Following are some of the most popular; be sure to check the Facebook page of the truck you have in mind before heading out, as locations and hours change frequently.

Daniel Thaiger (Map p282; ☎084 549 0995; www.facebook.com/danielthaiger; Soi 23, Th Sukhumvit; mains from 139B; 🕒5-10.30pm; [M]Sukhumvit exit 2, [S]Asok exit 3) Bangkok's best burgers are served from this American-run truck that, at the time of research, had a long-standing stint on Soi 23.

Full Moon Food Truck (www.facebook.com/fullmoonfoodtruckbkk; mains from 150B; 🕒5-11.30pm) Cheesy, American-style dishes – think mac 'n cheese and Philly-style cheesesteak sandwiches – are what you can expect at this truck that often sets up along Th Sukhumvit.

Orn The Road (☎095 628 0416; www.facebook.com/orntheroadbkk; mains from 160-300B; 🕒11am-7pm; 🌿) Allegedly the city's first food truck, this bright orange vehicle serves a variety of burgers at a variety of locations, occasionally on Th Sukhumvit; check the Facebook page to see where Orn's setting up shop when you're in town.

Taco Taxi (Map p282; ☎086 787 8064; Soi 11, Th Sukhumvit; mains from 60B; 🕒8.30pm-3.30am; [S]Nana exit 3) Scratch that late-night itch with tacos and 'Mexican smoothies' (aka margaritas). At the time of research, Taco Taxi was setting up in front of the Ambassador Hotel, but search online to see if this has changed.

Jungle Juice + Kebabs (☎087 147 5550; www.facebook.com/junglejuiceasia; mains from 60B; 🕒10am-10pm) An odd combo of fruit slushies and kebabs that sets up in various locations, including along Th Sukhumvit.

S Asok exit 2) Located on the ground floor of Sukhumvit Plaza (the multistorey complex also known as Korean Town), this restaurant is the city's best destination for authentic Seoul food. Go for the tasty prepared dishes or, if you've got a bit more time, the excellent DIY Korean-style barbecue.

BEI OTTO
GERMAN $$$

Map p282 (02 260 0869; www.beiotto.com; 1 Soi 20, Th Sukhumvit; mains 185-995B; ⊙11am-midnight; ; M Sukhumvit exit 2, S Asok exit 4) Claiming a Bangkok residence for more than 30 years, Bei Otto's major culinary bragging point is its pork knuckles, reputedly the best in town. A good selection of German beers and an attached delicatessen with brilliant breads and super sausages make it even more attractive to go Deutsch.

SOUL FOOD MAHANAKORN
THAI $$$

Map p282 (02 714 7708; www.soulfood mahanakorn.com; 56/10 Soi 55/Thong Lor, Th Sukhumvit; mains 140-300B; ⊙5.30pm-midnight; ; S Thong Lo exit 3) Soul Food gets its interminable buzz from its dual nature as both an inviting restaurant – the menu spans tasty interpretations of rustic Thai

SUKHUMVIT'S JAPANESE SCENE

Bangkok is home to a huge Japanese expat population, many of whom live around mid-Sukhumvit (indeed, on Google Maps this area is labelled as 'Japaness [sic] Village'). Along with these Japanese expats has come a sophisticated array of restaurants, some representing the only branches of certain chains outside of Japan. Not surprisingly, the dining options go way beyond sushi. Some of our favourites:

Jidori-Ya Kenzou (Map p282; off Soi 26, Th Sukhumvit; dishes 60-350B; ⊙5pm-midnight Mon-Sat; S Phrom Phong exit 4) This cosy restaurant does excellent tofu dishes, delicious salads and great desserts – basically everything here is above average – but the highlight are the sublimely smoky, perfectly seasoned chicken skewers.

Ginzado (Map p282; 02 392 3247; Panjit Tower, 117 Soi 55/Thong Lor, Th Sukhumvit; dishes 120-900B; ⊙5-11pm; S Thong Lo exit 3) Make a reservation or queue for some really excellent *yakitori* (DIY grilled beef) not to mention a mean *bibimbap* (rice and toppings served in a sizzling stone bowl). Ginzado is located between Soi Thong Lor 3 and Soi Thong Lor 5, through the large white archway.

Teppen (Map p282; www.facebook.com/TeppenThailand; 14/2 Soi 61, Th Sukhumvit; dishes 140-960B; ⊙6pm-midnight; S Ekkamai exit 1) This is one of our favourite Bangkok *izakaya* (Japanese-style pub), and the menu here has a bit of everything, from Western-influenced salads to Japanese-style beef offal stew.

Ippudo (Map p282; www.ippudo.co.th/en; 4th fl, Emporium, cnr Soi 24 & Th Sukhumvit; mains 130-310B; ⊙10.30am-10pm; S Phrom Phong exit 2) This Japanese ramen chain with a cult-like following has reached Thailand; expect queues during lunch and dinner.

Nirai-Kanai (Map p282; www.facebook.com/niraikanaibangkok; Soi Thong Lor 13; dishes 80-480B; ⊙5pm-midnight; S Phrom Phong exit 3 & taxi) Think you know Japanese food? Prepared to be schooled at this open-air restaurant serving the specialities of the southern island of Okinawa. With ingredients such as bitter gourd and yes, Spam, you're in for a surprise.

Imoya (Map p282; 3rd fl, Terminal Shop Cabin, 2/17-19 Soi 24, Th Sukhumvit; mains 40-400B; ⊙6pm-midnight; S Phrom Phong exit 4) A visit to this well-hidden Japanese restaurant, with its antique ads, wood panelling and wall of sake bottles, is like taking a trip in a time machine. Even the prices of the Japanese-style pub grub haven't caught up with modern times.

Fuji Super (Map p282; www.ufmfujisuper.com; 593/29-39, Soi 33/1, Th Sukhumvit; ⊙8am-10pm; S Phrom Phong exit 5) Central Bangkok or suburban Tokyo? It's hard to tell when inside this well-stocked supermarket; it has additional branches around town.

Gateway Ekamai (Map p282; www.gatewayekamai.com/en; 982/22 Th Sukhumvit; ⊙10am-10pm; S Ekkamai exit 4) Much of this huge mall is dedicated to Japanese-style fast food, including several restaurant outlets and shops selling Japanese snacks and sweets.

ℹ️ SUKHUMVIT'S INTERNATIONAL SUPERMARKETS

Are you an American in need of a peanut-butter fix or an Aussie craving Vegemite? Don't fret: Th Sukhumvit is home to Bangkok's best-stocked international grocery stores.

Villa Market (Map p282; www.villamarket.com; Soi 33/1, Th Sukhumvit; ⏰24hr; 🚇Phrom Phong exit 5) The main branch of this long-standing international grocery store is the place to pick up culinary 'necessities' from Cheerios to cheddar cheese. There are additional Th Sukhumvit branches at **Soi 11** (Map p282; Soi 11, Th Sukhumvit; ⏰24hr; 🚇Nana exit 3), **Soi 49** (Map p282; Soi 49, Th Sukhumvit; ⏰24hr; 🚇Phrom Phong exit 3 & taxi) and off **Soi 55/Thong Lor** (Map p282; Soi Thong Lor 15; ⏰24hr; 🚇Thong Lo exit 3 & taxi). Check the website for other locations.

Gourmet Market (Map p282; 5th fl, Emporium, cnr Soi 24 & Th Sukhumvit; ⏰10am-10pm; 🚇Phrom Phong exit 2) Emporium's Gourmet Market carries a wide range of Western-style staples.

Foodland (Map p282; www.foodland.co.th; 87 Soi 5, Th Sukhumvit; ⏰24hr; 🚇Nana exit 1) Well-stocked grocery store with several branches across town.

---

dishes – and a bar serving deliciously boozy, Thai-influenced cocktails. Reservations recommended.

ROAST INTERNATIONAL $$$
Map p282 (www.roastbkk.com; 1st fl, Seen Space, 251/5 Soi Thong Lor 13; mains 280-420B; ⏰10am-11pm Mon-Thu & 9am-11pm Fri & Sat, 9am-10pm Sun; 🚇Thong Lo exit 3 & taxi) With great coffee and comforting, American-style dishes, Roast is a no-brainer brunch option. Yet an open and airy atmosphere and a diverse menu make it a good choice for any time, day or night.

BACCO – OSTERIA DA SERGIO ITALIAN $$$
Map p282 (www.bacco-bkk.com; 35/1 Soi 53, Th Sukhumvit; antipasti 200-800B, mains 350-1200B; ⏰11.30am-2.30pm & 5.30pm-midnight Mon-Fri, 11am-midnight Sat & Sun; 🅿; 🚇Thong Lo exit 1) The slightly cheesy interior of this *osteria* (Italian-style wine bar) serves as something of a cover for one of Bangkok's better Italian menus. There's an abundance of delicious antipasti, but the emphasis here is on breads, from pizza to *piada* (flatbread), all of which are exceptional.

🍷 DRINKING & NIGHTLIFE

⭐WTF BAR
Map p282 (www.wtfbangkok.com; 7 Soi 51, Th Sukhumvit; ⏰6pm-1am Tue-Sun; 📶; 🚇Thong Lo exit 3) Wonderful Thai Friendship – what did you think it stood for? – is a funky and friendly neighbourhood bar that also packs

in a gallery space. Arty locals and resident foreigners come for the old-school cocktails, live music and DJ events, poetry readings, art exhibitions and tasty bar snacks. And we, like them, give WTF our vote for Bangkok's best bar.

TUBA BAR
Map p282 (www.facebook.com/tubabkk; 34 Room 11-12 A, Soi Thong Lor 20/Soi Ekamai 21; ⏰11am-2am; 🚇Ekkamai exit 1 & taxi) Part storage room for over-the-top vintage furniture, part restaurant, part friendly local boozer; this quirky bar certainly doesn't lack in diversity – nor fun. Indulge in a whole bottle (if you don't finish it, they'll hold onto it for your next visit) and don't miss the moreish chicken wings or the delicious deep-fried *lâhp* (a tart, spicy salad of minced meat).

SUGAR RAY BAR
Map p282 (www.facebook.com/pages/Sugar-Ray-Youve-Just-Been-Poisoned/234918586711793; off Soi Ekamai 21; ⏰8pm-2am Wed, Fri & Sat; 🚇Ekkamai exit 1 & taxi) Run by a team of fun and funky Thai dudes who make flavoured syrups, Sugar Ray is a fun, funky hidden bar serving fun, funky cocktails. Think: an Old Fashioned made with aged rum, orange and cardamom syrup, and garnished with a piece of caramelised bacon.

BADMOTEL BAR
Map p282 (www.facebook.com/badmotel; 331/4-5 Soi 55/Thong Lor, Th Sukhumvit; ⏰5pm-1am; 🚇Thong Lo exit 3 & taxi) Badmotel blends the modern and the kitschy, the cosmopolitan and the Thai, in a way that has struck a nerve among Bangkok hipsters. This is

SUKHUMVIT DRINKING & NIGHTLIFE

A SUKHUMVIT NIGHTLIFE CHEAT SHEET

Th Sukhumvit is home to many of Bangkok's best bars, clubs and live-music venues. So many, in fact, that it can be hard to decide on a venue. So based on the type of night you'd like to have (or avoid), we've put together a handy cheat sheet:

For a uniquely Thai night out: Lam Sing (p153), Nung-Len, Parking Toys' Watt (p152), Bangkok Bar

For creative cocktails: Sugar Ray (p149), Badmotel (p149), J. Boroski Mixology, Alchemist

For a unique soundtrack: WTF (p149), Studio Lam, Happy Monday (p152)

For live music: Titanium (p153), Bangkok Bar, Fat Gut'z (p153), Apoteka (p153)

For good bar snacks: Tuba (p149), Walden, Above 11

For a sophisticated night out: A R Sutton & Co Engineers Siam, Living Room (p152), Mikkeller, Black Amber Social Club (p151)

For a budget night out: Cheap Charlie's, Bar 23

For a late night out: Narz (p152), Levels (p152), Scratch Dog (p152)

manifested in drinks that combine Hale's Blue Boy, a Thai childhood drink staple, with rum, and bar snacks such as *naam prik ong* (a northern Thai–style dip), here served with pappadams.

MIKKELLER BAR

Map p282 (www.mikkellerbangkok.com; 26 Yaek 2, Soi Ekamai 10; ⏲5pm-midnight; Ⓢ Ekkamai exit 1 & taxi) These buzz-generating Danish 'gypsy' brewers have set up shop in Bangkok, granting us more than 30 beers on tap. Expect brews ranging from the local (Sukhumvit Brown Ale) to the insane (Beer Geek, a 13% alcohol oatmeal stout), as well as an inviting atmosphere and good bar snacks.

STUDIO LAM BAR

Map p282 (www.facebook.com/studiolambangkok; Soi 51, Th Sukhumvit; ⏲6pm-1am Tue-Sun; Ⓢ Thong Lo exit 3) This new venue is an extension of uberhip record label ZudRangMa (see p153), with a Jamaican-style sound system custom-built for world and retro-Thai DJ sets and the occasional live show. Thai-influenced signature drinks bring Studio Lam to the present day.

J. BOROSKI MIXOLOGY BAR

Map p282 (www.josephboroski.com; off Soi 55/Thong Lor, Th Sukhumvit; ⏲7pm-2am; 📶; Ⓢ Thong Lo exit 3 & taxi) The eponymous mixologist here has done away with both addresses and cocktail menus to arrive at the modern equivalent of the speakeasy. Tell the boys behind the bar what flavours you fancy and, using top-shelf liquor and unique ingredients, they'll create something memorable.

Located in an unmarked street near Soi Thong Lor 7; refer to the website for the exact location.

A R SUTTON & CO ENGINEERS SIAM BAR

Map p282 (Parklane, Soi 63/Ekamai, Th Sukhumvit; ⏲6pm-midnight; Ⓢ Ekkamai exit 2) Skeins of copper tubing, haphazardly placed one-of-a-kind antiques, zinc ceiling panels, and rows of glass vials and baubles culminate in one of the most unique and beautifully fantastical bars in Bangkok – if not anywhere. And best of all, the short menu of classic cocktails complements the lost-in-time vibe.

WALDEN BAR

Map p282 (7/1 Soi 31, Th Sukhumvit; ⏲6.30pm-1am Mon-Sat; Ⓢ Phrom Phong exit 5) Get past the hyper-minimalist *Kinfolk* vibe, and the thoughtful Japanese touches of this new bar make it one of the more welcoming places in town. The brief menu of drinks spans Japanese-style 'highballs', craft beers from the US, and simple, delicious bar snacks.

CHEAP CHARLIE'S BAR

Map p282 (Soi 11, Th Sukhumvit; ⏲4.30-11.45pm Mon-Sat; Ⓢ Nana exit 3) There's never enough seating, and the design concept is best described as 'junkyard', but on most nights this chummy, open-air beer corner is a great place to meet everybody from package tourists to resident English teachers.

BLACK AMBER SOCIAL CLUB   BAR

Map p282 (www.facebook.com/blackamber socialclub; Soi Thong Lor 6; ☺6.30pm-midnight; ⓢThong Lo exit 3 & taxi) Promise us you won't tell anybody else about Black Amber, one of our new favourite bars in town. A dark, sumptuous ambience (furnishings include an entire ostrich skeleton), moustached and/or coiffed staff (Black Amber is linked to a barber shop of the same name), and a drinks list that doesn't stray far from scotch give Black Amber an authentically retro, speakeasy atmosphere.

GREASE   CLUB

Map p282 (www.greasebangkok.com; 46/12 Soi 49, Th Sukhumvit; ☺6pm-2am Mon-Sat; ⓢPhrom Phong exit 3 & taxi) Bangkok's hottest, youngest-feeling nightclub is also one of its biggest – you could get lost here in the four floors of dining venues, lounges and dance floors.

ROOT GARDEN   CAFE

Map p282 (www.facebook.com/Rootgarden. thonglor; Soi Thong Lor 3; ☺9am-9pm Tue-Sun; 🛜; ⓢThong Lo exit 3) Harking back to a time when this corner of Bangkok was fields, not condos, is this open-air-cafe-slash-urban farm. Come for coffee, organic fruit drinks or the frequent events – see the website for details.

ABOVE 11   BAR

Map p282 (www.aboveeleven.com; 33rd fl, Fraser Suites Sukhumvit, Soi 11, Th Sukhumvit; ☺6pm-2am; ⓢNana exit 3) This sophisticated roof-topper combines downward glances of Bangkok's most cosmopolitan neighbourhood with Peruvian/Japanese bar snacks.

ARENA 10   CLUB

Map p282 (Soi Thong Lor 10/Soi Ekamai 5; ⓢEkkamai exit 2 & taxi) This open-air entertainment zone is the destination of choice for Bangkok's young and beautiful – well, for the moment, at least. **Demo** (Map p282; www.facebook.com/demobang kok; ☺9pm-2am) combines blasting beats and a New York City warehouse vibe, while **Funky Villa** (Map p282; www.face book.com/funkyvillabkk; ☺7pm-2am), with its outdoor seating and Top 40 soundtrack, is more chilled.

There's a 400B entrance fee for non-Thais on Friday and Saturday.

ALCHEMIST   BAR

Map p282 (www.thealchemistbkk.com; 1/19 Soi 11, Th Sukhumvit; ☺5pm-midnight Tue-Sun; ⓢNana exit 3) A tiny bar with a big emphasis on cocktails, the Alchemist claims to do Bangkok's best Old Fashioned, and we don't tend to disagree.

BAR 23   BAR

Map p282 (www.facebook.com/bkkbar23; Soi 16, Th Sukhumvit; ☺9pm-2am Tue-Sat; ⓜSukhumvit exit 2, ⓢAsok exit 6) The foreign NGO crowd and indie Thai types flock to this warehouse-like bar on weekends; cold Beerlao and a retro-rock soundtrack keep them there until the late hours.

Bar 23 is about 500m down Soi 16, which is accessed from Th Ratchadaphisek.

NUNG-LEN   CLUB

Map p282 (www.nunglen.net; 217 Soi 63/Ekamai, Th Sukhumvit; ☺6pm-1am Mon-Sat; ⓢEkkamai exit 1 & taxi) Young, loud and Thai, Nung-Len (literally 'sit and chill') is a ridiculously popular den of live music and uni students on buzzy Th Ekamai. Get there before 10pm or you won't get in at all.

SHADES OF RETRO   BAR

Map p282 (www.facebook.com/shadesofretro bar; Soi Thararom 2, Soi 55/Thong Lor, Th Sukhumvit; ☺2pm-1am; ⓢThong Lo exit 3 & taxi) As the name suggests, this eclectic place takes Bangkok's vintage fetish to the max. You'll have to climb around Vespas and Naugahyde sofas to reach your seat, but you'll be rewarded with friendly service, free popcorn and a varied domestic soundtrack (the people behind Shades also run the domestic indie label Small Room).

IRON FAIRIES   BAR

Map p282 (www.theironfairies.com; 394 Soi 55/ Thong Lor, Th Sukhumvit; ☺6pm-2am; ⓢThong Lo exit 3 & taxi) Imagine, if you can, an abandoned fairy factory in Paris c 1912, and you'll begin to get an idea of the vibe at this popular pub/wine bar. If you manage to wrangle one of the handful of seats, you can test their claim of serving Bangkok's best burgers. There's live music after 9.30pm.

BANGKOK BAR   BAR

Map p282 (www.facebook.com/BangkokBar Thonglor; rooftop, The Opus, Soi Thong Lor 10; ☺5pm-2am; ⓢThong Lo exit 3 & taxi) Bounce with Thai indie kids at this fun but astonishingly uncreatively named rooftop

SUKHUMVIT DRINKING & NIGHTLIFE

bar. There's live music, the eats are strong enough to make Bangkok Bar a dinner destination in itself, and we double-dog-dare you to walk a straight line after downing two Mad Dogs, Bangkok Bar's infamous house drink.

THE DISTRICT CLUB

Map p282 (34 Soi 11, Th Sukhumvit; admission from 250B; ⏲9pm-2am; [S]Nana exit 3) The former Q Bar has been reworked into this nightlife complex with four different zones. If you've come for drinking, not dancing, Qup, the rooftop bar, allegedly has the biggest selection of booze in Thailand, while the Vault boasts a 1920s-era speakeasy vibe.

NARZ CLUB

Map p282 (www.narzclubbangkok.net; 112 Soi 23; admission from 400B; ⏲9pm-2am; [M]Sukhumvit exit 2, [S]Asok exit 3) Like a small clubbing neighbourhood, Narz consists of three vast zones boasting an equal variety of music. It's largely a domestic scene, but the odd guest DJ can pull a large crowd. Open later than most.

LONG TABLE BAR

Map p282 (www.longtablebangkok.com; 25th fl, Column Bldg, 48 Soi 16, Th Sukhumvit; ⏲5pm-2am; [M]Sukhumvit exit 2, [S]Asok exit 6) Come to this slick, 25th-floor balcony to sip fruity cocktails and gloat at the poor sods stuck in traffic below. In addition to views, there's a menu of Thai-inspired dishes and generous happy-hour specials.

It's located about 200m down Soi 16, which is accessible via Th Ratchadaphisek.

HAPPY MONDAY BAR

Map p282 (Ekkamai Shopping Mall, Soi Ekamai 10, Soi 63/Ekamai, Th Sukhumvit; ⏲7pm-1am Mon-Sat; [S]Ekkamai exit 1 & taxi) This somewhat concealed pub follows the tried and true Ekamai–Thong Lor formula of retro furniture, a brief bar-snack menu and bizarrely named house drinks. The diverse soundtrack, spun by local and visiting DJs, sets it apart.

LEVELS CLUB

Map p282 (www.levelsclub.com; 6th fl, Aloft, 35 Soi 11, Th Sukhumvit; admission 500B; ⏲9pm-late; [S]Nana exit 3) Come 1am, when most Soi 11 bars are beginning to close up, folks begin to file into this popular hotel nightclub. See the website for info about guest DJs and other promotions.

GLOW CLUB

Map p282 (96/415 Soi Prasanmit; admission from 350B; ⏲10pm-1am Mon-Wed, 10pm-3am Thu, 10pm-4am Fri & Sat; [M]Sukhumvit exit 2, [S]Asok exit 3) This self-proclaimed 'boutique' club starts things early in the evening as a lounge boasting an impressive spectrum of vodkas. As the evening progresses, enjoy tunes ranging from hip hop (Fridays) to electronica (Saturdays) and everything in between.

OSKAR BAR

Map p282 (www.oskar-bistro.com; 24 Soi 11, Th Sukhumvit; ⏲4pm-2am; [S]Nana exit 3) It touts itself as a bistro, but Oskar is more like a cocktail bar dressed as a club – with food. Correspondingly, the drinks and eats are all over the map, but are satisfying and cost less than you'd expect from a place this flashy.

SCRATCH DOG CLUB

Map p282 (basement, Windsor Suites Hotel, 8-10 Soi 20, Th Sukhumvit; admission 400B; ⏲midnight-late; [M]Sukhumvit exit 2, [S]Asok exit 4) It's pretty much as corny as the name and the Goofy-as-DJ logo suggest, but Scratch Dog pulls a relatively mixed crowd and is probably the least dodgy of Bangkok's late-late nightclubs. Don't bother showing up before 2am.

☆ ENTERTAINMENT

LIVING ROOM LIVE MUSIC

Map p282 (☎02 649 8888; www.thelivingroomatbangkok.com/en; Level 1, Sheraton Grande Sukhumvit, 250 Th Sukhumvit; ⏲6pm-midnight; [M]Sukhumvit exit 3, [S]Asok exit 2) Don't let looks deceive you: every night this bland hotel lounge transforms into the city's best venue for live jazz. True to the name, there's comfy, sofa-based seating, all of it within earshot of the music. Enquire ahead of time to see which sax master or hide-hitter is in town.

PARKING TOYS' WATT LIVE MUSIC

Map p287 (www.facebook.com/Wattparkingtoys; 164 Soi Sun Wichai 14; ⏲6pm-2am; [S]Ekkamai exit 4 & taxi) Resembling a Moroccan souk stuffed with kitschy Thai furniture, this is one of Bangkok's quirkier options for a night of live music. And like its mother venue, Parking Toys (p164), it's also a great

WORTH A DETOUR

LAM SING

Even Ziggy Stardust–era David Bowie has nothing on **Lam Sing** (www.facebook.com/iSanLamSing; 57/5 Th Phet Phra Ram; ⏲9.30pm-4am; [S]Ekkamai exit 1 & taxi). A dark, decadent, rhinestone-encrusted den, it's one of Bangkok's best venues for *mŏr lam* and *lôok tûng*, music with roots in Thailand's rural northeast. Come for raucous live performances accompanied by tightly choreographed, flagrantly costumed backup dancers. There's no English-language sign here, but most taxi drivers are familiar with the place.

place to eat; don't miss tasty Thai-style drinking snacks such as 'larb pork balls'.

TITANIUM LIVE MUSIC

Map p282 (www.titaniumbangkok.com; 2/30 Soi 22, Th Sukhumvit; ⏲8pm-1am; [S]Phrom Phong exit 6) Many come to this cheesy 'ice bar' for the chill, the skimpily dressed working girls and the flavoured vodka, but we come for Unicorn, the all-female house band that rocks the place every night from 9.30pm to 12.30am.

APOTEKA LIVE MUSIC

Map p282 (www.apotekabangkok.com; Soi 11, Th Sukhumvit; ⏲5pm-1am Mon-Thu, 5pm-2am Fri & Sat, 3pm-1am Sun; [S]Nana exit 3) Antiques and a shophouse-like setting give Apoteka a fun, old-school feel. Solid mixed drinks and blues-oriented bands every night from around 7pm make it one of the better places in the area to sip to live music.

FAT GUT'Z LIVE MUSIC

Map p282 (www.facebook.com/fatgutzsaloon; 264 Soi Thong Lor 12; ⏲5pm-2am; [S]Thong Lo exit 3 & taxi) This closet-sized 'saloon' combines live music and, er, fish and chips. Despite (or perhaps thanks to?) the odd whiff of chip oil, the odd combo works. Live blues every night from 9pm to midnight.

FRIESE-GREEN CLUB CINEMA

Map p282 (FGC; ☎087 000 0795; www.facebook.com/The-Friese-GreeneClub/371737282944797; 259/6 Soi 22, Th Sukhumvit; [S]Phrom Phong exit 6) You couldn't find a bigger contrast with Bangkok's huge, mall-bound cinemas than this private theatre with just eight seats. Check the Facebook page for a schedule of upcoming films.

SOI COWBOY RED-LIGHT DISTRICT

Map p282 (Soi Cowboy; ⏲4pm-2am; [M]Sukhumvit exit 2, [S]Asok exit 3) This single-lane strip of raunchy bars claims direct lineage to the post-Vietnam War R&R era. A real flesh trade functions amid the flashing neon.

NANA ENTERTAINMENT PLAZA RED-LIGHT DISTRICT

Map p282 (Soi 4, Th Sukhumvit; ⏲4pm-2am; [S]Nana exit 2) Nana is a three-storey go-go bar complex where the sexpats are separated from the gawking tourists. It's also home to a few *gà·teu·i* (transgender person; also spelt *kàthoey*) bars.

SHOPPING

For a list of recommended tailors along Th Sukhumvit, see p 46.

SHOP @ TCDC HANDICRAFTS

Map p282 (www.tcdc.or.th/shop; 5th fl, Emporium, cnr Soi 24 & Th Sukhumvit; ⏲10.30am-9pm Tue-Sun; [S]Phrom Phong exit 2) This shop, attached to the TCDC design library and museum, is a great place to pick up one-of-a-kind souvenirs, such as soaps and candles, kitchen aprons resembling Thai boxing shorts, unique postcards and cheeky housewares – all dreamt up by Thai designers.

ANOTHER STORY HANDICRAFTS

Map p282 (4th fl, Emquartier, Th Sukhumvit; ⏲10am-10pm; [S]Phrom Phong exit 1) A self-proclaimed 'lifestyle concept store', Another Story is probably more accurately described as an engaging assemblage of cool stuff. Even if you're not planning to buy, it's fun to flip through the unique, domestically made items such as ceramics from Prempacha in Chiang Mai, leather goods from brands like labrador, and fragrant soaps, oils and candles from BsaB.

ZUDRANGMA RECORDS MUSIC

Map p282 (www.zudrangmarecords.com; 7/1 Soi 51, Th Sukhumvit; ⏲2-9pm Tue-Sun; [S]Thong Lo exit 1) The headquarters of this retro/world label is a chance to finally combine the university-era pastimes of record-browsing and drinking. Come to snicker at corny old Thai vinyl covers or invest in some of the label's highly regarded compilations of classic *mŏr lam* and *lôok tûng* (Thai-style country music).

TERMINAL 21 SHOPPING CENTRE

Map p282 (www.terminal21.co.th; cnr Th Sukhumvit & Soi 21/Asoke; ⏰10am-10pm; [M]Sukhumvit exit 3, [S]Asok exit 3) Seemingly catering to a Thai need for wacky objects to be photographed in front of, this new mall is worth a visit for the spectacle as much as the shopping. Start at the basement-level 'airport' and proceed upwards through 'Paris', 'Tokyo' and other city-themed floors. Who knows, you might even buy something.

SOP MOEI ARTS HANDICRAFTS

Map p282 (www.sopmoeiarts.com; Soi 49/9, Th Sukhumvit; ⏰9.30am-5pm Tue-Sat; [S]Phrom Phong exit 3 & taxi) The Bangkok showroom of this non-profit organisation features the vibrant cloth creations of Karen weavers in Mae Hong Son, in northern Thailand.

It's located at the end of Soi 49/9, in the Racquet Club complex.

ALMETA HANDICRAFTS

Map p282 (www.almeta.com; 20/3 Soi 23, Th Sukhumvit; ⏰10am-6pm; [M]Sukhumvit exit 2, [S]Asok exit 3) If the verdant colours of Thai silk evoke frumpy society matrons, then you're a candidate for Almeta's earth-tones similar in hue to raw sugar or lotus blossoms.

THANON SUKHUMVIT MARKET SOUVENIRS

Map p282 (btwn Soi 3 & Soi 15, Th Sukhumvit; ⏰11am-11pm Tue-Sun; [S]Nana exits 1 & 3) Knock-off clothes and watches, stacks of adult DVDs, martial arts throwing stars and other questionable items dominate this market that caters mainly to package tourists.

DASA BOOK CAFÉ BOOKS

Map p282 (www.dasabookcafe.com; 714/4 Th Sukhumvit; ⏰10am-8pm; [S]Phrom Phong exit 4) Boasting more than 16,000 books, Dasa is one of Bangkok's best-stocked used bookstores. A frequently updated list of stock (also available online) makes it easy to find that title you've been searching for; an attached cafe provides an excuse to linger.

SPORTS & ACTIVITIES

HELPING HANDS COOKING COURSE

(☎080 434 8686; www.cookingwithpoo.com; courses 1500B; ⏰lessons 8.30am-1pm) This popular cooking course was started by a native of Khlong Toey's slums and is held in her neighbourhood. Courses, which must be booked in advance, span three dishes and include a visit to Khlong Toey Market and transport to and from Emporium Shopping Centre.

YUNOMORI ONSEN & SPA ONSEN

Map p282 (www.yunomorionsen.com; 120/5 Soi 26, Th Sukhumvit; onsen 450B, massage per hr 350B; ⏰10.30am-11pm; [S]Phrom Phong exit 3 & taxi) Bangkok as a whole can often seem like a sauna, but for a more refined approach to sweating, consider this *onsen* (Japanese-style hot-spring bath). The thermal water is trucked up from southern Thailand and employed in the gender-divided, open pools. In addition to sauna, steam bath and soak pools, massage and other spa treatments are also available.

PHUSSAPA THAI MASSAGE SCHOOL MASSAGE

Map p282 (☎02 204 2922; www.thaimassage-bangkok.com/nuat1_egl.htm; 25/8 Soi 26, Th Sukhumvit; tuition from 6000B; ⏰massage 11am-11pm, lessons 9am-4pm; [S]Phrom Phong exit 4) Run by a long-time Japanese resident

THAICRAFT FAIR

The twice-monthly **ThaiCraft Fair** (Map p282; www.thaicraft.org; 3rd fl, Jasmine City Bldg, cnr Soi 23 & Th Sukhumvit; ⏰10am-3pm; [M]Sukhumvit exit 2, [S]Asok exit 3) is a great chance to browse through the products of more than 60 community groups. For 20 years, ThaiCraft has marketed quality handicrafts made by artisans across all parts of Thailand, and recent fairs have seen products such as handmade baskets and mulberry-bark notebooks. Check the website to see if the next one is being held during your visit.

SUKHUMVIT'S SPAS

Th Sukhumvit is home to many of Bangkok's recommended and reputable massage studios, including the following:

Health Land (Map p282; ☑02 261 1110; www.healthlandspa.com; 55/5 Soi 21/Asoke, Th Sukhumvit; Thai massage 2hr 500B; ☺9am-11pm; ⓜSukhumvit exit 1, ⓢAsok exit 5) A winning formula of affordable prices, expert treatments and pleasant facilities has created a small empire of Health Land centres, including branches on **Soi Ekamai 10** (Map p282; ☑02 392 2233; www.healthlandspa.com; 96/1 Soi Ekamai 10; Thai massage 2hr 500B; ☺9am-11pm, with herbal compress; ⓢEkkamai exit 2 & taxi) and **Th Sathon** (p141).

Asia Herb Association (Map p282; ☑02 261 7401; www.asiaherbassociation.com; 33/1 Soi 24, Th Sukhumvit; Thai massage per hr 500B, Thai massage with herbal compress 1½hr 1100B; ☺9am-2am; ⓢPhrom Phong exit 4) This Japanese-owned chain specialises in massage using *bràkóp* (traditional Thai herbal compresses) filled with 18 different herbs. There are multiple branches along Th Sukhumvit, including at **Soi 31** (Map p282; ☑02 261 2201; www.asiaherbassociation.com; 20/1 Soi 31, Th Sukhumvit; Thai massage per hr 500B, with herbal compress 1½hr 1100B; ☺9am-2am; ⓢPhrom Phong exit 5) and **Soi 55/Thong Lor** (Map p282; ☑02 392 3631; www.asiaherbassociation.com; 58/19-25 Soi 55/Thong Lor, Th Sukhumvit; Thai massage per hr 500B, with herbal compress 1½hr 1100B; ☺9am-2am; ⓢThong Lo exit 3).

Divana Massage & Spa (Map p282; ☑02 261 6784; www.divanaspa.com; 7 Soi 25, Th Sukhumvit; massage from 1100B, spa packages from 2650B; ☺11am-11pm Mon-Fri, 10am-11pm Sat & Sun; ⓜSukhumvit exit 2, ⓢAsok exit 6) Divana retains a unique Thai touch with a private and soothing setting in a garden house.

Coran (Map p282; ☑02 726 9978; www.coranbangkok.com; 94-96/1 Soi Ekamai 10, Soi 63/Ekamai, Th Sukhumvit; Thai massage per hr 600B; ☺11am-10pm; ⓢEkkamai exit 4 & taxi) A classy, low-key spa housed in a Thai villa. Aroma and Thai-style massage are available.

Lavana (Map p282; ☑02 229 4510; www.lavanabangkok.com; 4 Soi 12, Th Sukhumvit; Thai massage per hr 450B; ☺9am-midnight; ⓜSukhumvit exit 3, ⓢAsok exit 2) Another spa with an emphasis on traditional Thai healing using *bràkóp*. Oil massage is also available.

Rakuten (Map p282; ☑02 258 9433; 94 Soi 33, Th Sukhumvit; Thai massage per hr 250B; ☺noon-midnight; ⓢPhrom Phong exit 5) A Japanese-themed spa that gets good reports for its Thai-style massage.

Baan Dalah (Map p282; ☑02 653 3358; www.baandalahmindbodyspa.com; 2 Soi 8, Th Sukhumvit; Thai massage per hr 350B; ☺10am-midnight; ⓢNana exit 4) A small, conveniently located spa with services ranging from foot massage to full-body Thai massage.

of Bangkok, the basic course in Thai massage here takes 30 hours spread over five days; there are shorter courses in foot massage and self massage. Thai massage is also available for 300B per hour.

KRUDAM GYM
MARTIAL ARTS

Map p282 (☑087 111 7115; www.krudamgym.com; Soi 24, Th Sukhumvit; per lesson adult/child 550/450B; ☺10am-9pm Mon-Fri, 10am-7.30pm Sat & Sun; ⓢPhrom Phong exit 2) Helmed by Dam Srichan, a former professional boxer, this small gym in downtown Bangkok offers 1½-hour walk-in lessons in *moo·ay tai* (Thai boxing; also spelt *muay thai*) for all skill levels, including for children. See the website for times.

ABC AMAZING
BANGKOK CYCLISTS
BICYCLE TOUR

Map p282 (☑081 812 9641; www.realasia.net; 10/5-7 Soi Aree, Soi 26, Th Sukhumvit; tours from 1300B; ☺daily tours at 8am, 10am, 1pm & 6pm; ⓢPhrom Phong exit 4) A long-running operation offering morning, afternoon and all-day bike tours of Bangkok and its suburbs.

FUN-ARIUM
PLAY CENTRE

Map p282 (☑02 665 6555; www.funarium.co.th; 111/1 Soi 26, Th Sukhumvit; admission 110-320B; ☺9am-6pm Mon-Thu, to 7pm Fri-Sun; ☏; ⓢPhrom Phong exit 1 & taxi) Bangkok's largest indoor playground, with coffee and wi-fi to keep parents happy while the kids play.

SUKHUMVIT SPORTS & ACTIVITIES

Greater Bangkok

Neighbourhood Top Five

1 Getting lost in **Chatuchak Weekend Market** (p158), one of the world's largest markets and a must-do Bangkok experience.

2 Partying at the bars and clubs on RCA/Royal City Ave, such as **Route 66** (p165).

3 Travelling back in time at retro-themed market **Talat Rot Fai** (p161).

4 Ditching the smog and traffic and heading to **Ko Kret** (p162).

5 Experiencing the charms of provincial Thailand at **Nonthaburi Market** (p161).

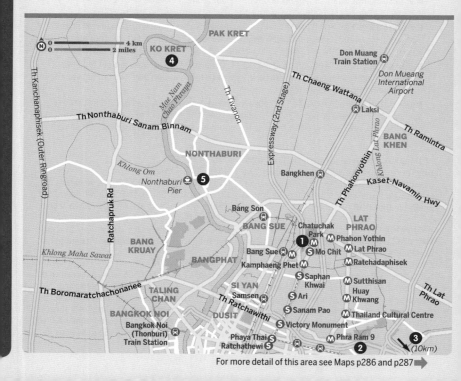

For more detail of this area see Maps p286 and p287 ➡

Explore: Greater Bangkok

There are several reasons to visit greater Bangkok, but most people come for the markets: the northern suburbs are home to some of the city's best. Chatuchak Weekend Market draws tens of thousands of shoppers and is a hectic but must-do Bangkok experience. Nonthaburi Market is an expansive wet market that shows the area's provincial side, while retro-themed Talat Rot Fai is a Bangkok-hipster magnet. Other reasons to visit Bangkok's suburbs include nightlife, with the RCA/Royal City Ave entertainment strip drawing thousands of weekend partiers.

For the day markets you'll want to arrive as early as possible. Set aside at least half a day for Chatuchak. Getting to Nonthaburi Market by boat takes at least an hour; keep in mind that the market has pretty much packed up by 9am. Talat Rot Fai is usually open until around 1am. Most clubs and live-music venues don't get going until 11pm and close at 2am.

Most of the markets are located within easy access of the northern extents of the BTS (Skytrain) and/or MRT (Metro). Reaching other destinations in Bangkok's 'burbs often involves a taxi ride from BTS or MRT terminal stations and a bit of luck. A smartphone with a mapping function is an invaluable tool for helping you arrive at the right place and on time.

Local Life

→**Chatuchak Weekend Market** It may be a huge draw for tourists, but it's still very much a local affair, with thousands of Thais shuffling between stalls.

→**RCA** For decades, the dance clubs, live-music venues and bars along Royal City Ave have been the first nightlife choice for most young Thais. In recent years the clientele has grown up – slightly, at least – and RCA now hosts locals and visitors of just about every age.

→**Local Style** Tattoo dudes, hipsters, hippies, punks and mods: Talat Rot Fai is the place to witness the various cliques of modern Thai youth.

→**Full-Flavoured Eats** An excursion to Bangkok's suburbs can be a profoundly tasty experience, with heaps of restaurants that don't tone down their flavours for foreigners. The city's outskirts are also a great place to sample regional Thai cuisine.

Getting There & Away

→**BTS** Ari, Bang Chak, Bang Na, Bearing, Chong Nonsi, Ekkamai, Mo Chit, Phra Khanong, Udom Suk.

→**MRT** Chatuchak Park, Huay Khwang, Kamphaeng Phet, Lat Phrao, Phetchaburi, Phra Ram 9, Sutthisan, Thailand Cultural Centre.

→**River ferry** Nonthaburi Pier.

→**Klorng Boat** Asoke-Phetchaburi Pier.

Lonely Planet's Top Tip

Make a point of arriving at Chatuchak Weekend Market as early as possible – about 10am is a good bet – as the crowds are much thinner and the temperatures slightly lower.

 Best Places to Eat

→ Chatuchak Weekend Market (p158)

→ Yusup (p163)

→ Khua Kling Pak Sod (p163)

→ Puritan (p163)

→ Or Tor Kor Market (p162)

→ Taksura (p165)

For reviews, see p163.➡

 Best Drinking & Entertainment

→ Parking Toys (p164)

→ Lumpinee Boxing Stadium (p164)

→ Route 66 (p165)

For reviews, see p164.➡

 Best Markets

→ Chatuchak Weekend Market (p158)

→ Talat Rot Fai (p161)

→ Nonthaburi Market (p161)

For reviews, see p158.➡

GREATER BANGKOK

TOP SIGHT
CHATUCHAK WEEKEND MARKET

Imagine all of Bangkok's markets fused together in a seemingly never-ending commerce-themed barrio. Now add a little artistic flair, a sauna-like climate and bargaining crowds and you've got a rough sketch of Chatuchak (also spelled 'Jatujak' or nicknamed 'JJ'). Once you're deep in its bowels, it will seem like there is no order and no escape, but Chatuchak is actually arranged into relatively coherent sections.

Antiques, Handicrafts & Souvenirs

Section 1 is the place to go for Buddha statues, old LPs and random antiques.

More secular arts and crafts, like musical instruments and hill-tribe items, can be found in Sections 25 and 26. **Meng** (Section 26, Stall 195, Soi 8) features a mish-mash of quirky antiques from Thailand and Myanmar.

Baan Sin Thai (Section 24, Stall 130, Soi 1) sells *kŏhn* masks and old-school Thai toys, while **Kitcharoen Dountri** (Section 8, Stall 464) specialises in Thai musical instruments, including flutes, whistles and drums, and CDs of classical Thai music.

Golden Shop (Section 17, Stall 36) is a one-stop souvenir shop, and boasts an equal blend of tacky and worthwhile items, ranging from traditionally dressed dolls to commemorative plates. For something quirkier, consider the lifelike plastic Thai fruit and vegetables at **Marché** (Section 17, Stall 254, Soi 1) or their scaled-down miniature counterparts nearby at **Papachu** (Section 17, Stall 23).

Section 7 is a virtual open-air art gallery; we particularly like the Bangkok-themed murals at **Pariwat A-nantachina** (Section 7, Stall 117, Soi 63/3).

Several shops in Section 10, including **Tuptim Shop** (Section 10, Stall 261, Soi 19), sell Burmese lacquerware.

DON'T MISS...

➡ Cheap clothes
➡ One-of-a-kind souvenirs
➡ A market meal

PRACTICALITIES

➡ ตลาดนัดจตุจักร, Talat Nat Jatujak
➡ Map p286, D1
➡ www.chatuchak.org
➡ Th Phahonyothin
➡ ⊘9am-6pm Sat & Sun
➡ ⓂChatuchak Park exit 1, Kamphaeng Phet exits 1 & 2, ⓈMo Chit exit 1

Clothing & Accessories

Clothing dominates much of Chatuchak, starting in Section 8 and continuing through the even-numbered sections to 24. Sections 5 and 6 deal in used clothing for every Thai youth subculture, from punks to cowboys; Soi 7, where it transects Sections 12 and 14, is heavy on hip-hop and skate fashions. Tourist-sized clothes and textiles are found in sections 8 and 10.

Sections 2 and 3, particularly the tree-lined Soi 2 of the former, is the Siam Sq of Chatuchak, and is home to heaps of trendy independent labels. Moving north, Soi 4 in Section 4 boasts several shops selling locally designed T-shirts. In fact, Chatuchak as a whole is a particularly good place to pick up quirky T-shirts of all types.

For something more rustic, **Khaki-Nang** (Section 8, Stall 267-268, Soi 17) sells canvas clothing and tote bags, many featuring old-school Thai themes. And if you can't make it up to Chiang Mai, **Roi** (Section 25, Stall 268, Soi 4) and similar shops nearby are where you'll find hand-woven cotton scarves, clothes and other accessories from Thailand's north.

For accessories, several shops in Sections 24 and 26, such as **Orange Karen Silver** (Section 26, Stall 229, Soi 34/8), specialise in chunky silver jewellery and uncut semiprecious stones.

Food & Drinks

Lots of Thai-style eating and snacking will stave off Chatuchak rage (cranky behaviour brought on by dehydration or hunger), and numerous food stalls are set up throughout the market, particularly between Sections 6 and 8. Long-standing standouts include **Foontalop** (Section 26, Stall 319, no roman-script sign; mains 20-70B; ☺10am-6pm Sat-Sun), an incredibly popular Isan restaurant; **Café Ice** (Section 7, Stall 267; mains 250-490B; ☺10am-6pm Sat-Sun), a Western-Thai fusion joint that does good, if overpriced, *pàt tai* (fried noodles) and tasty fruit shakes; **Saman Islam** (Section 16, Stall 34, Soi 24; mains 40-100B; ☺10am-6pm Sat-Sun), a restaurant that serves a tasty chicken biriani, in addition to other Thai-Muslim dishes; and **Toh-Plue** (opposite Section 17; mains 150-400B; ☺noon-8pm Sat & Sun) for all the Thai standards. Alternatively, cross Th Kamphaeng Phet 1 to the food court at Or Tor Kor Market (p162).

Viva 8 (www.facebook.com/Viva8JJ; Section 8, Stall 371, mains 150-300B; ☺9am-10pm Sat & Sun) features a bar, a DJ and, when we stopped by, a Spanish chef making huge platters of paella. As evening draws near, down a beer at **Viva's** (Section 26, Stall 161; ☺10am-10pm Sat & Sun), a cafe-bar that features live music and stays open late.

IMPORTANT STUFF

There's an information centre and several banks with ATMs and foreign-exchange booths at the Chatuchak Park office near the northern end of the market's Soi 1, Soi 2 and Soi 3. Pay toilets are located sporadically throughout the market.

Several vendors – largely those selling clothing, accessories and food – open up shop on Friday nights from around 8pm to midnight.

FINDING YOUR WAY AROUND

Schematic maps are located throughout Chatuchak; if you need more detail (not to mention insider tips), consider purchasing Nancy Chandler's Map of Bangkok (www.nancychandler.net), available at most Bangkok bookshops.

CHATUCHAK MARKET

Th Kamphaengphet 2

JJ Mall

Section 7
Entrance 2

Chatuchak Park

Mo Chit $

Section 8

Section 9 Section 6 Ⓜ Chatuchak Park

Section 11

Section 13 Section 10

Section 15 Section 12

Section 14

Th Phahonyothin

Section 17 Clock Tower Section 5

Section 19 Entrance 3

Entrance 1 Section 22 Section 16

Section 25 Section 18

Section 1 Section 4

Section 26 Section 20

Section 24 Section 21

Section 23

Kamphaeng Phet Ⓜ Section 2 Section 3

Th Kamphaengphet 1

Antiques, Handicrafts & Souvenirs

Housewares & Decor

Clothing & Accessories

Pets

Plants & Gardening

Housewares & Decor

The western edge of the market, particularly sections 8 to 26, features all manner of housewares, from cheap plastic buckets to expensive brass woks. This area is a particularly good place to stock up on inexpensive Thai ceramics, ranging from celadon to the traditional rooster-themed bowls from Lampang. **PL Bronze** (Section 25, Stall 185, Soi 4) has a huge variety of stainless-steel flatware, and **Ton-Tan** (Section 8, Stall 460, Soi 15/1) deals in coconut- and sugar-palm-derived plates, bowls and other utensils.

Those looking to spice up the house should stop by **Spice Boom** (Section 26, Stall 246, Soi 8), where you can find dried herbs and spices for both consumption and decoration. Other notable olfactory indulgences include the handmade soaps, lotions, salts and scrubs at **D-narn** (Section 19, Stall 203) and the fragrant perfumes and essential oils at **AnyaDharu Scent Library** (Section 3, Stall 3, Soi 43/2).

Pets

Puppies and kittens are sold in sections 13 and 15. Soi 9 of the former features several shops that deal solely in clothing for pets. It's worth noting that this section has, in the past, been associated with the sale of illegal wildlife, although much of this trade has been driven underground.

Plants & Gardening

The interior perimeter of sections 2 to 4 features a huge variety of potted plants, flowers, herbs and fruits, and the accessories needed to maintain them. Some of these shops are also open on weekday afternoons.

SIGHTS

CHATUCHAK WEEKEND MARKET — MARKET

See p158.

ANCIENT CITY — MUSEUM

(เมืองโบราณ, Muang Boran; www.ancientcitygroup.net/ancientsiam/en; 296/1 Th Sukhumvit, Samut Prakan; adult/child 9am-4pm 700/350B, 4-7pm 350/175B; ⏰9am-7pm; [S]Bearing exit 1) Don't have the time to see Thailand's most famous historic monuments? Then consider visiting scaled-down versions of them in what claims to be the largest open-air museum in the world. It's an excellent place to explore by bicycle (daily hire 50B) as it's usually quiet and rarely crowded.

Ancient City lies east of Bangkok outside Samut Prakan, which is most conveniently accessed via the park's shuttle bus from BTS Bearing station (see website for departure times).

TALAT ROT FAI — MARKET

(ตลาดรถไฟ; www.facebook.com/taradrodfi; Soi 51, Th Srinakharin; ⏰6pm-1am Thu-Sun; [S]Udom Suk exit 2 & taxi) The emphasis at this night market is on the retro, from vintage clothes to kitschy antiques. And with stalls and food trucks, VW-van-based bars and land-bound pubs, and even a few hipster barber shops, it's also much more than just a shopping destination.

If this isn't enough vintage for you, consider the recently opened and slightly smaller (yet more convenient to reach) **Talat Rot Fai 2** (Map p287; Esplanade Complex, 99 Th Ratchadaphisek; ⏰6pm-1am Thu-Sun; [S]Thailand Cultural Centre exit 4), on Th Ratchadaphisek. To get here, take the MRT to Thailand Cultural Centre and walk through the Esplanade mall.

NONTHABURI MARKET — MARKET

(ตลาดนนทบุรี; Tha Nam Nonthaburi, Nonthaburi; ⏰5-9am; ⛴Nonthaburi Pier) Exotic fruits, towers of dried chillies, smoky grills and the city's few remaining rickshaws form a very un-Bangkok backdrop at this, one of the most expansive and atmospheric produce markets in the area. Come early though, as most vendors are gone by 9am.

To get to the market, take the Chao Phraya Express Boat to Nonthaburi Pier,

GREATER BANGKOK'S KID-ORIENTED ATTRACTIONS

The suburbs north of Bangkok are home to a handful of kid-oriented museums and theme parks. All of the following are accessible via taxi from Mo Chit BTS station or Chatuchak Park MRT station.

Children's Discovery Museum (Map p286; Th Kamphaengphet 4, Queen Sirikit Park; ⏰9am-5pm Tue-Fri, 10am-6pm Sat & Sun; 👪; [M]Chatuchak Park exit 1, [S]Mo Chit exit 1) [FREE] Learning is well-disguised as fun at this museum, open again after a lengthy renovation. The interactive exhibits range in topic from construction to culture, although we suspect most will be drawn to the Dino Detective Zone, where kids can dig in sand to find and reassemble dinosaur bones.

Safari World (☎02 518 1000; www.safariworld.com; 99 Th Ramindra 1; adult/child 580/480B; ⏰9am-5pm; [M]Chatuchak Park exit 2 & taxi, [S]Mo Chit exit 3 & taxi) Claiming to be the world's largest 'open zoo', Safari World is divided into two parts: a drive-through Safari Park and a Marine Park. In the Safari Park, visitors take a bus tour (windows remain closed) through an 'oasis for animals' separated into different habitats. The Marine Park focuses on stunts by dolphins and other trained animals; note that dolphin performances have received criticism by animal-welfare groups who claim the captivity of cetaceans is debilitating and stressful for the animals, and that this is exacerbated by human interaction.

Siam Park City (☎02 919 7200; www.siamparkcity.com; 203 Th Suansiam; adult/child 900/750B; ⏰10am-6pm; [M]Chatuchak Park exit 2 & taxi, [S]Mo Chit exit 1 & taxi) Features more than 30 rides and a water park with the largest wave pool in the world.

Dream World (☎02 577 8666; www.dreamworld.co.th/en; 62 Mu 1, Th Rangsit-Nakornnayok, Pathum Thani; admission 1200B; ⏰10am-5pm Mon-Fri, to 7pm Sat & Sun; [M]Chatuchak Park exit 2 & taxi, [S]Mo Chit exit 1 & taxi) Expansive amusement park that boasts a snow room.

KO KRET

An easy rural getaway from Bangkok, Ko Kret is an artificial 'island', the result of a canal having been dug nearly 300 years ago to shorten an oxbow bend in Mae Nam Chao Phraya. The area is one of Thailand's oldest settlements of Mon, who were a dominant people of central Thailand between the 6th and 10th centuries AD. Today, Ko Kret is a popular weekend escape, known for its hand-thrown terracotta pots and its busy weekend market.

A 6km paved path circles the island, and can be easily completed on foot or by bicycle, the latter available for hire from Ko Kret's main pier (40B per day). Alternatively, it's possible to charter a long-tail boat for up to 10 people for 500B; the typical island tour stops at a batik workshop, a sweets factory and, on weekends, a floating market.

Ko Kret's most identifiable landmark is the curiously leaning stupa at **Wat Poramai Yikawat** (วัดปรมัยยิกาวาส; Ko Kret, Nonthaburi; ⊙9am-5pm; ⊠river-crossing ferry from Wat Sanam Neua) FREE. The temple is also home to an interesting Mon-style marble Buddha statue and a simple **museum** (Wat Poramai Yikawat, Ko Kret, Nonthaburi; ⊙1-4pm Mon-Fri, 9am-5pm Sat & Sun; ⊠river-crossing ferry from Wat Sanam Neua) FREE. From here, go in either direction to find both abandoned kilns and working pottery centres on the island's east and north coasts. Yet even more prevalent than temples or pottery is food. On weekends, droves of Thais flock to Ko Kret to eat deep-fried savoury snacks and Thai-style sweets. One dish to look for is *khâw châa*, an unusual but delicious Mon concoction of savoury titbits served with chilled, fragrant rice. **Pa Ka Lung** (Restaurant River Side; Ko Kret, Nonthaburi; mains 30-60B; ⊙8am-4pm Mon-Fri, to 6pm Sat & Sun; ⊠cross-river ferry from Wat Sanam Neua), an open-air food court with an English-language menu and sign, serves *khâw châa* and other dishes. Arrive on a weekday and the eating options are much fewer, but you'll have the island to yourself.

Ko Kret is in Nonthaburi, about 15km north of central Bangkok. To get there, take bus 166 from the Victory Monument or a taxi to Pak Kret, before boarding the cross-river ferry (2B, from 5am to 9pm) that leaves from Wat Sanam Neua.

the northernmost stop for most lines. The market is a two-minute walk east along the main road from the pier.

OR TOR KOR MARKET
MARKET

Map p286 (องค์การตลาดเพื่อเกษตรกร; Th Kamphaengphet 1; ⊙8am-6pm; MKamphaeng Phet exit 3) Or Tor Kor is Bangkok's highest-quality fruit and agricultural market, and taking in the toddler-sized mangoes and dozens of pots full of curries amounts to culinary trainspotting. The vast majority of vendors' goods are takeaway only, but a small food court and a few informal restaurants can also be found.

To get here, take the MRT to Kamphaeng Phet station and exit on the side opposite Chatuchak (the exit says 'Marketing Organization for Farmers').

BANGKOK UNIVERSITY ART GALLERY
ART GALLERY

(BUG; www.facebook.com/bangkokuniversity gallery; 3rd fl, Bldg 9, City Campus, Th Phra Ram IV; ⊙10am-7pm Tue-Sat; ⓢEkkamai exit 4 & taxi)

FREE This spacious, modern compound is located at what is currently the country's most cutting-edge art school. Recent exhibitions have encompassed a variety of media by some of the country's top names, as well as the work of internationally recognised artists.

ERAWAN MUSEUM (CHANG SAM SIAN)
MUSEUM

(พิพิธภัณฑ์ช้างเอราวัณ (ช้างสามเศียร); www.ancient citygroup.net/erawan/en/home; Soi 119, Th Sukhumvit; adult/child 9am-5pm 400/200B, 5-8pm 200/100B; ⊙9am-8pm; ⓢBearing exit 1) Located on the way to Ancient City and created by the same visionary, this museum is actually a five-storey sculpture of Erawan, Indra's three-headed elephant mount from Hindu mythology. The interior is filled with antique sculptures but is most impressive for the stained-glass ceiling.

The museum is most conveniently accessed via a shuttle bus from BTS Bearing station (see website for departure times).

🍴 EATING

YUSUP THAI, HALAL $

(531/12 Kaset-Navamin Hwy; mains 50-120B; ⏲8.30am-3pm; [S]Mo Chit exit 3 & taxi) The Thai-language sign in front of this restaurant boldly says *rah·chah kôw mòk* (King of Biriani) and Yusup indeed backs it up with flawless biriani, not to mention sour oxtail soup and decadent *gaang mát·sà·màn* ('Muslim curry'). For dessert try *roh·đee wăhn,* a paratha-like crispy pancake with sweetened condensed milk and sugar – a dish that will send most carb-fearing Westerners running away screaming.

To get here, take a taxi heading north from BTS Mo Chit and tell the driver to take you to the Kaset intersection and turn right on Th Kaset-Navamin. Yusup is on the left-hand side, about 1km past the first stoplight.

AJH VEGETARIANS VEGETARIAN, THAI $

Map p286 (Banana Family Park, Th Phahonyothin; mains 15-30B; ⏲7am-2pm Tue-Sun; 🌿; [S]Ari exit 1) Vegetarians trek to this food-court-bound, open-air stall north of central Bangkok for meat-free Thai dishes. Fresh juices and naturally derived soaps and lotions are also available at the adjacent stalls and shops. To find it, take exit 1 at Ari BTS and turn right down the narrow alleyway just before Esso station.

KHUA KLING PAK SOD SOUTHERN THAI $$

Map p286 (☎02 617 2553; www.khuaklingpaksod.com; 24 Soi 5, Th Phahonyothin; mains 150-380B; ⏲11am-2.30pm & 5.30-9.30pm; [S]Ari exit 1) Southern Thai is probably the country's spiciest regional cuisine, so if you're going to sweat over dinner, why not do so in white-tablecloth comfort. Recommended dishes include the eponymous *khua kling,* minced meat fried in an incendiary curry paste, or *moo hong,* fragrant, almost candy-like braised pork belly, a Chinese-Thai specialty of Phuket.

PURITAN DESSERTS $$

Map p286 (46/1 Soi Ari 5; cakes & pastries from 120B; ⏲noon-10pm Tue-Fri, 10am-10pm Sat & Sun; [S]Ari exit 1) In an attempt to describe the vibe of this uniquely bizarre dessert cafe, the words 'a knight wearing a tiara' have

EATING & DRINKING IN ARI

Ari has been touted as one of Bangkok's up-and-coming 'hoods for years now, and we think its time has finally arrived. Yet unlike most of Bangkok's nightlife areas, which tend to draw a clear line between eateries and bars, Ari seems to excel at places that blend the two genres. Some of our favourites:

➡ **Fatbird** (Map p286; ☎02 619 6609; www.facebook.com/fatbird; Soi 7/Ari, Th Phahonyothin; mains 160-300B; ⏲5.30pm-midnight Tue-Sun; [S]Ari exit 3) The dishes here, which range from tater tots to 'tom-yum-kung fried rice', don't quite cut it for dinner. But approach them as bar snacks, especially when combined with Fatbird's great drinks, eclectic shophouse atmosphere and fun soundtrack, and you have yourself a winner.

➡ **Casa Azul** (Map p286; www.facebook.com/casaazulbkk; 2/23 Soi 7/Ari, Th Phahonyothin; dishes 150-250B; ⏲11am-midnight; [S]Ari exit 3) A short menu of Tex-Mex staples, a huge list of imported microbrews and a fun atmosphere (check the Facebook page for theme nights) make up this new place that can't seem to decide if it's a restaurant or bar.

➡ **Salt** (Map p286; ☎02 619 6886; www.saltbangkok.com; Soi 7/Ari, Th Phahonyothin; mains 220-1350B; ⏲5pm-midnight Mon-Sat; [S]Ari exit 1) Flashing a strategically placed copy of *Larousse Gastronomique*, and serving dishes ranging from sushi to wood-fired pizza, Salt is the epitome of the type of contemporary, eclectic restaurant-bar that has come to define Ari. Be sure to book ahead if dining or drinking on a weekend.

➡ **The Yard** (Map p286; 51 Soi 5, Th Phahonyothin; ⏲5pm-midnight; [S]Ari exit 1) The open-air lawn of this hostel functions as a fun, informal bar, while **Paper Butter and the Burger** (Map p286; www.facebook.com/PaperButter; The Yard, 51 Soi 5, Th Phahonyothin; mains 120-190B; ⏲11am-10pm Mon-Sat; [S]Ari exit 1), an on-site burger shack, is its restaurant.

been used. Oddly enough this is a pretty accurate summary of Puritan, although there's also 16-plus chandeliers, taxidermied animals, cherubs and other antiquated, Europhile touches. Most importantly, however, there are excellent and authentic cakes and pies.

YANG GAO GORN
THAI $$

Map p286 (📞081 930 5260; www.facebook.com/YangGaoGorn; 1st fl, Frank & Release, 97 Soi 8, Th Phahonyothin; mains 70-320B; ⏱11.30am-10pm; ⓢAri exit 3 & taxi) The setting and location – a relatively bare dining room overlooking a covered football field – couldn't be more of a contrast with the home-style, hard-to-find Thai dishes at this family-run restaurant. When we visited, Yang Gao Gorn hadn't yet finalised its English-language menu, but the friendly, English-speaking owners can help in the ordering process.

Yang Gao Gorn has no English-language sign, but is located in the Frank & Release football complex, the second left turn down Soi 8.

ROSDEE
CHINESE-THAI $$

(2357 Th Sukhumvit; mains 70-2800B; ⏱8am-9pm; ⓢBang Chak exit 1) This decades-old staple is known for its consistently tasty, well-executed Chinese-Thai favourites, such as the garlicky *or sòo·an* (oysters fried with egg and a sticky batter), or the house speciality, braised goose; we also like the uniformed service staff.

Rosdee is located on the corner with Soi 95/1, a short walk from the BTS stop at Bang Chak.

ANOTAI
VEGETARIAN $$

Map p287 (www.facebook.com/pages/Anotai/40116588503; 976/17 Soi Rama 9 Hospital, Th Phra Ram IX; mains 150-300B; ⏱10am-9.30pm Thu-Tue; 🖉; ⓜPhra Ram 9 exit 3 & taxi) Upscale-ish Thai- and Italian-style vegie eats can be found at this long-standing restaurant, which also has its own vegetable market and organic farm.

🍷 DRINKING & NIGHTLIFE

O'GLEE
BAR

Map p286 (www.facebook.com/ogleeari1; Soi Ari 1; ⏱5.30pm-midnight; ⓢAri exit 3) The name and decor of this new bar vaguely call to mind an Irish pub. But rather than shamrocks and clichés, you get an astonishing selection of imported microbrews – both in bottles and draught – served by a charming Thai family.

AREE
BAR

Map p286 (cnr Soi Ari 4/Nua & Soi 7/Ari, Th Phahonyothin; ⏱6pm-1am; ⓢAri exit 3) Exposed brick, chunky carpets and warm lighting give Aree a cosier feel than your average Bangkok bar. It also offers live music (from 8pm, Tuesday to Sunday), contemporary Thai drinking snacks, and a relatively sophisticated drinks list.

FAKE CLUB THE NEXT GEN
CLUB, GAY

(www.facebook.com/fakeclubthenextgen; 222/32 Th Ratchadaphisek; ⏱9pm-3am; ⓜSutthisan exit 3) This long-standing, popular gay staple is now in new digs. Expect live music, cheesy choreography and lots of lasers.

☆ ENTERTAINMENT

★PARKING TOYS
LIVE MUSIC

(📞02 907 2228; www.parkingtoys.in.th; 17/22 Soi Mayalap, off Kaset-Navamin Hwy; ⏱4pm-2am; ⓜChatuchak Park exit 2 & taxi, ⓢMo Chit exit 3 & taxi) One of Bangkok's best venues for live music, Parking Toys hosts an eclectic revolving cast of fun bands ranging in genre from rockabilly to electro-funk jam acts.

To get here, take a taxi heading north from BTS Mo Chit (or the MRT Chatuchak Park) and tell the driver to take you to the Kaset intersection and turn right on Th Kaset-Navamin; Parking Toys is just past the second stoplight on this road.

LUMPINEE BOXING STADIUM
SPECTATOR SPORT

(📞02 282 3141; www.muaythailumpinee.net/en; 6 Th Ramintra; tickets 3rd-class/2nd-class/ringside 1000/1500/2000B; ⓜChatuchak Park exit 2 & taxi, ⓢMo Chit exit 3 & taxi) Bangkok has two premier Thai boxing rings: Ratchadamnoen Stadium (p98) and Lumpinee Boxing Stadium. Recently, Lumpinee moved to fancy new digs north of town. Matches occur here on Tuesdays and Fridays from 6.30pm to 11pm, and on Saturdays at 4pm to 8.30pm and from 9pm to 12.30am. At the time of research there were plans underway for a Thai boxing museum and a school for foreign fighters.

RCA/ROYAL CITY AVENUE

By day a bland-looking strip of offices, come Friday and Saturday nights, Royal City Ave – known by everybody as RCA – transforms into one of Bangkok's most popular nightlife zones. Although some of the bigger clubs can draw thousands, keep in mind that they often require an ID check and also maintain a dress code (no shorts or sandals).

The easiest way to approach RCA is via taxi from the MRT stop at Phra Ram 9; taxis generally can't enter RCA itself, so you'll have to U-turn or cross busy Th Phet Uthai on foot. Approaching the strip from Th Phet Uthai, you'll find the following venues:

Onyx (Map p287; www.facebook.com/onyxbkk; RCA/Royal City Ave; admission from 400B; ⊗8pm-3.30am; ⊠Phra Ram 9 exit 3 & taxi) Probably the most sophisticated club along RCA – evidenced by the hefty entry fee and the coiffed and coddled clientele. Check the Facebook page for upcoming DJ events.

Beer Cap (Map p287; www.facebook.com/beercapbkk; 21/66 RCA/Royal City Ave; ⊗6pm-2am; ⊠Phra Ram 9 exit 3 & taxi) The beats and bright lights of EDM not your thing? Prefer craft beer to vodka shots? Then head to this casual beer bar with heaps of imported brews and a menu with helpful tasting notes to ease the decision-making process.

Route 66 (Map p287; www.route66club.com; 29/33-48 RCA/Royal City Ave; admission 300B; ⊗8pm-2am; ⊠Phra Ram 9 exit 3 & taxi) This vast club has been around just about as long as RCA has, but frequent facelifts and expansions have kept it relevant. Top 40 hip hop rules the main space here, although there are several different themed 'levels', featuring anything from Thai pop to live music.

Castro (Map p287; www.facebook.com/Castro.rca.bangkok; RCA/Royal City Ave; admission 200B; ⊗9.30pm-2am; ⊠Phra Ram 9 exit 3 & taxi) Coyote boys, late hours and a dark, anything-goes lounge: RCA's biggest gay bar has all the essentials for a night you might love to regret.

Vesbar (Map p287; www.facebook.com/GoVesBar; RCA/Royal City Ave; ⊗11am-midnight; ⊠Phra Ram 9 exit 3 & taxi) This Vespa-themed bar-restaurant serves up international dishes, imported beers and jazzy live music (Wednesday, Friday and Saturday).

Taksura (Map p287; RCA/Royal City Avenue; ⊗6pm-2am; ⊠Phra Ram 9 exit 3 & taxi) Existing somewhere between restaurant and pub is retro-themed Taksura. If you're fuelling up for the clubs, the spicy *gàp glâem* (Thai drinking snacks) won't disappoint.

It's located well north of central Bangkok; the best way to get here is via taxi from BTS Mo Chit or MRT Chatuchak Park.

MAMBO CABARET   CABARET

(☎02 294 7381; 59/28 Yannawa Tat Mai; tickets 800-1000B; ⊗show times 7.15pm & 8.30pm; ⓢChong Nonsi exit 2 & taxi) This transgender cabaret venue hosts choreographed stage shows featuring Broadway high-kicks and lip-synched pop tunes.

HOUSE   CINEMA

Map p287 (www.houserama.com; 3rd fl, RCA Plaza, RCA/Royal City Ave; ⊠Phetchaburi exit 1 & taxi) Bangkok's first and biggest art-house cinema, House shows lots of foreign flicks of the non-Hollywood type.

HOLLYWOOD   LIVE MUSIC

Map p287 (72/1 Soi 8, Th Ratchadaphisek; ⊗8pm-2am; ⊠Phra Ram 9 exit 3) Like taking a time machine back to the previous century, Hollywood is a holdover from the days when a night out in Bangkok meant corny live stage shows, wiggling around the whisky-set table and neon, neon, neon. As is the case with many of its counterparts, you'll need to purchase a bottle of whisky at the door to gain entry.

SIAM NIRAMIT   THEATRE

Map p287 (☎02 649 9222; www.siamniramit. com; 19 Th Thiam Ruammit; tickets 1500-2350B; ⊗shows 8pm; ⊠Thailand Cultural Centre exit 1 & access by shuttle bus) A cultural theme park, this enchanted kingdom transports visitors to a Disneyfied version of ancient Siam with a brightly coloured stage show of traditional

WORTH A DETOUR

PHRAPRADAENG PENINSULA

If you've been to any of Bangkok's rooftop bars, you may have noticed the rural-looking zone just southeast of the city centre. Known in English as the Phrapradaeng Peninsula, the conspicuously green finger of land is surrounded on three sides by Mae Nam Chao Phraya, a feature that seems to have shielded it from development.

Most people visit the peninsula for the **Bang Nam Pheung Market** (ตลาดบางน้ำผึ้ง; Bang Kachao, Phrapradaeng; ⏰8am-3pm Sat & Sun; [S]Bang Na exit 2 & taxi), a fun, weekends-only market with an emphasis on food. While you're there, also check out the wonderfully dilapidated **Wat Bang Nam Pheung Nok** (วัดบางน้ำผึ้งนอก; Bang Kachao, Phrapradaeng, Samut Prakan; ⏰dawn-dusk; [S]Bang Na exit 2 & taxi) [FREE], a 250-year old Buddhist temple.

For something more active, the area is on the itinerary of many Bangkok bike tours, which take advantage of the peninsula's elevated walkways. Alternatively, there's **Si Nakhon Kheun Khan Park** (สวนศรีนครเขื่อนขันธ์; Bang Kachao, Phrapradaeng, Samut Prakan; ⏰6am-7pm; [S]Bang Na exit 2 & taxi) [FREE], a vast botanical park with a large lake and birdwatching tower.

If you're really enjoying the Phrapradaeng Peninsula, you can extend your stay by overnighting at **Bangkok Tree House** (p204).

To get to Phrapradaeng, take the BTS to Bang Na and jump in a taxi for the short ride to the pier at Wat Bang Na Nork via Th Sanphawut. From there, take the river-crossing ferry (4B) followed by a short motorcycle taxi (10B) ride, if you're going to Bang Nam Pheung Market.

performance depicting the Lanna Kingdom, the Buddhist heaven and Thai festivals.

A free shuttle-bus service is available at Thailand Cultural Centre MRT station, running every 15 minutes from 6pm to 7.45pm.

SHOPPING

FORTUNE TOWN ELECTRONICS

Map p287 (Th Ratchadaphisek; ⏰10am-9pm; [M]Phra Ram 9 exit 1) If you need to supplement your digital life with cheap software, a camera or computer peripherals, this multi-storey mall is a much saner alternative to Pantip Plaza (p123).

SPORTS & ACTIVITIES

BAIPAI THAI COOKING SCHOOL COOKING COURSE

(☎02 561 1404; www.baipai.com; 8/91 Soi 54, Th Ngam Wong Wan; courses 2200B; ⏰lessons 9.30am-1.30pm & 1.30-5.30pm) Housed in an attractive suburban villa, with classes taught by a small army of staff, Baipai offers two daily lessons of four dishes each. Transport there is provided.

HOUSE OF DHAMMA MEDITATION

(☎02 511 0439; www.houseofdhamma.com; 26/9 Soi 15, Th Lat Phrao; fee by donation; ⏰lessons 10am-5pm Wed-Sun; [M]Lat Phrao exit 3) Helen Jandamit has opened her suburban Bangkok home to meditation retreats and two-day classes in *vipassana* (insight meditation). Check the website to see what workshops are on offer and be sure to reserve a spot at least a week in advance.

MUAYTHAI INSTITUTE MARTIAL ARTS

(☎02 992 0096; www.muaythai-institute.net; Rangsit Stadium, 336/932 Th Prachatipat, Pathum Thani; 10-day course from 8000B; [M]Chatuchak Park exit 2 & taxi, [S]Mo Chit exit 3 & taxi) Associated with the respected World Muay Thai Council, the institute offers a fundamental course in Thai boxing (consisting of three levels of expertise), as well as courses for instructors, referees and judges.

FAIRTEX MUAY THAI MARTIAL ARTS

(☎086 776 0488; www.fairtexbangplee.com; 99/5 Mu 3, Soi Buthamanuson, Th Thaeparak, Samut Prakan; tuition & accommodation per day 1450-1850B; [S]Chong Nonsi exit 2 & taxi) A popular, long-running Thai-boxing camp south of Bangkok.

Excursions from Bangkok

Ayuthaya Historical Park p168
Thailand's heroic former capital, Ayuthaya is a Unesco World Heritage site and a major pilgrimage site for anyone interested in ancient history.

Ko Samet p171
This island, only a few hours from Bangkok, has famously squeaky sand beaches and accommodation to fit any budget.

Amphawa p174
Amphawa's canal-side setting and ancient wooden houses look like they are straight out of a movie; its homestays provide an up-close experience of this unique community.

Phetchaburi (Phetburi) p176
Phetchaburi's temples and peak-roofed wooden houses combine to form the epitome of central Thai life.

Kanchanaburi p181
Recent history is only a train ride away in Kanchanaburi, where vivid museums and touching monuments bring home the area's history as a WWII labour camp.

Khao Yai p185
Home to Khao Yai National Park, one of Thailand's biggest and best reserves, where mountainous monsoon forests boast hundreds of resident species.

TOP SIGHT
AYUTHAYA HISTORICAL PARK อุทยานประวัติศาสตร์อยุธยา

Ancient ruins, a rural Thai vibe, tasty food, good-value accommodation – and all this only 70km from Bangkok: Ayuthaya is the easiest and most worthwhile escape from the Big Mango.

The riverside city served as the seat of one of ancient Thailand's most powerful kingdoms until 1767, when it was destroyed in warfare by the Burmese. Today the ruins of the former capital, **Ayuthaya Historical Park**, are one of Thailand's biggest tourist sites. They're separated into two distinct districts: the ruins 'on the island', in the central part of town west of Th Chee Kun, are most easily visited on bicycle (40B to 50B per day) or motorbike (250B to 300B per day); those 'off the island', opposite the river from the centre, are best visited by evening boat tour (200B per person). For more detailed descriptions of the ruins, pick up the *Ayuthaya* booklet from the Ayutthaya Tourist Center.

On the Island

Ayutthaya Tourist Center

This **museum** (ศูนย์ท่องเที่ยวอยุธยา; ☎035 246076; ◷8.30am-4.30pm) **FREE** should be your first stop in Ayuthaya, as the excellent upstairs exhibition hall puts everything in context and describes the city's erstwhile glories, while the ground-floor TAT office has lots of maps and good advice.

Wat Phra Si Sanphet

This was once the largest **temple** (วัดพระศรีสรรเพชญ์; admission 50B; ◷8am-6pm) in Ayuthaya and was used as the royal temple/palace by several kings. Built in the late 15th century, the compound contained a 16m standing Buddha coated with up to 250kg of gold, later melted down and carted off by the Burmese conquerors. Its three Ayuthaya-style *chedi* (stupas) have come to be identified with Thai art more than any other style.

Wihan Phra Mongkhon Bophit

This **sanctuary hall** (วิหารพระมงคลบพิตร; ◷8am-5pm) **FREE** houses one of the largest bronze Buddha images in Thailand. This 12.5m-high figure (17m with the base) was badly damaged by a lightning-induced fire around 1700 and then again when the Burmese sacked the city. The Buddha and the building were repaired in the 20th century.

Wat Phra Ram

Wat Phra Ram (วัดพระราม; admission 50B; ◷8am-6pm) may mark the cremation site of King U Thong, though its history is unclear. It has one of the tallest *brahng* (Khmer-style tower) in Ayuthaya, though the surrounding grounds are less extensive than the better known sites. One good reason to visit is that few other people do.

Wat Ratchaburana

Wat Ratchaburana (วัดราชบูรณะ; admission 50B; ◷8am-6pm) dates back to the early 15th century and contains *chedi* and faded murals that are among the oldest in the country.

Wat Mahathat

This **wát** (วัดมหาธาตุ; Th Chee Kun; admission 50B; ◷8am-6pm) features one of the first *brahng* built in the capital and an evocative Buddha head engulfed by finger-like tree roots – the most photographed site in Ayuthaya.

DON'T MISS...

➡ A crash course in local history at the Ayutthaya Tourist Center

➡ Wat Phra Si Sanphet

➡ The riverside setting at Wat Chai Wattanaram

➡ Ancient murals at Wat Ratchaburana

PRACTICALITIES

➡ อุทยานประวัติศาสตร์ อยุธยา

➡ individual sites 50B, day passes 220B

➡ ◷8am-5pm

Wat Lokayasutharam

This **temple** (วัดโลกยสุธาราม; off Th Khlong Thaw; ⊙dawn-dusk) FREE features an impressive 28m-long reclining Buddha, ostensibly dating back to the early Ayuthaya period. A visit is worth the short bike trip it takes to reach it.

Wat Suwandararam

The two main structures of this **wát** (วัดสุวรรณดาราราม; ⊙dawn-dusk) FREE boast attractive murals, including a modern-era depiction of a famous Ayuthaya-era battle in the *wí-hǎhn* (central sanctuary), and classic *Jataka* (stories from the Buddha's lives) in the adjacent *bòht* (ordination hall). Nearby **Pom Phet Fortress** (ป้อมเพชร) served as the island's initial line of defence for centuries. Only crumbling walls remain today, but the spot features breezy views and is also home to a ferry to the mainland.

Chao Sam Phraya National Museum

The city's largest **museum** (พิพิธภัณฑสถานแห่งชาติเจ้าสามพระยา; cnr Th Rotchana & Th Si Sanphet; adult/child 150B/free; ⊙9am-4pm; P) has 2400 items on show, ranging from a 2m-high bronze-cast Buddha head to glistening treasures found in the crypts of Wat Mahathat and Wat Ratchaburana.

Chantharakasem National Museum

Inside this national **museum** (พิพิธภัณฑสถานแห่งชาติจันทรเกษม; Th U Thong; admission 100B; ⊙9am-4pm Wed-Sun) is a collection of Buddhist art, sculptures, ancient weapons and lacquered cabinets. The museum is within the grounds of Wang Chan Kasem (Chan Kasem Palace), which was built for King Naresuan by his father in 1577.

Wat Thammikarat

Wat Thammikarat (วัดธรรมิกราช; ⊙8am-7pm) FREE features overgrown *chedi* ruins and lion sculptures.

Off the Island

Wat Chai Wattanaram

The ruined Ayuthaya-style tower and *chedi* of **Wat Chai Wattanaram** (วัดไชยวัฒนาราม; admission 50B; ⊙8am-6pm), on the western bank of Mae Nam Chao Phraya, boast the most attractive setting of any of the city's temples. The manicured Thai-style compound across the river belongs to the Thai royal family.

Wat Phanan Choeng

Southeast of town on Mae Nam Chao Phraya, this **wát** (วัดพนัญเชิง; admission 20B; ⊙dawn-dusk) was built before Ayuthaya became a Siamese capital. The

GETTING THERE & AWAY

Ayuthaya is 70km north of Bangkok. Minivans depart from a stall east of Bangkok's Victory Monument (60B, one hour, every 30 minutes from 6am to 9pm) and from the Northern & Northeastern Bus Terminal (50B, one hour, hourly 5am to 7pm). Northbound trains leave Bangkok's Hualamphong Station (15B to 185B, 1½ to 2½ hours) every 30 minutes from 6.20am to 9pm (less frequently from 9.30am to 4pm). A taxi to Ayuthaya costs around 1500B.

Most visitors are on a big bus and a tight schedule. Instead, explore by túk-túk (pronounced đúk đúk), boat or bicycle.

INFORMATION

The **Tourism Authority of Thailand office** (TAT; ☎035 246076; tatyutya@tat.or.th; Th Si Sanphet; ⊙8.30am-4.30pm) is in an Art Deco building west of the park.

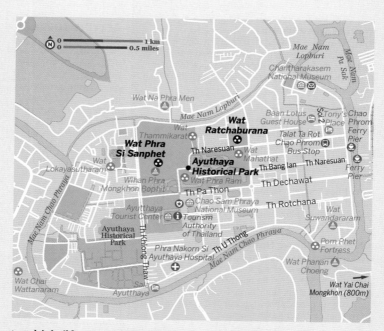

temple's builders are unknown, but it appears to have been constructed in the early 14th century, so it's possibly Khmer. The main *wí·hǎhn* contains a highly revered, 19m-high sitting Buddha image from which the wát derives its name.

Wat Yai Chai Mongkhon

Also southeast of town, this **wát** (วัดใหญ่ชัยมงคล; admission 20B; ☺6am-6pm) is a quiet place built in 1357 by King U Thong and was once famous as a meditation centre. The compound contains a large *chedi,* and a community of *mâa chee* (Buddhist nuns) lives here.

Wat Na Phra Men

This **temple** (วัดหน้าพระเมรุ; admission 20B; ☺dawn-dusk; ℗) is notable because it escaped destruction when the Burmese army overran and sacked the city in 1767. The main *bòht* was built in 1546 and features fortress-like walls and pillars. The *bòht* interior contains an impressive carved wooden ceiling and a splendid 6m-high sitting Buddha in royal attire. Inside a smaller *wí·hǎhn* behind the *bòht* is a green-stone, European-pose (sitting in a chair) Buddha from Sri Lanka, said to be 1300 years old. The walls of the *wí·hǎhn* show traces of 18th- or 19th-century murals.

Elephant Kraal

North of the city, the **Elephant Kraal** (เพนียดคล้องช้าง) **FREE** is a restoration of the wooden stockade once used for the annual round-up of wild elephants. A fence of huge teak logs enclosed the elephants. The king had a raised observation pavilion for the event.

SLEEPING IN AYUTHAYA

Baan Lotus Guest House (☑035 251988; Th Pamaphrao; dm/s/d & tw 200/250/350-600B; ⓟ☒☎⊞) Set in large, leafy grounds, this converted teak schoolhouse has a cool, clean feel and remains our favourite place to crash. Staff are as charmingly old-school as the building itself.

Tony's Place (☑035 252578; www.tonyplace-ayutthaya.com; Soi 2, Th Naresuan; r 200-1200B; ☒☎⊞) Budget rooms still offer just the basics, but the true flashpacker can hang out in renovated rooms that verge on the palatial, relatively speaking.

Sala Ayutthaya (☑035 242588; www.salaayutthaya.com; Th U Thong; r incl breakfast 4700-9400B; ☒☎⊞) Artistically combining Ayutthaya's ancient aesthetic with modern flair, Sala Ayutthaya is a beautiful place that also packs stunning views of the river and ruins.

Ko Samet   เกาะเสม็ด

Explore

It takes at least five hours to reach Ko Samet from Bangkok, so schedule in at least two nights if you really want to experience the island's famously fine sands. Long weekends can be particularly busy, with thousands of Bangkokians beelining for the island; arrive on a weekday and you'll probably have Ko Samet to yourself.

The Best...

⇒**Place to Eat** Red Ginger (p173)
⇒**Place to Drink** Baywatch Bar (p173)
⇒**Beach** Ao Wong Deuan (p107)

Top Tip

Ko Samet is a relatively dry island, making it an excellent place to visit during the rainy season (approximately June to October) when other tropical paradises might be underwater.

Getting There & Away

⇒**Minivan** Minivans to Ban Phe (the pier for ferries to Ko Samet) depart from a stall southeast of Bangkok's Victory Monument (200B, three hours, hourly from 6am to 8pm).

⇒**Bus** Buses to Ban Phe leave from Bangkok's Eastern Bus Terminal (166B, four hours, every two hours from 7am to 6pm).

⇒**Boat** Boats to Ko Samet leave from Ban Phe's many piers. Most boats go to Na Dan Pier (return 100B, 40 minutes, hourly from 8am to 5pm). You can also charter a speedboat (about 2500B depending on demand) for up to 10 people.

Need to Know

⇒**Location** 200km southeast of Bangkok
⇒**National Parks Main Office** (btwn Na Dan & Hat Sai Kaew; ☉sunrise-sunset) There's also another office at Ao Wong Deuan.

⊙ SIGHTS

KHAO LAEM YA/MU KO SAMET NATIONAL PARK   NATIONAL PARK

(อุทยานแห่งชาติเขาแหลมหญ้า-หมู่เกาะเสม็ด; ☑038 653034; reserve@dnp.go.th; adult/child 200/100B; ☉8.30am-4.30pm) **Ko Man Klang, Ko Kudee** and **Ko Man Nok,** along with **Ko Man Nai** to the west, are part of Khao Laem Ya/Mu Ko Samet National Park. This official status hasn't kept away all development, only moderated it. Ko Kudee has a small, pretty sandy stretch, clear water for decent snorkelling and a nice little hiking trail. The best way to visit is to join a boat tour from Ko Samet.

Beaches

Ko Samet is shaped like a golf tee, with the wide part in the north tapering away along a narrow strip to the south. Most boats from the mainland arrive at Na Dan Pier in the north, which is little more than a transit point for most visitors. Starting just south of Na Dan Pier and moving clockwise, the island's most noteworthy beaches include:

Hat Sai Kaew (หาดทรายแก้ว) On the northeastern coast is the most developed

Ko Samet

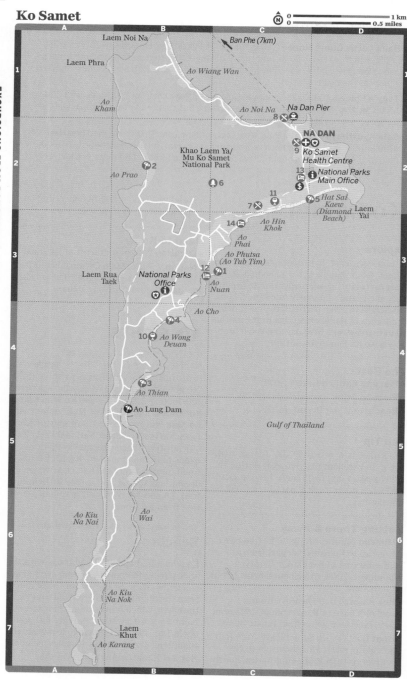

N

0 _____ 1 km
0 _____ 0.5 miles

Laem Noi Na

Laem Phra

Ao Wiang Wan

Ban Phe (7km)

Ao Kham

Ao Noi Na

Na Dan Pier

8

NA DAN

9

Ko Samet
Health Centre

Khao Laem Ya/
Mu Ko Samet
National Park

Ao Prao

6

13

National Parks
Main Office

11

7

5   *Hat Sai
Kaew
(Diamond
Beach)*   Laem
Yai

14

*Ao Hin
Khok*

*Ao
Phai*

*Ao Phutsa
(Ao Tub Tim)*

Laem Rua
Taek

National Parks
Office

12

1

*Ao
Nuan*

Ao Cho

4

10

*Ao Wong
Deuan*

3

Ao Thian

Ao Lung Dam

Gulf of Thailand

*Ao Kiu
Na Nai*

*Ao
Wai*

*Ao Kiu
Na Nok*

Laem
Khut

Ao Karang

Ko Samet

stretch of beaches and the best place for nightlife. Wealthy Bangkokians with their designer sunglasses and designer dogs file straight into Hat Sai Kaew's air-con bungalows.

Ao Hin Khok & Ao Phai (อ่าวหินโคก/อ่าวไผ่) Scattered south along the eastern shore are a scruffier set of beaches that were once populated solely by backpackers but are increasingly catering to flashpackers and Bangkok expats.

Ao Phutsa (อ่าวพุทรา (อ่าวทับทิม); Ao Tub Tim) This wide and sandy beach is a favourite for solitude seekers, families and gay men who need access to 'civilisation' but not a lot of other stimulation.

Ao Wong Deuan (อ่าววงเดือน) Immediately to the south is the prom queen of the bunch, with a graceful stretch of sand that is home to an entourage of sardine-packed sun-worshippers, package tourists, screaming jet-skis and honky-tonk bars.

Ao Thian (อ่าวเทียน) This beach is punctuated by big boulders that shelter small sandy spots, creating a castaway feel. Thai college kids claim these for all-night guitar jam sessions and if you're also on a tight budget, this beach is your best bet.

Ao Wai (อ่าวหวาย) A lovely beach far removed from everything else (though in reality it is 2km from Ao Thian).

Ao Prao The only developed beach on the steeper western side of the island, it hosts three upmarket resorts and moonlights as 'Paradise Beach' to those escaping winter climates.

✕ EATING & DRINKING

Every hotel and guesthouse has a restaurant, and choosing one can be as difficult as a walk along the beach inspecting menus along the way. There are several food stalls along the main drag between Na Dan Pier and Hat Sai Kaew, and it's worth looking out for the nightly beach barbecues, particularly along Ao Hin Khok and Ao Phai.

Likewise, every hotel has a beachside bar, and there are plenty of stand-alone bar-restaurants that occupy the beachfront at Hat Sai Kaew and Ao Wong Deuan.

RABEANG BAAN THAI $
(Na Dan; dishes 70-120B; ◷8am-9pm) Right by the ferry terminal, this spot has good enough food to make you forget you have to leave the island. It is busier at lunch than dinner.

JEP'S RESTAURANT INTERNATIONAL $
(Ao Hin Khok; mains 60-150B; ◷7am-11pm) Canopied by the branches of an arching tree decorated with pendant lights, this pretty place does a wide range of international, and some Thai, dishes. Be sure to leave room for dessert.

RED GINGER INTERNATIONAL, THAI $$
(Na Dan; dishes 120-320B; ◷11am-11pm) A small but select menu of the French-Canadian chef's favourite dishes star at this atmospheric eatery between the pier and Hat Sai Kaew. Good salads, great oven-baked ribs, and some Thai food.

BAYWATCH BAR BAR
(Ao Wong Deuan; beers from 80B; ◷sunset-late) A good spot for after-dark beach-gazing, with a fun crowd and strong cocktails.

NAGA BAR BAR
(Ao Hin Khok; beers from 70B; ◷sunset-late) This busy beachfront bar is covered in Day-Glo art and run by a friendly bunch of locals who offer good music, lots of whisky and vodka/Red Bull buckets.

🛏 SLEEPING

Due to the high demand, Ko Samet's prices can seem elevated compared with the amenities on offer, especially on weekends. A ramshackle hut starts at about 600B and with air-con this can climb to 1000B. Reservations aren't always honoured, so at peak times (most weekends and especially public-holiday weekends) it is advisable to arrive early, poised for the hunt.

MOSSMAN HOUSE   GUESTHOUSE $
(📞038 644017; Hat Sai Kaew; r 800-1300B; 🕸🛜) On the main street, just before the national park ticket office, is this sound guesthouse, with large, comfortable rooms and leafy grounds. Choose a spot at the back for some quiet.

AO NUAN BUNGALOWS   BUNGALOW $$
(📞081 781 4875; bungalow with fan 800-1200, with air-con 1500-3000B; 🕸) Ao Nuan is Samet's one remaining bohemian bay, with no internet and access only via a dirt track. Guests hang in hammocks outside their wooden bungalows here or chill in the attached restaurant. Tents are also available (450B).

⭐SAMED PAVILION RESORT
BOUTIQUE HOTEL $$$
(📞038 644420; www.samedpavilionresort.com; Ao Phai; r incl breakfast 3500-5500B; 🕸@🛜🏊) This gorgeous boutique resort has 85 elegant, spacious rooms set around a pool.

Amphawa อัมพวา

Explore

Amphawa is located within day-trip distance from Bangkok, but is probably best approached as an overnighter. The trip is easy enough by bus or minivan or via a more circuitous route, and after you've seen the town, Amphawa is a good jumping-off point for other floating markets such as Damnoen Saduak (p180) and Tha Kha (p180).

The Best...
➡**Sight** Amphawa

➡**Place to Eat** Amphawa Floating Market (p176)

➡**Place to Stay** ChababaanCham Resort (p176)

Top Tip

Amphawa is mobbed with tourists from Bangkok every weekend. For cheaper accommodation and a calmer environment, make a point of hitting the town during the week.

Getting There & Away
➡**Minivan** Frequent minivans run from a stop north of Bangkok's Victory Monument to Samut Songkhram (also known as Mae Klong; 70B, 1½ hours, frequent from 6am to 9pm). From there, you can hop in a *sŏrng·tăa·ou* (passenger pick-up truck; 8B) near the market for the 10-minute ride to Amphawa.

➡**Bus** From Bangkok's Southern Bus Terminal, board any bus bound for Damnoen Saduak and ask to get off at Amphawa (80B, two hours, frequent from 6am to 9pm).

Need to Know
➡**Location** 80km southwest of Bangkok

➡**Tourist Office** (📞034 752847; www.amphawatourism.com; 71 Th Prachasret, Amphawa; ⏱8.30am-4.30pm)

◉ SIGHTS

AMPHAWA   VILLAGE
(อัมพวา) This canal-side village has become a popular destination among city folk who seek out what many consider its quintessentially 'Thai' setting. This urban influx has sparked quite a few signs of gentrification, but the canals, old wooden buildings, atmospheric cafes and quaint water-borne traffic still retain heaps of charm. At weekends, Amphawa puts on a fun floating market that's a good spot for eating or shopping for souvenirs.

FIREFLIES GUIDED TOURS   BOAT TOUR
(หิ่งห้อย; Amphawa; ⏱dusk) At night, long-tail boats zip through Amphawa's sleepy canals and rivers to watch the Christmas-tree-like light dance of the *hìng hôy* (fireflies), most populous during the wet season. From Friday to Sunday, a number of operators from several piers lead tours, charging 60B for a seat. Outside of these days, it costs 500B for a two-hour charter.

THE LONG WAY TO AMPHAWA

Amphawa is only 80km from Bangkok, but if you play your cards right, you can reach the town via a long journey involving trains, boats, a motorcycle ride and a short jaunt in the back of a truck. Why? Because sometimes the journey is just as important as the destination.

The adventure begins at Thonburi's **Wong Wian Yai** (☎02 465 2017, call centre 1690; www.railway.co.th; off Th Phra Jao Taksin; [S]Wongwian Yai exit 4 & taxi) train station. Just past the Wong Wian Yai traffic circle is a fairly ordinary food market that camouflages the unspectacular terminus of this commuter line. Hop on one of the hourly trains (10B, one hour, from 5.30am to 8.10pm) to Samut Sakhon.

After 15 minutes on the rattling train the city density yields to squat villages. From the window you can peek into homes, temples and shops built a carefully considered arm's length from the passing trains. Further on, palm trees, patchwork rice fields, and marshes filled with giant elephant ears and canna lilies line the route, punctuated by whistle-stop stations.

The backwater farms evaporate quickly as you enter **Samut Sakhon**, popularly known as Mahachai because it straddles the confluence of Mae Nam Tha Chin and Khlong Mahachai. This is a bustling port town, several kilometres upriver from the Gulf of Thailand, and the end of the first rail segment. Before the 17th century it was called Tha Jiin (Chinese Pier) because of the large number of Chinese junks that called here.

After working your way through one of the most hectic fresh markets in the country, you'll come to a vast harbour clogged with water hyacinths and wooden fishing boats. A few rusty cannons pointing towards the river testify to the existence of the town's crumbling fort, built to protect the kingdom from sea invaders.

Take the ferry across to Baan Laem (3B to 5B), jockeying for space with motorcycles that are driven by school teachers and people running errands. If the infrequent 5B ferry hasn't already deposited you there, take a motorcycle taxi (10B) for the 2km ride to **Wat Chawng Lom** (วัดช่องลม; Ban Laem, Samut Sakhon; 🕗dawn-dusk) [FREE], home to the **Jao Mae Kuan Im Shrine**, a 9m-high fountain in the shape of the Mahayana Buddhist Goddess of Mercy that is popular with regional tour groups. Beside the shrine is Tha Chalong, a train stop with three daily departures for Samut Songkhram at 8.10am, 12.05pm and 4.40pm (10B, one hour). The train rambles out of the city on tracks that the surrounding forest threatens to engulf, and this little stretch of line genuinely feels a world away from the big smoke of Bangkok.

The jungle doesn't last long, and any illusion that you've entered a parallel universe free of concrete is shattered as you enter **Samut Songkhram**. And to complete the seismic shift you'll emerge directly into a hubbub of hectic market stalls. Between train arrivals and departures these stalls set up directly on the tracks, and must be hurriedly cleared away when the train arrives – it's quite an amazing scene.

Commonly known as Mae Klong, Samut Songkhram is a tidier version of Samut Sakhon and offers a great deal more as a destination. Owing to flat topography and abundant water sources, the area surrounding the provincial capital is well suited to the steady irrigation needed to grow guava, lychee and grapes. From Mae Klong Market pier *(tâh đà·làht mâa glorng)*, you can charter a boat (1000B) or hop in a *sŏrng·tăa·ou* (8B) near the market for the 10-minute ride to Amphawa.

WAT AMPHAWAN CHETIYARAM BUDDHIST TEMPLE

(วัดอัมพวันเจติยาราม; off Rte 6006, Amphawa; 🕗dawn-dusk) [FREE] Steps from Amphawa's central footbridge is this graceful temple thought to be located at the place of the family home of Rama II (King Phraphutthaloetla Naphalai; r 1809–24), and which features accomplished murals.

KING BUDDHALERTLA (PHUTTHA LOET LA) NAPHALAI MEMORIAL PARK MUSEUM

(อุทยานพระบรมราชานุสรณ์ พระบาทสมเด็จพระพุทธเลิศหล้านภาลัย (อุทยาน ร. ๒); off Rte 6006, Amphawa; admission 20B; 🕗8.30am-5pm) This park is a museum housed in a collection of traditional central Thai-style houses set on four landscaped acres. Dedicated to Rama II, who was born in the area, the

museum contains rare Thai books and antiques from early 19th-century Siam.

DON HOI LOT BEACH
(คอนหอยหลอด) The area's second-most famous tourist attraction is a bank of fossilised shells at the mouth of Mae Nam Mae
Klong, not far from Samut Songkhram.
These shells come from *hǒy lòrt* (clams
with a tube-like shell). While nearby seafood restaurants are popular with city folk
year-round, the shell bank is best seen during April and May when the river surface
has receded to its lowest level.

To get there hop into a *sǒrng·tǎa·ou* (10B,
about 15 minutes) in front of Samut Songkhram's Somdet Phra Phuttalertla Hospital
at the intersection of Th Prasitpattana and
Th Tamnimit. Or charter a boat from Mae
Klong Market pier *(tâh dà·làht mâa glorng)*, a scenic journey of around 45 minutes
(about 1000B).

EATING

In addition to the below, there are several
basic Thai restaurants in Amphawa; many
more are open on weekends.

AMPHAWA FLOATING MARKET MARKET $
(ตลาดน้ำอัมพวา; Amphawa; dishes 20-40B; ⊙4-
9pm Fri-Sun) If you're in Amphawa on a
weekend, plan your meals around this fun
market where grilled seafood and other
dishes are served directly from boats.

SEAFOOD RESTAURANTS SEAFOOD $
(Don Hoi Lot, Samut Songkhram; mains 70-200B;
⊙10am-10pm) The road leading to Don Hoi
Lot is lined with seafood restaurants, nearly all serving dishes made with *hǒy lòrt,* the
area's eponymous shellfish.

🛏 SLEEPING

Amphawa is popular with Bangkok's weekend warriors and virtually every other
house has opened its door to tourists in the
form of homestays. These can range from
little more than a mattress and a mosquito
net to upmarket guesthouse-style accommodation. Fan rooms start at about 250B
while air-con rooms, many of which share
bathrooms, begin at about 1000B. Prices
are half this on weekdays. If you prefer

something a bit more private, consider one
of the following.

BAAN KU PU HOTEL $$
(☑034 725920; Th Rim Khlong; bungalows incl
breakfast 800-4000B; ✳) A Thai-style 'resort'
featuring wooden bungalows in a relatively
peaceful enclave.

CHABABAANCHAM RESORT HOTEL $$$
(☑081 984 1000; www.chababaancham.com; Th
Rim Khlong; r incl breakfast 1500-2400B; ✳⊛)
Located just off the canal, this place has attractive, modern and spacious duplex-style
rooms, the more expensive of which come
equipped with a rooftop lounge area.

PLOEN AMPHAWA RESORT HOTEL $$$
(☑081 458 9411; www.ploenamphawa.com; Th
Rim Khlong; r incl breakfast 1400-3000B; ✳⊛)
Not a resort at all, but rather a handful of
rooms in a refurbished wooden home in the
thick of the canal area.

Phetchaburi (Phetburi) เพชรบุรี

Explore

Phetchaburi (colloquially known as Phet-
buri) is only about two hours from Bang-
kok. It is probably best approached as an
overnighter, although it's worth noting that
the town's hotels are a dreary lot. Regard-
less, despite the number of worthwhile
sights, very few foreign tourists make it to
Phetchaburi, and you'll likely have the town
to yourself.

If you have time, consider extending your
stay to take in the jungle at Kaeng Krachan
National Park.

The Best...
➡**Sight** Phra Nakhon Khiri Historical Park
➡**Place to Eat** Rabieng Rim Nam (p179)
➡**Place to Stay** 2N Guesthouse (p179)

Top Tip
The train is the slowest but arguably the
most scenic way to reach Phetchaburi.

Getting There & Away

➡ **Minivan** Frequent minivans ply from a stop just east of Bangkok's Victory Monument to Phetchaburi (100B, two hours, every 45 minutes from 5.15am to 8pm).

➡ **Bus** Air-con buses run to/from Bangkok's Southern Bus Terminal (120B, two hours, frequent).

➡ **Train** There are frequent services from Bangkok's Hualamphong Train Station, and fares vary depending on the train and class (34B to 388B, three to four hours, 11 daily from 1.51am to 4.46pm).

Need to Know

➡ **Location** 166km south of Bangkok

◉ SIGHTS

PHRA NAKHON KHIRI
HISTORICAL PARK   HISTORIC SITE

(อุทยานประวัติศาสตร์พระนครคีรี; ☎032 401006; admission 150B, tram return adult/child 50/15B; ⊗park & tram 8.30am-4.30pm) This national historical park sits regally atop Khao Wang (Palace Hill), surveying the city with subdued opulence. Rama IV (King Mongkut) built the palace, in a mix of European and Chinese styles, and surrounding temples in 1859 as a retreat from Bangkok. The hilltop location allowed the king to pursue his interest in astronomy and stargazing.

Each breezy hall of the palace is furnished with royal belongings. Cobblestone paths lead from the palace through the forested hill to three summits, each topped by a *chedi* (stupa). The white spire of **Phra That Chom Phet** skewers the sky and can be spotted from the city below.

There are two entrances to the site. The front entrance is across from Th Ratwithi and involves a strenuous footpath that passes a troop of unpredictable monkeys. The back entrance is on the opposite side of the hill and has a **tram** that glides up and down the summit. This place is a popular school-group outing and you'll be as much of a photo-op as the historic buildings.

A **Monday night market** lines the street in front of Khao Wang with the usual food and clothing stalls.

WAT MAHATHAT
WORAWIHAN   BUDDHIST TEMPLE

(วัดมหาธาตุวรวิหาร; Th Damnoen Kasem) **FREE** Centrally located, gleaming white Wat Mahathat is a lovely example of an everyday temple with as much hustle and bustle as the busy commercial district around it. The showpiece is a five-tiered Khmer-style *prang* (stupa) decorated in stucco relief, a speciality of Phetchaburi's local artisans, while inside the main *wí·hǎhn* (shrine hall or sanctuary) are contemporary murals.

THAM KHAO LUANG   CAVE

(ถ้ำเขาหลวง; ⊗8am-6pm) **FREE** About 4km north of town is Tham Khao Luang, a dramatic stalactite-stuffed chamber that's one of Thailand's most impressive cave shrines, and a favourite of Rama IV. Accessed via steep stairs, its central Buddha figure is often illuminated with a heavenly glow when sunlight filters in through the heart-shaped skylight.

Guides lurk in the car park, but they're not essential and aren't always forthcoming about their fees (usually 100B per person). You'll need to arrange transport here from town (around 150B return).

WAT YAI SUWANNARAM   BUDDHIST TEMPLE

(วัดใหญ่สุวรรณาราม; Th Phongsuriya; ⊗7am-6pm) **FREE** This expansive temple compound was originally built in Ayuthaya during the 17th century and was moved to Phetchaburi and renovated during the reign of Rama V (King Chulalongkorn; r 1868–1910). Legend has it that the gash in the ornately carved wooden doors of the lengthy wooden *sǎh·lah* (often spelt as *sala*) dates from the Burmese attack. The faded murals inside the *bòht* date back to the 1730s.

WARNING: MONKEY BUSINESS

Note that Phra Nakhon Khiri Historical Park is home to hundreds of monkeys that are, according to numerous signs, 'not afraid anyone'. You will make yourself a particular target of their aggression by carrying any sort of food or drink. If you're hungry or thirsty, consume your food or drink at the stalls (the vendors are equipped to defend against attacks) and be sure to discard any cans, peels or wrappers before proceeding.

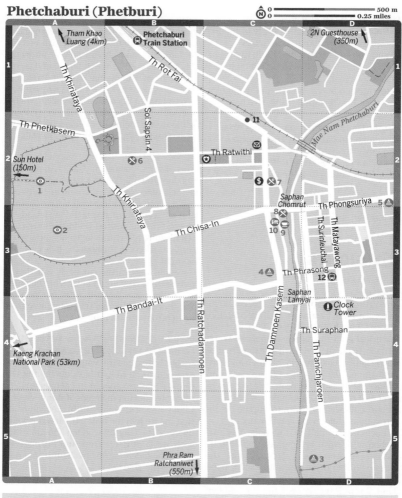

Phetchaburi (Phetburi)

Next to the *bòht*, set on a murky pond, is a beautifully designed old *hŏr drai* (*Tripitaka* library), though these days it's home only to pigeons.

PHRA RAM RATCHANIWET HISTORIC SITE
(พระรามราชนิเวศน์; ☏032 428083; Ban Peun Palace; admission 50B; ☺8.30am-4.30pm Mon-Fri) An incredible art nouveau creation, construction of this elegant summer palace began in 1910 at the behest of Rama V (who died just after the project was started). It was designed by German architects, who used the opportunity to showcase contemporary design innovations; inside there are spacious sun-drenched rooms decorated with exquisite glazed tiles, stained glass, parquet floors and plenty of wrought-iron details.

The palace is on a military base 1km south of town; you may be required to show your passport.

WAT KO KAEW SUTHARAM BUDDHIST TEMPLE
(วัดเกาะแก้วสุทธาราม, Wat Ko; off Th Matayawong; ☺7am-6pm) Buddhist temple with elaborate 18th-century murals.

⊙ Around Phetchaburi (Phetburi)

KAENG KRACHAN
NATIONAL PARK NATIONAL PARK
(อุทยานแห่งชาติแก่งกระจาน; ☏032 459291; www.dnp.go.th; admission 300B; ☺visitors centre 8.30am-4.30pm) At 3000 sq km, Thailand's largest national park is home to the stunning **Pa La-U** waterfalls, and includes long-distance hiking trails that snake through forests and savannah-like grasslands, past cliffs, caves and mountains. Two rivers, Mae Nam Phetchaburi and Mae Nam Pranburi, a large lake and abundant rainfall keep the place green year-round. Animal life includes wild elephants, deer, tigers, bears, gibbons, boars, hornbills, dusky langurs, gaurs, wild cattle and 400 species of birds.

✗ EATING & DRINKING

Phetchaburi is especially famous for its desserts, many of which can claim a royal pedigree. The desserts get their sweetness from the fruit of the sugar palms that dot the countryside around here. Two of the most famous sweets on offer include *môr gaang* (an egg-and-coconut-milk custard) and *kà·nŏm đahn* (bright yellow steamed buns sweetened with sugar-palm kernels).

★**RABIENG RIM NAM** INTERNATIONAL, THAI $
(☏032 425707; 1 Th Chisa-In; dishes 50-100B; ☺8am-midnight; ☎) This riverside restaurant serves up terrific food in an agreeable atmosphere, and the English-speaking owner is a fount of tourist information. The affiliated guesthouse has a few run-down but bearable rooms (120B), all with shared bathrooms.

JEK MENG THAI $
(www.jekmeng-noodle.com; 85 Th Ratwithi; dishes 50-100B; ☺7am-5pm) A cut above your average hole-in-the-wall joint, you can get curries and dumplings here, as well as fried rice and noodles. It's opposite the Shell petrol station. Look for the black-and-white chequered tablecloths.

NE & NAL THAI $
(Th Damnoen Kasem; dishes 30-50B; ☺8am-4pm) Great slow-cooked soups in claypots are the signature dishes at this casual place. Their *gŏo·ay đĕe·o gài* (chicken noodles) comes southern style with a whole chicken drumstick.

PAGODA CAFE CAFE
(95 Th Klongkrachang; tea/coffee from 35B; ☺9am-6pm Tue-Sun; ☎) Pagoda is a hip cafe that draws lots of students and makes a fine, air-conditioned retreat from the afternoon sun.

🛏 SLEEPING

Once bereft of guesthouses, Phetchaburi's accommodation options have improved significantly in recent years. But there aren't many places, so it's worth booking ahead, especially in high season.

2N GUESTHOUSE GUESTHOUSE $
(☏081 817 1134; two_nguesthouse@hotmail.com; 98/3 Mu 2, Tambol Bankoom; d & tw 580B; ﹡☎) In a secluded location away from the centre of town, the six rooms here are big and bright and come with small balconies. The friendly staff are a solid source of information and offer free pick-ups and bicycles.

WHITE MONKEY GUESTHOUSE **$$**
(☑032 898238; whitemonkey.guesthouse@
gmail.com; 78/7 Th Klongkrachang; r 600-
1000B; ✳🛜) New, if pricey, guesthouse with
bright, spacious, spick-and-span rooms (the
more expensive have air-con and private
bathrooms), a fine communal terrace and
helpful English-speaking staff who can or-
ganise trips in the area.

FLOATING MARKETS

Pictures of floating markets (dà·làht nám) jammed full of wooden canoes pregnant with colourful exotic fruits have defined the official tourist profile of Thailand for decades. The idyllic scenes are as iconic as the Grand Palace or the Reclining Buddha, but they are also almost completely contrived for, and dependent upon, foreign and domestic tourists – roads and motorcycles have long moved Thais' daily errands onto dry ground. That said, if you can see them for what they are, a few of Thailand's floating markets are worth a visit.

Tha Kha Floating Market (ตลาดน้ำท่าคา; Tha Kha, Samut Songkhram; ☺7am-noon, 2nd, 7th & 12th day of waxing & waning moons plus Sat & Sun) This, the most 'real'-feeling floating market, is also the most difficult to reach. A handful of vendors coalesce along an open rural klorng (canal, also spelt khlong) lined with coconut palms and old wooden houses. **Boat rides** (20B per person, 45 minutes) can be arranged along the canal, and there are lots of tasty snacks and fruits for sale. Contact Amphawa's tourist office (p174) to see when the next one is. To get here, take one of the morning sŏrng·tǎa·ou (passenger pick-up trucks, 20B, 45 minutes) from Samut Songkhram's market area.

Amphawa Floating Market (p176) The Amphawa Floating Market, located in Samut Songkhram Province, convenes near Wat Amphawa. The emphasis is on edibles and tourist knick-knacks, and because the market is only there on weekends and is popular with tourists from Bangkok, things can get pretty hectic.

Taling Chan Floating Market (ตลาดน้ำตลิ่งชัน; Khlong Bangkok Noi, Thonburi; ☺7am-4pm Sat & Sun; ⓈWongwian Yai exit 3 & taxi) Located just outside Bangkok on the access road to Khlong Bangkok Noi, Taling Chan looks like any other fresh-food market busy with produce vendors from nearby farms. But the twist emerges at the canal where several floating docks serve as informal dining rooms, and the kitchens are canoes tethered to the docks. Taling Chan is in Thonburi and can be reached via taxi from Wongwian Yai BTS station or via air-con bus 79 (16B, 25 minutes), which makes stops on Th Ratchadamnoen Klang. Long-tail boats from any large Bangkok pier can also be hired for a trip to Taling Chan and the nearby Khlong Chak Phra.

Damnoen Saduak Floating Market (ตลาดน้ำดำเนินสะดวก; Damnoen Saduak, Ratchaburi; ☺7am-noon) This 100-year-old floating market – the country's most famous – is now essentially a floating souvenir stand filled with package tourists. This in itself can be a fascinating insight into Thai culture, as the vast majority of tourists here are Thais, and watching the approach to this cultural 'theme park' is instructive. But beyond the market, the residential canals are quite peaceful and can be explored by hiring a boat (100B per person) for a longer duration. Trips stop at small family businesses, including a Thai candy maker, a pomelo farm and a knife crafter. Air-con bus 79 (with stops on Th Ratchadamnoen Klang) and minivans from the Victory Monument both connect to the Southern Bus Terminal in Thonburi, from where you can find buses to Damnoen Saduak (80B, two hours, frequent from 6am to 9pm).

Don Wai Market (ตลาดดอนหวาย; Don Wai, Nakhon Pathom; ☺6am-6pm) Not technically a swimmer, this market claims a riverbank location in Nakhon Pathom Province, having originally started out in the early 20th century as a floating market for pomelo and jackfruit growers and traders. As with many tourist attractions geared towards Thais, the main attraction is food, including fruit, traditional sweets and bèt pah·lóh (five-spice stewed duck), which can be consumed aboard large boats that cruise Mae Nam Nakhorn Chaisi (60B, one hour). The easiest way to reach Don Wai Market is to take a minibus (45B, 35 minutes) from beside **Central Pinklao** (Th Somdet Phra Pin Klao; ☺10am-10pm; ⒮Talat Phlu exit 3 & taxi, or Victory Monument exit 3 & taxi) in Thonburi.

SUN HOTEL   HOTEL $$
(☎032 401000; www.sunhotelthailand.com; 43/33 Soi Phetkasem; r 950B; ❄@🛜) Sitting opposite the back entrance to Phra Nakhon Khiri, the Sun Hotel has professional staff and large, modern but uninspiring rooms. There's a pleasant cafe downstairs and you can rent bikes for 20B per hour.

Kanchanaburi

กาญจนบุรี

Explore

There are multiple ways to approach Kanchanaburi's sights. Many choose to charter a boat, which for 800B will take up to six people on a 1½-hour tour of the area's big sights. With a bit more time, bike (50B per day) and motorcycle (200B per day) are cheaper overall, and still viable ways to get around. And if you also have the time for this option, there are tourist trains that (slowly) whisk visitors over the Death Railway Bridge to the Hellfire Pass Memorial. In fact, it's worth staying overnight in Kanchanaburi, as there's good-value accommodation, and after the sun sets, the river boom-booms its way through the night with disco and karaoke barges packed with Bangkokians letting their hair down, especially at weekends.

The Best...

➡**Sight** Death Railway Bridge
➡**Place to Eat** Blue Rice (p184)
➡**Place to Drink** Sugar Member (p184)

Top Tip

Try as you might, you will find very few Thais who have ever heard of the River Kwai. The river over which the Death Railway trundled is pronounced like 'quack' without the '-ck'.

Getting There & Away

➡**Minivan** Frequent minivans depart from a stop just east of Bangkok's Victory Monument to Kanchanaburi (120B, two hours, hourly from 6am to 6pm).

➡**Bus** Buses leave from the Southern Bus Terminal in Thonburi (110B, about two hours, every 30 minutes from 4am to 8pm).
➡**Train** Trains leave Bangkok Noi Train Station in Thonburi at 7.45am and 1.35pm (100B, two hours). Returning to Bangkok, trains depart Kanchanaburi at 7.19am and 2.48pm.

Need to Know

➡**Location** 130km west of Bangkok
➡**Tourism Authority of Thailand Office** (TAT; ☎034 511200; tatkan@tat.or.th; Th Saengchuto; ⏱8.30am-4.30pm)

👁 SIGHTS

⭐**DEATH RAILWAY BRIDGE**   HISTORIC SITE
(สะพานข้ามแม่น้ำแคว; Bridge Over the River Kwai) The famous 300m railway bridge still retains its power and symbolism, especially if you visit early or late enough in the day to bypass the tourist scrum. Its centre was destroyed by Allied bombs in 1945, so only the outer curved spans are original. Nothing remains of a second (wooden) bridge the Japanese built 100m downstream. You're free to roam over the bridge. Stand in one of the safety points along the bridge if a train appears.

⭐**THAILAND–BURMA RAILWAY CENTRE**   MUSEUM
(ศูนย์รถไฟไทย-พม่า; www.tbrconline.com; 73 Th Jaokannun; adult/child 140/60B; ⏱9am-5pm) This modern, informative museum explains Kanchanaburi's role in WWII and ensures that the deaths remain a tragedy, not a statistic. The galleries tell the history of the railway, how prisoners were treated and what happened after the line was completed. Upstairs is a display of wartime artefacts, including one POW's darts fashioned from old razors, and a diorama showing how Hellfire Pass got its name. Be sure to take time to watch the poignant video from POW survivors.

⭐**KANCHANABURI WAR CEMETERY**   CEMETERY
(สุสานทหารพันธมิตรดอนรัก; Th Saengchuto; ⏱24hr) The largest of Kanchanaburi's two war cemeteries, immaculately maintained by the Commonwealth War Graves Commission, is right in town. Of the 6981

Kanchanaburi

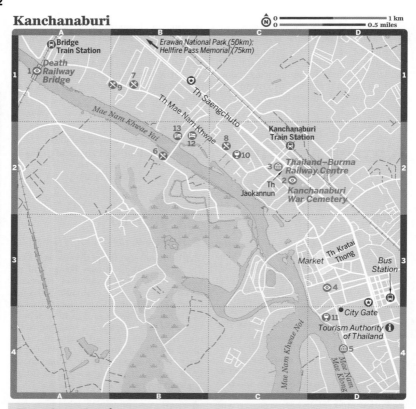

Kanchanaburi

soldiers buried here, nearly half were British; the rest came mainly from Australia and the Netherlands. As you stand at the cemetery entrance, the entire right-hand side contains British victims, the front-left area contains Australian graves, the rear left honours Dutch soldiers and unknown soldiers and those who were cremated lie at the furthest spot to the left.

HERITAGE WALKING STREET   AREA
(ถนนปากแพรก) This wonderful old street offers a glimpse of a bygone Kanchanaburi. Many shops date from the turn of the 20th century and the variety of buildings include Sino-Portuguese, Thai, Vietnamese and Chinese styles. Yellow signs reveal the history and architecture of nearly 20 of them. During WWII the Japanese rented several

THE DEATH RAILWAY

Kanchanaburi's history includes a brutal cameo (later promoted to starring) role in WWII. The town was home to a Japanese-run prisoner-of-war camp, from which Allied soldiers and many others were used to build the notorious Death Railway, linking Bangkok with Burma (now Myanmar). Carving a rail bed out of the 415km stretch of rugged terrain was a brutally ambitious plan by the Japanese, intended to meet an equally remarkable goal of providing an alternative supply route for the Japanese conquest of Burma and other countries to the west. Japanese engineers estimated that the task would take five years to complete. But the railway was completed in a mere 14 months, entirely by forced labour that had little access to either machines or nutrition. A Japanese brothel train inaugurated the line.

Close to 100,000 labourers died as a result of the hard labour, torture or starvation; 13,000 of them were POWs, mainly from Britain, Australia, the Netherlands, New Zealand and America, while the rest were Asians recruited largely from Burma, Thailand and Malaysia. The POWs' story was chronicled in Pierre Boulle's novel *The Bridge on the River Kwai* and later popularised by the movie of the same name. Many visitors come here specifically to pay their respects to the fallen POWs at the Allied cemeteries.

The original bridge was used by the Japanese for 20 months before it was bombed by Allied planes in 1945. As for the railway itself, only the 130km stretch from Bangkok to Nam Tok remains. The rest was either carted off by Karen and Mon tribespeople for use in the construction of local buildings and bridges, recycled by Thai Railways or reclaimed by the jungle.

buildings here as offices, residences, a prison and a brothel.

JEATH WAR MUSEUM MUSEUM
(พิพิธภัณฑ์สงคราม; Th Wisuttharangsi; admission 50B; ⊘8am-5pm) This small museum contains correspondence and artwork from former POWs that detail their harsh living conditions, plus various personal effects and war relics, including an Allied bomb dropped to destroy the bridge that didn't explode. The main reason to come, however, is that one of the three galleries is built from bamboo in the style of the shelters (called *attap*) the POWs lived in.

◉ Around Kanchanaburi

ERAWAN NATIONAL PARK NATIONAL PARK
(อุทยานแห่งชาติเอราวัณ; ☑034 574222; adult/child 300/200B) Famed for its seven-tiered waterfall, Erawan National Park is an extremely popular (ie crowded) place for locals and visitors alike. **Erawan waterfall** (trail open 8am to 5pm) gets its name as some people think the top level resembles Erawan, the three-headed elephant of Hindu mythology. Walking to the first three tiers is easy, but after that walking shoes and some endurance are needed to complete the 2km hike.

HELLFIRE PASS MEMORIAL MUSEUM
(ช่องเขาขาด; ☑034 919605; Rte 323; ⊘museum 9am-4pm, grounds 7.30am-6pm) FREE This poignant memorial is a beautiful tribute to those who died building the WWII Burma-Thailand Railway. Start your visit at the museum and get the free audio guide, which has detailed descriptions of the area and fascinating anecdotes from survivors. Then walk down a long staircase to the trail that follows the original rail bed. Near the start is the infamous cutting known as Hellfire Pass (locally referred to as Konyu Cutting), which is the largest along the railway's length.

✖ EATING & DRINKING

Kanchanaburi is not a culinary destination, and guesthouse-style and tourist-oriented restaurants serving bland Thai standards seem to dominate. It is, however, something of a nightlife town, and bars extend nearly the entire length of Th Mae Nam Khwae. Of these, tacky hostess bars dominate the southern end, backpacker-friendly pubs define the middle, and open-air bar-restaurants for the Thai crowd can be found at the street's northern end.

TIGER SANCTUARY OR TOURIST TRAP?

Kanchanaburi's so-called Tiger Temple is perhaps the most controversial tourist attraction in Thailand. It started in 1999 as a rescue shelter for orphaned tiger cubs, but later it became a very profitable tourist attraction, and a breeding program has increased the tiger population to near 150.

Despite having allegedly been caught breaking the law and providing substandard care for its tigers (not following even the most basic conservation protocols), and long facing accusations (including by the temple's former veterinarian) that tigers have been sold to overseas buyers for pets and body parts, the Tiger Temple continues to draw throngs of tourists.

The alleged misdeeds have been widely reported in both Thai and foreign media, and the Department of National Parks, Wildlife and Plant Conservation has threatened to remove the tigers (they have previously removed Asiatic black bears and other illegally held animals from the temple), but no actual charges have ever been filed and the temple denies all allegations.

If this isn't enough reason to stay away, it should also be pointed out that many travel insurance companies do not cover visits here or to other places like it. While tiger attacks are rare, they do happen, and in May 2015 a tiger mauled the Tiger Temple's abbot.

★**BLUE RICE**　　　　　　　　　　　　THAI **$**
(www.applesguesthouse.com; 153/4 Mu 4 Ban Tamakahm; dishes 135B; ⊙11am-2pm & 6-10pm; 🛜🍴) A perfect riverside setting, brilliant menu and fantastic flavours make this a winner. Chef Apple puts a fresh, gourmet spin on Thai classics such as the eponymous rice, *yam sôm oh* (pomelo salad) and chicken-coconut soup with banana plant.

PAI-KAN　　　　　　　　　　　　　THAI **$**
(Th Mae Nam Khwae; dishes 35-159B; ⊙11am-10pm; 🛜) Scribble down your order in the little notebook then watch as the cooks go to work in the open kitchen. Thai dishes are simple but flavoursome and wholly authentic. There are many less-common dishes such as seaweed soup and *sôm·đam* made from cucumber instead of papaya.

ON'S THAI-ISSAN　　　　　VEGETARIAN **$**
(☏087 364 2264; www.onsthaiissan.com; Th Mae Nam Khwae; dishes 50B; ⊙10am-10pm; 🍴) The Thai (and a little Isan) vegetarian and vegan food on offer here is so good that there are many carnivorous diners. Friendly On will even be happy to teach you how to make it. A two-hour, three-dish cookery course costs 600B.

MEAT & CHEESE　　　　INTERNATIONAL, THAI **$$**
(Th Mae Nam Khwae; dishes 70-3300B; ⊙11am-11pm; 🛜) This popular place prides itself on its steaks, but the wood-fired pizzas are the real stars. There's a live band after 9pm.

SUGAR MEMBER　　　　　　　　　　　BAR
(Th Mae Nam Khwae) Has hip, friendly staff who will sip whisky buckets with you all night.

TAM NAN　　　　　　　　　　　　　　BAR
(Th Song Khwae) The best of the bars along this strip, with live music and a country vibe.

🛏 SLEEPING

Travellers tend to navigate towards a 1km stretch of Th Mae Nam Khwae, where budget guesthouses offer riverfront views on raft houses. In contrast, there are several new boutique midrange spots on this strip and just out of town.

BLUE STAR GUEST HOUSE　　　GUESTHOUSE **$**
(☏034 624733; www.bluestar-guesthouse.com; 241 Th Mae Nam Khwae; r 200-750B; 🅿🌀🛜) Nature wraps itself around Blue Star's super-basic but fairly priced waterside huts, creating a jungly vibe. Better, more modern rooms sit up on solid land. Overall, one of the best budget choices in town.

★**GOOD TIMES RESORT**　　　　　　HOTEL **$$**
(☏087 162 4949; www.good-times-resort.com; r incl breakfast 1150-2700B; 🅿🌀🛜🏊) Although the road to the resort doesn't inspire confidence, get past the car park and you'll find

a little riverside oasis with large, attractive rooms plus good service and dining.

★ **ORIENTAL KWAI RESORT** RESORT **$$$**
(☏034 588168; www.orientalkwai.com; 194/5 Mu 1, Tambon Lat Ya; r incl breakfast 2300-4900B; ❈☎❄) This wonderful Thai-Dutch-run spot, 13km northwest of town, almost 2km off the road to Erawan National Park, has lovely, well-appointed cottages in a semi-wild garden full of birds. Two of the cottages are designed for families and can sleep up to six people. It should be no surprise that it's often full, so book in advance if possible.

Khao Yai เขาใหญ่

Explore

Khao Yai is only about 200km from Bangkok, but the area is best approached as an overnight trip. There are two strategies for doing this, depending on your interests. If you've come for the nature, the logical option is to sleep at the park (or at a guesthouse that provides tours to the park), which can be reached via public transport. If you're looking for a more leisurely weekend getaway to take in the restaurants, resorts, wineries and other attractions that surround the actual park, you'll need to hire a car.

The Best...

➡**Sight** Khao Yai National Park
➡**Place to Eat** Khrua Khao Yai (p186)
➡**Place to Stay** Hotel des Artists (p186)

Top Tip

The best time to visit the park is in the dry season (December to June), but during the rainy season river rafting and waterfall-spotting will be more dramatic.

Getting There & Away

➡**Minivan** Frequent minivans ply from a stop southwest of Bangkok's Victory Monument to Pak Chong (160B, 2½ hours, hourly 7am to 8pm). From Pak Chong, take a *sŏrng·tăa·ou* (40B, 45 minutes, every 30 minutes from 6am to 5pm) to the park entrance. From there, it's another 14km to the visitor centre, which can be reached by chartering a vehicle (500B).

➡**Bus** From Bangkok's Northern & Northeastern Bus Terminal, buses to Khorat (Nakhon Ratchasima) stop in Pak Chong (128B, three hours).

➡**Hire Car** For more freedom, hire a car and drive.

Need to Know

➡**Location** 196km northeast of Bangkok
➡**Visitor Centre** (☏086 092 6529; ◷8am-7pm)

◉ SIGHTS

★ **KHAO YAI**
NATIONAL PARK NATIONAL PARK
(อุทยานแห่งชาติเขาใหญ่; ☏086 092 6529; adult/child 400/200B, car 50B; ◷6am-6pm) Cool and lush, Khao Yai National Park is an easy escape into the primordial jungle. The 2168-sq-km park, part of a Unesco World Heritage site, spans five forest types, from rainforest to monsoon. The park's centrepiece is **Nam Tok Haew Suwat** (น้ำตกเหวสุวัต), a 25m-high cascade that puts on a thundering show in the rainy season. **Nam Tok Haew Narok** (น้ำตกเหวนรก) is its larger cousin, with three pooling tiers and a towering 150m drop.

PALIO SHOPPING CENTRE
(www.palio-khaoyai.com; Th Thanarat Km 17; ◷10am-7pm Mon-Fri, 9am-9pm Sat & Sun) We can't imagine a more jarring contrast to one of the world's premier protected natural areas than this wacky open-air shopping centre. Modelled after a Tuscan village, Palio is indicative of what the Khao Yai area has increasingly become over the last decade or so: a weekend playground for upper-middle-class Thais. Inside, you'll find shops, cafes, bars and hordes of Thais taking photos of each other with digital SLRs. There's plenty to eat and, on weekends, live music until 9pm.

✖ EATING

In recent years, the area surrounding Khao Yai National Park has become a minor culinary destination, with restaurants featuring cuisines ranging from upmarket Italian

THAILAND'S NAPA VALLEY

The cool highlands surrounding Khao Yai are home to a nascent wine industry. These have been dubbed the 'New Latitude' wines because, at between 14 and 18 degrees north, they fall far outside the traditional wine-grape-growing latitudes of between 30 and 50 degrees north or south of the equator. **PB Valley Khao Yai Winery** (☎036 226415; www.khaoyaiwinery.com; tours 300B; ☺tours 10.30am, 1.30pm & 3.30pm) and **GranMonte Estate** (☎044 009543; www.granmonte.com; tours adult/under 20yr 300/220B; ☺tours 10am, 11.30am, 1pm, 2.30pm & 4.30pm Sat, Sun & holidays Nov-Feb, 10.30am, 1.30pm & 3.30pm Mar-Oct) are among the winemakers managing to coax shiraz and chenin blanc grapes from the relatively tropical climate. The wines do seem to improve year by year, though they still have a way to go. Both offer free tastings and GranMonte also has some appealing rooms overlooking the vineyards from 4200B.

to Muslim-Thai. The towns that surround the park have lively night markets; but if you don't have a car, you'll find restaurants within the park.

KHRUA KHAO YAI
INTERNATIONAL, THAI $

(Th Thanarat Km 13.5; mains 60-150B; ☺9am-8pm Sun-Thu, to 10pm Fri & Sat) This open-air hut is hugely popular with visiting Bangkokians because it serves a hefty menu of satisfying Thai and *fa·ràng* dishes. The English-language menu is limited, so we recommend pointing to whatever the table next to you is eating, which is likely to be the delicious home-smoked ham or a mushroom dish.

DAIRY HOME
INTERNATIONAL, THAI $

(Th Mitraphab/Rte 2 Km 144; mains 50-300B; ☺9am-8pm) If a weekend of intense jungle exploring or wine tasting has left you with a need for Western eats, stop by this organic dairy for a country breakfast of homemade sausages, farm-fresh eggs and good coffee.

NARKNAVA
THAI, HALAL $

(Khao Mok Hi So; www.narknavafarm.com; Th Phansuk-Kud Khala Km 8; mains 50-150B; ☺8am-7pm Tue-Sun) Islamic world–influenced cuisine is unexpected in this neck of the woods, but Narknava is an established favourite for its infamous chicken biriani – infamous, because at 100B it's superexpensive by Thai standards. Unusually, the food is much better than the website images suggest.

🛏 SLEEPING

Th Thanarat, the road that links Pak Chong and the park, is home to several midrange to upmarket resorts targeted at Thai tourists.

★KHAOYAI GARDEN LODGE
HOTEL $

(☎044 365178; www.khaoyaigardenlodgekm7.com; Th Thanarat, Km 7; r with fan 350B, with aircon 2000-3200B, f 2800B; P❋@🤖🏊) This friendly, family-run place offers a variety of rooms (the cheapest are large, have shared hot-water bathrooms and fans, and are better value than other cheapies in the area), all spread out around an attractive garden. It's great value and the restaurant-lounge in front encourages interaction with fellow guests.

PARK LODGING
BUNGALOW $

(☎02 562 0760; www.dnp.go.th/parkreserve; r & bungalows 800-9000B, 30% discount Mon-Thu) These lodgings are rustic – no air-con, fridges or TVs – but comfortable. Note that you must book them through the national park website.

★HOTEL DES ARTISTS
HOTEL $$$

(☎044 297444; hoteldesartists@gmail.com; Th Thanarat, Km 22; r 3200-4200B, villas incl breakfast 5000-6000B; P❋@🤖🏊) Breaking from the Khao Yai norm, this tasteful hotel goes for French-colonial chic rather than a nature theme, though with its mountain views out the back you won't forget where you are. The rooms are gorgeous and the villas sit right by the large swimming pool.

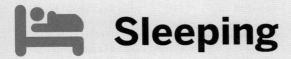

Sleeping

If your idea of the typical Bangkok hotel was influenced by The Hangover Part II, *you'll be pleased to learn that the city is home to a variety of modern hostels, guesthouses and hotels. To make matters better, much of Bangkok's accommodation offers excellent value, and competition is so intense that fat discounts are almost always available.*

Hostels

Those counting every baht can get a dorm bed (or a closet-like room) with a shared bathroom for as little as 230B. The latest trend in Bangkok is slick 'flashpacker' hostels that blur the line between budget and midrange. A bed at these will cost between around 400B and 800B.

Guesthouses

In Bangkok, this designation usually refers to any sort of budget accommodation rather than a room in a family home, although we use it to describe the latter. Guesthouses and similar budget hotels are generally found in somewhat inconveniently located corners of old Bangkok (Banglamphu, Chinatown and Thewet), which means the money you're saving in rent will probably go on taxi fares. Rates begin at about 500B.

Hotels

Bangkok's midrange hotels often have all the appearance of a Western-style hotel, but without the predictability. If you're on a lower-midrange budget, and don't care much about aesthetics, some very acceptable rooms can be had for between 1200B and 2000B. If your budget is higher, it pays to book ahead, as online discounts can be substantial. You'll find several midrange hotels along lower Th Sukhumvit, near Siam Sq and in Banglamphu.

Luxury, Business & Boutique Hotels

Bangkok is home to a huge number of top-end hotels ranging from boutique (small but cosy) to luxury (big and brash). Most hotels of this type are located on Th Sukhumvit and Th Silom, or along Mae Nam Chao Phraya. Rooms generally start between 5000B and 9000B before hefty online discounts.

Amenities

Wi-fi is nearly universal across the spectrum, but air-conditioning and lifts are not.

BUDGET

The cheapest hostels and guesthouses often share bathrooms and may not even supply a towel. Some remain fan-cooled or, in the case of dorms, will only run the air-con between certain hours. Wi-fi, if available, is typically free at budget places. If on offer, breakfast at most Bangkok hostels and budget hotels is little more than instant coffee and toast.

MIDRANGE

Increasingly, midrange has come to mean a room with air-con, a fridge, hot water, TV and free wi-fi. It's not uncommon for a room to boast all of these but lack a view, or even windows. Breakfast can range from 'buffets' based on toast and fried eggs to healthier meals with yoghurt or tropical fruit.

TOP END

Top-end hotels in Bangkok supply all the facilities you'd expect at this range, though it's not uncommon to have to pay a premium for wi-fi. In sweaty Bangkok, pools are almost standard, not to mention fitness and business centres, restaurants and bars. Breakfast is often buffet-style.

NEED TO KNOW

Price Ranges
Accommodation in this book is broken down into three categories. We've listed high-season walk-in rates, excluding the 'plus-plus' that most top-end places charge, which in Thailand is made up of 10% service and 7% government tax.

$	less than 1000B a night
$$	1000B to 3000B a night
$$$	more than 3000B a night

The best time for discounts is outside of Bangkok's peak seasons, which are from November to March and from July to August.

Accommodation Websites
➔ **Agoda** (www.agoda. com/city/bangkok-th. html) Asia-based hotel booking site that offers a lowest-price guarantee.

➔ **Lonely Planet** (www. lonelyplanet.com/thai land/bangkok/hotels) Find reviews and make bookings.

➔ **Travelfish** (www. travelfish.org/country/ thailand) Independent reviews with lots of reader feedback.

Lonely Planet's Top Choices

AriyasomVilla (p202) Sumptuous refurbished villa with a classy B&B vibe.

Phra-Nakorn Norn-Len (p194) A unique, fun and thoughtful hotel in a refreshingly untouristed 'hood.

Siam Heritage (p199) Homely touches and warm service make this the closest you may come to sleeping in a Thai home.

Best by Budget

$
Lub*d (p191) Youthful feeling hostel with two convenient locations in central Bangkok.

Chern (p190) Surprisingly sophisticated dorms and rooms for the price.

Silom Art Hostel (p191) Eclectic, eccentric budget digs.

$$
Smile Society (p199) A homely haven in the middle of Bangkok's financial district.

Feung Nakorn Balcony (p195) Former school turned cute midranger.

Sam Sen Sam Place (p194) Spotless, welcoming rooms in a refurbished house.

$$$
Metropolitan by COMO (p200) Urban sophistication and excellent dining.

Mandarin Oriental (p200) Bangkok's oldest hotel remains one of its best.

Peninsula Hotel (p200) Sky-high standards of service.

Best for Romantics

Old Capital Bike Inn (p193) Refurbished shophouse with a secluded, seductive vibe.

Arun Residence (p196) Cosy rooms overlooking Mae Nam Chao Phraya.

Loy La Long (p196) Forget about the rest of the world at this tiny, concealed hotel on the river.

Best Affordable Luxury

Hansar (p197) Spacious, good-value, apartment-like rooms.

S31 (p203) Conveniently located, contemporary accommodation at a fair price.

Glow Trinity Silom (p200) Top-end style and service for a tariff that's just above midrange.

Best Artsy Stays

Beat Hotel (p204) One-of-a-kind wall-sized murals and bright colours shape the vibe here.

Hotel Indigo (p197) Local history and culture are reinterpreted as design at this new hotel.

Inn A Day (p190) Former factory blending industrial and retro Thai touches.

Best Rooms with Views

Millennium Hilton (p201) Tall riversider featuring some of Bangkok's best watery views.

Bangkok Tree House (p204) Take in the greenery and river from these elevated bungalows in Bangkok's 'green lung'.

Sofitel So (p201) Rooms peering over the urban oasis that is Lumphini Park.

Where to Stay

Neighbourhood	For	Against
Ko Ratanakosin & Thonburi	Bangkok's most famous sights at your door; occasional river views; (relatively) fresh air; old-school Bangkok feel.	Difficult to reach; few budget options; lack of dining and drinking venues; touts.
Banglamphu	Close to main sights; proximity to classic Bangkok 'hood; lots of good-value budget beds; fun, intergalactic melting-pot feel; virtually interminable dining options; one of the city's best nightlife areas.	Getting to and from the area can be troublesome; Th Khao San can be noisy and rowdy; budget places can have low standards; relentless touts.
Thewet & Dusit	Good budget options; riverside village feel; fresh air; close to a handful of visit-worthy sights.	Few midrange and upmarket options; not very convenient access to rest of Bangkok; relatively few dining and drinking options; comatose at night.
Chinatown	Some interesting budget and midrange options; off the beaten track; easy access to worthwhile sights and some of the city's best food; close to Bangkok's main train station.	Noisy; polluted; touts; hectic; few non-eating-related nightlife options; access to rest of Bangkok not very convenient.
Siam Square, Pratunam, Phloen Chit & Ratchathewi	Wide spread of accommodation alternatives; mega-convenient access to shopping (and air-conditioning); steps away from BTS.	Touts; unpristine environment; relative lack of dining and entertainment options in immediate area; lacks character.
Riverside, Silom & Lumphini	Some of the city's best upmarket accommodation; river boats and river views; super-convenient access to BTS and MRT; lots of dining and nightlife options; gay-friendly.	Can be noisy and polluted; budget options can be pretty dire; hyper-urban feel away from the river.
Sukhumvit	Some of the city's most sophisticated hotels; lots of midrange options; easy access to BTS and MRT; international dining; easy access to some of the city's best bars; home to several reputable spas and massage parlours.	Annoying street vendors and sexpat vibe; noisy; hyper-touristy.
Greater Bangkok	Less hectic setting; good value; depending on location, convenient airport access.	Transport can be inconvenient; lack of drinking and entertainment options.

🛏 Ko Ratanakosin & Thonburi

AROM D HOSTEL   HOSTEL $
Map p265 (📞02 622 1055; www.aromdhostel.com; 336 Th Maha Rat; incl breakfast dm 800B, r 2250-2500B; ❄@🛜; 🚤Tien Pier) Dorm beds and rooms are united by a cutesy design theme and a host of inviting communal areas including a rooftop deck, computers, a ground-floor cafe and TV room. Private rooms don't have much space, but they do have style. The posted rates are typically subject to hefty discounts.

ROYAL THA TIEN VILLAGE   HOTEL $$
Map p265 (📞095 151 5545; www.facebook.com/theroyalthatienvillage; 392/29 Soi Phen Phat; r 1200B; ❄@🛜; 🚤Tien Pier) These 12 rooms spread over two converted shophouses are relatively unassuming, but TV, fridge, air-con, lots of space and shiny wood floors, not to mention a cosy homestay atmosphere, edge this place into the recommendable category. It's popular, so be sure to book ahead.

INN A DAY   HOTEL $$$
Map p265 (📞02 221 0577; www.innaday.com; 57-61 Th Maha Rat; incl breakfast r 3500-4200B, ste 7500-9000B; ❄@🛜; 🚤Tien Pier) Inn A Day wows with its hyper-cool retro/industrial theme (the hotel is located in a former sugar factory) and its location (it towers over the river and Wat Arun). The 11 rooms aren't huge, but they include unique touches such as clear neon shower stalls, while the top-floor suites have two levels and huge claw-foot tubs.

CHAKRABONGSE VILLAS   HOTEL $$$
Map p265 (📞02 622 1900; www.chakrabongsevillas.com; 396/1 Th Maha Rat; incl breakfast r 5000B, ste 10,000-25,000B; ❄@🛜❄; 🚤Tien Pier) This almost fairy-tale-like compound incorporates three sumptuous but cramped rooms and four larger suites and villas, some with great river views, all surrounding a still-functioning royal palace dating back to 1908. There's a pool, jungle-like gardens and an elevated deck for romantic riverside dining. No walk-ins.

SALA RATANAKOSIN   HOTEL $$$
Map p265 (📞02 622 1388; www.salaresorts.com/rattanakosin; Soi Tha Tian; incl breakfast r 4000-6300B; ste 12,100B; ❄@🛜; 🚤Tien Pier) Sala boasts a sleek, modernist feel – a somewhat jarring contrast with the former warehouse it's located in. The 15 rooms are decked out in black and white, and boast open-plan bathrooms and big windows looking out on the river and Wat Arun – they can't be described as vast, but will satisfy the fashion-conscious.

IBRIK RESORT   BOUTIQUE HOTEL $$$
Map p265 (📞02 848 9220; www.ibrikresort.com; 256 Soi Wat Rakhang; r incl breakfast 4000B; ❄🛜; 🚤Wang Lang/Siriraj Pier, or river-crossing ferry to Wat Rakhang Pier) With only three rooms, it doesn't get much smaller than this hotel. It's also hard to get closer to Mae Nam Chao Phraya than this, although it's worth noting that the Moonlight Room has neither river views nor balcony.

AURUM: THE RIVER PLACE   HOTEL $$$
Map p265 (📞02 622 2248; www.aurum-bangkok.com; 394/27-29 Soi Pansuk; r incl breakfast 3700-4600B; ❄@🛜; 🚤Tien Pier) The 12 rooms here don't necessarily reflect the grand European exterior of this refurbished shophouse. Nonetheless they're comfortable, modern and well appointed, and most offer fleeting views of Mae Nam Chao Phraya.

🛏 Banglamphu

⭐CHERN   HOSTEL $
Map p268 (📞02 621 1133; www.chernbangkok.com; 17 Soi Ratchasak; dm 400B, r 1400-1900B; ❄@🛜; 🚤klorng boat to Phanfa Leelard Pier) The vast, open spaces and white, over-exposed tones of this hostel converge in an almost afterlife-like feel. The eight-bed dorms are above average, but we particularly like the private rooms, which, equipped with attractively minimalist touches, a vast desk, TV, safe, fridge and heaps of space, are a steal at this price.

FORTVILLE GUESTHOUSE   HOTEL $
Map p268 (📞02 282 3932; www.fortvilleguesthouse.com; 9 Th Phra Sumen; r 870-1120B; ❄@🛜; 🚤Phra Athit/Banglamphu Pier) With an exterior that combines elements of a modern church and/or castle, and an interior that relies on mirrors and industrial themes, the design concept of this hotel – undergoing a renovation at the time of research – is tough to pin down. The rooms themselves are stylishly minimal, and the

BANGKOK'S BEST HOSTELS

If you're on a shoestring budget, Bangkok has heaps of options for you, ranging from high-tech, pod-like dorm beds in a brand-new hostel to cosy bunk beds in a refurbished Chinatown shophouse. (And if you decide that you need a bit more privacy, nearly all of Bangkok's hostels also offer private rooms.) And best of all, at the places listed here, we found the bathrooms to be clean and convenient, and sharing will hardly feel like a compromise. Some of our picks:

Lub*d (Map p274; ☎02 634 7999; www.siamsquare.lubd.com; Th Phra Ram I; dm 590B, r 1550-2000B; ❄@📶; [S]National Stadium exit 1) The title is a play on the Thai *làp dee*, meaning 'sleep well', but the fun atmosphere at this modern-feeling hostel might make you want to stay up all night. Diversions include an inviting communal area stocked with games and a bar, and thoughtful facilities range from washing machines to a theatre room. If this one's full, there's another branch just off **Th Silom** (Map p278; ☎02 634 7999; www.silom.lubd.com; 4 Th Decho; dm 550-600B, r 1250-1900B; ❄@📶; [S]Chong Nonsi exit 2).

Silom Art Hostel (Map p278; ☎02 635 8070; www.silomarthostel.com; 198/19-22 Soi 14, Th Silom; dm 380-450B, r 1200B; ❄@📶; [S]Chong Nonsi exit 3) Quirky, artsy, bright and fun, Silom Art Hostel combines recycled materials, unconventional furnishings and colourful wall paintings to culminate in a hostel that's quite unlike anywhere else in town. It's not all about style though: beds and rooms are functional and comfortable, with lots of appealing communal areas.

Loftel 22 (Map p271; www.loftel22bangkok.com; 952 Soi 22, Th Charoen Krung; dm 350B, r 900-1350B; ❄@📶; ⛴Marine Department Pier, [M]Hua Lamphong exit 1) Stylish, inviting dorms and private rooms (all with shared bathrooms) have been coaxed out of these two adjoining shophouses. Friendly service and a location in one of Chinatown's most atmospheric corners round out the package.

NapPark Hostel (Map p268; ☎02 282 2324; www.nappark.com; 5 Th Tani; dm 440-650B; ❄@📶; ⛴Phra Athit/Banglamphu Pier) This popular hostel features dorm rooms of various sizes, the smallest and most expensive of which boasts six pod-like beds outfitted with power points, mini-TV, reading lamp and wi-fi. Cultural-based activities and inviting communal areas ensure that you may not actually get the chance to plug in.

Saphaipae (Map p278; ☎02 238 2322; www.saphaipae.com; 35 Th Surasak; incl breakfast dm 450B, r 1000-1600B; ❄@📶; [S]Surasak exit 1) The bright colours, chunky furnishings and bold murals in the lobby of this hostel give it the feel of a day-care centre for travellers – a vibe that continues through to the playful communal areas and rooms. Dorms and rooms are thoughtful and well equipped, and there's heaps of helpful travel resources and facilities.

Suneta Hostel Khaosan (Map p268; ☎02 629 0150; www.sunetahostel.com; 209-211 Th Kraisi; incl breakfast dm 490-590B, r 1180B; ❄@📶; ⛴Phra Athit/Banglamphu Pier) A pleasant, low-key atmosphere, a unique, retro-themed design (some of the dorm rooms resemble sleeping car carriages), a location just off the main drag, and friendly service are what make Suneta stand out.

Yim Huai Khwang Hostel (Map p287; ☎02 118 6038; www.yimhuaikhwang.com; 70 Th Pracha Rat Bamphen; incl breakfast dm 450-550B, r 1556-3000B; ❄📶; [M]Huay Khwang exit 1) A new suburban hostel decked out in an eclectic, colourful fashion, with dorm rooms ranging in size from four to six comfortable, high-tech bunk beds. Yes, it's far from any sights, but it is very close to the MRT.

S1 Hostel (Map p277; ☎02 679 7777; www.facebook.com/S1hostelBangkok; 35/1-4 Soi Ngam Du Phli; dm 330-380B, r 700-1300B; ❄@📶; [M]Lumphini exit 1) A huge new hostel with dorm beds decked out in a simple yet attractive primary-colour scheme. A host of facilities (laundry, kitchen, rooftop garden) and a convenient location within walking distance of the MRT make it great value.

more expensive ones include perks such as a fridge and balcony.

KHAOSAN IMMJAI
HOSTEL $

Map p268 (☑02 629 3088; www.khaosanimmjai.com; 240 Soi 1, Th Samsen; dm incl breakfast 350-420B; ✳@⍥; ⌨Phra Athit/Banglamphu Pier) There's nothing flashy or particularly exceptional about this hostel. But a homely feel and positive feedback edge it into the recommendable column. Dorms, which range from four to 14 beds, are clean, done out in pastel tones and have ample natural light. There is access to lots of convenient amenities (washing machines, computers, etc), although none of these are free.

WILD ORCHID VILLA
HOTEL $

Map p268 (☑02 629 4378; www.wildorchidvilla.com; 8 Soi Chana Songkhram; r 300-1800B; ✳⍥; ⌨Phra Athit/Banglamphu Pier) The cheapies here (fan-cooled and with share bathrooms) are some of the tiniest we've seen anywhere, but like most of the rooms at Wild Orchid are clean and neat, and come in a bright, friendly package. It's popular, so be sure to book ahead.

★LAMPHU TREEHOUSE
HOTEL $$

Map p268 (☑02 282 0991; www.lamphutreehotel.com; 155 Wanchat Bridge, off Th Prachathipatai; incl breakfast r 1650-2500B; ste 3500-4500B; ✳@⍨; ⌨klorng boat to Phanfa Leelard Pier) Despite the name, this attractive midranger has its feet firmly on land, and as such represents brilliant value. The wood-panelled rooms are attractive and inviting, and the rooftop bar, pool, internet cafe, restaurant and quiet canal-side location ensure that you may never feel the need to leave. An annexe a couple blocks away increases your odds of snagging an elusive reservation.

THE WAREHOUSE
HOTEL $$

Map p268 (☑02 622 2935; www.thewarehousebangkok.com; 120 Th Bunsiri; r incl breakfast 2380-2680B; ✳@⍨; ⌨klorng boat to Phanfa Leelard Pier) Wooden pallets as furniture, yellow and black wall art, and exposed fittings and other industrial elements contribute to the factory theme here. Against all odds, the Warehouse pulls it off, and what you get are 36 rooms that are fun, functional and relatively spacious, if not stupendous value.

SOURIRE
HOTEL $$

Map p268 (☑02 280 2180; www.sourirebangkok.com; Soi Chao Phraya Si Phiphat; r incl breakfast 1500-3500B; ✳@⍥; ⌨klorng boat to Phanfa Leelard Pier) More home than hotel, the 38 rooms here exude a calming, matronly vibe. Soft lighting, comfortable and sturdy wood furniture, and the friendly, aged owners complete the package.

To reach the hotel, follow Soi Chao Phraya Si Phiphat to the end and knock on the tall brown wooden door immediately on your left.

VILLA CHA-CHA
HOTEL $$

Map p268 (☑02 280 1025; www.villachacha.com; 36 Th Tani; r 1400-2200B; ✳⍥⍨; ⌨Phra Athit/Banglamphu Pier) Wind your way between Balinese statues, lounging residents, a rambling restaurant and a tiny pool to emerge at this seemingly hidden but popular hotel. Rooms are capable – bar the frequently clumsy stabs made at interior design (think art-school nude portraits) – but the real draw here is the hyper-social, resort-like atmosphere.

DIAMOND HOUSE
HOTEL $$

Map p268 (☑02 629 4008; www.thaidiamondhouse.com; 4 Th Samsen; r 1100-1700B; ✳@⍥; ⌨Phra Athit/Banglamphu Pier) Despite sharing real estate with a Chinese temple, there's no conflict of design at this eccentric hotel. Most rooms have raised-platform beds and are outfitted with stained glass, dark, lush colours and eclectic furnishings. There's a lack of windows, and some of the rooms can seem pretty tight, but a rooftop deck and an outdoor jacuzzi are attempts to make up for this.

HOTEL DÉ MOC
HOTEL $$

Map p268 (☑02 282 2831; www.hoteldemoc.com; 78 Th Prachathipatai; r incl breakfast 1650-1850B; ✳@⍥⍨; ⌨klorng boat to Phanfa Leelard Pier) With high ceilings and generous windows, the rooms at this 1960s-era hotel seem spacious, although the furnishings, like the exterior, are still stuck in the previous century. The grounds include an inviting and retro-feeling pool and cafe, and complimentary transport to Th Khao San and free use of bikes are thoughtful perks.

RAMBUTTRI VILLAGE INN
HOSTEL $$

Map p268 (☑02 282 9162; www.rambuttrivillage.com; 95 Soi Ram Buttri; r incl breakfast 850-2350B; ✳⍥⍨; ⌨Phra Athit/Banglamphu Pier)

Located just off the main drag, this mid-sized hotel has an abundance of relatively characterless, yet clean, comfortable good-value rooms. A ground-floor courtyard with restaurants and shops also makes it a convenient place to stay.

PANNEE RESIDENCE
HOTEL **$$**

Map p268 (✆02 629 4560; 117 Th Din So; r incl breakfast 1100-1700B; ❄@🛜; 🚤klorng boat to Phanfa Leelard Pier) Pannee is a multistorey hotel offering tidy, if somewhat character-anaemic, rooms. The cheapest rooms are small, but like all the others include a safe, TV and fridge. An upper-floor patio with outdoor rain showers and daybeds for sunbathing provides a bit more room to stretch, and proximity to Bangkok's big sights makes the decision easy.

RIKKA INN
HOTEL **$$**

Map p268 (✆02 282 7511; www.rikkainn.com; 259 Th Khao San; r 1150-1750B; ❄@🛜⬜; 🚤Phra Athit/Banglamphu Pier) Boasting tight but attractive rooms, a rooftop pool and a location right in the middle of all the action on Th Khao San, the Rikka is one of the area's most conveniently located – and better-value – midrangers.

BAAN DINSO
@ RATCHADAMNOEN
HOTEL **$$**

Map p268 (✆086 815 3300; www.baandinso.com; 78/3 Th Ratchadamnoen Klang; r incl breakfast 800-2570B; ❄🛜; 🚤klorng boat to Phanfa Leelard Pier) Overlooking what is arguably the most famous intersection in Bangkok, the rooms here run the spectrum from modern but tiny singles with shared bathrooms to the more spacious Grand rooms, most of which offer fleeting views of the Democracy Monument.

RAJATA HOTEL
HOTEL **$$**

Map p268 (✆02 628 8084; www.rajatahotel.com; 46 Soi 6, Th Samsen; r 1000B; ❄@🛜; 🚤Phra Athit/Banglamphu Pier) This defiantly old-school hotel is an unassuming but comfortable choice for those who'd rather not stay on Th Khao San, but who don't want to be too far away. Rooms have tall ceilings, but not heaps of horizontal space nor much natural light.

ROYAL HOTEL
HOTEL **$$**

Map p268 (✆02 222 9111; www.rattanakosin hotel.com; cnr Th Ratchadamnoen Klang & Th Atsadang; r incl breakfast 1300-2400B; ❄🛜⬜; 🚤Phra Athit/Banglamphu Pier) If you cherish history over style, then consider a stay at this landmark hotel dating back to 1942, also known as the Rattanakosin Hotel. Be sure to ask for one of the recently renovated rooms, don't miss the funky pool, and relish the fact that you're steeped in history and staying basically across the street from most of Bangkok's big-hitter sights.

NEW SIAM RIVERSIDE
HOTEL **$$**

Map p268 (✆02 629 3535; www.newsiam.net; 21 Th Phra Athit; r incl breakfast 1490-3990B; ❄@🛜; 🚤Phra Athit/Banglamphu Pier) One of a handful of places along Th Phra Athit taking advantage of the riverside setting, this hotel has comfortable rooms with tiny bathrooms. But the real value comes from the on-site amenities (internet, travel agent, restaurant) and a location on one of the city's more pleasant streets. Book ahead.

BUDDY BOUTIQUE HOTEL
HOTEL **$$**

Map p268 (✆02 629 4477; www.buddylodge.com; 256 Th Khao San; r 2000-3000B; ❄@🛜⬜; 🚤Phra Athit/Bangamphu Pier) This gigantic complex, which includes a pool, fitness room and, ahem, a branch of McDonald's, is, as far as we're aware, the most expensive place to stay on Th Khao San. Correspondingly, rooms are comfortable, well equipped and evocative of a breezy, tropical manor house.

OLD CAPITAL BIKE INN
HOTEL **$$$**

Map p268 (✆02 629 1787; www.oldcapitalbkk.com; 609 Th Phra Sumen; r incl breakfast 3190-6590B; ❄@🛜; 🚤klorng boat to Phanfa Leelard Pier) The dictionary definition of a honeymoon hotel, this antique shophouse has 10 rooms that are decadent and sumptuous, blending rich colours and heavy wood furnishings. A recent management change and refurbishment has seen the introduction of a bicycle theme, and bikes can be borrowed for free.

PRAYA PALAZZO
HOTEL **$$$**

Map p268 (✆02 883 2998; www.prayapalazzo.com; 757/1 Somdej Prapinklao Soi 2; incl breakfast r 4145-5334B, ste 7118-11,282B; ❄🛜⬜; 🚤hotel shuttle boat from Phra Athit/Banglamphu Pier) After lying dormant for nearly 30 years, this elegant 19th-century mansion in Thonburi has been reborn as an attractive riverside boutique hotel. The 17 rooms can seem rather tight, and river views can be elusive, but the meticulous renovation, handsome antique furnishings and bucolic atmosphere convene in a boutique with authentic old-world charm.

RIVA SURYA
HOTEL $$$

Map p268 (📞02 633 5000; www.rivasuryabang kok.com; 23 Th Phra Athit; r incl breakfast 6950-10,350B; ❄️@🛜; 🚤Phra Athit/Banglamphu Pier) A former condo has been transformed into one of the more design-conscious hotels in this part of town. The 68 rooms are decked out in greys and blacks, with contemporary furnishings, and in the case of the Riva Rooms, great river views, although not always tonnes of space.

VILLA PHRA SUMEN
HOTEL $$$

Map p268 (📞080 085 0085; www.villaphra sumen.com; 457 Th Phra Sumen; incl breakfast r 3000-3300B; ste 4500-6000B; ❄️@🛜; 🚤klorng boat to Phanfa Leelard Pier) Surrounding a garden and edging the canal, the new Villa Phra Sumen boasts a secluded, secret feel. Gain access to the compound and inside you'll find 34 rooms that range from somewhat tight (and likewise overpriced) standard rooms to dual-level suites, all of which come equipped with balconies and contemporary amenities, and are looked after by service-minded staff.

🛏 Thewet & Dusit

HI BAAN THEWET
HOTEL $

Map p270 (📞02 281 0361; www.hi-baanthewet.com; 25/2 Th Phitsanulok; r incl breakfast 500-750B; ❄️@🛜; 🚤Thewet Pier) The rather institutional lobby here stands in contrast to the 14 pleasant, vaguely old-school-themed rooms. Some are on the small side and could use windows, but inviting communal areas and the leafy, quiet, off-the-beaten-track location make up for this.

PENPARK PLACE
HOTEL $

Map p270 (📞02 628 8896; www.penparkplace.com; 22 Soi 3, Th Samsen; r 330-1650B; ste 2200B; ❄️@🛜; 🚤Thewet Pier) This former factory has been turned into a good-value budget hotel. A room in the original building is little more than a bed and a fan, but an adjacent add-on sees a handful of well-equipped apartment-like rooms and suites.

⭐SAM SEN SAM PLACE
GUESTHOUSE $$

Map p270 (📞02 628 7067; www.samsensam.com; 48 Soi 3, Th Samsen; r incl breakfast 590-2400B; ❄️@🛜; 🚤Thewet Pier) One of the homeliest places in this area, if not Bangkok, this colourful, refurbished antique villa gets glowing reports about its friendly service and quiet location. The 18 rooms here all are extremely tidy, and the cheapest are fan-cooled and share a bathroom.

BAAN MANUSARN
GUESTHOUSE $$

Map p270 (📞02 281 2976; www.facebook.com/baanmanusarn; Th Krung Kasem; r incl breakfast 1400B; ❄️@🛜; 🚤Thewet Pier) Steps from Thewet Pier is this inviting vintage shophouse with four rooms. All feature beautiful wood floors and lots of space. The two family rooms are the most generously sized, and half the rooms have balconies.

SSIP BOUTIQUE
HOTEL $$

Map p270 (📞02 282 6489; www.ssiphotelthailand.com; 42 Th Phitsanulok; r incl breakfast 2200-3500B; ❄️@🛜; 🚤Thewet Pier) Handsome tiles, heavy wood furniture, antique furnishings: the 20 rooms here have been meticulously styled to emulate an old-school Bangkok feel. But modern amenities (TV, fridge, safe) and thoughtful staff ensure a thoroughly contemporary stay.

⭐PHRA-NAKORN NORN-LEN
HOTEL $$$

Map p270 (📞02 628 8188; www.phranakorn-nornlen.com; 46 Soi Thewet 1; r incl breakfast 2200-4200B; ❄️@🛜; 🚤Thewet Pier) Set in an enclosed garden compound decorated like the Bangkok of yesteryear, this bright and cheery hotel is fun and atmospheric, if not necessarily a stupendous-value place to stay. Although the 31 rooms are attractively furnished with antiques and paintings, it's worth noting that they don't include TV or in-room wi-fi, a fact made up for by daily activities, massage and endless opportunities for peaceful relaxing.

THE SIAM
HOTEL $$$

Map p270 (📞02 206 6999; www.thesiamhotel.com; 3/2 Th Khao; incl breakfast r 14,950-22,327B, villa 26,271-36,912B; ❄️@🛜❄️; 🚤Thewet Pier, or hotel shuttle boat from Sathon/Central Pier) Zoom back to the 1930s in this modern riverside hotel, where Art Deco influences, copious marble and beautiful antiques define the look. Rooms are spacious and well appointed, while villas up the ante with rooftop balcony and plunge pool. Yet it's not just about navel-gazing, with activities ranging from Thai boxing lessons to a private theatre to keep you busy.

CASA NITHRA
HOTEL $$$

Map p270 (02 628 6228; www.casanithra.com; 176 Th Samsen; incl breakfast r 3500-4300B; ste 5000B; @⊕; Thewet Pier) The 73 rooms in this new hotel come in earthy shades of brown, with subtle furnishings and flourishes that intertwine contemporary and Thai design themes. Deluxe rooms throw in a bit more space, as well as an inviting, free-standing bathtub. Online discounts chip away at the tariff.

Chinatown

SIAM CLASSIC
GUESTHOUSE $

Map p271 (02 639 6363; 336/10 Trok Chalong Krung; r incl breakfast 450-1200B; @; Ratchawong Pier, Hua Lamphong exit 1) The rooms here don't include much furniture, and the cheapest don't include air-con or en suite bathrooms, but an effort has been made at making them feel comfortable, tidy and even a bit stylish. An inviting ground-floor communal area encourages meeting and chatting, and the whole place exudes a welcoming homestay vibe.

OLDTOWN
HOSTEL $

Map p271 (02 639 4879; www.oldtown hostelbkk.com; 1048-1054 Soi 28, Th Charoen Krung; dm 230-270B, r 800B; @⊕; Marine Department Pier, Hua Lamphong exit 1) The dorms and rooms at this new, shophouse-bound hostel all share bathrooms and are relatively plain, but this is made up for by lots of communal space, including a vast lobby with a pool table, kitchen, computers and comfy chairs, and an adjoining cafe.

★ FEUNG NAKORN BALCONY
HOTEL $$

Map p271 (02 622 1100; www.feungnakorn. com; 125 Th Fuang Nakhon; incl breakfast dm/r 700/1650B, ste 2100-4700B; @⊕; Saphan Phut/Memorial Bridge Pier, Pak Klong Taladd Pier) Located in a former school, the 42 rooms here surround an inviting garden courtyard and are generally large, bright and cheery. Amenities such as a free minibar, safe and flat-screen TV are standard, and the hotel has a quiet and secluded location away from the strip, with capable staff. A charming and inviting (if not particularly great-value) place to stay.

SHANGHAI MANSION
HOTEL $$$

Map p271 (02 221 2121; www.shanghaimansion. com; 479-481 Th Yaowarat; incl breakfast r 3000-4000B, ste 4500B; @⊕; Ratchawong Pier, Hua Lamphong exit 1 & taxi) Easily the most consciously stylish place to stay in Chinatown, if not in all of Bangkok. This award-winning boutique hotel screams Shanghai circa 1935 with stained glass, an abundance of lamps, bold colours and cheeky Chinatown kitsch. If you're willing to splurge, ask for one of the bigger street-side rooms with tall windows that allow more natural light.

Siam Square, Pratunam, Phloen Chit & Ratchathewi

WENDY HOUSE
HOSTEL $

Map p274 (02 214 1149; www.wendyguest house.com; 36/2 Soi Kasem San 1; r incl breakfast 750-2000B; @⊕; National Stadium exit 1) The rooms at this long-standing budget option are small and basic, but are exceedingly clean and relatively well equipped (TV, fridge) for this price range.

BOXPACKERS HOSTEL
HOSTEL $

Map p271 (02 656 2828; www.boxpackers hostel.com; 39/3 Soi 15, Th Phetchaburi; incl breakfast dm 500-800B, r 1260-1530B; ⊕; Ratchathewi exit 1 & taxi) A contemporary, sparse hostel with dorms ranging in size from four to 12 double-decker pods – some of which are double beds. Communal areas are inviting, and include a ground-floor cafe and a lounge with pool table. A linked hotel also offers 14 small but similarly attractive private rooms.

BIZOTEL
HOTEL $$

Map p271 (02 245 2424; www.bizotelbkk.com; 104/40 Th Rang Nam; r incl breakfast 1800B; @⊕; Victory Monument exit 4) Attractive, bright and stuffed with useful amenities: you could be fooled into believing that the rooms at this new hotel cost twice this much. A location in a relatively quiet part of town is another bonus, and helpful, friendly staff seal the deal.

INDRA REGENT HOTEL
HOTEL $$

Map p271 (02 208 0022; www.indrahotel.com; 120/126 Th Ratchaprarop; incl breakfast r 2500-4200B, ste 5000-12,500; ⊕; Ratchathewi exit 1 & taxi) A classic Bangkok hotel dating back to 1971, nearly half of its 500 rooms have been renovated, but the Indra Regent still retains charming touches of its past.

BANGKOK'S BEST SMALL HOTELS

Although the big chains dominate the skyline, Bangkok is also home to several attractive hotels and guesthouses with fewer than 10 rooms. Some of our faves:

Arun Residence (Map p265; ☏02 221 9158; www.arunresidence.com; 36-38 Soi Pratu Nokyung; incl breakfast r 3500-4200B, ste 5800B; ❋@⚡; ⛴Tien Pier) Although strategically located on the river directly across from Wat Arun, this multilevel wooden house boasts much more than just great views. The six rooms here manage to feel both homey and stylish, some being tall and loft-like, while others cojoin two rooms (the best are the top-floor, balcony-equipped suites).

Loy La Long (Map p271; ☏02 639 1390; www.loylalong.com; 1620/2 Th Songwat; incl breakfast dm 1300B, r 2100-4000B; ❋@⚡; ⛴Ratchawong Pier, Ⓜ Hua Lamphong exit 1 & taxi) Rustic, retro, charming – the six rooms in this 100-year-old wooden house can lay claim to more than their fair share of personality. And united by a unique location elevated over Mae Nam Chao Phraya complete with breezy, inviting nooks and crannies, the whole place is also privy to a hidden, almost secret, feel. The only hitch is in finding it; to get here, proceed to Th Songwat and cut directly through Wat Patumkongka Rachaworawiharn to the river.

W Home (☏02 291 5622; www.whomebangkok.com; Yaek 8, Soi 79, Th Charoen Krung; r incl breakfast 1500-1600; ❋@⚡; Ⓢ Saphan Taksin exit 2 & taxi) It's admittedly off the grid, but that's part of the charm at this 60-year-old renovated house. Welcoming hosts, four small but attractive and thoughtfully furnished rooms (although only one with en suite bathroom), inviting communal areas and an authentic homestay atmosphere round out the package. Soi 79 branches off Th Charoen Krung about 1km south of Saphan Taksin; W Home is about 250m east of the main road.

Bhuthorn (Map p268; ☏02 622 2270; www.thebhuthorn.com; 96-98 Th Phraeng Phuthon; r incl breakfast 4500-6300B; ❋@⚡; ⛴Saphan Phut/Memorial Bridge Pier, Pak Klong Taladd Pier) Travel a century back in time by booking one of the three rooms in this beautiful antique shophouse in a classic Bangkok neighbourhood. They're not particularly huge, but are big on atmosphere and come with both antique furnishings and modern amenities. The sister hotel, **Asadang** (Map p271; ☏085 180 7100; www.theasadang.com; 94-94/1 Th Atsadang; r incl breakfast 3900-6000B; ❋@⚡; ⛴Saphan Phut/Memorial Bridge Pier, Pak Klong Taladd Pier), a couple of blocks away, offers a similar package.

Café Ice Residence (Map p278; ☏02 636 7831; cafeiceresidences@gmail.com; 44/4 Soi Phiphat 2; r incl breakfast 2100-3000B; ❋@⚡; Ⓢ Chong Nonsi exit 2) This spotless, classy villa is more home than hotel, with nine inviting, spacious and comfortable rooms. Outfitted with subtle yet attractive furnishings, they share a location with a Thai restaurant on a quiet street.

Loog Choob Homestay (Map p270; ☏085 328 2475; www.loogchoob.com; 463/5-8 Th Luk Luang; incl breakfast r 2100B, ste 3600-4400B; ❋@⚡; ⛴Thewet Pier, Ⓢ Phaya Thai exit 3 & taxi) Five rooms in a former gem factory outside the tourist zone might sound iffy, but the rooms here are stylish and inviting, and come supplemented by a huge array of thoughtful amenities and friendly, heartfelt service.

Baan Noppawong (Map p268; ☏02 224 1047; www.facebook.com/baannoppawong; 112-114 Soi Damnoen Klang Tai; incl breakfast r 2500-3200, ste 4200-4990; ❋⚡; ⛴klorng boat to Phanfa Leelard Pier) If your grandma ran a hotel in Bangkok, it might resemble the seven rooms in this fastidiously tidy antique house. Rooms don't have much space, but are light-filled, comfortable and homely, and attractively decorated with antique furnishings. A secluded location augments the homestay vibe.

Baan Dinso (Map p268; ☏02 621 2808; www.baandinso.com; 113 Trok Sin; incl breakfast dm 650B, r 1000-2600B; ❋@⚡; ⛴klorng boat to Phanfa Leelard Pier) This antique wooden villa may not represent the best value in Bangkok, but for accommodation with a nostalgic vibe and palpable sense of place, it's almost impossible to beat. Of the nine small-yet-spotless rooms, only five have en suite bathrooms, while all have access to functional and inviting communal areas.

Rooms are comfortable, spacious and well equipped – if somewhat conservative – and with the cheapest just squeezing into the midrange, represent decent value.

LEMONTEA HOTEL HOTEL $$
Map p271 (☏02 693 5499; www.lemonteahotel. com; 55 Soi 15, Th Phetchaburi; r incl breakfast 1890-3440; ✻@🛜; Ⓢ Ratchathewi exit 1 & taxi) Located down a narrow, hectic street in a frenetic part of town, this new, charming and peaceful small hotel is something of an oasis. Rooms may not be as fashionable as the exterior/lobby suggest, but are attractive and comfortable, and service gets positive feedback.

VISTA RESIDENCE HOTEL $$
Map p274 (☏02 612 3911; www.vistaresidence bkk.com; 80 Soi Kasem San 3; r incl breakfast 1700-1900; ✻🛜; Ⓢ National Stadium exit 1) The 15 rooms here boast a feminine, homely vibe; think matronly service, the smell of potpourri, and paintings of flowers on the walls. Added bonuses are the hotel's proximity to public transport and shopping.

SIAM@SIAM HOTEL $$$
Map p274 (☏02 217 3000; www.siamatsiam. com; 865 Th Phra Ram I; r incl breakfast 5467-9200B; ✻@🛜; Ⓢ National Stadium exit 1) A seemingly random mishmash of colours and industrial/recycled materials in the lobby here result in a style one could only describe as 'junkyard chic' – but in a good way, of course. The rooms, which largely continue the theme, are found between the 14th and 24th floors, and offer terrific city views. There's a spa, a rooftop restaurant and an 11th-floor pool.

HANSAR HOTEL $$$
Map p274 (☏02 209 1234; www.hansarbangkok. com; 3 Soi Mahadlekluang 2; ste incl breakfast 5000-24,000B; ✻@🛜; Ⓢ Ratchadamri exit 4) The Hansar can claim that elusive intersection of style and value. All 94 rooms here are handsome and feature huge bathrooms and giant desks, but the smallest (and cheapest) studios are probably the best deal, as they have a kitchenette, washing machine, stand-alone tub, free wi-fi and, in most, a balcony.

OKURA PRESTIGE HOTEL $$$
Map p274 (☏02 687 9000; www.okurabangkok. com; 57 Th Witthayu/Wireless Rd; incl breakfast r 14,000-25,000B; ste 29,000-150,000B;

Ⓟ✻@🛜; Ⓢ Phloen Chit exit 5) The Bangkok venture of this Japanese chain – the first branch outside of its homeland – is, unlike other recent, big-name openings in Bangkok, distinctly unflashy. But we like the minimalist, almost contemplative feel of the lobby and the 240 rooms, and the subtle but thoughtful, often distinctly Japanese touches. Significant online discounts are available.

HOTEL INDIGO HOTEL $$$
Map p274 (☏02 207 4999; www.ihg.com; 81 Th Witthayu/Wireless Rd; incl breakfast r 3599-8599, ste 15,599-20,599B; ✻@🛜; Ⓢ Phloen Chit exit 5) An international chain with local flavour, the Indigo has borrowed from the history and culture of this corner of Bangkok to arrive at a hotel that is retro, modern, Thai and artsy all at the same time. Many of the 192 rooms overlook some of the greener areas of Bangkok's embassy district, and all are decked out with colourful furnishings and functional amenities.

HOTEL MUSE HOTEL $$$
Map p274 (☏02 630 4000; www.hotelmuse bangkok.com; 55/555 Th Lang Suan; incl breakfast r 7515-9015B, ste 12,515-48,765B; ✻@🛜; Ⓢ Ratchadamri exit 2) Gaining inspiration from the golden era of travel of the late 19th century, this unique hotel straddles the past and the present. Rooms are dark and decadent – the vibe set by the faux-antique furniture, textured wallpaper and clawfoot tubs – but also feature modern amenities and great city views. It's run by Accor, so the service is on par with the surroundings.

K MAISON HOTEL $$$
Map p271 (☏02 245 1953; www.kmaisonboutique. com; Soi Ruam Chit; incl breakfast r 2675-3975B, ste 8375B; ✻🛜; Ⓢ Victory Monument exit 4) The lobby, with its virginal white, swirling marble and streaks of blue, sets the tone of this new boutique. The 21 rooms follow suit, and are handsome in a delicate and attractively sparse way. Lest you think it's all about image, K Maison appears to be functional and comfortable.

CONRAD HOTEL BANGKOK HOTEL $$$
Map p274 (☏02 690 9999; www.conradhotels. com; 87 Th Witthayu/Wireless Rd; incl breakfast r 5000-8000B, ste 12,000-80,000B; ✻@🛜; Ⓢ Phloen Chit exit 1) When built in 2003, the Conrad was one of the first hotels in Bangkok to consciously make an effort to appeal

to the young and hip. It has since been surpassed in this area, but still offers attractive and comfortable accommodation for the mature-and-hip crowd.

LIT BANGKOK HOTEL & RESIDENCE HOTEL **$$$**

Map p274 (☎02 612 3456; www.litbangkok.com; 36/1 Soi Kasem San 1; incl breakfast r 7000-8000B, ste 9000-10,000B; ❄@📶🏊; [S]National Stadium exit 1) This modern, architecturally striking hotel has a variety of room styles united by a light theme. Check out a few, as they vary significantly, and some features, such as a shower that can be seen from the living room, aren't necessarily for everybody.

PULLMAN BANGKOK KING POWER HOTEL **$$$**

Map p271 (☎02 680 9999; www.pullmanbangkokkingpower.com; 8/2 Th Rang Nam; incl breakfast r 4000-6000B, ste 7000B; ❄@📶🏊; [S]Victory Monument exit 2) The Pullman is a great choice for those who want to stay in a business-class hotel, but who would rather not stay 'downtown'. Rooms are smart and modern, and the Pullman's restaurants are among the best-value Western dining options in town. It's located a brief walk from the BTS stop at Victory Monument.

Riverside, Silom & Lumphini

HQ HOSTEL HOSTEL **$**

Map p278 (☎02 233 1598; www.hqhostel.com; 5/3-4 Soi 3, Th Silom; incl breakfast dm 330-520B, r 890-990B; ❄@📶; [M]Si Lom exit 2, [S]Sala Daeng exit 2) HQ is a flashpacker hostel in the polished-concrete-and-industrial-style mould. It includes four- to 10-bed dorms, a few private rooms (some with en suite bathroom) and inviting communal areas in a narrow multistorey building in the middle of Bangkok's financial district.

ETZZZ HOSTEL HOSTEL **$**

Map p277 (☎02 286 9424; www.etzhostel.com; 5/3 Soi Ngam Du Phli; dm 250-350B, r 900B; ❄@📶; [M]Lumphini exit 1) This narrow shophouse includes dorms ranging in size from four to 12 beds, and two private rooms (the

HOTEL ALTERNATIVES IN BANGKOK

If you're planning on staying longer than a few days, or you're somebody who doesn't need maid service, there are ample alternatives to the traditional hotel in Bangkok.

At the time of research the most talked about alternative, Airbnb (www.airbnb.com/s/Bangkok--Thailand), had heaps of listings in the city, ranging from condos and apartments to small hotels masquerading as condos and apartments. For something a bit more established there's **House by the Pond** (Map p282; ☎02 259 3543; www.housebythepond.com; 230/3 Soi Sainumthip 2; r per night 1400-2500B; ❄@📶🏊; [S]Phrom Phong exit 6 & taxi), an old-school-style Bangkok apartment that offers nightly, weekly and monthly stays.

On the other hand, if you've got a bit more money and don't want to forgo the perks of staying at a hotel, a clever route is the ubiquitous serviced apartment. Bangkok is loaded with apartments that offer long-stay options with the benefits of a hotel (doormen, maids, room service, laundry). But what few people realise is that most serviced apartments are happy to take short-term guests as well as longer stayers – and that by booking ahead you can get a luxury apartment with much more space and facilities (kitchen, washing machine etc) than a hotel room, for the same or less money. It's really a great way to stay in town, especially if you're a family who needs more space than two hotel rooms. Recommended outfits include the following:

Siri Sathorn (Map p277; ☎02 266 2345; www.sirisathorn.com; 27 Soi Sala Daeng 1; r 3312-16,992B; ❄@📶🏊; [M]Si Lom exit 2, [S]Sala Daeng exit 2) Chic modern apartments starting at 60 sq metres; also includes shuttle bus, spa and professional service.

Centrepoint (☎02 630 6345; www.centrepoint.com; r & ste incl breakfast 2523-7200B) One of Bangkok's biggest managers of serviced apartments, with five properties across the city.

Urbana (☎02 227 9999; www.urbanahospitality.com; ste 2100-7000B) Reputable serviced-apartment provider with two properties in Bangkok.

latter equipped with en suite bathroom), all of which are united by a neat, primary colour theme and a convenient location near the MRT.

★ SMILE SOCIETY
HOTEL **$$**

Map p278 (📞081 442 5800, 081 444 1596; www.smilesocietyhostel.com; 30/3-4 Soi 6, Th Silom; incl breakfast dm 420B, r 900-1880B; ✴@🛜; MSi Lom exit 2, SSala Daeng exit 1) Part boutique, part hostel, this four-storey shophouse combines small but comfortable and well-equipped rooms and dorms with spotless shared bathrooms. A central location, overwhelmingly positive guest feedback, and helpful, English-speaking staff are other perks. And a new and virtually identical annexe next door helps with spillover as Smile Society gains more fans.

AMBER
HOTEL **$$**

Map p278 (📞02 635 7272; www.amberboutiquesilom.com; 200 Soi 14, Th Silom; r incl breakfast 1650-2150B; ✴🛜; SChong Nonsi exit 3) Spanning design themes such as Moroccan, Sino-Portuguese and Modern, it's easy to assume that Amber might emphasise style over comfort. But nothing here is flashy or overwrought, and what you'll get are 19 excellent value, spacious rooms with lots of amenities and natural light, in a quiet location.

SILOM ONE
HOTEL **$$**

Map p278 (📞02 635 5130; www.silomone.com; 281/15 Soi 1, Th Silom; r 2500-3500; ✴🛜; MSi Lom exit 2, SSala Daeng exit 2) Barely squeezing into the midrange bracket is this hotel with 10 rooms that boast an almost Japanese minimalism. You can't beat its convenient location in a dead-end alley, steps away from public transport and heaps of street food.

LUXX XL
HOTEL **$$**

Map p277 (📞02 684 1111; www.staywithluxx.com; 82/8 Th Lang Suan; incl breakfast r 2033-2990B, ste 3670-11,962B; ✴@🛜✉; SRatchadamri exit 2) LUXX oozes with a contemporary, minimalist hipness that wouldn't be out of place in London or New York. Floor-to-ceiling windows allow heaps of natural light, suites have an added kitchenette, and all rooms are decked out with appropriately stylish furnishings. There's another slightly cheaper (and smaller) **Th Decho branch** (Map p278; 📞02 635 8844; www.staywithluxx.com; 6/11 Th Decho; incl breakfast r 1536-2119B,

ste 2172-2278; ✴@🛜; SChong Nongsi exit 3), off Th Silom.

URBAN HOUSE
HOTEL **$$**

Map p278 (📞081 492 7778; www.urbanh.com; 35/13 Soi Yommarat; incl breakfast r/ste 1200/1480B; ✴🛜; MSi Lom exit 2, SSala Daeng exit 4) There's nothing showy about this shophouse with six rooms, but that's exactly what we like about it. Rooms are subtle, comfortable and relatively spacious, and the place boasts a peaceful, homely atmosphere, largely due to the kind host and the quiet residential street it's located on.

SWAN HOTEL
HOTEL **$$**

Map p280 (📞02 235 9271; www.swanhotelbkk.com; 31 Soi 36/Rue de Brest, Th Charoen Krung; r incl breakfast 1200-2000B; ✴@🛜✉; ⛴Oriental Pier) The 1960s-era furnishings date this classic Bangkok hotel despite relatively recent renovations. But the rooms are airy and virtually spotless, and the antiquated vibe provides the Swan, in particular its pool area, with a fun, groovy vibe.

BANGKOK CHRISTIAN GUEST HOUSE
HOTEL **$$**

Map p278 (📞02 233 2206; www.bcgh.org; 123 Soi Sala Daeng 2; r incl breakfast 1100-2860B; ✴🛜♿; MSi Lom exit 2, SSala Daeng exit 2) This resolutely institutional-feeling guesthouse is a wise choice for families on a budget, as some rooms have as many as five beds, and include access to a 2nd-floor children's play area.

CHAYDON SATHORN
HOTEL **$$**

Map p277 (📞02 343 6333; www.chaydonsathorn.com; 31 Th Sathon Tai/South; r incl breakfast 1500-2500B; ✴@🛜; MLumphini exit 2) The former King's Hotel has been reborn as a no-frills midranger, located right in the middle of the embassy district. The primary colours and bold lines of the design scheme make up for the lack of natural light in some rooms. Online discounts available through the website.

★ SIAM HERITAGE
HOTEL **$$$**

Map p278 (📞02 353 6101; www.thesiamheritage.com; 115/1 Th Surawong; incl breakfast r 4900-5700B, ste 7000-13,500B; ✴@🛜✉; MSi Lom exit 2, SSala Daeng exit 1) &Tucked off busy Th Surawong, this hotel overflows with homey Thai charm – probably because the owners also live in the same building. The 73 rooms are decked out in silk and dark woods with classy design touches and thoughtful amenities. There's an inviting rooftop garden/pool/spa, and it's all cared for by a team of professional, accommodating staff. Highly recommended.

★METROPOLITAN BY COMO
HOTEL $$$

Map p277 (☑02 625 3333; www.comohotels.com/metropolitanbangkok; 27 Th Sathon Tai/South; incl breakfast r 4500-6500B, ste 7500-40,000B; ✻@🛜☒; MLumphini exit 2) The exterior of Bangkok's former YMCA has changed relatively little, but a peek inside reveals one of the city's sleekest, sexiest hotels. A 2014 renovation has all 171 rooms looking better than ever in striking tones of black, white and yellow. It's worth noting that the City rooms tend to feel a bit tight, while in contrast the two-storey penthouse suites are like small homes.

MANDARIN ORIENTAL
HOTEL $$$

Map p280 (☑02 659 9000; www.mandarinorientaltal.com; 48 Soi 40/Oriental, Th Charoen Krung; incl breakfast r 14,150-30,000B, ste 26,700-160,000B; ✻@🛜☒; 🚢Oriental Pier, or hotel shuttle boat from Sathon/Central Pier) For the true Bangkok experience, a stay at this grand old riverside hotel is a must. The majority of rooms are in the modern and recently refurbished New Wing, but we prefer the old-world ambience of the Garden and Authors' Wings, the latter of which was

undergoing a significant renovation at the time of research.

The hotel is also home to one of the region's most acclaimed spas (p141), a legendary fine-dining restaurant (p131) and a cooking school (p141).

PENINSULA HOTEL
HOTEL $$$

Map p280 (☑02 861 2888; www.peninsula.com; 333 Th Charoen Nakhon; incl breakfast r 17,000-25,000B, ste 30,000-140,000B; ✻@🛜☒; 🚢hotel shuttle boat from Sathon/Central Pier) After nearly 20 years in Bangkok, the Pen still seems to have it all: the location (towering over the river), the rep (it's consistently one of the top-ranking luxury hotels in the world) and one of the highest levels of service in town. If money is no obstacle, stay on one of the upper floors where you literally have all of Bangkok at your feet.

GLOW TRINITY SILOM
HOTEL $$$

Map p278 (☑02 231 5050; www.glowbyzinc.com/trinity-silom; 150 Soi Phiphat 2; r incl breakfast 3500-4200B; ✻@🛜☒; 🔵Chong Nonsi exit 2) A sophisticated hotel with rates that weigh in at just above midrange, Glow has spacious-feeling, modern, tech-equipped rooms, professional service, and pool and fitness facilities just next door.

SUKHOTHAI HOTEL
HOTEL $$$

Map p277 (☑02 344 8888; www.sukhothai.com; 13/3 Th Sathon Tai/South; incl breakfast r 12,800-16,800B, ste 17,800-80,000B; ✻@🛜☒;

FROM LITERATI TO GLITTERATI

Now a famous grande dame, the Mandarin Oriental started its career as the seafarers' version of a Th Khao San guesthouse. The original owners, two Danish sea captains, traded the nest to Hans Niels Andersen, the founder of the formidable East Asiatic Company. Andersen transformed the hotel into a civilised palace of grand architecture and luxurious standards. He hired an Italian architect, S Cardu, to design what is now the Authors' Wing, which was the city's most fantastic building not commissioned by the king.

The rest of the hotel's history relies on its famous guests. A Polish-born sailor named Joseph Conrad stayed here in 1888. The hotel brought him good luck: he got his first command on the ship *Otago,* from Bangkok to Port Adelaide, Australia, which in turn gave him ideas for several early stories. W Somerset Maugham stumbled into the hotel with an advanced case of malaria. In his feverish state, he heard the German manager arguing with the doctor about how a death in the hotel would hurt business. Maugham's overland Southeast Asian journey is recorded in *The Gentleman in the Parlour: A Record of a Journey from Rangoon to Haiphong,* which gave literary appeal to the hotel. Other notable guests have included Noël Coward, Graham Greene, John le Carré, James Michener, Gore Vidal and, er, Barbara Cartland. Some modern-day writers claim that a stay here will overcome writer's block – though we suspect any writer booking in these days would need a very generous advance indeed.

Ⓜ Lumphini exit 2) This is one of Bangkok's classiest luxury options, and, as the name suggests, the Sukhothai employs brick stupas, courtyards and antique sculptures to create a peaceful, almost temple-like atmosphere. The rooms contrast this with high-tech TVs, phones and in some cases, toilets.

MILLENNIUM HILTON HOTEL $$$
Map p280 (📞02 442 2000; www.bangkok.hilton. com; 123 Th Charoen Nakhon; incl breakfast r 4300-6200B, ste 6800-34,300B; ✱@🛜🏊; 🚤 hotel shuttle boat from Sathon/Central Pier) As soon as you enter the dramatic lobby, it's obvious that this is Bangkok's youngest, most modern riverside hotel. Rooms, all of which boast widescreen river views, carry on the theme and are decked out with funky furniture and Thai-themed photos. A glass lift and an artificial beach are just some of the fun touches.

TRIPLE TWO SILOM HOTEL $$$
Map p278 (📞02 627 2222; www.tripletwosilom. com; 222 Th Silom; incl breakfast r 3200-3500B, ste 7900B; ✱@🛜; 🚇 Chong Nonsi exit 3) A renovation has left the rooms here resembling sleek modern offices – in a good way. With all the space, huge bathrooms and inviting-looking beds, you'll be inspired to relax, not work. Guests can use the rooftop garden, but have to go next door to the sister Narai Hotel for the swimming pool and fitness centre.

W BANGKOK HOTEL $$$
Map p278 (📞02 344 4000; www.whotels. com/bangkok; 106 Th Sathon Neua/North; incl breakfast r 9000-10,350B, ste 11,250-154,350B; ✱@🛜🏊; 🚇 Chong Nonsi exit 1) A bold, brash, big-chain newbie, the W has correspondingly youngish rooms with cheeky touches (think Thai-boxing-themed furnishings) and high-tech amenities. Glitter and glass, a lobby bar and a pool that glows are some of the other touches that make this a front-runner for Bangkok's clubbiest hotel.

SHANGRI-LA HOTEL HOTEL $$$
Map p280 (📞02 236 7777; www.shangri-la.com; 89 Soi 42/1; incl breakfast r 10,000-14,100B, ste 14,800-124,800B; ✱@🏊; 🚇 Saphan Taksin exit 1) A convenient location near the BTS, generous rates, a resort-like riverside atmosphere, a huge selection of rooms (with more than 800, it's one of the city's largest hotels),

and ample activities and amenities make the Shangri-La a clever choice for families.

SOFITEL SO HOTEL $$$
Map p277 (📞02 624 0000; www.sofitel.com; 2 Th Sathon Neua/North; incl breakfast r 7750-10,700B, ste 13,200-50,000B; ✱@🛜🏊; Ⓜ Lumphini exit 2) Taking inspiration from (and featuring amazing views of) adjacent Lumphini Park, this is one of a handful of large-yet-hip name-brand hotels to open in Bangkok over the last few years. The four elements–inspired design theme has no two rooms looking quite the same, but all are spacious and stylish, contemporary and young.

ANANTARA SATHORN HOTEL $$$
Map p278 (📞02 210 9000; www.bangkok-sathorn.anantara.com; 36 Th Naradhiwas Rajanagarindra/Chong Nonsi; incl breakfast r 3900-4200B, ste 4400-9400B; ✱@🛜🏊; 🚇 Chong Nonsi exit 1) If you're the type who prefers an apartment over a hotel room, consider this branch of the Anantara chain. Deluxe rooms are spacious, come equipped with a (relatively) functional kitchenette and dining room, and share inviting facilities ranging from a pool to tennis court.

🛏 Sukhumvit

SUK 11 HOSTEL $
Map p282 (📞02 253 5927; www.suk11.com; 1/33 Soi 11, Th Sukhumvit; r incl breakfast 535-1712B; ✱@🛜; 🚇 Nana exit 3) Extremely well run and equally popular, this rustic guesthouse is an oasis of woods and greenery in the urban jungle that is Th Sukhumvit. The rooms are basic, clean and comfy, if a bit dark, while the cheapest of them share bathrooms. Although the building holds nearly 70 rooms, you'll still need to book at least two weeks ahead.

PAUSE HOSTEL HOSTEL $
Map p282 (📞02 108 8855; www.onedaybkk.com; Oneday, 51 Soi 26, Th Sukhumvit; incl breakfast dm 450-550B, r 1300-2000B; ✱@🛜; 🚇 Phrom Phong exit 4) Attached to a cafe/co-working space in this modern, open-feeling hostel. Dorms span four to eight beds, and like the private rooms (only some of which have en suite bathrooms) are united by a handsome industrial-design theme and inviting, sun-soaked communal areas.

ATLANTA
HOTEL **$**

Map p282 (☏02 252 1650; www.theatlantahotel
bangkok.com; 78 Soi 2, Th Sukhumvit; incl breakfast r 750-1050B, ste 950-1950B; ❄@☎≋;
ⓈNana exit 2) Defiantly antiquated and
equal parts frumpy and grumpy, this crumbling gem has changed very little since its
1952 construction. The opulent lobby stands
in stark contrast to the simple rooms, and
the anti-sex-tourist warnings are frantic
in tone, but the inviting pool (allegedly the
country's first hotel pool) and delightful
restaurant (for guests only) are just enough
incentive to get past these.

NAPA PLACE
HOTEL **$$**

Map p282 (☏02 661 5525; www.napaplace.com;
11/3 Soi Napha Sap 2; incl breakfast r 2200-
3100B, ste 3400-4100B; ❄@☎; ⓈThong Lo
exit 2) Hidden in the confines of a typical
Bangkok urban compound is what must be
the city's homeliest accommodation. The 12
expansive rooms have been decorated with
dark woods from the family's former lum-
ber business and light-brown cloths from
the hands of Thai weavers, while the cosy
communal areas might not be much dif-
ferent from the suburban living room you
grew up in.

S-BOX
HOTEL **$$**

Map p282 (☏02 262 0991; www.sboxhotel.com; 4
Soi 31, Th Sukhumvit; r incl breakfast 1000-2524B;
❄@☎; ⓈPhrom Phong exit 5) The name says
it all: the rooms here are little more than
boxes – albeit attractive, modern boxes with
stylish furniture and practical amenities.
The cheapest are pod-like and lack natural
light, while the more expensive have floor-
to-ceiling windows.

FUSION SUITES
HOTEL **$$**

Map p282 (☏02 665 2644; www.fusionbangkok.
com; 143/61-62 Soi 21/Asoke, Th Sukhumvit; r
incl breakfast 1700-2400B; ❄@☎; ⓜSukhum-
vit exit 1, ⓈAsok exit 1) A disproportionately
funky hotel for this price range, with un-
conventional furnishings providing the
rooms here with heaps of style, although
the cheapest can be a bit dark.

BAAN SUKHUMVIT
HOTEL **$$**

Map p282 (☏02 258 5630; www.baansukhum
vit.com; 392/38-39 Soi 20, Th Sukhumvit; r incl
breakfast 1320-1650B; ❄@☎; ⓜSukhumvit exit
1, ⓈAsok exit 1) With only 12 rooms, this hotel
exudes an approachable, cosy feel. Rooms

lack bells and whistles, but are subtly attractive; the more expensive include a bit
more space, a bathtub and a safe. There's
another branch nearby on Soi 18.

RETROASIS
HOTEL **$$**

Map p282 (☏02 665 2922; www.retroasishotel.
com; 503 Th Sukhumvit; r incl breakfast 1663-
2323B; ❄☎≋; ⓜSukhumvit exit 2, ⓈAsok exit
6) This former tryst hotel dating back to the
'60s has been converted to a fun midranger.
Bright paint and an inviting central pool
give the hotel a young, fresh vibe, while
vintage furniture and architecture serve as
reminders of its real age.

STABLE LODGE
HOTEL **$$**

Map p282 (☏02 653 0017; www.stablelodge.com;
39 Soi 8, Th Sukhumvit; r 1766-1980B; ❄☎≋;
ⓈNana exit 4) To be honest, we were slightly
disappointed that the faux-Tudor theme of
the downstairs restaurant didn't carry on
into the rooms, but could find few other
faults. Rooms are plain, but are also relatively spacious, conveniently located and
offer access to an inviting pool.

★ARIYASOMVILLA
HOTEL **$$$**

Map p282 (☏02 254 8880; www.ariyasom.com;
65 Soi 1, Th Sukhumvit; r incl breakfast 6650-
14,750B; ❄@☎≋; ⓈPhloen Chit exit 3) Lo-
cated at the end of Soi 1 behind a wall of
tropical greenery, this beautifully renovat-
ed 1940s-era villa is one of the worst-kept
accommodation secrets in Bangkok. The
24 rooms are spacious and meticulously
outfitted with thoughtful Thai design
touches and sumptuous, beautiful antique
furniture. There's also a spa and an inviting
tropical pool. Book well in advance.

Breakfast is vegetarian and served in the
villa's stunning glass-encased dining room.

SHERATON GRANDE SUKHUMVIT
HOTEL **$$$**

Map p282 (☏02 649 8888; www.sheraton
grandesukhumvit.com; 250 Th Sukhumvit; incl
breakfast r 11,000-13,800B, ste 19,00-56,000B;
❄@☎≋; ⓜSukhumvit exit 3, ⓈAsok exit 2)
A conveniently located, business-oriented
hotel that offers some of the biggest rooms
in town and fills them with a generous
spread of amenities. Guest feedback is overwhelmingly positive, and by the time you
read this, ongoing renovations will be making what was already a very good hotel an
excellent one.

MA DU ZI HOTEL $$$

Map p282 (☑02 615 6400; www.maduzihotel.
com; cnr Th Ratchadaphisek & Soi 16, Th Sukhum-
vit; incl breakfast r 7062-7651B, ste 10,593-
15,301B; ✼@☂; MSukhumvit exit 3, SAsok
exit 6) The name is Thai for 'come take a
look', somewhat of a misnomer for this
reservations-only, no-walk-ins hotel. If
you've gained access, behind the gate you'll
find a modern, sophisticated midsized
hotel steeped in dark, chic tones and de-
signs. We particularly like the immense
bathrooms, equipped with a walk-in tub
and minimalist shower.

S31 HOTEL $$$

Map p282 (☑02 260 1111; www.s31hotel.com;
545 Soi 31, Th Sukhumvit; incl breakfast r 6000-
7000B; ste 9000-10,000B; ✼☂☂; SPhrom
Phong exit 5) The bold patterns and graphics of its interior and exterior make the S31
a fun, youthful choice. Thoughtful touches
such as kitchenettes with large fridge,
super-huge beds and Thai boxing and yoga
courses prove that the style also has sub-
stance. Significant discounts can be found
online, and additional branches are on Soi
15 and Soi 33.

SPA AUBERGE EUGENIA HOTEL $$$

Map p282 (☑02 205 0111; www.facebook.
com/asiaherbassociation.eugenia; 267 Soi 31,
Th Sukhumvit; r incl breakfast 8000-12,500B;
✼@☂✛; SPhrom Phong exit 6 & taxi) Art
deco prints, worn wooden floors and an-
tique furniture spur the retro vibe at this
boutique place. As such, you won't find TVs
or tonnes of modern amenities, but the ho-
tel is linked to one of Bangkok's best spa
chains.

⌚ Greater Bangkok

SIAMAZE HOSTEL $

(☑02 693 6336; www.siamaze.com; Soi 17, Th
Ratchadaphisek; incl breakfast dm 390-490B,
r 1200-1960B; ✼@☂; MSutthisan exit 4) Si-
amaze is an unflashy, casual budget hotel
with spacious private rooms and tech-
outfitted bunk-bed dorms. The latter share
big, clean bathrooms and access to thought-
ful, convenient facilities. If you're OK with
staying away from the main tourist drag,
it's an excellent deal.

THE YARD HOSTEL $

Map p286 (☑089 677 4050; www.theyardhostel.
com; 51 Soi 5, Th Phahonyothin; incl breakfast dm
550-650B, r 1500B; ✼☂; SAri exit 1) This fun
hostel is comprised of 10 converted ship-
ping containers. Predictably, neither the
dorm nor private rooms are huge (nor great
value), but are attractive and cosy, and have
access to inviting communal areas ranging
from the eponymous lawn (which also func-
tions as a bar) to a kitchen.

REFILL NOW! HOSTEL $

(☑02 713 2044; www.refillnow.co.th; 191 Yaek
5, Soi Pridi Bhanom Yong 42, Soi 71, Th Sukhum-
vit; dm 402B, r 770-3885B; ✼@☂✛; SPhra
Khanong exit 3 & taxi) This is the kind of place
that might make you think twice about

AIRPORT ACCOMMODATION

The vast majority of visitors to Bangkok need not consider the airport hotel riga-
marole as taxis are cheap and plentiful, and early-morning traffic means the trip
shouldn't take too long. That said, those worried about a super-early departure or late
arrival may consider a stay at one of the following:

Novotel Suvarnabhumi Airport Hotel (☑02 131 1111; www.novotelairportbkk.com;
Suvarnabhumi International Airport; incl breakfast r 5613-6200B, ste 8043B; ✼@☂; SPhra
Khanong exit 3 & taxi, ⊟Suvarnabhumi Airport & hotel shuttle bus) Has 600-plus luxurious
rooms; located within the Suvarnabhumi International Airport compound.

The Cottage (☑02 727 5858; www.thecottagesuvarnabhumi.com; 888/8 Th Lad Krabang; r
incl breakfast 900-2700B; ✼@☂✛; SPhra Khanong exit 3 & taxi, ⊟Suvarnabhumi Airport
& hotel shuttle bus) Near the airport compound and within walking distance of food and
shopping is this solid midranger with airport shuttle.

Amari Airport Hotel (☑02 566 1020; www.amari.com/donmuang; 333 Th Choet Wut-
thakat; r 2190-2590B; ste 2590-3590B; ✼@☂✛; MChatuchak Park exit 2 & taxi, SMo Chit
exit 3 & taxi) Located directly opposite Don Mueang International Airport.

sleeping in a dorm. Rooms and dorms are stylishly minimalist and the latter have flirtatious pull screens between each double-bunk; women-only dorms are also available. There's an achingly hip chill-out area and, upstairs, a massage centre.

BEAT HOTEL HOTEL **$$**
(☎02 178 0077; www.beathotelbangkok.com; 69/1 Th Sukhumvit; r incl breakfast 2000-2500B; ❄@📶🏊; [S]Phra Khanong exit 3) This new, art-themed hotel has a vibrant, youthful vibe that kicks off in the lobby. The 54 rooms continue this feeling, ranging in design from those with colourful floor-to-ceiling wall art to others painted in a monochromatic bold hue. It's worth shelling out for the super-huge Deluxe rooms.

MYSTIC PLACE HOTEL **$$**
Map p286 (☎02 270 3344; www.mysticplacebkk.com; 224/5-9 Th Pradiphat; r incl breakfast 1530-1870B; ❄@📶; [S]Saphan Khwai exit 2 & taxi) This hotel unites 36 rooms, each of which is individually and playfully designed. One we checked out combined a chair upholstered with stuffed animals and walls covered with graffiti, while another was swathed in eye-contorting op art. Heaps of fun and perpetually popular, so be sure to book ahead.

BE MY GUEST BED & BREAKFAST GUESTHOUSE **$$**
Map p287 (☎02 692 4037; www.bemyguestbnb.com; 212/4 Soi 1, Soi 7, Th Ratchadaphisek; r incl breakfast 900-1400B; ❄@📶; [M]Thailand Cultural Centre exit 4 & taxi) With only four rooms and the owner living upstairs, you really are the eponymous guest at this friendly, tidy guesthouse. Rooms are neat but simple, and supplemented by user-friendly communal areas, personal service and a genuinely homey vibe. Contact in advance, both to ensure vacancy and to ask for detailed instructions on locating the place.

★**BANGKOK TREE HOUSE** HOTEL **$$$**
(☎082 995 1150; www.bangkoktreehouse.com; near Wat Bang Na Nork, Phrapradaeng; bungalow incl breakfast 6000-10,000B; ❄@📶🏊; [S]Bang Na exit 2 & taxi) Located in the lush green zone known as the Phrapradaeng Peninsula (see p166). To get to Bangkok Tree House, take the BTS to Bang Na and then a taxi for the short ride to the pier at Wat Bang Na Nork. From there, take the river-crossing ferry (4B, 5am to 9.30pm), and continue by motorcycle taxi (10B) or on foot (call ahead for directions).

The 12 multilevel bungalows here are stylishly sculpted from sustainable and recycled materials, resulting in a vibe that calls to mind a sophisticated, eco-friendly summer camp. Thoughtful amenities include private computers equipped with movies, free mobile-phone and bicycle use, and free ice cream. Significant online discounts are available.

Understand Bangkok

Bangkok Today

Bangkok is nothing if not resilient. Recent years have brought explosive protests and army curfews to Thailand's capital. But the city keeps grinding onwards. Bangkok, Thailand's seat of power since the era of direct palace rule, has taken on added prominence now that the staunchly royalist and Bangkok-centric military rules the country outright. But the city remains anxious over everyday woes, such as traffic and flooding, and harbours larger worries over the monarch's health.

Best on Film

Monrak Transistor (directed by Pen-Ek Ratanaruang; 2001) An aspiring *loôk tûng* (Thai country music) singer trades his bucolic life for one of struggle in the big city.

Nang Nak (directed by Nonzee Nimibutr; 1999) This classic Thai tale is a fascinating peek at Thai beliefs, as well as the provincial village that existed before Bangkok was taken over by concrete.

Best in Print

Sightseeing (Rattawut Lapcharoensap; 2004) Written by an American-born Thai who later moved to Bangkok, the short stories in this book provide a look at the lives of normal Thais who live in the type of suburbs and towns most visitors will never see.

Four Reigns (Kukrit Pramoj; Thai 1953, English 1981) Follows the fictional life of Phloi, a minor courtier during the Bangkok palace's last days of absolute monarchy.

Return to Authoritarian Rule

Thailand's strongman ruler, army general Prayut Chan-o-cha, has quipped that the country is '99 percent democratic' now that his junta reigns supreme. But that's not remotely true. The country is best described as a dictatorship – albeit one with a much lighter touch than North Korea's Kim dynasty.

The lives of Bangkok's workaday residents have not changed radically since the coup in 2014. The junta's soaring vows to eliminate corruption and 'return happiness' to all Thais are largely unfulfilled. The economy is stagnant. The currency has weakened. And the mysterious bombing of a heavily touristed shrine indicates that Bangkok is not immune to the threat of international terrorism. But most of the city keeps chugging along as it always has.

The junta's darker side is mostly felt by the political class: deposed officials, academics, activists and dissidents. The military government has rounded up critics for 'attitude adjustment', which translates to forcible confinement on an army base.

But 'attitude adjustment' is a dream compared to the fate of those convicted of slandering the royal family. Thailand's sentences for violations of lèse-majesté laws (insulting the throne) were already among the world's harshest. Under the junta, which projects itself as the valiant defender of the palace's eminence, they've grown even more severe.

Thailand's elderly king now requires frequent medical treatment, and his passing is almost unthinkable for reverent subjects who view him as the pinnacle of Thai society and the nation's guiding moral force. Exactly how the nation will react is unknown (and open discussion of the king's death is highly taboo), but the event will likely usher in a period of intense mourning and bring Bangkok to a halt.

Car-mageddon

Thailand is the wealthiest nation on Southeast Asia's mainland and, thanks in large part to last decade's economic boom, cars are now obtainable for lower-middle-class families. Yet, while many perceive Bangkok as a city on the go, it's often ground to a stop. Traffic, the curse of every tropical megacity, is particularly painful in Bangkok. Studies place Bangkok on global top 10 worst traffic lists, and its road fatalities are higher in only two nations: Libya and Iraq.

All those vehicles ply narrow routes laid out in the Siamese era when locals travelled around on a network of Venice-style canals. Some of those canals are still fetid channels overrun with giant lizards; others were drained, paved and turned into the thoroughfares that are now jammed with cars. Along Bangkok's main drag, Th Sukhumvit, the traffic quagmire is worsened by the city's craze for mega-malls. Glitzy shopping complexes have swallowed up much of the real estate alongside the old road. Open-air markets have been replaced with air-conditioned malls (and several malls devour more electricity per year than Thailand's poorest provinces). Mall-goers dump even more cars on badly clogged roads and, yet, the malls continue to swell in size.

Thankfully, some of the city's traffic woes should be relieved by Bangkok's growing twin rail services – the BTS (Skytrain) and MRT (Metro) – which are expanding into previously remote sections of the city.

Sinking into the Earth

All of Bangkok's glitz and grime, its glowing mall districts and drab cement slums, sit on squishy ground. Centuries ago the region was a mucky marshland. Today, that's the foundation upon which Bangkok rests – and the city is literally sinking into the earth.

Thailand's disaster specialists have long predicted the city's sinking problem. Rising sea levels are partially to blame, as are factories on the city's outskirts that suck up groundwater and hasten the massive city's descent into the ground. Experts warn that, by 2100, much of the city may be flooded and unliveable.

But far-off doomsday scenarios are overshadowed by more immediate concerns: the annual ritual of panicking over floods. Monsoons can transform Bangkok's side streets into streams. A 2011 tropical storm was among the worst in recent memory, leaving millions homeless, killing around 800 people and causing more than US$45 billion in damages.

Wracked by political turmoil, Thailand's leaders – both the junta and the elected party they ousted – have done little to prepare for the next flooding calamity. A proposed solution to the long-term sinking problem, a seawall in the Gulf of Thailand that would cost billions, remains far-fetched.

Bangkok Today was written by a Bangkok-based correspondent

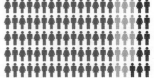

if Bangkok were 100 people

75 would be Thai
14 would be Chinese
11 would be other

belief systems
(% of population)

94 Buddhist
3 Muslim
2 Christian
1 other

population per sq km

BANGKOK THAILAND

≈ 130 people

History

Since the late 18th century, the history of Bangkok has essentially been the history of Thailand. Many of the country's defining events have unfolded here, and today the language, culture and food of the city have come to represent those of the entire country. This situation may once have seemed impossible, given the city's origins as little more than an obscure Chinese trading port, but with a population of more than 10 million, Bangkok will continue to shape Thailand's history for some time to come.

From the Beginning

King Taksin's execution was in the custom reserved for royalty – sealing him inside a velvet sack to ensure no royal blood touched the ground before beating him to death with a scented sandalwood club.

Ayuthaya & Thonburi

Before it became the capital of Siam – as Thailand was then known – in 1782, the tiny settlement known as Bang Makok was merely a backwater village opposite the larger Thonburi Si Mahasamut on the banks of Mae Nam Chao Phraya, not far from the Gulf of Siam.

Thonburi had been founded by a group of wealthy Siamese during the reign of King Chakkraphat (r 1548–68) as an important relay point for sea- and river-borne trade between the Gulf of Siam and Ayuthaya, 86km upriver. Ayuthaya served as the royal capital of Siam from 1350 to 1767, and throughout this time European powers tried without success to colonise the kingdom.

Eventually, an Asian power subdued the capital when the Burmese sacked Ayuthaya in 1767. Many Siamese were marched off to Pegu (Bago, Myanmar today), where they were forced to serve the Burmese court. However, the remaining Siamese regrouped under Phraya Taksin, a half-Chinese, half-Thai general who decided to move the capital further south along Mae Nam Chao Phraya, closer to the Gulf of Siam. Thonburi was a logical choice for the new capital.

The Chakri Dynasty & the Birth of Bangkok

Taksin eventually succumbed to mental illness and was executed, and one of his key generals, Phraya Chakri, came to power and was crowned in 1782 as Phraphutthayotfa. Fearing Thonburi to be vulnerable to Bur-

TIMELINE	1548–68	1768	1779
	Thonburi Si Mahasamut, at the time little more than a Chinese trading post on the right bank of Mae Nam Chao Phraya, is founded.	King Taksin the Great moves the Thai capital from Ayuthaya to Thonburi Si Mahasamut, a location he regarded as beneficial for both trade and defence.	After a brutal war of territorial expansion, the Emerald Buddha, Thailand's most sacred Buddha image, is brought to Bangkok from Laos, along with hundreds of Laotian slaves.

mese attack from the west, Chakri moved the Siamese capital across the river to Bang Makok (Olive Plum riverbank), named for the trees that grew there in abundance. As the first monarch of the new Chakri royal dynasty – which continues to this day – Phraya Chakri was posthumously dubbed Rama I.

The first task set before the planners of the new city was to create hallowed ground for royal palaces and Buddhist monasteries. Astrologers divined that construction of the new royal palace should begin on 6 May 1782, and ceremonies consecrated Rama I's transfer to a temporary new residence a month later.

In time, Ayuthaya's control of tribute states in Laos and western Cambodia was transferred to Bangkok, and thousands of prisoners of war were brought to the capital to work. Bangkok also had ample access to free Thai labour via the *prâi lŏoang* (commoner/noble) system, under which all commoners were required to provide labour to the state in lieu of taxes.

Using this immense pool of labour, Rama I augmented Bangkok's natural canal and river system with hundreds of artificial waterways feeding into Thailand's hydraulic lifeline, the broad Mae Nam Chao Phraya. Rama I also ordered the construction of 10km of city walls and *klorng rôrp grung* (canals around the city) to create a royal 'island' – Ko Ratanakosin – between Mae Nam Chao Phraya and the canal loop.

Temple and canal construction remained the highlight of early development in Bangkok until the reign of Rama III (King Phranangklao; r 1824–51), when attention turned to upgrading the port for international sea trade. The city soon became a regional centre for Chinese trading ships, slowly surpassing in importance even the British port at Singapore.

> Rama IV was the first monarch to show his face to the Thai public.

The Age of Politics

European Influence & the 1932 Revolution

Facing increasing pressure from British colonies in neighbouring Burma and Malaya, in 1855 Rama IV (King Mongkut; r 1851–68) signed the Bowring Treaty with Britain. This agreement marked Siam's break from exclusive economic involvement with China, a relationship that had dominated the previous century.

The signing of this document, and the subsequent ascension of Rama V (King Chulalongkorn; r 1868–1910), led to the largest period of European influence on Siam. Wishing to head off any potential invasion plans, Rama V ceded Laos and Cambodia to the French, and northern Malaya to the British between 1893 and 1910. The two European powers, for their part, were happy to use Siam as a buffer state between their respective colonial domains.

1782	1783	1785	1821
Rama I re-establishes the Siamese court across the river from Thonburi, resulting in the creation of both the current Thai capital and the Chakri dynasty.	Chinese residents of the present-day Ko Ratanakosin area are relocated upriver along Mae Nam Chao Phraya to today's Yaowarat district, resulting in the city's Chinatown.	The majority of the construction of Ko Ratanakosin, Bangkok's royal district, including famous landmarks such as the Grand Palace and Wat Phra Kaew, is finished.	A boatload of opium marks the visit of the first Western trader to Bangkok; the trade of this substance is eventually banned nearly 20 years later.

EXTENDED FAMILIES IN THAILAND'S ROYAL COURT

Until polygamy was outlawed by Rama VI (King Vajiravudh; r 1910–25), it was expected of Thai monarchs to maintain a harem consisting of numerous 'major' and 'minor' wives and the children of these relationships. This led to some truly vast families: Rama I (King Phraphutthayotfa; r 1782–1809) had 42 children by 28 mothers; Rama II (King Phraphutthaloetla Naphalai; r 1809–24), 73 children by 40 mothers; Rama III (King Phranangklao; r 1824–51), 51 children by 37 mothers (he would eventually accumulate a total of 242 wives and consorts); Rama IV (King Mongkut; r 1851–68), 82 children by 35 mothers; and Rama V (King Chulalongkorn; r 1868–1910), 77 children by 40 mothers. In the case of Rama V, his seven 'major' wives were all half-sisters or first cousins, a conscious effort to maintain the purity of the bloodline of the Chakri dynasty. Other consorts or 'minor' wives were often the daughters of families wishing to gain greater ties with the royal family.

In contrast to the precedent set by his predecessors, Rama VI had one wife and one child, a girl born only a few hours before his death. As a result, his brother, Prajadhipok, was appointed as his successor. Rama VII also had only one wife and failed to produce any heirs. After abdicating in 1935 he did not exercise his right to appoint a successor, so lines were drawn back to Rama V, and the grandson of one of his remaining 'major' wives, nine-year-old Ananda Mahidol, was chosen to be the next king.

Rama V gave Bangkok 120 new roads during his reign, inspired by street plans from Batavia (the Dutch colonial centre now known as Jakarta), Calcutta, Penang and Singapore. Germans were hired to design and build railways emanating from the capital, while the Dutch contributed the design of Bangkok's Hualamphong train station, today considered a minor masterpiece of civic Art Deco.

In 1893 Bangkok opened its first railway line, extending 22km from Bangkok to Pak Nam, where Mae Nam Chao Phraya enters the Gulf of Siam. A 20km electric tramway opened the following year, paralleling the left bank of Mae Nam Chao Phraya.

Americans established Siam's first printing press along with the kingdom's first newspaper in 1864. The first Siamese-language newspaper, *Darunovadha,* came along in 1874, and by 1900 Bangkok boasted three daily English-language newspapers: the *Bangkok Times, Siam Observer* and *Siam Free Press.*

As Bangkok prospered, many wealthy merchant families sent their children to study in Europe. Students of humbler socio-economic status who excelled at school had access to government scholarships for overseas study. In 1924 a handful of Siamese students in Paris formed the Promoters of Political Change, a group that met to discuss ideas for a future Siamese government modelled on Western democracy.

In 1861 Bangkok's European diplomats and merchants delivered a petition to Rama IV requesting roadways so they could enjoy horse riding for physical fitness and pleasure. The royal government acquiesced, and established a handful of roads suitable for horse-drawn carriages and rickshaws.

1851	1855	1868	1893
Rama IV, the fourth king of the Chakri dynasty, comes to power, courts relations with the West and encourages the study of modern science in Siam.	Bangkok, now Siam's major trading centre, begins to feel pressure from colonial influences; Rama IV signs the Bowring Treaty, which liberalises foreign trade in Siam.	At the age of 15, Chulalongkorn, the oldest son of Rama IV, becomes the fifth king of the Chakri dynasty upon the death of his father.	After a territorial dispute, France sends gunboats to threaten Bangkok, forcing Siam to give up most of its territory east of the Mekong River; Siam gains its modern boundaries.

A bloodless revolution in 1932, initiated by the Promoters of Political Change and a willing Rama VII (King Prajadhipok; r 1925–35), transformed Siam from an absolute monarchy into a constitutional one. Bangkok thus found itself the nerve centre of a vast new civil service, which, coupled with its growing success as a world port, transformed the city into a mecca for Siamese seeking economic opportunities.

Military Dictatorships

Phibul Songkhram, appointed prime minister by the People's Party in December 1938, changed the country's name from Siam to Thailand and introduced the Western solar calendar. Phibul, who in 1941 allowed Japanese regiments access to the Gulf of Thailand, resigned in 1944 under pressure from the Thai underground resistance, and was eventually exiled to Japan. Bangkok resumed its pace towards modernisation, even after Phibul returned to Thailand in 1948 and took over the leadership again via a military coup. Over the next 15 years, bridges were built over Mae Nam Chao Phraya, canals were filled in to provide space for new roads, and multistorey buildings began crowding out traditional teak structures.

In 1957 Phibul's successor General Sarit Thanarat subjected the country to a true military dictatorship: abolishing the constitution, dissolving the parliament and banning all political parties. In the 1950s, the US partnered with Sarit and subsequent military dictators, Thanom Kittikachorn and Praphat Charusathien (who controlled the country from 1964 to 1973), to allow the US military to develop bases in Thailand during the war in Vietnam in exchange for economic incentives. During this time Bangkok gained notoriety as a 'rest and recreation' (R&R) spot for foreign troops stationed in Southeast Asia.

In 1973 an opposition group of left-wing activists, mainly intellectuals and students, organised political rallies demanding a constitution from the military government. On 14 October that year the military brutally suppressed a large demonstration in Bangkok, killing 77 people and wounding more than 800. The event is commemorated by a monument on Th Ratchadamnoen Klang in Bangkok, near the Democracy Monument. King Bhumibol stepped in and refused to support further bloodshed, forcing Thanom and Praphat to leave Thailand.

In the following years, the left-oriented student movement grew more radical, creating fears among working-class and middle-class Thais of home-grown communism. In 1976 Thanom returned to Thailand (ostensibly to become a monk) and was received warmly by the royal family. In response, protesters organised demonstrations at Thammasat University against the perceived perpetrator of the 14 October

HISTORY THE AGE OF POLITICS

Water-borne traffic, supplemented by a meagre network of footpaths, dominated Bangkok well into the middle of the 19th century.

1910	1914	1917	1932
Vajiravudh becomes the sixth king of the Chakri dynasty after the death of his older brother; he fails to produce a male heir during his reign.	Don Mueang, Thailand's first international airport, officially opens. It remains the country's main domestic and international airport until the opening of Suvarnabhumi in 2006.	Bangkok's first Western-style institute of higher education, Chulalongkorn University, is founded; it's still regarded as the country's most prestigious.	A bloodless coup transforms Siam from an absolute to a constitutional monarchy; the deposed king, Rama VII, remains on the throne until he abdicates three years later.

massacre. Right-wing, anti-communist civilian groups clashed with the students, resulting in bloody violence. In the aftermath, many students and intellectuals were forced underground, and joined armed communist insurgents – known as the People's Liberation Army of Thailand (PLAT) – based in the jungles of northern and southern Thailand.

Military control of the country continued through the 1980s. The government of the 'political soldier', General Prem Tinsulanonda, enjoyed a period of political and economic stability. Prem dismantled the communist insurgency through military action and amnesty programs. But the country's new economic success presented a challenging rival: prominent business leaders who criticised the military's role in government and their now-dated Cold War mentality.

The Recent Past

It's Just Business

In 1988 Prem was replaced in elections by Chatichai Choonhavan, leader of the Chat Thai Party, who created a government dominated by well-connected provincial business people. His government shifted power away from the bureaucrats and set about transforming Thailand into an 'Asian Tiger' economy. But the business of politics was often bought and sold like a commodity and Chatichai was overthrown by the military on grounds of extreme corruption. This coup demarcated an emerging trend in Thai politics: the Bangkok business community and educated classes siding with the military against provincial business-politicians and their money politics.

In May 1992 several huge demonstrations demanding the resignation of the next in a long line of military dictators, General Suchinda Kraprayoon, rocked Bangkok and the large provincial capitals. Charismatic Bangkok governor Chamlong Srimuang, winner of the 1992 Magsaysay Award (a humanitarian service award issued in the Philippines) for his role in galvanising the public to reject Suchinda, led the protests. After confrontations between the protesters and the military near the Democracy Monument resulted in nearly 50 deaths and hundreds of injuries, Rama IX summoned both Suchinda and Chamlong for a rare public scolding. Suchinda resigned, having been in power for less than six weeks.

Bangkok approached the new millennium riding a tide of events that set new ways of governing and living in the capital. The most defining moment occurred in July 1997 when – after several months of warning signs that nearly everyone in Thailand and the international community ignored – the Thai currency fell into a deflationary tailspin

1935–46	1939	1946	1951–63
Ananda Mahidol, grandson of one of Rama V's 'major' wives, is appointed king; his reign ends abruptly when he is shot dead in his room in mysterious circumstances.	The country's name is changed from Siam to Thailand.	Pridi Phanomyong becomes Thailand's first democratically elected prime minister; after a military coup, Pridi is forced to flee Thailand, returning only briefly one more time.	Field marshal Sarit Thanarat wrests power from Phibun Songkhram, abolishes the constitution and embarks on one of the most authoritarian regimes in modern Thai history.

RAMA IX

A common backdrop in Bangkok are images of King Bhumibol Adulyadej, Thailand's longest-reigning monarch and the longest-reigning living monarch in the world. Also known in English as Rama IX (the ninth king of the Chakri dynasty), Bhumibol Adulyadej was born in 1927 in the USA, where his father, Prince Mahidol, was studying medicine at Harvard University.

Fluent in English, French, German and Thai, Bhumibol ascended the throne in 1946 following the death of his brother Rama VIII (King Ananda Mahidol; r 1935–46), who reigned for just over 11 years before dying under mysterious circumstances. An ardent jazz composer and saxophonist when he was younger, Rama IX has hosted jam sessions with the likes of jazz greats Woody Herman and Benny Goodman. His compositions are often played on Thai radio. Today, the king is predominately recognised for his extensive development projects, particularly in rural areas of Thailand. For a relatively objective English-language biography of the king's accomplishments, *King Bhumibol Adulyadej: A Life's Work* (Editions Didier Millet, 2010) is available in most Bangkok bookshops.

Rama IX and Queen Sirikit have four children: Princess Ubol Ratana (b 1951), Crown Prince Maha Vajiralongkorn (b 1952), Princess Maha Chakri Sirindhorn (b 1955) and Princess Chulabhorn (b 1957).

After more than 60 years in power, and having spent most of the last few years in hospital with very few public appearances, Rama IX is thought to be preparing for his succession. In recent years the Crown Prince has performed most of the royal ceremonies the king would normally perform, such as presiding over the Royal Ploughing Ceremony, changing the attire on the Emerald Buddha and handing out academic degrees at university commencements.

Along with nation and religion, the monarchy is very highly regarded in Thai society – negative comment about the king or any member of the royal family is a social as well as legal taboo.

and the national economy screeched to a virtual halt. The country's economy was plagued by foreign-debt burdens, an overextension in the real-estate sector and a devalued currency. Within months of the crisis, the Thai currency plunged from 25B to 56B per US$1. Bangkok, which rode at the forefront of the 1980s double-digit economic boom, suffered more than elsewhere in the country in terms of job losses and massive income erosion. The International Monetary Fund (IMF) stepped in to impose financial and legal reforms and economic liberalisation programs in exchange for more than US$17 billion to stabilise the Thai currency.

1962	1973	1981	1985
US involvement in the Indochina War leads to the economic and infrastructural expansion of Bangkok; dissatisfaction with the Thai government leads to communist insurgency.	Student protests lead to violent military suppression; 1971 coup leader Thanom Kittikachorn is exiled by Rama IX; and Kukrit Pramoj's civilian government takes charge.	General Prem Tinsulanonda is appointed prime minister after a military coup and is largely able to stabilise Thai politics over the next eight years.	Chamlong Srimuang is elected mayor of Bangkok; three years later, after forming his own largely Buddhist-based political group, the Palang Dharma Party, he is re-elected mayor.

The Rise & Fall of the Shinawatras

In January 2001, billionaire and former police colonel Thaksin Shinawatra became prime minister after winning a landslide victory in nationwide elections – the first in Thailand under the strict guidelines established in the 1997 constitution. Thaksin's new party, called Thai Rak Thai (TRT; Thais Love Thailand), swept into power on a populist agenda that seemed at odds with the man's enormous wealth and influence. Self-styled as a CEO-politician, Thaksin swiftly delivered on his campaign promises for rural development, including agrarian debt relief, village capital funds and cheap health care.

In 2011 Yingluck Shinawatra became the first female prime minister in Thai history.

Despite numerous controversies, during the February 2005 general elections Thaksin became the first Thai leader in history to be elected to a consecutive second term. His popularity among the working class and rural voters was immense. However, time was running short for Thaksin and his party. In 2006 Thaksin was accused of abusing his powers and of conflicts of interest, most notably in his family's sale of their Shin Corporation to the Singaporean government for 73 billion baht (US$1.88 billion), a tax-free gain thanks to legislation he helped craft. Demonstrations in Bangkok called for his ousting, and many of the PM's most highly placed supporters also turned against him.

On the evening of 19 September 2006, while Thaksin was attending a UN conference in New York City, the Thai military took power in a bloodless coup. Calling themselves the Council for Democratic Reform under the Constitutional Monarch, the junta cited the TRT government's alleged violations of lèse-majesté laws (royal treason), corruption, interference with state agencies and creation of social divisions as justification for the coup. Thaksin quickly flew to London, where he remained in exile until his UK visa was revoked in 2008.

In a nationwide referendum held on 19 August 2007, Thais approved a military-drafted constitution. Under the new constitution, elections were finally held in late 2007. After forming a loose coalition with several other parties, parliament chose veteran politician and close Thaksin ally Samak Sundaravej as prime minister. This was an unsatisfactory outcome to the military and the anti-Thaksin group known as the People's Alliance for Democracy (PAD), comprised of mainly urban elites nicknamed 'Yellow Shirts' because they wore yellow (the king's birthday colour). It was popularly believed that Thaksin was consolidating power during his tenure so that he could interrupt royal succession.

In September 2008, Samak Sundaravej was unseated by the Constitutional Court on a technicality: while in office, he hosted a TV cooking show deemed to be a conflict of interest. Concerned that another election would yield another Thaksin win, on 25 November hundreds

1992	1997	1999	2001
Protests led by Chamlong Srimuang against 1991 coup leader Suchinda Kraprayoon lead to violent confrontations; Suchinda resigns following a public scolding by Rama IX.	Thailand devalues the baht, triggering the Asian economic crisis; massive unemployment, personal debt and a crash of the Thai stock market follow.	The BTS (Skytrain), Bangkok's first expansive public transport system, opens in commemoration of Rama IX's 6th cycle (72nd birthday).	Thaksin Shinawatra, Thailand's richest man, is elected prime minister on a populist platform in what some have called the most open, corruption-free election in Thai history.

of armed PAD protesters stormed Bangkok's Suvarnabhumi and Don Mueang Airports, entering the passenger terminals and taking over the control towers. Thousands of additional PAD sympathisers eventually flooded Suvarnabhumi, leading to the cancellation of all flights and leaving as many as 230,000 domestic and international passengers stranded. The stand-off lasted until 2 December, when the Supreme Court wielded its power yet again in order to ban Samak's successor, Prime Minister Somchai Wongsawat, from politics and ordered his political party and two coalition parties dissolved.

In December 2008 a tenuous new coalition was formed, led by Oxford-educated Abhisit Vejjajiva, leader of the Democrat Party. Despite Abhisit being young, photogenic, articulate and allegedly untainted by corruption, his perceived association with the PAD did little to placate the United Front for Democracy against Dictatorship (UDD), a loose association of red-shirted Thaksin supporters, who by 2010 were holding large-scale protests in central Bangkok to demand that he stand down. Thailand, which had mostly experienced a relatively high level of domestic stability and harmony throughout its modern history, was now effectively polarised between the predominately middle- and upper-class, urban-based PAD and the largely working-class, rural UDD.

THAILAND'S COLOURS OF PROTEST

Most Thais are aware of the day of the week they were born, and in Thai astrology each day is associated with a particular colour. However, in the aftermath of the 2006 coup, these previously benign hues started to take on a much more political meaning.

To show their alleged support for the royal family, the anti-Thaksin People's Alliance for Democracy (PAD) adopted yellow as their uniform. This goes back to 2006, when in an effort to celebrate the 60th anniversary of Rama IX's ascension to the throne, Thais were encouraged to wear yellow, the colour associated with Monday, the king's birthday. A couple of years later, pink was added to the repertoire as a nod to a previous occasion when the king safely emerged from a lengthy hospital visit wearing a bright pink blazer.

To differentiate themselves, the pro-Thaksin United Front for Democracy against Dictatorship (UDD) began to wear red, and soon thereafter became known colloquially as the 'Red Shirts'. To add to the political rainbow, during riots in 2009, a blue-shirted faction emerged, apparently aligned with a former Thaksin ally and allegedly sponsored by the Ministry of the Interior. During the political crisis of 2010, a 'no colour' group of peace activists and a 'black shirt' faction, believed to consist of rogue elements of the Thai military, also emerged. And during the protests in 2013 and 2014, anti-government protesters ditched yellow shirts in favour of the Thai flag, the red, white and blue stripes of which were co-opted on ribbons, buttons, shirts and iPhone cases.

2004	9 June 2006	19 September 2006	August 2007
The MRT (Metro), Bangkok's first underground public transport system, is opened; an accident the next year injures 140 and causes the system to shut down for two weeks.	Thailand celebrates the 60th anniversary of Rama IX's ascension to the throne; the Thai king continues to be the longest-serving monarch in the world.	A bloodless coup sees the Thai military take power from Thaksin while he is at a UN meeting in New York; at the time of research he remains in exile.	In a nationwide referendum, voters agree to approve a military-drafted constitution, Thailand's 17th since becoming a constitutional monarchy in 1932.

THAILAND'S CONSTITUTIONAL CRISES

Since transitioning to a constitutional monarchy in 1932, Thailand has seen a staggering 18 constitutions (20 by some counts) – on average a new charter every four years, thought to be the most constitutional instability of any country.

The most lauded of Thailand's charters is the 1997 constitution. Often called the 'people's constitution', the charter fostered great hope in a population left emotionally battered by the 1997 economic crisis by guaranteeing – at least on paper – more human and civil rights than had ever been granted in Thailand. The document, which was drafted largely by elected officials and subject to public scrutiny, called for the upper and lower chambers of parliament to be fully elected by popular vote, essentially strengthening the influence of voters and the role of prime minister. It was this power to the people that paved the way for Thaksin and his well-loved Thai Rak Thai party to win just short of half of the seats of parliament in 2001, and nearly complete control of parliament in 2005.

Subsequent constitutions, largely drafted under the gaze of military regimes, have grown notably thicker (the draft constitution proposed in 2015 spanned a whopping 194 pages and 315 articles) and have moved in the opposite direction of the spirit of the 1997 charter, essentially weakening the executive branch while increasing the influence and power of the judiciary. The current interim constitution, drafted by the National Council for Peace and Order (NCPO), the military junta, includes controversial provisions that allow for an unelected prime minister, grants the military sweeping powers and enshrines its amnesty from past and future actions.

In 2015 the NCPO hand-picked a council to draft a new constitution, only to swiftly reject it, thought by many a delaying tactic to prolong their rule. The selection of a new panel, the drafting of a new charter and a proposed referendum means that Thailand's next elections aren't likely until early 2017.

In April 2010 violent clashes between police and protesters (numbering in the tens of thousands) resulted in 25 deaths. Red-shirted protesters barricaded themselves into an area stretching from Lumphini Park to the shopping district near Siam Sq, effectively shutting down parts of central Bangkok. In May the protesters were eventually dispersed by force, but not before at least 36 buildings were set alight and at least 15 people killed. Crackdown-related arson damage was estimated at US$1.5 billion, and the death toll from the 2010 conflicts amounted to nearly 100 people, making it Thailand's most deadly and costly political unrest in 20 years.

Parliamentary elections in 2011 saw the election of Yingluck Shinawatra, the younger sister of the still-exiled Thaksin. A former businesswoman, Yingluck had no prior political experience and was described by her older brother as his 'clone'. Yingluck's leadership was tested almost immediately, when in mid-2011 the outskirts of Bangkok were hit by the most devastating floods in decades. Although nearly all

November 2008	April 2010	July 2011	5 August 2011
Thousands of yellow-shirted anti-Thaksin protesters – the People's Alliance for Democracy (PAD) – take over Bangkok's airports; tourist numbers drop.	Pro-Thaksin supporters clash with troops in central Bangkok, leading to 25 deaths, several hundred injuries and the torching of several buildings.	Heavy monsoonal rains lead to floods covering much of central Thailand, including parts of Bangkok, although protective measures spare nearly all the city's central districts.	The Thai parliament approves the election of Yingluck Shinawatra, younger sister of deposed former prime minister Thaksin Shinawatra and the country's first female prime minister.

of central Bangkok was spared from flooding, it was largely perceived that this was done at the expense of upcountry regions.

Yingluck's tenure progressed relatively uneventfully until 2013, when she had to deal with the fallout from both a botched rice scheme and a proposed bill that would have granted amnesty to her brother, thus potentially allowing Thaksin to return to Thailand without facing trial for previous corruption convictions. The bill was rejected, but Yingluck's intentions were made clear. Within weeks, anti-government protesters were staging frequent rallies, eventually taking over sections of central Bangkok in early 2014. After violent clashes that led to dozens of deaths and a nullified election, in May 2014 Thailand's Constitutional Court found Yingluck and nine members of her cabinet guilty of abuse of power, forcing them to stand down.

The 2014 Coup

The military quickly filled the vacuum after Yingluck's ousting, declaring martial law on May 20, and two days later officially announcing that it had seized power of the country, carrying out Thailand's 12th successful military coup since 1932. Yingluck was subsequently impeached (thus banning her from participating in politics for five years) and at the time of research was facing criminal charges.

In August 2014 former Commander in Chief of the Royal Thai Army Prayut Chan-o-cha shed his uniform to become Thailand's prime minister – the country's 29th since 1932. To date, Prayut's rule has been heavy-handed, quickly squashing protests and incarcerating political opponents in the name of 'attitude adjustment'. Press freedom in Thailand is highly restricted and lèse-majesté-related convictions have spiked.

On 17 August, 2015, a bomb planted at Bangkok's Erawan Shrine exploded, killing 20 people, mostly Chinese tourists. At the time of research, two suspects had been arrested for the apparent act of terrorism. Their nationalities and motives remain unknown, but the incident is thought to be tied to Uighur militants, ostensibly in revenge for Thailand's forced repatriation of 109 Uighurs to China earlier in the year.

Thailand's inclusion in the ASEAN Economic Community (AEC) in 2015 could have signalled a transition towards increased involvement in the international community and potentially a leading role for Thailand. Instead it coincided with the country's most insular, undemocratic government in decades. And incidents such as the Erawan Shrine bombing prove that military rule has made Thailand no more stable nor safe, at least to the threats of international terrorism. Yet the military's iron fist and Rama IX's ailing health mean that, as of this writing, it is impossible to say how long Prayut and the National Council for Peace and Order (NCPO) will cling to power.

A mere 13 sq km in 1900, today the Bangkok Metropolitan Region (which includes Nakhon Pathom, Nonthaburi, Pathum Thani, Samut Prakan, Samut Sakhon and Thonburi) spans an astounding 7762 sq km.

October 2013 – February 2014	22 May 2014	17 August 2015	2015
Anti-goverment protesters seize key sections of Bangkok; violent incidents lead to 825 injuries and 28 deaths.	The Thai military seizes control of the country in what is Thailand's 12th coup d'état since abolishing absolute monarchy in 1932.	A bomb is set off at Erawan Shrine, killing 20. At the time of research, two suspects had been arrested for the apparent act of terrorism, although their motives were unknown.	Thailand becomes a member of the ASEAN Economic Community (AEC), an initiative to integrate the economies of 10 countries in Southeast Asia.

People & Culture

Bangkok is both utterly Thai and totally foreign. Old and new ways clash and mingle, constantly redrawing the lines of what it means to be 'Thai'. Despite the international veneer, a Thai value system – built primarily on religious and monarchical devotion – guides every aspect of life. Almost all Thais, even the most conspicuously consuming, are dedicated Buddhists aiming to be reborn into a better life by making merit (giving donations to temples or feeding monks), regarding this as the key to their earthly success.

People of Bangkok

Thailand Demographics

Population: 67.22 million

Fertility Rate: 1.4

Percentage of people over 65: 10%

Urbanisation rate: 49%

Life expectancy: 74 years

Bangkok accommodates every rung of the economic ladder, from the aristocrat to the slum dweller. It is the new start for the economic hopefuls and the last chance for the economic refugees. The lucky ones from the bottom rung – taxi drivers, food vendors, maids, nannies and even prostitutes – form the working-class backbone of the city. Many hail from the northeastern provinces and send hard-earned baht back to their families in small rural villages. At the very bottom are the dispossessed, who live in squatter communities on marginal, often polluted land. While the Thai economy has surged, a truly comprehensive social net has yet to be constructed. Meanwhile, Bangkok is also the great incubator for Thailand's new generation of young creatives, from designers to architects, and has long nurtured the archetype of the country's middle class.

The city has also represented economic opportunity for foreign immigrants. Approximately half of its population claims some Chinese ancestry, be it Cantonese, Hainanese, Hokkien or Teochew. Although the first Chinese labourers faced discrimination from the Thais, their descendants' success in business, finance and public affairs helped to elevate the status of Chinese and Thai-Chinese families.

Immigrants from South Asia also migrated to Bangkok and comprise the second-largest Asian minority. Sikhs from northern India typically make their living in tailoring, while Sinhalese, Bangladeshis, Nepalis and Pakistanis can be found in the import-export or retail trade.

The Thai Character

Much of Thailand's cultural value system is hinged upon respect for the family, religion and monarchy. Within that system each person knows his or her place, and Thai children are strictly instructed in the importance of group conformity, respecting elders and suppressing confrontational views. In most social situations, establishing harmony often takes a leading role and Thais take personal pride in making others feel at ease.

Other notable cultural characteristics include a strong belief in the concept of saving face and an equally strong regard for *sà·nùk,* Thai-style fun.

Religion

Theravada Buddhism

Around 90% of Bangkokians are Buddhists, who believe that individuals compound merit through a combination of good works, meditation and study of the *dhamma* (Buddhist philosophy).

The social and administrative centre for Thai Buddhism is the wát (temple or monastery), a walled compound containing several buildings constructed in the traditional Thai style with steep, swooping roof lines and colourful interior murals; the most important structures contain solemn Buddha statues cast in bronze.

Walk the streets of Bangkok early in the morning and you'll catch the flash of shaved heads bobbing above bright ochre robes, as monks all over the city engage in *bin·tá·bàht,* the daily house-to-house alms-food gathering. Thai men are expected to shave their heads and don monastic robes temporarily at least once in their lives.

Guardian Spirits

Animism predates the arrival of all other religions in Bangkok, and it still plays an important role in the everyday life of most city residents. Believing that *prá poom* (guardian spirits) inhabit rivers, canals, trees and other natural features, and that these spirits must be placated whenever humans trespass upon or make use of these features, the Thais build spirit shrines to house the displaced spirits. These dollhouse-like structures perch on wood or cement pillars next to their homes and receive daily offerings of rice, fruit, flowers and water.

Other Religions

Thai royal ceremony remains almost exclusively the domain of one of the most ancient religious traditions still functioning in the kingdom,

Cultural Readings

Being Dharma: The Essence of the Buddha's Teachings (2001; Ajahn Chah)

Very Thai (2013; Philip Cornwel-Smith)

Sacred Tattoos of Thailand (2011; Joe Cummings)

PEOPLE & CULTURE RELIGION

THE CHINESE INFLUENCE

In many ways Bangkok is a Chinese, as much as a Thai, city. The presence of the Chinese in Bangkok dates back to before the founding of the city, when Thonburi Si Mahasamut was little more than a Chinese trading outpost on Mae Nam Chao Phraya. In the 1780s, during the construction of the new capital under Rama I (King Phraphutthayotfa; r 1782–1809), Hokkien, Teochew and Hakka Chinese were hired as labourers. The Chinese already living in the area were relocated to the districts of Yaowarat and Sampeng, today known as Bangkok's Chinatown.

During the reign of Rama I, many Chinese began to move up in status and wealth. They controlled many of Bangkok's shops and businesses, and because of increased trading ties with China, were responsible for an immense expansion in Thailand's market economy. Visiting Europeans during the 1820s were astonished by the number of Chinese trading ships on Mae Nam Chao Phraya, and some assumed that the Chinese formed the majority of Bangkok's population.

The newfound wealth of certain Chinese trading families created one of Thailand's first elite classes that was not directly related to royalty. Known as *jôw sŏo·a*, these 'merchant lords' eventually obtained additional status by accepting official posts and royal titles, as well as offering their daughters to the royal family.

During the reign of Rama III (King Phranangklao; r 1824–51), the Thai capital began to absorb many elements of Chinese food, design, fashion and literature. This growing ubiquity of Chinese culture, coupled with the tendency of Chinese men to marry Thai women and assimilate into Thai culture, had, by the beginning of the 20th century, resulted in relatively little difference between the Chinese and their Siamese counterparts. By the turn of the 21st century, approximately half the people in Bangkok were able to lay claim to some Chinese ancestry.

WHAT'S A WÁT?

Bangkok is home to hundreds of wáts, temple compounds that have traditionally been at the centre of community life.

Buildings & Structures

Even the smallest wát will usually have a *bòht*, *wí·hăhn* and monks' living quarters.

Bòht The ordination hall, the most sacred prayer room at a wát. Aside from the fact it does not house the main Buddha image, you'll know the *bòht* because it is usually more ornately decorated and has eight cornerstones to mark its boundary.

brahng A towering phallic spire of Khmer origin serving the same religious purpose as a *chedi*.

Chedi (stupa) A large bell-shaped tower usually containing five structural elements symbolising (from bottom to top) earth, water, fire, wind and void; depending on the wát, relics of the Buddha, a Thai king or some other notable are typically housed inside.

Drum Tower Elevates the ceremonial drum beaten by novices.

Gù·đì Monks' living quarters.

Hŏr đrai The manuscript library: a structure for holding Buddhist scriptures. As these texts were previously made from palm leaves, *hŏr đrai* were typically elevated or built over water to protect them from flooding and/or termites.

Mon·dòp An open-sided, square building with four arches and a pyramidal roof, used to worship religious objects or texts.

Săh·lah (sala) A pavilion, often open-sided, for relaxation, lessons or miscellaneous activities.

Wí·hăhn (vihara) The sanctuary for the temple's main Buddha image and where lay-people come to make their offerings. Classic architecture typically has a three-tiered roof representing the triple gems: the Buddha (the teacher), Dharma (the teaching) and Sangha (the followers).

Buddha Images

Elongated earlobes, no evidence of bone or muscle, arms that reach to the knees, a third eye: these are some of the 32 characteristics, originating from 3rd-century India, that govern the depiction of the Buddha in sculpture and denote his divine nature. Other symbols to be aware of are the various hand positions and 'postures', which depict periods in the life of the Buddha.

Sitting Teaching or meditating. If the right hand is pointed towards the earth, the Buddha is subduing the demons of desire. If the hands are folded in the lap, the Buddha is meditating.

Reclining The exact moment of the Buddha's passing into *parinibbana* (post-death nirvana).

Standing Bestowing blessings or taming evil forces.

Walking The Buddha after his return to earth from heaven.

Brahmanism. White-robed, topknotted priests of Indian descent keep alive an arcane collection of rituals that, it is generally believed, must be performed at regular intervals to sustain the three pillars of Thai nationhood: sovereignty, religion and the monarchy.

Green-hued onion domes looming over rooftops belong to mosques and mark the immediate neighbourhood as Muslim, while brightly painted and ornately carved cement spires indicate a Hindu temple. Wander down congested Th Chakkaraphet in Bangkok's Phahurat district to find Gurdwara Siri Guru Singh Sabha, a Sikh temple where visitors are very welcome. A handful of steepled Christian churches, including a few historic ones, have been built over the centuries and can be found near the banks of Mae Nam Chao Phraya. In Chinatown, large round doorways topped with heavily inscribed Chinese characters and flanked by red paper lanterns mark the location of *săhn jôw,* Chinese temples dedicated to the worship of Buddhist, Taoist and Confucian deities.

Monarchy

The Thais' relationship with their king is deeply spiritual and intensely personal. All Thai kings are referred to as 'Rama', one of the incarnations of the Hindu god Vishnu, and are seen as a father figure (the king's birthday is the national celebration of Father's Day). The reigning monarch, King Bhumibol Adulyadej, also known as Rama IX, celebrated his 60th year on the throne in 2006, an event regarded by many Thais as bittersweet because the ageing king may soon leave the helm of the Thai nation. His son, Crown Prince Maha Vajiralongkorn, has been chosen to succeed him, but it is the king's daughter, Princess Maha Chakri Sirindhorn, that many Thais feel a deeper connection with because she has followed in her father's philanthropic footsteps.

It's worth mentioning that, in Thai society, not only is criticising the monarchy an extreme social faux pas, it's also illegal.

Visual Arts

Divine Inspiration

The wát served as a locus for the highest expressions of Thai art for roughly 800 years, from the Lanna to Ratanakosin eras. Accordingly, Bangkok's 400-plus Buddhist temples are brimming with the figuratively imaginative, if thematically formulaic, art of Thailand's foremost muralists. Always instructional in intent, such painted images range from the depiction of the *Jataka* (stories of the Buddha's past lives) and scenes from the Indian Hindu epic *Ramayana,* to elaborate scenes detailing daily life in Thailand.

The development of Thai religious art and architecture is broken into different periods defined by the patronage of the ruling capital. The best examples of a period's characteristics are seen in the variations of the *chedi* shape and in the features of the Buddhist sculpture, including facial features, the top flourish on the head, the dress and the position of the feet in meditation.

The Modern Era

Adapting traditional themes to the secular canvas began around the turn of the 20th century as Western influence surged in the region. In general, early contemporary Thai painting favoured abstraction over realism, and often preserved the one-dimensional perspective of traditional mural paintings. In the 1970s, Thai artists tackled the modernisation of Buddhist themes through abstract expressionism. In the 1990s, there was a push to move art out of museums and into public spaces. Today, there are two major trends in contemporary Thai art: the updating of religious themes and tongue-in-cheek social commentary. Thai sculpture is often considered to be the strongest of the contemporary arts.

Music

Classical Thai

Classical central-Thai music *(pleng tai deum)* features a dazzling array of textures and subtleties, hair-raising tempos and pastoral melodies. The classical orchestra *(ʼbèe-pâht)* can include as few as five players or might have more than 20. Leading the band is *ʼbèe,* a straight-lined woodwind instrument with a reed mouthpiece and an oboe-like tone; you'll hear it most at *moo·ay tai* (Thai boxing; also spelt *muay thai*) matches. The four-stringed *phin,* plucked like a guitar, lends subtle counterpoint, while *rá·nâht èhk,* a bamboo-keyed percussion instrument resembling the xylophone, carries the main melodies. The slender *sor,* a bowed instrument with a coconut-shell soundbox, provides soaring embellishments, as does the *klòo·i,* a wooden Thai flute.

Lôok Tûng & Mŏr Lam

Popular Thai music has borrowed much from Western music, particularly in instrumentation, but retains a distinct flavour of its own. The bestselling of all modern musical genres in Thailand remains *lôok tûng.* Literally 'children of the fields', *lôok tûng* dates back to the 1940s, is comparable to country and western in the USA, and tends to appeal most to working-class Thais. Subject matter almost always concerns tales of lost love, tragic early death and the dire circumstances of farmers who work day in and day out and still owe money to the bank.

Another genre more firmly rooted in northeastern Thailand, and nearly as popular in Bangkok, is *mŏr lam.* Based on the songs played on the Lao-Isan *kaan,* a reed instrument devised of a double row of bamboo-like reeds fitted into a hardwood soundbox, *mŏr lam* features a simple but insistent bass beat and plaintive vocal melodies.

In recent years, *lôok tûng* and *mŏr lam* from the 1960s and '70s have seen a resurgence of popularity in Thailand and have also garnered a cult following abroad, largely aided by successful retro compilations.

Songs for Life

The 1970s ushered in a new music style inspired by the politically conscious folk rock of the US and Europe, which the Thais dubbed *pleng pêu·a chee·wít* (literally 'music for life') after Marxist Jit Phumisak's earlier Art for Life movement. Closely identified with the Thai band Caravan – who still perform – the introduction of this style was the most significant musical shift in Thailand since *lôok tûng* arose in the 1940s.

Pleng pêu·a chee·wít has political and environmental topics rather than the usual love themes. During the authoritarian dictatorships of the '70s many of Caravan's songs were banned. Following the massacre of student demonstrators in 1976, some members of the band fled to the hills to take up with armed communist groups.

T-Pop & Indie

For nearly three decades, Thailand has had a thriving teen-pop industry – sometimes referred to as T-Pop – centred on artists chosen for their good looks, and then matched with syrupy song arrangements. Thongchai 'Bird' McIntyre, who released his first album in 1986, is arguably the king of this genre. In the 1990s, labels such as GMM Grammy and RS Productions released a flood of T-pop copycat acts, often emulating Western-style boy bands or Japanese or Taiwanese musical trends. The current crop of Thai pop stars can be seen imitating the signature dance moves of Korean pop stars (Japan pop, or J-pop, is out).

In the 1990s an alternative pop scene – known as *glorng sěh·ree* ('free drum'); also *pleng dâi din* ('underground music') – grew in Bangkok. Moderndog, a Britpop-inspired band of four Chulalongkorn University graduates, is generally credited with bringing independent Thai music into the mainstream, and their success prompted an explosion of similar bands and indie recording labels. Although some of the influential indie labels have been bought out by bigger conglomerates, today the alt scene lives on in a variety of other forms – lounge pop, garage rock and electronica.

Cinema

When it comes to Thai cinema, there are usually two concurrent streams: movies that are financially successful and those that are considered cinematically meritorious. Only occasionally do these overlap.

Bangkok Film launched Thailand's film industry with the first Thai-directed silent movie, *Chok Sorng Chan,* in 1927. Perhaps partially influenced by India's famed masala movies – which enjoyed a strong following in post-WWII Bangkok – early Thai films blended romance, comedy, melodrama and adventure to give audiences a little bit of everything. Popular Thai cinema ballooned in the 1960s and '70s, especially when the government levied a tax on Hollywood imports, which spawned a home-grown industry.

However, the Thai movie industry almost died during the '80s and '90s, swamped by Hollywood extravaganzas and the boom era's taste for anything imported. From a 1970s peak of about 200 releases per year, by 1997 the Thai output shrank to an average of only 10 films a year. The Southeast Asian economic crisis that year threatened to further bludgeon the ailing industry, but the lack of funding coupled with foreign competition brought about a new emphasis on quality rather than quantity.

Thai cinema graduated into international film circles in the late 1990s and early 2000s, with directors like Apichatpong Weerasethakul earning accolades from critics, including at Cannes. Film-fest fare has been bolstered by independent film clubs and self-promotion through social media. This is how low-budget filmmakers are bypassing the big studios, the censors (who are ever-vigilant) and the controversy-averse movie theatres. At the same time, Thailand's big studios continue to put out ghost stories, horror flicks, sappy love stories and camp comedies. Popular and elaborate historical movies serve a dual purpose: making money and promoting national identity.

Thai Movies

Nang Nak (1999; Nonzee Nimibutr)

Ong Bak (2003; Prachya Pinkaew)

Uncle Boonmee Who Can Recall His Past Lives (2010; Apichatpong Weerasethakul)

PEOPLE & CULTURE CINEMA

Traditional Theatre & Dance

Kŏhn

Scenes performed in traditional *kŏhn* (and *lá·kon* performances) – a dance drama formerly reserved for court performances – come from the 'epic journey' tale of the *Ramakian* (the Thai version of the Hindu epic, the *Ramayana*), with parallels in the Greek Odyssey and the myth of Jason and the Argonauts. In all *kŏhn* performances, four types of characters are represented – male humans, female humans, monkeys and demons. Monkey and demon figures are always masked with the elaborate head coverings often seen in tourist promo material. Behind the masks and make-up, all actors are male. Traditional *kŏhn* is very expensive to produce – Ravana's retinue alone (Ravana is the *Ramakian's* principal villain) consists of more than 100 demons, each with a distinctive mask.

Lá·kon

The more formal *lá·kon nai* (inner *lá·kon,* which means that it is performed inside the palace) was originally performed for lower nobility by all-female ensembles. Today it's a dying art, even more so than royal *kŏhn*. In addition to scenes from the *Ramakian, lá·kon nai* performances may include traditional Thai folk tales; whatever the story, the text is always sung. *Lá·kon nôrk* (outer *lá·kon,* performed outside the palace) deals exclusively with folk tales and features a mix of sung and spoken text, sometimes with improvisation. Male and female performers are permitted. Like *kŏhn* and *lá·kon nai,* performances of *lá·kon nôrk* are increasingly rare.

Translations of Thai short stories and novels can be downloaded as e-books at www.thaifiction.com.

BANGKOK FICTION

Visitors to virtually any of Bangkok's English-language bookshops will notice an abundance of novels with titles such as *Confessions of a Bangkok Private Eye, Even Thai Girls Cry, Fast Eddie's Lucky 7 A Go Go, Lady of Pattaya, The Go Go Dancer Who Stole My Viagra, My Name Lon You Like Me?, The Pole Dancer* and *Thai Touch.* Welcome to the Bangkok school of fiction, a genre defined by its obsession with crime, exoticism and Thai women.

The birth of this genre can be traced back to Jack Reynolds' 1956 novel, *A Woman of Bangkok.* Recently reprinted, it continues to be an influence for many Bangkok-based writers, and Reynolds' formula of Western-man-meets-beautiful-but-dangerous-Thai-woman – occasionally spiced up with some crime – is a staple of the modern genre.

Standouts include John Burdett's *Bangkok 8* (2003), a page-turner in which Sonchai Jitpleecheep, a half-Thai, half-*fa·ràng* (Westerner) police detective investigates the python-and-cobras murder of a US marine in Bangkok. Along the way we're treated to vivid portraits of Bangkok's gritty nightlife and insights into Thai Buddhism. The book's five sequels have sold well internationally.

Christopher G Moore, a Canadian and longtime resident of Bangkok, has authored more than 20 mostly Bangkok-based crime novels to positive praise both in Thailand and abroad. His description of Bangkok's sleazy Thermae Coffee House (called 'Zeno' in *A Killing Smile*) is the closest literature comes to evoking the perpetual male adolescence to which such places cater.

Private Dancer, by English thriller author Stephen Leather, is another classic example of Bangkok fiction, despite having only been available via download until recently.

Jake Needham's 1999 thriller *The Big Mango* has tongue-in-cheek references to the Bangkok bar-girl scene and later became the first expat novel to be translated into Thai.

A variation on *lá·kon* that has evolved specifically for shrine worship, *lá·kon gâa bon* involves an ensemble of about 20, including musicians. At an important shrine such as Bangkok's Lak Meuang, four troupes may alternate, each for a week at a time, as each performance lasts from 9am to 3pm and there is usually a long list of worshippers waiting to hire them.

Lí·gair

In outlying working-class neighbourhoods of Bangkok you may be lucky enough to come across the gaudy, raucous *lí·gair*. This theatrical art form is thought to have descended from drama-rituals brought to southern Thailand by Arab and Malay traders. The first native public performance in central Thailand came about when a group of Thai Muslims staged *lí·gair* for Rama V in Bangkok during the funeral commemoration of Queen Sunantha. *Lí·gair* grew very popular under Rama VI, peaked in the early 20th century and has been fading slowly since the 1960s.

Lá·kon Lék

A form of Thai puppet theatre, *hùn grà·bòrk* (cylinder puppets), is based on popular Hainanese puppet shows. It uses 30cm hand puppets carved from wood and viewed only from the waist up.

Lá·kon lék (little theatre; also known as *hùn lõo·ang*, or royal puppets), like *kõhn*, was once reserved for court performances. Metre-high marionettes made of *kòi* paper and wire, wearing elaborate costumes, were used to convey similar themes, music and dance movements.

Two or three puppet masters were required to manipulate each *hùn lõo·ang* – including arms, legs, hands, even fingers and eyes – by means of wires attached to long poles. Stories were drawn from Thai folk tales, particularly *Phra Aphaimani* (a classical Thai literary work), and occasionally from the *Ramakian*. Surviving examples of a smaller, 30cm court version called *hùn lék* (little puppets) are occasionally used in live performances; only one puppeteer is required for each marionette in *hùn lék*.

Eating in Thailand

There's a universe of amazing dishes once you get beyond 'pad Thai' and green curry, and for many travellers food is one of the main reasons for visiting Thailand. Even more remarkable, however, is the love for Thai food among locals: Thais become just as excited with a bowl of well-prepared noodles at a renowned hawker stall as tourists do. This unabashed enthusiasm for eating, not to mention an abundance of fascinating ingredients and influences, has generated one of the most fun and diverse food scenes in the world.

How Thais Eat

Aside from the occasional indulgence in deep-fried savouries, most Thais sustain themselves on a varied and relatively healthy diet of fruits, rice and vegetables mixed with smaller amounts of animal protein and fat. Satisfaction seems to come not from eating large amounts of food at any one meal, but rather from nibbling at a variety of dishes with as many different flavours as possible throughout the day.

Nor are certain kinds of food restricted to certain times of day. Practically anything can be eaten first thing in the morning, whether it's sweet, salty or chilli-ridden. *Kôw gaang* (curry over rice) is a very popular breakfast, as are *kôw nĕe·o mŏo tôrt* (deep-fried pork with sticky rice) and *kôw man gài* (sliced chicken served over rice cooked in chicken broth). Lighter morning choices, especially for Thais of Chinese descent, include *ʉ̌ah·tôrng·gŏh* (deep-fried fingers of dough) dipped in warm *nám đow·hôo* (soy milk). Thais also eat noodles, whether fried or in soup, with great gusto in the morning, or as a substantial snack at any time of the day or night.

As the staple with which almost all Thai dishes are eaten (noodles are still seen as a Chinese import), *kôw* (rice) is considered an indispensable part of the daily diet. Most Bangkok families will put on a pot of rice, or start the rice cooker, just after rising in the morning to prepare a base for the day's menu.

Finding its way into almost every meal is *ʉ̌lah* (fish), even if it's only in the form of *nám ʉ̌lah* (a thin amber sauce made from fermented anchovies; see p227), which is used to salt Thai dishes, much as soy sauce is used in eastern Asia. Pork is undoubtedly the preferred protein, with chicken in second place. Beef is seldom eaten in Bangkok, particularly by Thais of Chinese descent who subscribe to a Buddhist teaching that forbids eating 'large' animals.

Thais are prodigious consumers of fruit. Vendors push glass-and-wood carts filled with a rainbow of fresh sliced papaya, pineapple, watermelon and mango, and a more muted palette of salt-pickled or candied seasonal fruits. These are usually served in a small plastic bag with a thin bamboo stick to use as an eating utensil.

Because many restaurants in Thailand are able to serve dishes at an only slightly higher price than they would cost to make at home, Thais dine out far more often than their Western counterparts. Dining with others is always preferred because it means everyone has a chance to

Appon's Thai Food (www. khiewchanta. com) features nearly 1000 authentic and well-organised Thai recipes – many with helpful audio recordings of their Thai names – written by a Thai.

sample several dishes. When forced to fly solo by circumstances – such as during lunch breaks at work – a single diner usually sticks to one-plate dishes such as fried rice or curry over rice.

The Four Flavours

Simply put, sweet, sour, salty and spicy are the parameters that define Thai food, and although many associate the cuisine with spiciness, virtually every dish is an exercise in balancing these four tastes. This balance might be obtained by a squeeze of lime juice, a spoonful of sugar and a glug of fish sauce, or a tablespoon of fermented soybeans and a splash of vinegar. Bitter also factors into many Thai dishes, and often comes from the addition of a vegetable or herb. Regardless of the source, the goal is the same: a favourable balance of four clear, vibrant flavours.

Staples & Specialities

Rice & Noodles

In Thailand, to eat is to eat rice, and for most of the country, a meal is not acceptable without this staple. Thailand maintains the world's fifth-largest amount of land dedicated to growing rice, an industry that employs more than half the country's arable land and a significant portion of its population. Rice is so central to Thai food culture that the most common term for 'eat' is *gin kôw* (literally, 'consume rice') and one of the most common greetings is *Gin kôw rĕu yang?* (Have you consumed rice yet?)

There are many varieties of rice in Thailand and the country has been among the world leaders in rice exports since the 1960s. The highest grade is *kôw hŏrm má·lí* (jasmine rice), a fragrant long grain that is so coveted by neighbouring countries that there is allegedly a steady underground business in smuggling out fresh supplies. The grain is customarily served alongside main dishes such as curries, stir-fries or soups, which are lumped together as *gàp kôw* (with rice). When you order plain rice in a restaurant you use the term *kôw blòw* ('plain rice') or *kôw sŏo·ay* ('beautiful rice'). Residents of Thailand's north and northeast eat *kôw nĕe·o*, 'sticky rice', a glutinous short-grained rice that is cooked by steaming, not boiling. And in Chinese-style eateries, *kôw đôm,* 'boiled rice', a watery porridge sometimes employing brown or purple rice, is a common carb.

For the scoop on Thai noodles and noodle dishes, see p32.

Curries & Soups

In Thai, *gaang* (it sounds somewhat similar to the English 'gang') is often translated as 'curry', but it actually describes any dish with a lot of liquid and can thus refer to soups (such as *gaang jèut*) as well as the classic chilli-paste-based curries for which Thai cuisine is famous. The preparation of the latter begins with a *krêu·ang gaang,* created by mashing, pounding and grinding an array of fresh ingredients with a stone mortar and pestle to form an aromatic, extremely pungent-tasting and rather thick paste. Typical ingredients in a *krêu·ang gaang* include dried chilli, galangal, lemongrass, kaffir lime zest, shallots, garlic, shrimp paste and salt.

Another food celebrity that falls into the soupy category is *đôm yam,* the famous Thai spicy-and-sour soup. Fuelling the fire beneath *đôm yam's* often velvety surface are fresh *prík kêe nŏo* (tiny chillies) or half a teaspoonful of *nám prík pŏw* (roasted chilli paste). Lemongrass, kaffir lime leaf and lime juice give *đôm yam* its characteristic tang.

Lonely Planet's *From the Source – Thailand* features authentic recipes from across the country, plus background information on the dishes and the regions they come from.

Thailand is the world's second-largest exporter of rice, and in 2014 exported approximately 10.8 million tonnes of the grain.

Stir-Fries & Deep-Fries

The simplest dishes in the Thai culinary repertoire are the various *pàt* (stir-fries) introduced to Thailand by the Chinese, who are world famous for being able to stir-fry a whole banquet in a single wok.

The list of *pàt* dishes seems endless. Many cling to their Chinese roots, such as the common *pàt pàk bûng fai daang* (morning glory flash-fried with garlic and chilli), while some are Thai-Chinese hybrids, such as *pàt pèt* (literally 'spicy stir-fry'), in which the main ingredients, typically meat or fish, are quickly stir-fried with red curry paste.

Tôrt (deep-frying in oil) is mainly reserved for snacks such as *glôo·ay tôrt* (deep-fried bananas) or *ʰò·ʰée·a* (egg rolls). An exception is *ʰlah tôrt* (deep-fried fish), which is a common way to prepare fish.

Thai Food by David Thompson is widely considered the most authoritative English-language book on Thai cooking. Thompson's follow up to the book, *Thai Street Food*, focuses on less-formal street cuisine.

EATING IN THAILAND STAPLES & SPECIALITIES

Hot & Tangy Salads

Standing right alongside curries in terms of Thai-ness is the ubiquitous *yam,* a hot and tangy 'salad' typically based around seafood, meat or vegetables.

Lime juice provides the tang, while the abundant use of chilli generates the heat. Most *yam* are served at room temperature or just slightly warmed by any cooked ingredients. The dish functions equally well as part of a meal, or on its own as *gàp glâam,* snack food to accompany a night of boozing.

Nám Prík

Although they're more home than restaurant food, *nám prík,* spicy chilli-based 'dips' are, for the locals at least, among the most emblematic of all Thai dishes. Typically eaten with rice and steamed or fresh vegetables and herbs, they're also among the most regional of Thai dishes, and you could probably pinpoint the province you're in by simply looking at the *nám prík* on offer.

Fruits

Being a tropical country, Thailand excels in the fruit department. *Má·môo·ang* (mangoes) alone come in a dozen varieties that are eaten at different stages of ripeness. Other common fruit include *sàp·ʰà·rót* (pineapple), *má·lá·gor* (papaya) and *daang moh* (watermelon), all of which are sold from vendor carts and accompanied by a dipping mix of salt, sugar and ground chilli.

A highlight of visiting Thailand is sampling the huge variety of fruit you probably never knew existed. Many are available year-round

SOMETHING'S FISHY

Westerners might scoff at the all-too-literal name of this condiment, but for much of Thai cooking, fish sauce is more than just another ingredient – it is *the* ingredient.

Essentially the liquid extracted from salted fish, *nám ʰlah,* as it's known in Thai, is one of the most common seasonings in the Thai kitchen, and takes various guises depending on the region. In northeastern Thailand, discerning diners prefer a thick, pasty mash of fermented freshwater fish and sometimes rice. Where people have access to the sea, fish sauce takes the form of a thin, amber liquid extracted from salted anchovies – much like with olive oil, the first extraction is considered the finest. In both cases the result has an admittedly pungent nose, but is generally salty, rather than fishy, in taste. Indeed, *prík nám ʰlah,* a tiny bowl of fish sauce, often supplemented with thinly sliced chillies and garlic – an item found on just about every restaurant table in Thailand – can be considered the Thai equivalent of the salt shaker.

nowadays, but April and May is peak season for several of the most beloved varieties, including durian, mangoes and mangosteen.

Following are some of the fruits available in Thailand:

Custard apple Known in Thai as *nóy nàh,* the knobbly green skin of this fruit conceals hard black seeds and sweet, gloopy flesh with a granular texture.

Durian Known in Thai as *tú·ree·an,* the king of fruit is also Thailand's most infamous, due to its intense flavour and odour, which can suggest everything from custard to onions.

Guava A native of South America, *fa·ràng* is a green, apple-like ball containing a pink or white flesh that's sweet and crispy.

Jackfruit The gigantic green pod of *kà·nŭn* – it's considered the world's largest fruit – conceals dozens of waxy yellow sections that taste like a blend of pineapple and bananas (it reminds us of Juicy Fruit chewing gum).

Langsat Strip away the yellowish peel of this fruit, known in Thai as *long·gong,* to find a segmented, perfumed pearlescent flesh with a lychee-like flavour.

Longan *Lam yai* takes the form of a tiny hard ball; it's like a mini-lychee with sweet, perfumed flesh. Peel it, eat the flesh and spit out the hard seed.

Lychee The pink skin of *lín·jèe* conceals an addictive translucent flesh similar in flavour to a grape; it's generally only available between April and June.

Mangosteen The hard purple shell of *mang·kút,* the queen of Thai fruit, conceals delightfully fragrant white segments, some containing a hard seed.

Pomelo Like a grapefruit on steroids, *sôm oh* takes the form of a thick pithy green skin hiding sweet, tangy segments; cut into the skin, peel off the pith and then break open the segments and munch on the flesh inside.

Rambutan People have different theories about what *ngó* look like, not all repeatable in polite company. Regardless, the hairy shell contains sweet translucent flesh that you scrape off the seed with your teeth.

Rose apple Known in Thai as *chom·pôo,* rose apple is an elongated pink or red fruit with a smooth, shiny skin and pale, watery flesh; a good thirst quencher on a hot day.

Salak Also known as snake fruit because of its scaly skin, the exterior of *sàlà* looks like a mutant strawberry and the soft flesh tastes like unripe bananas.

Starfruit The star-shaped cross-section of *má·feu·ang* is the giveaway; the yellow flesh is sweet and tangy and believed by many to lower blood pressure.

Sweets

English-language Thai menus often have a section called 'Desserts', but Thai-style sweets are generally consumed as breakfast or a sweet snack, not directly following a meal. Sweets also take two slightly different forms in Thailand. *Kŏrng wăhn,* which translates as 'sweet things', are small, rich sweets that often boast a slightly salty flavour. Prime ingredients for *kŏrng wăhn* include grated coconut, coconut milk, rice flour (from white rice or sticky rice), cooked sticky rice, tapioca, mung-bean starch, boiled taro and various fruits. Egg yolks are a popular ingredient for many *kŏrng wăhn,* including the ubiquitous *fŏy torng* (literally 'golden threads'), probably influenced by Portuguese desserts and pastries introduced during the early Ayuthaya era.

Thai sweets roughly similar to the European concept of pastries are called *kà·nŏm.* Probably the most popular type of *kà·nŏm* in Thailand are the bite-sized items wrapped in banana leaves, especially *kôw đôm gà·tí* and *kôw đôm mát.* Both consist of sticky rice grains steamed with *gà·tí* (coconut milk) inside a banana-leaf wrapper to form a solid, almost taffy-like, mass.

Maintained by a Thai woman living in the US, She Simmers (www.shesimmers.com) is an excellent source of recipes for those making Thai food outside Thailand.

Bangkok's Top 50 Street Food Stalls by Chawadee Nualkhair also functions well as a general introduction and guide to Thai-style informal dining.

(CON)FUSION CUISINE

A popular dish at restaurants across Thailand is *kôw pàt à·me·rí·gan,* 'American fried rice'. Taking the form of rice fried with ketchup, raisins and peas, sides of ham and deep-fried hot dogs, and topped with a fried egg, the dish is, well, every bit as revolting as it sounds. But at least there's an interesting history behind it: American fried rice allegedly dates back to the Vietnam War era, when thousands of US troops were based in northeastern Thailand. A local cook is said to have taken the 'American Breakfast' (also known as ABF: fried eggs with ham and/or hot dogs, and white bread, typically eaten with ketchup) and made it 'Thai' by frying the various elements with rice.

This culinary cross-pollination is only one example of the tendency of Thai cooks to pick and choose from the variety of cuisines at their disposal. Other (significantly more palatable) examples include *gaang mát·sà·màn,* 'Muslim curry', a classic blend of Thai and Middle Eastern cooking styles, and the famous *pàt tai,* essentially a blend of Chinese cooking methods and ingredients (frying, rice noodles) with Thai flavours (fish sauce, chilli, tamarind).

Drinks
Coffee, Tea & Fruit Drinks

Thais are big coffee drinkers, and good-quality arabica and robusta are cultivated in the hilly areas of northern and southern Thailand. The traditional filtering system is nothing more than a narrow cloth bag attached to a steel handle. This type of coffee is served in a glass, mixed with sugar and sweetened with condensed milk – if you don't want either, be sure to specify *gah·faa dam* (black coffee) followed with *mâi sài nám·đahn* (without sugar).

Black tea, both local and imported, is available at the same places that serve real coffee. *Chah tai,* Thai-style tea, derives its characteristic orange-red colour from ground tamarind seed added after curing.

Fruit drinks appear all over Thailand and are an excellent way to rehydrate after water becomes unpalatable. Most *nám pŏn·lá·mái* (fruit juices) are served with a touch of sugar and salt and a whole lot of ice. Many foreigners object to the salt, but it serves a metabolic role in helping the body to cope with tropical temperatures.

Beer & Spirits

There are several brands of beer in Thailand, ranging from domestic brands (Singha, Chang, Leo) to foreign-licensed labels (Heineken, Asahi, San Miguel). They are all largely indistinguishable in terms of taste and quality.

Domestic rice whisky and rum are favourites of the working class, struggling students and at family gatherings as they're more affordable than beer. Once spending money becomes a priority, Thais often upgrade to imported whiskies. These are usually drunk with lots of ice, soda water and a splash of Coke. On a night out, buying a whole bottle is the norm in most of Thailand. If you don't finish it, it will simply be kept at the bar for your next visit.

Vegetarians & Vegans

Vegetarianism isn't a widespread trend in Thailand, but many of the tourist-oriented restaurants cater to vegetarians, and there are also a handful of *ráhn ah·hăhn mang·sà·wí·rát* (vegetarian restaurants) in Bangkok where the food is served buffet-style and is very inexpensive.

The downloadable *Vegetarian Thai Food Guide* (www.eating thaifood.com/vegetarian-thai-food-guide) is a handy resource for vegetarians visiting Thailand.

Pok Pok, by Andy Ricker with JJ Goode, features recipes for the rustic, regional Thai dishes served at Ricker's eponymous Portland, Oregon, New York City and Los Angeles restaurants.

Dishes are almost always 100% vegan (ie no meat, poultry, fish or fish sauce, dairy or egg products).

During the Vegetarian Festival, celebrated by Chinese Buddhists in September/October, many restaurants and street stalls in Bangkok go meatless for one month.

The phrase 'I'm vegetarian' in Thai is *pŏm gin jair* (for men) or *dì·chăn gin jair* (for women). Loosely translated this means 'I eat only vegetarian food', which includes no eggs and no dairy products – in other words, total vegan.

Habits & Customs

Like most of Thai culture, eating conventions appear relaxed and informal but are orchestrated by many implicit rules.

Whether at home or in a restaurant, Thai meals are always served 'family-style', that is, from common serving platters, and the plates appear in whatever order the kitchen can prepare them. When serving yourself from a common platter, put no more than one spoonful onto your plate at a time. Heaping your plate with all 'your' portions at once will look greedy to Thais unfamiliar with Western conventions. Another important factor in a Thai meal is achieving a balance of flavours and textures. Traditionally, the party orders a curry, a steamed or fried fish, a stir-fried vegetable dish and a soup, taking great care to balance cool and hot, sour and sweet, salty and plain.

Originally Thai food was eaten with the fingers, and it still is in certain regions of the kingdom. In the early 1900s, Thais began setting their tables with fork and spoon to affect a 'royal' setting, and it wasn't long before fork-and-spoon dining became the norm in Bangkok and later spread throughout the kingdom. To use these tools the Thai way, use a serving spoon, or your own, to take a single mouthful-size of food from a central dish, and ladle it over a portion of your rice. The fork is then used to push the now food-soaked portion of rice back onto the spoon before entering the mouth.

If you're not offered chopsticks, don't ask for them. Chopsticks are reserved for eating Chinese-style food from bowls, or for eating in all-Chinese restaurants. In either case you will be supplied with chopsticks without having to ask. Unlike their counterparts in many Western countries, restaurateurs in Thailand won't assume you don't know how to use them.

The Sex Industry in Thailand

Thailand has had a long and complex relationship with prostitution that persists today. It is also an international sex tourism destination, a designation that began around the time of the Vietnam War. The industry targeted to foreigners is very visible, with multiple red-light districts in Bangkok alone, but there is also a more clandestine domestic sex industry and myriad informal channels of sex-for-hire.

An Illegal & Vast Industry

Prostitution is technically illegal in Thailand. However, anti-prostitution laws are often ambiguous and unenforced. Some analysts have argued that the high demand for sexual services in Thailand limits the likelihood of the industry being curtailed; however, limiting abusive practices within the industry is the goal of many activists and government agencies.

It is difficult to determine the number of sex workers in Thailand, the demographics of the industry or its economic significance. This is because there are many indirect forms of prostitution, the illegality of the industry makes research difficult, and different organisations use varying approaches to collect data. In 2003, measures to legalise prostitution cited the Thai sex industry as being worth US$4.3 billion (about 3% of GDP), and employing roughly 200,000 sex workers. A study conducted in 2003 by Thailand's Chulalongkorn University estimated 2.8 million sex workers, of which 1.98 million were adult women, 20,000 were adult men and 800,000 were children (defined as any person under the age of 18). A 2007 report compiled by the Institute for Population and Social Research at Mahidol University estimated that there are between 200,000 and 300,000 active female sex workers in Thailand at any given time.

The Coalition Against Trafficking in Women (CATW; www.catwinternational.org) is an NGO that works internationally to combat prostitution and trafficking of women and children.

History & Cultural Attitudes

Prostitution has been widespread in Thailand since long before the country gained a reputation among international sex tourists. Throughout Thai history the practice was accepted and common among many sectors of society, though it has not always been respected by society as a whole.

Due to international pressure from the UN, prostitution was declared illegal in 1960, though entertainment places (go-go bars, beer bars, massage parlours, karaoke bars and bathhouses) are governed by a separate law passed in 1966. These establishments are licensed and can legally provide nonsexual services (such as dancing, massage, a drinking buddy); sexual services occur through these venues, but they are not technically the businesses' primary purpose.

With the arrival of the US military in Southeast Asia during the Vietnam War era, enterprising forces adapted the existing framework to suit foreigners, in turn creating an international sex tourism industry

PROS & CONS

Women's rights groups take oppositional approaches to the question of prostitution. Abolitionists see prostitution as exploitation and an infraction of basic human rights. Meanwhile, mitigators recognise that there is demand and supply, and try to reduce the risks associated with the activity through HIV/AIDS prevention and education programs (especially for economic migrants). Sex-worker organisations argue that prostitution is a legitimate job and the best way to help women is to treat the issue from a workers' rights perspective, demanding fair pay and compensation, legal redress and mandatory sick and vacation time. Also, according to pro-sex-worker unions, the country's quasi-legal commercial sex establishments provide service-industry jobs (dishwashers, cooks, cleaners) to non-sex-worker staff who would otherwise qualify for employment protection if the employer were a restaurant or a hotel.

that persists today. Indeed, this foreigner-oriented sex industry is still a prominent part of Thailand's tourist economy.

In 1998 the International Labour Organization, a UN agency, advised Southeast Asian countries, including Thailand, to recognise prostitution as an economic sector and income generator. It is estimated that one third of the entertainment establishments are registered with the government and the majority pay an informal tax in the form of police bribes.

Economic Motivations

Regardless of their background, most women in the sex industry are there for financial reasons: many find that sex work is one of the highest-paying jobs for their level of education, and they have financial obligations (be it dependents or debts). The most comprehensive data on the economics of sex workers comes from a 1993 survey by Kritaya Archavanitkul. The report found that sex workers made a mean income of 17,000B per month (US$18 per day), the equivalent of a mid-level civil-servant job, a position acquired with advanced education and family connections. At the time of the study, most sex workers did not have a high-school degree.

The International Labour Organization estimates a Thai sex workers' salary at 270B (US$9) a day, the average wage of a Thai service-industry worker. These economic factors provide a strong incentive for rural, unskilled women (and to a lesser extent, men) to engage in sex work.

As with many workers in Thai society, a large percentage of sex workers' wages are remitted back to their home villages to support their families (parents, siblings and children). Kritaya's 1993 report found that between 1800B and 6100B per month was sent back home to rural communities. The remittance-receiving households typically bought durable goods (TVs and washing machines), bigger houses and motorcycles or automobiles. Their wealth displayed their daughters' success in the industry and acted as a free advertisement for the next generation of sex workers.

Working Conditions

The unintended consequence of prostitution prohibition is the lawless working environment it creates for women who enter the industry. Sex work becomes the domain of criminal networks that are often involved in other illicit activities and circumvent the laws through bribes and violence.

Sex workers are not afforded the rights of other workers: there is no minimum wage; no required vacation pay, sick leave or break time; no deductions for social security or employee-sponsored health insurance; and no legal redress.

Bars can set their own punitive rules that fine a worker if she doesn't smile enough, arrives late or doesn't meet the drink quota. Empower, an NGO that fights for safe and fair standards in the sex industry, reported that most sex workers will owe money to the bar at the end of the month through these deductions. In effect, the women have to pay to be prostitutes and the fines disguise a pimp relationship.

Through lobbying efforts, groups such as Empower hope that lawmakers will recognise all workers at entertainment places (including dishwashers and cooks as well as 'working girls') as employees subject to labour and safety protections.

Other commentators, such as the Coalition Against Trafficking in Women (CATW), argue that legalising prostitution is not the answer, because such a move would legitimise a practice that is always going to

> Help stop child-sex tourism by reporting suspicious behaviour on a dedicated hotline (⌨1300), or by reporting perpetrators directly to the embassy of their home country.

THE SEX INDUSTRY IN THAILAND WORKING CONDITIONS

DR WIWAT, MR CONDOM & THE PREVENTION OF HIV/AIDS

In Thailand in 1990, there were approximately 100,000 new cases of HIV. In the three years that followed, that number leapt to an estimated one million. A progressive-minded regional bureaucrat, Dr Wiwat Rojanapithayakorn, noted that the vast majority of these cases were among sex workers, and kick-started a local campaign to encourage the use of condoms. This was a herculean task, as not only did most Thai men at the time eschew condoms, but the central government essentially did not acknowledge the existence of Thailand's sex industry. So collaborating with local authorities and venue owners, Dr Wiwat distributed free condoms and established a 'no condom, no sex' policy among sex venues that, within months, caused transmission rates to plummet dramatically.

Given his success and the immense threat that HIV/AIDS posed to Thailand in the early 1990s, Dr Wiwat proposed implementing his initiative on a national scale. The government enlisted the help of a charismatic family-planning advocate known colloquially as Mr Condom, Mechai Viravaidya. By 1993, the government budget for anti-AIDS programs was increased nearly twentyfold, and a massive anti-AIDS public awareness campaign was launched, with frequent messages broadcast on TV and radio, and free condoms distributed nationwide. In less than three years, condoms were essentially de-stigmatised in Thailand, and their use among sex workers went from an estimated 25% to more than 90%; indeed, for a while, condoms were known as *mechai* in Thai. Between 1991 and 2001 new transmissions of HIV in Thailand dropped from 143,000 per year to fewer than 14,000, and Thailand's methods in tackling the problem became a model for other countries, both in the region and elsewhere.

Thailand's campaign continues to be successful today. According to the Joint United Nations Programme on HIV/AIDS (UNAIDS), in 2000 there were an estimated 683,841 people in Thailand living with HIV; by 2014 this number had dropped to an estimated 445,504, and during the same period, new transmissions of HIV plummeted by approximately 75%. Likewise, during the same period, the rate of HIV infection among female sex workers in Thailand continued to drop, and in 2014 was at an estimated 1.1%.

Indeed, some feel that Thailand's anti-HIV/AIDS campaign has been too successful, in effect leading Thais to believe that the disease no longer poses a risk and that they don't need to protect themselves. A UNAIDS report from 2010 estimates that only 50% of venue-based sex workers had undergone an HIV test in the last year, and after an alarming spike around 2005, Thailand's rate of HIV infection among men who have sex with men remains relatively high at an estimated 9.2%, according to a 2014 report compiled by the same agency.

be dangerous and exploitative for the women involved. Instead, these groups focus on how to enable the women to leave prostitution and make their way into different types of work.

Child Prostitution & Human Trafficking

Organisations working across borders to stop child prostitution include Ecpat (End Child Prostitution & Trafficking; www. ecpat.net) and its Australian affiliate Child Wise (www.childwise. org.au).

Urban job centres such as Bangkok have large populations of displaced and marginalised people (immigrants from Myanmar, ethnic hill-tribe members and impoverished rural Thais). Children of these fractured families often turn to street begging, which is a pathway to prostitution, often through low-level criminal gangs. According to a report released by Ecpat (End Child Prostitution & Trafficking), in 2007 there were an estimated 60,000 children involved in prostitution in Thailand.

In 1996, Thailand passed a reform law to address the issue of child prostitution (defined in two tiers: 15 to 18 years old and under 15). Fines and jail time are assigned to customers, establishment owners and even parents involved in child prostitution (under the old law only prostitutes were culpable). Many countries also have extraterritorial legislation that allows nationals to be prosecuted in their own country for such crimes committed in Thailand.

Thailand is also a conduit and destination for people trafficking (including children) from Myanmar, Laos, Cambodia and China. As stated by the UN, human trafficking is a crime against humanity and involves recruiting, transporting, harbouring and receiving a person through force, fraud or coercion for purposes of exploitation. In 2015, the US State Department labelled Thailand as a Tier 3 country, meaning that it does not comply with the minimum standards for prevention of human trafficking, and is not making significant efforts to do so.

Survival Guide

Transport

ARRIVING IN BANGKOK

Most travellers will arrive in Bangkok via air, but for those entering the city on ground transport, or who have plans to move onward, following is a summary of the city's major transport hubs.

Flights, cars and tours can be booked online at lonely planet.com.

Suvarnabhumi International Airport

Located 30km east of central Bangkok, **Suvarnabhumi International Airport** (☏02 132 1888; www.suvarna bhumiairport.com) began commercial international and domestic service in 2006. The airport's name is pronounced *sù·wan·ná·poom*, and it inherited the airport code (BKK) previously held by the old airport at Don Mueang. The airport website has real-time details of arrivals and departures.

Train

The **Airport Rail Link** (☏call centre 1690; www.srtet. co.th) connects Suvarnabhumi International Airport with the BTS (Skytrain) stop at Phaya Thai (45B, 30 minutes, from 6am to midnight) and the MRT (Metro) stop at Phetchaburi (45B, 25 minutes, from 6am to midnight).

Taxi

➡ Metered taxis are available kerbside at Floor 1 – ignore the 'official airport taxi' touts who approach you inside the terminal.

➡ Typical metered fares from Suvarnabhumi include 200B to 250B to Th Sukhumvit; 250B to 300B to Th Khao San; and 400B to Mo Chit. Toll charges (paid by passengers) vary between 25B and 70B. Note that there's also a 50B surcharge added to all fares departing from the airport, payable directly to the driver.

Bus & Minivan

➡ A public transport centre is 3km from the airport and includes a bus terminal with buses to a handful of provinces and inner-city-bound buses and minivans. A free airport shuttle connects the transport centre with the passenger terminals.

➡ Bus lines that city-bound tourists are likely to use include line 551 to BTS Victory Monument station (40B, frequent from 5am to 10pm) and 552 to BTS On Nut (20B, frequent from 5am to 10pm). From these points, you can continue by public transport or taxi to your hotel.

Don Mueang International Airport

Bangkok's other airport, **Don Mueang International Airport** (☏02 535 1253; www. donmueangairportthai.com), 25km north of central Bangkok, was retired from service in 2006 only to reopen later as the city's de facto budget hub.

Bus

➡ From outside the arrivals hall, there are two airport bus lines from Don Mueang: A1 makes a stop at BTS Mo Chit (30B, frequent from 7.30am to 11.30pm); while the less frequent A2 makes stops at BTS Mo Chit and BTS Victory Monument (30B, every 30 minutes from 7.30am to 11.30pm).

➡ Public buses stop on the highway in front of the airport. Useful lines include 29, with a stop at Victory Monument BTS station before terminating at Hualamphong Train Station (24 hours); line 59, with a stop near Th Khao San (24 hours); and line 538, stopping at Victory Monument BTS station (4am to 10pm); fares are about 23B.

Taxi

As at Suvarnabhumi, public taxis leave from outside the arrivals hall and there is a

50B airport charge added to the meter fare.

Train

The walkway that crosses from the airport to the Amari Airport Hotel also provides access to Don Muang Train Station, which has trains to Hualamphong Train Station every one to 1½ hours from 4am to 11.30am and then roughly every hour from 2pm to 9.30pm (from 5B to 10B).

Eastern Bus Terminal

Eastern Bus Terminal (Map p282; ☎02 391 2504; Soi 40, Th Sukhumvit; [S]Ekkamai exit 2) The departure point for buses to Pattaya, Rayong, Chanthaburi and other points east, except for the border crossing at Aranya Prathet. Most people call it *sà·tăh·nee èk·gà·mai* (Ekamai station).

BTS

The Eastern Bus Terminal is a brief walk to Ekkamai BTS station, from where it's easy to connect to other points in Bangkok.

Northern & Northeastern Bus Terminal

Northern & Northeastern Bus Terminal (Mo Chit; ☎northeastern routes 02 936 2852, ext 602/605, northern routes 02 936 2841, ext 325/614; Th Kamphaeng Phet; [M]Kamphaeng Phet exit 1 & taxi, [S]Mo Chit exit 3 & taxi) Located just north of Chatuchak Park, this hectic bus station is also commonly called *kŏn sòng mŏr chít* (Mo Chit station) – not to be confused with Mo Chit BTS station. Buses depart from here for all northern and northeastern destinations, as well as international destinations including Pakse (Laos), Phnom Penh (Cambodia), Siem Reap (Cambodia) and Vientiane (Laos).

BTS

The Northern & Northeastern Bus terminal is a short taxi or motorcycle taxi ride from the BTS station at Mo Chit, from where it's easy to connect to other points in Bangkok.

MRT

The terminal is a short taxi or motorcycle taxi ride from the MRT station at Chatuchak Park.

Southern Bus Terminal

Southern Bus Terminal (Sai Tai Mai; ☎02 422 4444, call centre 1490; Th Boromaratchachonanee) The city's southern bus terminal, commonly called *săi đâi mài,* lies a long way west of the centre of Bangkok. Besides serving as the departure point for all buses south of Bangkok, transport to Kanchanaburi and western Thailand also departs from here.

Bus

From the Southern Bus Terminal, buses 79, 159, 201 and 516 connect to Th Ratchadamnoen Klang (near Th Khao San), and bus 40 connects to the Victory Monument, from where there's a BTS stop.

Minivan

A frequent minivan runs between the Southern Bus Terminal and Bangkok's Victory Monument, where there's a BTS stop.

Taxi

There's a taxi stall at the terminal; a trip into central Bangkok will cost around 120B.

Hualamphong Train Station

Hualamphong (☎02 220 4334, call centre 1690; www.railway.co.th; off Th Phra Ram IV; [M]Hua Lamphong exit 2) The city's main train terminus. It's advisable to ignore all touts here and avoid the travel agencies. Call or check the website to get destination timetable and price information.

MRT

Hualamphong Train Station is connected to the MRT (Metro) system, through which it's easy to access other parts of Bangkok.

CLIMATE CHANGE & TRAVEL

Every form of transport that relies on carbon-based fuel generates CO_2, the main cause of human-induced climate change. Modern travel is dependent on aeroplanes, which might use less fuel per kilometre per person than most cars but travel much greater distances. The altitude at which aircraft emit gases (including CO_2) and particles also contributes to their climate change impact. Many websites offer 'carbon calculators' that allow people to estimate the carbon emissions generated by their journey and, for those who wish to do so, to offset the impact of the greenhouse gases emitted with contributions to portfolios of climate-friendly initiatives throughout the world. Lonely Planet offsets the carbon footprint of all staff and author travel.

GETTING AROUND BANGKOK

Bangkok may seem chaotic and impenetrable at first, but its transport system is gradually improving, and although you'll almost certainly find yourself stuck in traffic at some point, the jams aren't as legendary as they used to be. For most of the day and night, Bangkok's 70,000 clean and dirt-cheap taxis are the most expedient choice – although it's important to note that Bangkok traffic is nothing if not unpredictable. During rush hour, the BTS, MRT, river ferries and *klorng* (canal, also spelt *khlong*) ferries are much wiser options. Locals and many local expats swear by the ubiquitous motorcycle taxis, but the accidents we've seen suggest that they're not really worth the risk.

BTS & MRT

➡ The elevated **BTS** (☎02 617 6000, tourist information 02 617 7341; www.bts.co.th), also known as the Skytrain (*rót fai fáa*), whisks you through 'new' Bangkok (Silom, Sukhumvit and Siam Sq). The interchange between the two lines is at Siam station, and trains run frequently from 6am to 11.45pm. Fares range from 15B to 52B, or 140B for a one-day pass. Most ticket machines only accept coins, but change is available at the information booths.

➡ Bangkok's **MRT** (☎02 354 2000; www.bangkokmetro. co.th) or Metro is most helpful for people staying in the Sukhumvit or Silom area to reach the train station at Hualamphong. Fares cost from 16B to 42B, or 120B for a one-day pass. The trains run frequently from 6am to midnight.

Taxi

➡ Although many first-time visitors are hesitant to use them, in general, Bangkok's taxis are new and spacious and the drivers are courteous and helpful, making them an excellent way to get around.

➡ All taxis are required to use their meters, which start at 35B, and fares to most places within central Bangkok cost 60B to 90B. Freeway tolls – 25B to 70B depending on where you start – must be paid by the passenger.

➡ **Taxi Radio** (☎1681; www. taxiradio.co.th) and other 24-hour 'phone-a-cab' services are available for 20B above the metered fare.

➡ If you leave something in a taxi your best chance of getting it back (still pretty slim) is to call ☎1644.

BANGKOK ADDRESSES

➡ Any city as large and unplanned as Bangkok can be tough to get around. Street names often seem unpronounceable, compounded by the inconsistency of romanised Thai spellings. For example, the street sometimes spelt as 'Rajdamri' is actually pronounced 'Ratchadamri' (with the appropriate tones, of course), or in abbreviated form as Rat damri. The 'v' in Sukhumvit should be pronounced like a 'w'. One of the most popular locations for foreign embassies is known both as Wireless Rd and Th Witthayu (*wí·tá·yú* is Thai for 'radio').

➡ Many street addresses show a string of numbers divided by slashes and hyphens, for example, 48/3-5 Soi 1, Th Sukhumvit. The reason is that undeveloped property in Bangkok was originally bought and sold in lots. The number before the slash refers to the original lot number. The numbers following the slash indicate buildings (or entrances to buildings) constructed within that lot. The pre-slash numbers appear in the order in which they were added to city plans, while the post-slash numbers are arbitrarily assigned by developers. As a result numbers along a given street don't always run consecutively.

➡ The Thai word *tà·nŏn* (usually spelt 'thanon') means road, street or avenue. Hence Ratchadamnoen Rd (sometimes referred to as Ratchadamnoen Ave) is always called Thanon (Th) Ratchadamnoen in Thai.

➡ A soi is a small street or lane that runs off a larger street. In our example, the address referred to as '48/3-5 Soi 1, Th Sukhumvit' will be located off Th Sukhumvit on Soi 1. Alternative ways of writing the same address include 48/3-5 Th Sukhumvit Soi 1, or even just 48/3-5 Sukhumvit 1. Some Bangkok soi have become so large that they can be referred to both as thanon and soi, eg Soi Sarasin/Th Sarasin and Soi Asoke/Th Asoke. Smaller than a soi is a *tròrk* (usually spelt 'trok') or alley. Well-known alleys in Bangkok include Chinatown's Trok Itsaranuphap and Banglamphu's Trok Rong Mai.

Taxi Alternatives

App-based alternatives to the traditional taxis that operate in Bangkok include the following:

→ **All Thai Taxi** (www.allthaitaxi.com)

→ **Easy Taxi** (www.easytaxi.com/th)

→ **GrabTaxi** (www.grabtaxi.com/bangkok-thailand)

→ **Uber** (www.uber.com/cities/bangkok)

Boat

River Ferries

→ The **Chao Phraya Express Boat** (☎02 623 6001; www.chaophrayaexpressboat.com) operates the main ferry service along Mae Nam Chao Phraya. The central pier is known as Tha Sathon, Saphan Taksin or sometimes Central Pier, and connects to the BTS at Saphan Taksin station.

→ Boats run from 6am to 8pm. Buy tickets (10B to 40B) at the pier or on board; hold on to your ticket as proof of purchase (an occasional formality).

→ The most common boats are the orange-flagged express boats. These run between Wat Rajsingkorn, south of Bangkok, to Nonthaburi, in the north, stopping at most major piers (15B, frequent from 6am to 7pm).

→ A blue-flagged tourist boat (40B, every 30 minutes from 9.30am to 5pm) runs from Sathon/Central Pier to Phra Athit/Banglamphu Pier, with stops at eight major sightseeing piers and a barely comprehensible English-language commentary. Vendors at Sathon/Central Pier tout a 150B all-day pass, but unless you plan on doing a lot of boat travel, it's not great value.

→ There are also dozens of cross-river ferries, which charge 3B and run every few minutes until late at night.

→ Private long-tail boats can be hired for sightseeing trips at Phra Athit/Banglamphu Pier, Chang Pier, Tien Pier and Oriental Pier.

Klorng Boats

→ Canal taxi boats run along Khlong Saen Saep (Banglamphu to Ramkhamhaeng) and are an easy way to get between Banglamphu and Jim Thompson House, the Siam Sq shopping centres (get off at Sapan Hua Chang Pier for both), and other points further east along Th Sukhumvit – after a mandatory change of boat at Pratunam Pier.

→ These boats are mostly used by daily commuters and pull into the piers for just a few seconds – jump straight on or you'll be left behind.

→ Fares range from 9B to 19B and boats run from 5.30am to 7.15pm from Mondays to Fridays, from 6am to 6.30pm on Saturdays, and from 6am to 6pm on Sundays.

Motorcycle Taxis

→ Motorcycle taxis (known as *motorsai*) serve two purposes in Bangkok.

→ Most commonly and popularly they form an integral part of the public transport network, running from the corner of a main thoroughfare, such as Th Sukhumvit, to the far ends of sois that run off that thoroughfare. Riders wear coloured, numbered vests and gather at either end of their soi, usually charging 10B to 20B for the trip (without a helmet unless you ask).

→ Their other purpose is as a means of beating the traffic. You tell your rider where you want to go, negotiate a price (from 20B for a short trip up to about 150B going across town), strap on the helmet (they will insist for longer trips) and say a prayer to whichever god you're into.

→ For more info, see p119.

Túk-Túk

→ Bangkok's iconic túk-túk (pronounced *dúk dúk;* a type of motorised rickshaw) are used

EXTENDING BANGKOK'S PUBLIC TRANSPORT

Weighing in at less than a paltry 50km of track, Bangkok's public transport network (the MRT and BTS) is admittedly a lightweight. Yes, it has much of 'downtown' Bangkok covered, but other than two relatively new BTS extensions east and west, it doesn't provide much help to those bound for the city's 'burbs. However, at the time of research, work was well underway on some significant extensions to both the MRT and BTS systems.

The MRT's 'blue line' and 'purple line' extensions will see the system pierce far-western Bangkok, east of Mae Nam Chao Phraya in Thonburi and northwest to Nonthaburi. Perhaps most beneficially, for tourists at least, the extensions will include much-needed stops in Ko Ratanakosin. The 'purple line' extension from Bang Sue northwest to Bang Yai is set to be the first to open in 2016. When finished, both extensions will essentially double the length of the current network, ultimately making it into a loop.

Similarly, the BTS is being extended in an easterly direction, from Bearing to Samut Prakan, set to be finished around 2017, as well as north from Mo Chit, set to be completed by 2019.

by Thais for short hops not worth paying the taxi flag fall for. For foreigners, however, these emphysema-inducing machines are part of the Bangkok experience, so despite the fact that they overcharge outrageously and you can't see anything due to the low roof, pretty much everyone takes a túk-túk at least once.

➡ It's worth knowing, however, that túk-túk are notorious for taking 'detours' to commission-paying gem and silk shops and massage parlours. En route to 'special' temples, you'll meet 'helpful' locals who will steer you to even more rip-off opportunities. Ignore anyone offering too-good-to-be-true 20B trips.

➡ Most túk-túk drivers ask too much from tourists (expat *fa·ràng* never use them). Expect to be quoted a 100B fare, if not more, for even the shortest trip. Try bargaining them down to about 60B for a short trip, preferably at night when the pollution (hopefully) won't be quite so bad. Once you've tried it, you'll find taxis are cheaper, cleaner, cooler and quieter.

Car

➡ For short-term visitors, you will find parking and driving a car in Bangkok more trouble

than it is worth. If you need private transport, consider hiring a car and driver through your hotel or hire a taxi driver that you find trustworthy. One reputable operator is **Julie Taxi** (☏091 098 4553, 081 846 2014; www.facebook.com/TourWithJulieTaxi), which offers a variety of vehicles and excellent service.

➡ But if you still want to give it a go, all the big car-hire companies have offices in Bangkok. Rates start around 1000B per day for a small car. A passport plus a valid licence from your home country (with English translation if necessary) or an International Driving Permit are required for all rentals.

➡ Reliable car-hire companies include the following, all of which also have counters at Suvarnabhumi and Don Mueang International Airports:

Avis (Map p277; ☏02 251 1131; www.avisthailand.com; 40 Th Sathon Neua/North; ⊙8am-6pm; ⓂLumphini exit 2)

Budget (Map p287; ☏02 203 9294; www.budget.co.th; 19/23 Bldg A, RCA/Royal City Ave; ⊙8am-7pm; ⓂPhra Ram 9 exit 3 & taxi)

Thai Rent A Car (Map p282; ☏02 737 8888; www.thairentacar.com; 2371 Th Phetchaburi Tat Mai;

⊙8.30am-5.30am Mon-Sat; ⓈThong Lo exit 3 & taxi)

Bus

➡ Bangkok's public buses are run by the **Bangkok Mass Transit Authority** (☏02 246 0973, call centre 1348; www.bmta.co.th).

➡ As the routes are not always clear, and with taxis being such a good deal, you'd really have to be pinching pennies to rely on buses as a way to get around.

➡ However, if you're determined, air-con bus fares range from 10B to 23B, and fares for fan-cooled buses start at 6.50B.

➡ Most of the bus lines run between 5am and 10pm or 11pm, except for the 'all-night' buses, which run from 3am or 4am to mid-morning.

➡ You'll most likely require the help of thinknet's *Bangkok Bus Guide*.

Bicycle

See p52 for details on getting around Bangkok by bicycle.

TOURS

See p51 for Bangkok's walking, biking, guided and river tours.

Directory A–Z

Customs Regulations

➡ White-uniformed customs officers prohibit the import or export of the usual array of goods – porn, weapons, drugs. If you're caught with drugs in particular, expect life never to be the same again. The usual 200 cigarettes or 250g of to-bacco are allowed in without duty, along with up to 1L of wine or spirits.

➡ For customs details, check out www.customs.go.th.

➡ Licences are required for exporting religious images and other antiquities (see p45).

Embassies

Australian Embassy (Map p277; ☑02 344 6300; www. thailand.embassy.gov.au; 37 Th Sathon Tai/South, Bangkok; ◑8.30am-4.30pm Mon-Fri; ⓜLumphini exit 2)

Cambodian Embassy (☑02 957 5851; 518/4 Th Pra-cha Uthit/Soi Ramkhamhaeng 39, Bangkok; ◑9am-noon Mon-Fri; ⓜPhra Ram 9 exit 3 & taxi)

Canadian Embassy (Map p277; ☑02 646 4300; www. thailand.gc.ca; 15th fl, Abdul-rahim Pl, 990 Th Phra Ram IV, Bangkok; ◑7.30am-12.15pm & 1-4.15pm Mon-Thu, to 1pm Fri; ⓜSi Lom exit 2, ⓢSala Daeng exit 4)

French Embassy (Map p280; ☑02 657 5100; www. ambafrance-th.org; 35 Soi 36, Th Charoen Krung, Bangkok; ◑8.30am-noon Mon-Fri; ⓔOriental Pier)

German Embassy (Map p277; ☑02 287 9000; www. bangkok.diplo.de; 9 Th Sathon Tai/South, Bangkok; ◑8.30-11.30am Mon-Fri; ⓜLumphini exit 2)

Irish Embassy (Map p274; ☑02 632 6720; www.ireland inthailand.com; 12th fl, 208 Th Witthayu/Wireless Rd, Bangkok; ◑8.30am-12.30pm Mon-Fri; ⓢPhloen Chit exit 1)

Laotian Embassy (☑02 539 6667; www.laoembassy bkk.gov.la/index.php/en; 502/1-3 Soi Sahakarnpramoon, Th Pracha Uthit/Soi Ramkham-haeng 39, Bangkok; ◑8am-noon & 1-4pm Mon-Fri; ⓜPhra Ram 9 exit 3 & taxi)

Malaysian Embassy (Map p277; ☑02 629 6800; www. kln.gov.my/web/tha_bangkok/ home; 33-35 Th Sathon Tai/ South, Bangkok; ◑8am-4pm Mon-Fri; ⓜLumphini exit 2)

Electricity

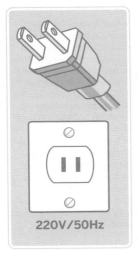

220V/50Hz

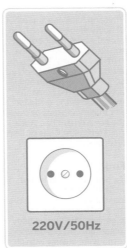

220V/50Hz

Myanmar Embassy (Map p278; ☎02 233 7250; www.myanmarembassybkk.com; 132 Th Sathon Neua/North, Bangkok; ⏲9am-noon & 1-3pm Mon-Fri; [S]Surasak exit 3)

Netherlands Embassy (Map p274; ☎02 309 5200; http://thailand.nlembassy.org; 15 Soi Ton Son, Bangkok; ⏲8.30-11.30am Mon-Thu; [S]Chit Lom exit 4)

New Zealand Embassy (Map p274; ☎02 254 2530; www.nzembassy.com/thailand; 14th fl, M Thai Tower, All Seasons Pl, 87 Th Witthayu/Wireless Rd, Bangkok; ⏲8am-noon & 1-2.30pm Mon-Fri; [S]Phloen Chit exit 5)

UK Embassy (Map p274; ☎02 305 8333; www.gov.uk/government/world/organisations/british-embassy-bangkok; 14 Th Witthayu/Wireless Rd, Bangkok; ⏲8am-4.30pm Mon-Thu, to 1pm Fri; [S]Phloen Chit exit 5)

US Embassy (Map p274; ☎02 205 4000; http://bangkok.usembassy.gov; 120-122 Th Witthayu/Wireless Rd, Bangkok; ⏲7am-4pm Mon-Fri; [S]Phloen Chit exit 5)

Emergencies

Police (☎191) The police contact number functions as the de facto universal emergency number in Thailand, and can also be used to call an ambulance or report a fire.

Tourist Police (☎24hr hotline 1155) The best way to deal with most problems requiring police (usually a rip-off or theft) is to contact the tourist police, who are used to dealing with foreigners and can be very helpful in cases of arrest. The English-speaking unit investigates criminal activity involving tourists and can act as a bilingual liaison with the regular police. Although they typically have no jurisdiction over the kinds of cases handled by regular cops, they should be able to help with translation, contacting your embassy and/or arranging a police report you can take to your insurer.

Health

While urban horror stories can make a trip to Bangkok seem frighteningly dangerous, few travellers experience anything more than an upset stomach and the resulting clenched-cheek waddles to the bathroom. If you do have a problem, Bangkok has some very good hospitals.

Air Pollution

Bangkok has a bad reputation for air pollution, and on bad days the combination of heat, dust and motor fumes can be a powerful brew of potentially toxic air.

The good news is that more efficient vehicles (and fewer of them thanks to the BTS/Skytrain and MRT/Metro) and less industrial pollution mean Bangkok's skies are much cleaner than they used to be.

Flu

Thailand has seen a number of nasty influenza strains in recent years, most notably the bird (H5N1) and swine (H1N1) varieties. That said, it's no worse than any other country in the region and is probably better prepared than most of the world for any major outbreak because the government has stockpiled tens of millions of Tamiflu doses.

Food

If a place looks clean and well run and the vendor also looks clean and healthy, then the food is probably safe. In general, the food in busy restaurants is cooked and eaten quite quickly with little standing around, and is probably not reheated. The same applies to street stalls.

For more on Bangkok's food, see the Eating chapter (p26). For an overview of Thailand's cuisine, see the Eating in Thailand chapter (p225).

Heat

➡ By the standards of most visitors Bangkok is somewhere between hot and seriously (expletive) hot all year round. Usually that will mean nothing more than sweat-soaked clothing, discomfort and excessive tiredness. However, heat exhaustion is not uncommon, and dehydration is the main contributor.

➡ Heat exhaustion symptoms include feeling weak, headache, irritability, nausea or vomiting, sweaty skin, a fast, weak pulse and a normal or slightly elevated body temperature.

➡ Treatment involves getting out of the heat and/or sun and cooling the victim down by fanning and applying cool, wet cloths to the skin, laying the victim flat with their legs raised and rehydrating with electrolyte drinks or water containing a quarter teaspoon of salt per litre.

➡ Heatstroke is more serious and requires more urgent action. Symptoms come on suddenly and include weakness, nausea, a hot, dry body with a temperature of more than 41°C, dizziness, confusion, loss of coordination, seizures and, eventually, collapse and loss of consciousness.

➡ Seek medical help for heatstroke and begin cooling by getting the victim out of the heat, removing their clothes, fanning them and applying cool, wet cloths or ice to their body, especially to the groin and armpits.

HIV & AIDS

➡ In Thailand, most cases of HIV transmission occur through sexual activity, and the remainder through natal transmission or intravenous drug use.

➡ HIV/AIDS can also be spread through infected blood transfusions, although this risk is virtually nil in Thailand due to rigorous blood-screening procedures.

➡ If you want to be pierced or tattooed, be sure to check that the needles are new.

Water & Ice

➡ Don't drink tap water, but do remember that all water served in restaurants or to guests in offices or homes in Bangkok comes from purified sources. It's not necessary to ask for bottled water in these places unless you prefer it.

➡ Ice is generally produced from purified water under hygienic conditions and is therefore theoretically safe.

Internet Access

➡ The ubiquity of smartphones has meant that internet cafes are an almost extinct species in Bangkok, although you can still find a couple in touristy areas such as Th Khao San.

➡ A convenient place to take care of your communication needs in the centre of Bangkok is the **TrueMove Shop** (Map p274; www.truemove.com; Soi 2, Siam Sq; 🕒7am-10pm; [S]Siam exit 4). It has high-speed internet computers equipped with Skype, sells phones and mobile subscriptions, and can also provide information on city-wide wi-fi access for computers and phones.

➡ Wi-fi, mostly free of charge, is ubiquitous in Bangkok these days, especially in mall-based cafes and restaurants.

Legal Matters

➡ Thailand's police don't enjoy a squeaky clean reputation, but as a foreigner, and especially a tourist, you probably won't have much to do with them. While some expats will talk of being targeted for fines while driving, most anecdotal evidence suggests Thai police will usually go out of their way not to arrest a foreigner breaking minor laws.

➡ Most Thai police view drug-takers as a social scourge and consequently see it as their duty to enforce the letter of the law; for others it's an opportunity to make untaxed income via bribes. Which direction they'll go often depends on drug quantities; small-time offenders are sometimes offered the chance to pay their way out of an arrest, while traffickers usually go to jail.

➡ Smoking is banned in all indoor spaces, including bars and pubs. The ban extends to open-air public spaces, which means lighting up outside a shopping centre, in particular, might earn you a polite request to butt out. If you throw your cigarette butt on the ground, however, you could then be hit with a hefty littering fine.

➡ If you are arrested for any offence, police will allow you to make a phone call to your embassy or consulate if you have one, or to a friend or relative. There's a whole set of legal codes governing the length of time and manner in which you can be detained before being charged or put on trial. Police have a lot of discretion and are more likely to bend these codes in your favour than the reverse. However, as with police worldwide, if you don't show respect you will only make matters worse, so keep a cool head.

Medical Services

More than Thailand's main health-care hub, Bangkok has become a major destination for medical tourism, with patients flying in for treatment from all over the world.

Hospitals

The following hospitals have English-speaking doctors.

Bangkok Christian Hospital (Map p278; ☎02 625 9000; www.bch.in.th/en; 124

PRACTICALITIES

Media

➡ Bangkok's predominant English-language newspapers are the *Bangkok Post* (www.bangkokpost.com) and the business-heavy *Nation* (www.nationmultimedia.com).

➡ The *International New York Times* and weeklies such as the *Economist* and *Time* are sold at numerous news stands.

➡ *Bangkok 101* (www.bangkok101.com) is a tourist-friendly listings magazine; *BK* (www.bk.asia-city.com) is a slightly more in-depth listings mag.

Weights & Measures

➡ The metric system is used.

Smoking

➡ Smoking is banned in all indoor places, including restaurants and bars, and all open-air public spaces.

Th Silom; Ⓜ️Si Lom exit 2, Ⓢ️Sala Daeng exit 1) Modern hospital in central Bangkok.

BNH (Map p278; ☏02 686 2700; www.bnhhospital.com; 9 Th Convent; Ⓜ️Si Lom exit 2, Ⓢ️Sala Daeng exit 2) Modern, centrally located hospital.

Bumrungrad International Hospital (Map p282; ☏02 667 1000; www.bumrungrad.com/thailandhospital; 33 Soi 3, Th Sukhumvit; Ⓢ️Phloen Chit exit 3) An internationally accredited hospital.

Samitivej Hospital (Map p282; ☏02 022 2222; www.samitivejhospitals.com; 133 Soi 49, Th Sukhumvit; Ⓢ️Phrom Phong exit 3 & taxi) Modern hospital in Bangkok.

Dentists

Business is good in the teeth game, partly because so many fa·ràng (Westerners) are combining their holiday with a spot of cheap root canal or some 'personal outlook' care – a teeth-whitening treatment by any other name. Prices are a bargain compared with Western countries, and the quality of dentistry is generally high.

Bangkok Dental Spa (Map p282; ☏02 651 0807; www.bangkokdentalspa.com; 2nd fl, Methawattana Bldg, 27 Soi 19, Th Sukhumvit; ⊘by appointment only; Ⓜ️Sukhumvit exit 3, Ⓢ️Asok exit 1) Dental-care centre with a spa-like environment.

DC-One the Dental Clinic (Map p277; ☏02 240 2800; www.dc-one.com; 31 Th Yen Akat; ⊘by appointment only; Ⓜ️Lumphini exit 2 & taxi) Dental clinic with reputation for excellent work and relatively high prices; popular with UN staff and diplomats.

Dental Hospital (Map p282; ☏02 260 5000; www.dentalhospitalbangkok.com; 88/88 Soi 49, Th Sukhumvit; ⊘9am-8pm Mon-Sat, to 4.30pm Sun; Ⓢ️Phrom Phong exit 3 & taxi) A private dental clinic with fluent English-speaking dentists.

Siam Family Dental Clinic (Map p274; ☏081 987 7700; www.siamfamilydental.com; 209 Th Phayathai; ⊘11am-8pm Mon-Fri, 10am-7pm Sat & Sun; Ⓢ️Siam exit 2) Private dental clinic in central Bangkok.

Pharmacies

Pharmacies are plentiful, and in central areas most pharmacists will speak English. If you don't find what you need in a Boots, Watsons or local pharmacy, try one of the hospitals.

Money

The basic unit of Thai currency is the baht. There are 100 satang in one baht – though the only place you'll be able to spend them is in the ubiquitous 7-Elevens. Coins come in denominations of 25 satang, 50 satang, 1B, 2B, 5B and 10B. Paper currency comes in denominations of 20B (green), 50B (blue), 100B (red), 500B (purple) and 1000B (beige).

ATMs

➡ You won't need a map to find an ATM in Bangkok – they're everywhere.

➡ Bank ATMs accept major international credit cards and many will also cough up cash (Thai baht only) if your card is affiliated with the Cirrus or Plus networks (typically for a fee of 150B).

➡ You can withdraw up to 20,000B per day from most ATMs.

Changing Money

➡ Banks or legal money-changers offer the optimum foreign-exchange rates.

➡ When buying baht, US dollars and euros are the most readily accepted currencies. British pounds, Australian dollars, Singapore dollars and Hong Kong dollars are also widely accepted.

➡ Most banks charge a commission and duty for each travellers cheque cashed.

Credit Cards

Credit cards as well as debit cards can be used for purchases at many shops and pretty much any hotel or restaurant, though you'll have to pay cash for your pàt tai. The most commonly accepted cards are Visa and MasterCard, followed by Amex and JCB. To report a lost or stolen card, call the following numbers:

Amex (☏02 273 5544)

MasterCard (☏001 800 11887 0663)

Visa (☏001 800 11 535 0660)

Tipping

Tipping is not a traditional part of Thai life and, except in big hotels and posh restaurants, tips are appreciated but not expected.

Opening Hours

All government offices and banks are closed on public holidays.

➡ **Banks** 9.30am to 3.30pm Monday to Friday; banks in shopping centres and tourist areas are often open longer hours (generally until 8pm), including weekends.

➡ **Bars & Nightclubs** Bars open from 6pm to midnight or 1am (officially); they close during elections and certain religious public holidays. Nightclubs open from 8pm to 2am; their closing times vary due to local enforcement of curfew laws.

➡ **Government Offices** 8.30am to 4.30pm Monday to Friday; some close between noon and

1pm, while others are open Saturday from 9am to 3pm.

➡ **Restaurants** Local Thai places open all day from 10am to 8pm or 9pm; formal restaurants from around 11am to 2pm and 6pm to 10pm.

➡ **Shops** Local stores open 10am to 7pm daily; malls and department stores from 10am to 10pm daily.

Post

Post offices are generally open from 8.30am to 4.30pm on weekdays, with larger branches also open from 9am to noon on Saturdays. Stamps are available at most 7-Eleven outlets.

Main Post Office (Map p280; ✆02 233 1050; Th Charoen Krung; ◷8am-8pm Mon-Fri, to 1pm Sat & Sun; ⛴Oriental Pier) Bangkok's main post office.

Public Holidays

Government offices and banks close their doors on the following public holidays. For the precise dates of lunar holidays, see the Events & Festivals page of the Tourism Authority of Thailand's (TAT) website: www.tourism thailand.org/see-do/event-festival.

1 January New Year's Day

February (date varies) Makha Bucha Day, Buddhist holy day

6 April Chakri Day, commemorating the founder of the Chakri dynasty, Rama I

13–14 April Songkran Festival, traditional Thai New Year and water festival

1 May Labour Day

5 May Coronation Day, commemorating the 1946 coronation of the king and queen

May/June (date varies) Visakha Bucha, Buddhist holy day

July (date varies) Asanha Bucha, Buddhist holy day

12 August Queen's Birthday

23 October Chulalongkorn Day

October/November (date varies) Ork Phansa, the end of Buddhist 'lent'

5 December King's Birthday/ Father's Day

10 December Constitution Day

31 December New Year's Eve

Safe Travel

As Thailand has recently been the site of both violent political protest and military coups, it's wise to check the situation before planning your trip. The following government websites offer travel advisories and information on current hotspots.

Australian Department of Foreign Affairs (www.smart traveller.gov.au)

British Foreign Office (www. gov.uk/foreign-travel-advice)

US State Department (www. travel.state.gov/content/ travel/en.html)

Generally, Bangkok is a safe city and incidents of violence against tourists are rare. That said, there is a repertoire of well-polished scams. But don't be spooked; commit the following to memory and you'll most likely enjoy a scam-free visit:

➡ **Gem scam** We're begging you, if you aren't a gem trader, then don't buy unset stones in Thailand – period.

➡ **Closed today** Ignore any 'friendly' local who tells you that an attraction is closed for a Buddhist holiday or for cleaning. These are set-ups for trips to a bogus gem sale.

➡ **Túk-túk rides for 20B** Say goodbye to your day's itinerary if you climb aboard this ubiquitous scam. These alleged 'tours' bypass all the sights and instead cruise to all the fly-by-night gem and tailor shops that pay commissions.

➡ **Flat-fare taxi ride** Flatly refuse any driver who quotes a flat fare (usually between 100B and 150B for in-town destinations), which will usually be three times more expensive than the reasonable meter rate. Walking beyond the tourist area will usually help in finding an honest driver. If the driver has 'forgotten' to put the meter on, just say, 'Meter, kha/khap'.

➡ **Friendly strangers** Be wary of smartly dressed men who approach you asking where you're from and where you're going. Their opening gambit is usually followed with: 'Ah, my son/daughter is studying at university in (your city)' – they seem to have an encyclopedic knowledge of major universities. As the tourist authorities here point out, this sort of behaviour is out of character for Thais and should be treated with suspicion.

Taxes & Refunds

➡ Thailand has a 7% Value Added Tax (VAT) on many goods and services. Midrange and top-end hotels and restaurants might also add a 10% service tax. When the two are combined this becomes the 17% king hit known as 'plus plus', or '++'.

➡ You can get a refund on VAT paid on shopping, though not on food or hotels, as you leave the country. See p48 for details.

Telephone

Domestic & International Calling

➡ Inside Thailand you must dial the area code no matter where you are. In effect, that means all numbers are nine digits; in Bangkok they begin with ✆02, then a seven-digit number. The only time you drop the initial ☎0 is when you're calling from outside Thailand. Calling the provinces will usually involve a three-digit code beginning with ☎0, then a six-digit number.

➡ To direct-dial an international number from a private phone, you can first dial ☎001, then the country code. However, you wouldn't do that, because ☎001 is the most expensive way to call internationally and numerous other prefixes give you cheaper rates. These include ☎007, ☎008 and ☎009, depending on which phone you're calling from. If you buy a local SIM card, which we recommend, the network provider will tell you which prefix to use; read the fine print.

USEFUL NUMBERS

Thailand country code ☎66

Bangkok city code ☎02

Mobile numbers ☎06, ☎08, ☎09

Operator-assisted international calls ☎100

Free local directory assistance call ☎1133

Mobile Phones

➡ If you have a GSM phone you will probably be able to use it on roaming in Thailand. If you have endless funds, or you only want to send text messages, you might be happy to do that. Otherwise, think about buying a local SIM card.

➡ If your phone is locked, head down to **MBK Center** (Map p274; www.mbk-center.com; cnr Th Phra Ram I & Th Phayathai; 🕙10am-10pm; [S]National Stadium exit 4) to get it unlocked or to shop for a new or cheap used phone (they start at less than 2000B).

➡ Buying a prepaid SIM is as easy as finding a 7-Eleven. The market is supercompetitive and deals vary so check websites first, but expect to get a SIM for as little as 49B. More expensive SIMs might come with preloaded talk time; if not, recharge cards are sold at the same stores and start from as little as 10B. Domestic per-minute rates start at less than 50 satang.

➡ The main networks:

AIS (1 2 Call; www.ais.co.th/12call/th)

DTAC (www.dtac.co.th)

TrueMove (Map p274; www.truemove.com; Soi 2, Siam Sq; 🕙7am-10pm; [S]Siam exit 4)

Time

➡ Thailand is seven hours ahead of GMT/UTC. Thus, noon in Bangkok is 9pm the previous night in Los Angeles, midnight the same day in New York, 5am in London, 6am in Paris, 1pm in Perth and 3pm in Sydney. Times are an hour later in countries or regions that are on Daylight Saving Time (DST). Thailand does not use daylight saving.

➡ The official year in Thailand is reckoned from the Western calendar year 543 BC, the beginning of the Buddhist Era (BE), so that AD 2016 is 2559 BE, AD 2017 is 2560 BE etc.

➡ All dates in this book refer to the Western calendar.

Toilets

➡ If you don't want to pee against a tree like the túk-túk (pronounced *đúk đúk*) drivers, you can stop at any shopping centre, hotel or fast-food restaurant for facilities. Shopping centres typically charge 3B to 5B for a visit.

➡ In older buildings and wát you'll still find squat toilets, but in modern Bangkok expect to be greeted by a throne.

➡ Toilet paper is rarely provided, so carry your own stash. Even in places where sit-down toilets are installed, the septic system may not be designed to take toilet paper. In such cases there will be a waste basket for used toilet paper and feminine hygiene products. Many toilets also come with a small spray hose – Thailand's version of the bidet.

Tourist Information

Bangkok has two organisations that handle tourism matters: the Tourism Authority of Thailand (TAT) for countrywide information, and Bangkok Information Center for city-specific information. Also be aware that travel agents in the train station and near tourist centres co-opt 'T.A.T.' and 'Information' as part of their name to lure in commissions. These places are not officially sanctioned information services, but just agencies registered with the TAT. So how can you tell the difference? Apparently it's all in the full stops – 'T.A.T.' means agency; 'TAT' is official.

Bangkok Information Center (Map p265; ☎02 225 7612-4; www.bangkoktourist.com; 17/1 Th Phra Athit; 🕙9am-7pm Mon-Fri, to 5pm Sat & Sun; ⛴Phra Athit/Banglamphu Pier) City-specific tourism office providing maps, brochures and directions. Kiosks and booths are found around town; look for the green-on-white symbol of a mahout on an elephant.

Tourism Authority of Thailand (TAT; ☎call centre 1672; www.tourismthailand.org) Has the following branches:

Head office (Map p282; ☎02 250 5500, call centre 1672; 1600 Th Phetchaburi Tat Mai; 🕙8.30am-4.30pm; [M]Phetchaburi exit 2)

Banglamphu (Map p268; ☎02 283 1500; cnr Th Ratchadamnoen Nok & Th Chakraphatdi Phong; ⊘8.30am-4.30pm; ⬛klorng boat Phanfa Leelard Pier)

Suvarnabhumi International Airport (⟁02 134 0040; 2nd fl, btwn Gates 2 & 5, Suvarnabhumi International Airport; ⊘24hr).

Travellers with Disabilities

➡ Bangkok presents one large, ongoing obstacle course for the mobility-impaired, with its high kerbs, uneven pavements and nonstop traffic. Many of the city's streets must be crossed via pedestrian bridges flanked with steep stairways, while buses and boats don't stop long enough to accommodate even the mildly disabled. Except for some BTS and MRT stations, ramps or other access points for wheelchairs are rare.

➡ A few top-end hotels make consistent design efforts to provide disabled access. Other deluxe hotels that have high employee-to-guest ratios are usually good about providing staff help where building design fails. For the rest, you're pretty much left to your own resources.

➡ Lonely Planet's free Accessible Travel guide can be downloaded here: http://lptravel.to/AccessibleTravel

➡ The following companies and websites might be useful:

Asia Pacific Development Centre on Disability (www.apcdfoundation.org)

Society for Accessible Travel & Hospitality (www.sath.org)
Wheelchair Holidays @ Thailand (www.wheelchairtours.com)

Visas

➡ Thailand's **Ministry of Foreign Affairs** (⟁02 203 5000; www.mfa.go.th) oversees immigration and visa issues. In the past several years there have been new rules almost annually regarding visas and extensions; the best online monitor is Thaivisa (www.thaivisa.com).

➡ Citizens of 62 countries (including most European countries, Australia, New Zealand and the USA) can enter Thailand at no charge. Depending on nationality, these citizens are issued a 14- to 90-day visa exemption if they arrive by air (most nationalities receive 30 days), or for 15 to 30 days by land.

Visa Extensions

➡ If you need more time in the country, apply for a 60-day tourist visa prior to arrival at a Thai embassy or consulate abroad. For business or study purposes, you can obtain 90-day nonimmigrant visas, but you'll need extra documentation. Officially, on arrival you must prove you have sufficient funds for your stay and proof of onward travel, but visitors are rarely asked about this.

➡ If you overstay your visa the penalty is 500B per day, with a 20,000B limit; fines can be paid

at any official exit point or at the **Bangkok Immigration Office** (⟁02 141 9889; www.bangkok.immigration.go.th/intro1.html; Bldg B, Government Centre, Soi 7, Th Chaeng Watthana; ⊘8.30am-noon & 1-4.30pm Mon-Fri; ⓂChatuchak Park exit 2 & taxi, ⓈMo Chit exit 3 & taxi). Dress in your Sunday best when doing official business in Thailand and do all visa business yourself (don't hire a third party). For all types of visa extensions, bring along two passport-sized photos and one copy each of the photo and visa pages of your passport.

➡ You can extend your stay, for the normal fee of 1900B, at the Immigration Office. Those issued with the visa exemption can extend their stay for an additional 30 days if the extension is handled before the visa expires. The 60-day tourist visa can be extended by up to 30 days at the discretion of Thai immigration authorities.

Women Travellers

➡ Everyday incidents of sexual harassment are much less common in Thailand than in India, Indonesia or Malaysia, and this might lull women familiar with those countries into thinking that Thailand is safer than it is. If you're a woman travelling alone it's worth pairing up with other travellers when moving around at night or, at the least, avoiding quiet areas.

➡ Whether it's tampons or any other product for women, you'll have no trouble finding it in Bangkok.

Language

Thailand's, and therefore Bangkok's, official language is effectively the dialect spoken and written in central Thailand, which has successfully become the lingua franca of all Thai and non-Thai ethnic groups in the kingdom.

In Thai the meaning of a single syllable may be altered by means of different tones. In standard Thai there are five: low tone, mid tone, falling tone, high tone and rising tone. The range of all five tones is relative to each speaker's vocal range, so there is no fixed 'pitch' intrinsic to the language.

➡ **low tone** – 'Flat' like the mid tone, but pronounced at the relative bottom of one's vocal range. It is low, level and has no inflection, eg bàht (baht – the Thai currency).

➡ **mid tone** – Pronounced 'flat', at the relative middle of the speaker's vocal range, eg dee (good). No tone mark is used.

➡ **falling tone** – Starting high and falling sharply, this tone is similar to the change in pitch in English when you are emphasising a word, or calling someone's name from afar, eg mâi (no/not).

➡ **high tone** – Usually the most difficult for non-Thai speakers. It's pronounced near the relative top of the vocal range, as level as possible, eg máh (horse).

➡ **rising tone** – Starting low and gradually rising, sounds like the inflection used by English speakers to imply a question – 'Yes?', eg săhm (three).

WANT MORE?

For in-depth language information and handy phrases, check out Lonely Planet's *Thai Phrasebook*. You'll find it at **shop.lonelyplanet.com**, or you can buy Lonely Planet's iPhone phrasebooks at the Apple App Store.

The Thai government has instituted the Royal Thai General Transcription System (RTGS) as a standard method of writing Thai using the Roman alphabet. It's used in official documents, road signs and on maps. However, local variations crop up on signs, menus etc. Generally, names in this book follow the most common practice.

In our coloured pronunciation guides, the hyphens indicate syllable breaks within words, and some syllables are further divided with a dot to help you pronounce compound vowels, eg mêu·a·rai (when).

The vowel a is pronounced as in 'about', aa as the 'a' in 'bad', ah as the 'a' in 'father', ai as in 'aisle', air as in 'flair' (without the 'r'), eu as the 'er' in 'her' (without the 'r'), ew as in 'new' (with rounded lips), oh as the 'o' in 'toe', or as in 'torn' (without the 'r') and ow as in 'now'.

Most consonants correspond to their English counterparts. The exceptions are b (a hard 'p' sound, almost like a 'b', eg in 'hip-bag'); đ (a hard 't' sound, like a sharp 'd', eg in 'mid-tone'); ng (as in 'singing'; in Thai it can occur at the start of a word) and r (as in 'run' but flapped; in everyday speech it's often pronounced like 'l'). If you read our coloured pronunciation guides as if they were English, you shouldn't have problems being understood.

BASICS

The social structure of Thai society demands different registers of speech depending on who you're talking to. To make things simple we've chosen the correct form of speech appropriate to the context of each phrase.

When being polite, the speaker ends his or her sentence with kráp (for men) or kâ (for women). It is the gender of the speaker that is being expressed here; it is also the common way to answer 'yes' to a question or show agreement.

In this chapter the masculine and feminine forms of phrases are indicated where relevant with 'm/f'.

Hello.	สวัสดี	sà-wàt-dee
Goodbye.	ลาก่อน	lah gòrn
Yes.	ใช่	châi
No.	ไม่	mâi
Please.	ขอ	kŏr
Thank you.	ขอบคุณ	kòrp kun
You're welcome.	ยินดี	yin dee
Excuse me.	ขออภัย	kŏr à-pai
Sorry.	ขอโทษ	kŏr tôht

How are you?
สบายดีไหม sà-bai dee măi

Fine. And you?
สบายดีครับ/ค่ะ sà-bai dee kráp/
แล้วคุณล่ะ kâ láa·ou kun lâ (m/f)

What's your name?
คุณชื่ออะไร kun chêu à-rai

My name is ...
ผม/ดิฉันชื่อ... pŏm/dì-chăn chêu ... (m/f)

Do you speak English?
คุณพูดภาษา kun pôot pah-săh
อังกฤษได้ไหม ang-grìt dâi măi

I don't understand.
ผม/ดิฉันไม่เข้าใจ pŏm/dì-chăn mâi kôw jai (m/f)

ACCOMMODATION

Where's a ...?	...อยู่ที่ไหน	...yòo têe năi
campsite	ค่ายพักแรม	kâi pák raam
guesthouse	บ้านพัก	bâhn pák
hotel	โรงแรม	rohng raam
youth hostel	บ้าน	bâhn
	เยาวชน	yow-wá-chon
Do you have	มีห้อง ...	mee hôrng ...
a ... room?	ไหม	măi
single	เดี่ยว	dèe·o
double	เตียงคู่	đee·ang kôo
twin	สองเตียง	sŏrng đee·ang
air-con	แอร์	aa
bathroom	ห้องน้ำ	hôrng nám
laundry	ห้องซักผ้า	hôrng sák pâh
mosquito net	มุ้ง	múng
window	หน้าต่าง	nâh đàhng

SIGNS

ทางเข้า	Entrance
ทางออก	Exit
เปิด	Open
ปิด	Closed
ห้าม	Prohibited
ห้องสุขา	Toilets
ชาย	Men
หญิง	Women

DIRECTIONS

Where's ...?
... อยู่ที่ไหน ... yòo têe năi

What's the address?
ที่อยู่คืออะไร têe yòo keu à-rai

Could you please write it down?
เขียนลงให้ได้ไหม kĕe·an long hâi dâi măi

Can you show me (on the map)?
ให้ดู (ในแผนที่) hâi doo (nai păn têe)
ได้ไหม dâi măi

Turn left/right.
เลี้ยวซ้าย/ขวา lée·o sái/kwăh

It's ...	อยู่ ...	yòo ...
behind	ที่หลัง	têe lăng
in front of	ตรงหน้า	đrong nâh
near	ใกล้ๆ	glâi glâi
next to	ข้างๆ	kâhng kâhng
straight ahead	ตรงไป	đrong bai

EATING & DRINKING

I'd like (the menu), please.
ขอ (รายการ kŏr (rai gahn
อาหาร) หน่อย ah-hăhn) nòy

What would you recommend?
คุณแนะนำอะไรบ้าง kun náa-nam à-rai bâhng

That was delicious!
อร่อยมาก à-ròy mâhk

Cheers!
ไชโย chai-yoh

Please bring the bill.
ขอบิลหน่อย kŏr bin nòy

I don't eat ...	ผม/ดิฉัน	pŏm/dì-chăn
	ไม่กิน ...	mâi gin ... (m/f)
eggs	ไข่	kài
fish	ปลา	ƀlah
red meat	เนื้อแดง	néu·a daang
nuts	ถั่ว	tòo·a

pork	หมู	mŏo
seafood	อาหารทะเล	ah-hăhn tá-lair
squid	ปลาหมึก	ƀlah mèuk

Key Words

bottle	ขวด	kòo·at
bowl	ชาม	chahm
breakfast	อาหารเช้า	ah-hăhn chów
cafe	ร้านกาแฟ	ráhn gah-faa
chopsticks	ไม้ตะเกียบ	mái đà-gèe·ap
cold	เย็น	yen
cup	ถ้วย	tôo·ay
dessert	ของหวาน	kŏrng wăhn
dinner	อาหารเย็น	ah-hăhn yen
drink list	รายการ	rai gahn
	เครื่องดื่ม	krêu·ang dèum
fork	ส้อม	sôrm
glass	แก้ว	gâa·ou
hot	ร้อน	rórn
knife	มีด	mêet
lunch	อาหาร	ah-hăhn
	กลางวัน	glahng wan
market	ตลาด	đà-làht
plate	จาน	jahn
restaurant	ร้านอาหาร	ráhn ah-hăhn
spicy	เผ็ด	pèt
spoon	ช้อน	chórn
vegetarian	คนกินเจ	kon gin jair
with/without	มี/ไม่มี	mee/mâi mee

Meat & Fish

beef	เนื้อ	néu·a
chicken	ไก่	gài
crab	ปู	ƀoo
duck	เป็ด	ƀèt
fish	ปลา	ƀlah
meat	เนื้อ	néu·a

Fruit & Vegetables

banana	กล้วย	glôo·ay
beans	ถั่ว	tòo·a
coconut	มะพร้าว	má-prów
eggplant	มะเขือ	má-kĕu·a
fruit	ผลไม้	pŏn-lá-mái
guava	ฝรั่ง	fa-ràng
lime	มะนาว	má-now
mango	มะม่วง	má-môo·ang
mangosteen	มังคุด	mang-kút
mushrooms	เห็ด	hèt
nuts	ถั่ว	tòo·a
papaya	มะละกอ	má-lá-gor
potatoes	มันฝรั่ง	man fa-ràng
rambutan	เงาะ	ngó
tamarind	มะขาม	má-kăhm
tomatoes	มะเขือเทศ	má-kĕu·a têt
vegetables	ผัก	pàk
watermelon	แตงโม	đaang moh

Other

chilli	พริก	prík
egg	ไข่	kài
fish sauce	น้ำปลา	nám ƀlah
noodles	เส้น	sên
oil	น้ำมัน	nám man
pepper	พริกไทย	prík tai
rice	ข้าว	kôw
salad	ผักสด	pàk sòt
salt	เกลือ	gleu·a

QUESTION WORDS		
What?	อะไร	à-rai
When?	เมื่อไร	mêu·a-rai
Where?	ที่ไหน	têe năi
Who?	ใคร	krai

soup	น้ำซุป	nám súp
soy sauce	น้ำซีอิ๊ว	nám see-éw
sugar	น้ำตาล	nám đahn
tofu	เต้าหู้	đôw hôo

Drinks

beer	เบียร์	bee·a
coffee	กาแฟ	gah-faa
milk	นมจืด	nom jèut
orange juice	น้ำส้ม	nám sôm
soy milk	น้ำเต้าหู้	nám đôw hôo
sugar-cane juice	น้ำอ้อย	nám ôy
tea	ชา	chah
water	น้ำดื่ม	nám dèum

EMERGENCIES

| Help! | ช่วยด้วย | chôo·ay dôo·ay |
| Go away! | ไปให้พ้น | bai hâi pón |

Call a doctor!
เรียกหมอหน่อย — rêe·ak mŏr nòy
Call the police!
เรียกตำรวจหน่อย — rêe·ak đam·ròo·at nòy
I'm ill.
ผม/ดิฉันป่วย — pŏm/dì-chăn bòo·ay (m/f)
I'm lost.
ผม/ดิฉัน — pŏm/dì-chăn
หลงทาง — lŏng tahng (m/f)
Where are the toilets?
ห้องน้ำอยู่ที่ไหน — hôrng nám yòo têe năi

SHOPPING & SERVICES

I'd like to buy ...
อยากจะซื้อ ... — yàhk jà séu ...

How much is it?
เท่าไร — tôw-rai

That's too expensive.
แพงไป — paang bai

Can you lower the price?
ลดราคาได้ไหม — lót rah-kah dâi măi

There's a mistake in the bill.
บิลใบนี้ผิด — bin bai née pìt ná
นะครับ/คะ — kráp/kâ (m/f)

TIME & DATES
What time is it?
กี่โมงแล้ว — gèe mohng láa·ou

morning	เช้า	chów
afternoon	บ่าย	bài
evening	เย็น	yen
yesterday	เมื่อวาน	mêu·a wahn
today	วันนี้	wan née
tomorrow	พรุ่งนี้	prûng née
Monday	วันจันทร์	wan jan
Tuesday	วันอังคาร	wan ang-kahn
Wednesday	วันพุธ	wan pút
Thursday	วันพฤหัสฯ	wan pá-réu-hàt
Friday	วันศุกร	wan sùk
Saturday	วันเสาร์	wan sŏw
Sunday	วันอาทิตย์	wan ah-tít

TRANSPORT

Public Transport

bicycle rickshaw	สามล้อ	săhm lór
boat	เรือ	reu·a
bus	รถเมล์	rót mair
car	รถเก๋ง	rót gĕng
motorcycle	มอร์เตอร์ไซค์	mor-đeu-sai
taxi	รับจ้าง	ráp jâhng
plane	เครื่องบิน	krêu·ang bin
train	รถไฟ	rót fai
túk-túk	ตุ๊ก ๆ	đúk đúk

When's	รถเมล์คัน ...	rót mair kan ...
the ... bus?	มาเมื่อไร	mah mêu·a rai
first	แรก	râak
last	สุดท้าย	sùt tái

A ... ticket,	ขอตั๋ว ...	kŏr đŏo·a ...
please.		
one-way	เที่ยวเดียว	têe·o dee·o
return	ไปกลับ	bai glàp

NUMBERS

1	หนึ่ง	nèung
2	สอง	sŏrng
3	สาม	săhm
4	สี่	sèe
5	ห้า	hâh
6	หก	hòk
7	เจ็ด	jèt
8	แปด	bàat
9	เก้า	gôw
10	สิบ	sìp
11	สิบเอ็ด	sìp-èt
20	ยี่สิบ	yêe-sìp
21	ยี่สิบเอ็ด	yêe-sìp-èt
30	สามสิบ	săhm-sìp
40	สี่สิบ	sèe-sìp
50	ห้าสิบ	hâh-sìp
60	หกสิบ	hòk-sìp
70	เจ็ดสิบ	jèt-sìp
80	แปดสิบ	bàat-sìp
90	เก้าสิบ	gôw-sìp
100	หนึ่งร้อย	nèung róy
1000	หนึ่งพัน	nèung pan
1,000,000	หนึ่งล้าน	nèung láhn

I'd like	ต้องการ	dôrng gahn
a/an ... seat.	ที่นั่ง ...	têe nâng ...
aisle	ติดทางเดิน	dìt tahng deun
window	ติดหน้าต่าง	dìt nâh dàhng
ticket window	ช่องขายตั๋ว	chôrng kăi dŏo·a
timetable	ตารางเวลา	dah-rahng wair-lah

What time does it get to (Chiang Mai)?

ถึง (เชียงใหม่)	tĕung (chee·ang mài)
กี่โมง	gèe mohng

Does it stop at (Saraburi)?

รถจอดที่ (สระบุรี)	rót jòrt têe (sà-rà-bù-ree)
ไหม	măi

I'd like to get off at (Saraburi).

ขอลงที่ (สระบุรี)	kŏr long têe (sà-rà-bù-ree)

Driving & Cycling

I'd like to	อยากจะ	yàhk jà
hire a/an ...	เช่า ...	chôw ...
4WD	รถโฟร์วีล	rót foh ween
car	รถเก๋ง	rót gĕng
motorbike	รถ มอร์เตอร์ไซค์	rót mor-đeu-sai

I'd like ...	ต้องการ ...	dôrng gahn ...
my bicycle	ซ่อมรถ	sôrm rót
repaired	จักรยาน	jàk-gà-yahn
to hire a	เช่ารถ	chôw rót
bicycle	จักรยาน	jàk-gà-yahn

Is this the road to (Ban Bung Wai)?

ทางนี้ไป (บ้านบุ่งหวาย) ไหม	tahng née bai (bâhn bùng wăi) măi

Where's a petrol station?

ปั๊มน้ำมันอยู่ที่ไหน	bám nám man yòo têe năi

How long can I park here?

จอดที่นี้ได้นานเท่าไร	jòrt têe née dâi nahn tôw-rai

I need a mechanic.

ต้องการช่างรถ	dôrng gahn châhng rót

I have a flat tyre.

ยางแบน	yahng baan

I've run out of petrol.

หมดน้ำมัน	mòt nám man

GLOSSARY

This glossary includes Thai, Pali (P) and Sanskrit (S) words and terms frequently used in this guidebook. For definitions of food and drink terms, see p30, p32 and p249.

baht – *(bàat)* the Thai unit of currency

bòht – central sanctuary in a Thai temple used for the monastic order's official business, such as ordinations; see also *wí·hǎhn*

Brahman – pertaining to Brahmanism, an ancient religious tradition in India and the predecessor of Hinduism; not to be confused with 'Brahmin', the priestly class in India's caste system

BTS – Bangkok Transit System (Skytrain); Thai: *rót fai fáh*

chedi – see *stupa*

đròrk – *(trok)* alley, smaller than a soi

fa·ràng –a Westerner (person of European origin); also guava

gà·teu·i – *(kàthoey)* Thailand's 'third gender', usually cross-dressing or transsexual males

hàht – beach; spelt 'Hat' in proper names

gǒo·ay đěe·o – *generic term for a noodle soup dish*

Isan – *(ee·sǎhn)* general term used for northeastern Thailand

jataka (P) – *(chah·dòk)* stories of the Buddha's previous lives

kàthoey – see *gà·teu·i*

klorng – canal; spelt 'Khlong' in proper nouns

kǒhn – masked dance-drama

lék – little, small (in size); see also *noi*

mâa nám – river; spelt Mae Nam in proper names

mahathat – *(má·hǎh tâht)* common name for temples containing Buddha relics; from the Sanskrit–Pali term *mahadhatu*

mâi ben rai – Thai expression meaning 'No problem' or 'It's OK'

masjid – *(mát·sà·yít)* mosque

meu·ang – city or principality

MRT – Metropolitan Rapid Transit, or Metro.

nám – water

nibbana (P/S) – nirvana; in Buddhist teachings, the state of enlightenment; escape from the realm of rebirth; Thai: *níp·pahn*

noi – *(nóy)* little, small (amount); see also *lék*

nôrk – outside, outer; spelt 'Nok' in proper names

ow – bay or gulf; spelt 'Ao' in proper nouns

prá – an honorific term used for monks, nobility and Buddha images; spelt 'Phra' in proper names

prang – *(brahng)* Khmer-style tower on temples

samsara (P) – in Buddhist teachings, the realm of rebirth and delusion

sangha – (P) the Buddhist community

satang – *(sà·dahng)* a Thai unit of currency; 100 satang equals 1 baht

soi – lane or small street

Songkran – Thai New Year, held in mid-April

sǒrng·tǎa·ou – (literally 'two rows') common name for small pick-up trucks with two benches in the back, used as buses/taxis; also spelt '*sǎwngthǎew*'

stupa – conical-shaped Buddhist monument used to inter sacred Buddhist objects

tâh – pier, boat landing; spelt 'Tha' in proper nouns

TAT – Tourism Authority of Thailand

Thammayut – one of the two sects of Theravada Buddhism in Thailand; founded by King Rama IV while he was still a monk

thanǒn – *(tà·nǒn)* street; spelt 'Thanon' in proper nouns and shortened to 'Th'

T-pop – popular teen-music

tràwk – see *đròrk*

Tripitaka (S) – Theravada Buddhist scriptures; (Pali: *Tipitaka*)

túk–túk – *(đúk–đúk)* motorised, three-wheeled rickshaw

wâi – palms–together Thai greeting

wang – palace

wát – temple–monastery; spelt 'Wat' in proper nouns

wí·hǎhn – *(wihan, viharn)* any large hall in a Thai temple, usually open to laity

yài – big

Behind the Scenes

SEND US YOUR FEEDBACK

We love to hear from travellers – your comments keep us on our toes and help make our books better. Our well-travelled team reads every word on what you loved or loathed about this book. Although we cannot reply individually to your submissions, we always guarantee that your feedback goes straight to the appropriate authors, in time for the next edition. Each person who sends us information is thanked in the next edition – the most useful submissions are rewarded with a selection of digital PDF chapters.

Visit **lonelyplanet.com/contact** to submit your updates and suggestions or to ask for help. Our award-winning website also features inspirational travel stories, news and discussions.

Note: We may edit, reproduce and incorporate your comments in Lonely Planet products such as guidebooks, websites and digital products, so let us know if you don't want your comments reproduced or your name acknowledged. For a copy of our privacy policy visit lonelyplanet.com/privacy.

OUR READERS

Many thanks to the travellers who used the last edition and wrote to us with helpful hints, useful advice and interesting anecdotes: Erik Dreyer, Marcia Freed, Hendrik Mueller-Ide, Paul Scott, Giovanni Serrapere, Ian Smith, Eddy Van Vaerenbergh

WRITER THANKS

Austin Bush

My thanks to the previous authors of this guide, Andrew Burke, Joe Cummings and China Williams – believe it or not, some of your words live on! Thanks also to destination editor Sarah Reid; this edition's Local Knowledgers Nima Chandler, Greg Jorgensen and Pongtawat 'Ian' Chalermkittichai; part-time research assistants Kathy MacLeod and Maher Sattar; and the rest of the kind folks on the ground in Bangkok.

ACKNOWLEDGMENTS

Illustrations pp62–3 and pp66–7 by Michael Weldon.

Cover photograph: Wat Pho, Shaun Egan/ AWL.

THIS BOOK

This 12th edition of Lonely Planet's *Bangkok* guidebook was researched and written by Austin Bush, who also wrote the previous two editions.

Destination Editor Sarah Reid

Coordinating Editor Nigel Chin

Product Editor Luna Soo

Senior Cartographer Diana Von Holdt

Book Designer Cam Ashley

Assisting Cartographer Valentina Kremenchutskaya

Assisting Editors Peter Cruttenden, Victoria Harrison, Tracy Whitmey

Cover Researcher Naomi Parker

Thanks to Grace Dobell, Bruce Evans, Ryan Evans, Kate Kiely, Wayne Murphy, Katie O'Connell, Kirsten Rawlings, Diana Saengkham, Ellie Simpson, Lauren Wellicome, Tony Wheeler, Patrick Winn

See also separate subindexes for:

🍴 **EATING P258**

🍺 **DRINKING & NIGHTLIFE P259**

☆ **ENTERTAINMENT P260**

🔒 **SHOPPING P260**

🏃 **SPORTS & ACTIVITIES P261**

🛏 **SLEEPING P261**

Index

Bangkok Maps

Sights
- Beach
- Bird Sanctuary
- Buddhist
- Castle/Palace
- Christian
- Confucian
- Hindu
- Islamic
- Jain
- Jewish
- Monument
- Museum/Gallery/Historic Building
- Ruin
- Shinto
- Sikh
- Taoist
- Winery/Vineyard
- Zoo/Wildlife Sanctuary
- Other Sight

Activities, Courses & Tours
- Bodysurfing
- Diving
- Canoeing/Kayaking
- Course/Tour
- Sento Hot Baths/Onsen
- Skiing
- Snorkelling
- Surfing
- Swimming/Pool
- Walking
- Windsurfing
- Other Activity

Sleeping
- Sleeping
- Camping

Eating
- Eating

Drinking & Nightlife
- Drinking & Nightlife
- Cafe

Entertainment
- Entertainment

Shopping
- Shopping

Information
- Bank
- Embassy/Consulate
- Hospital/Medical
- Internet
- Police
- Post Office
- Telephone
- Toilet
- Tourist Information
- Other Information

Geographic
- Beach
- Gate
- Hut/Shelter
- Lighthouse
- Lookout
- Mountain/Volcano
- Oasis
- Park
- Pass
- Picnic Area
- Waterfall

Population
- Capital (National)
- Capital (State/Province)
- City/Large Town
- Town/Village

Transport
- Airport
- Border crossing
- Bus
- Cable car/Funicular
- Cycling
- Ferry
- Metro/MTR/MRT station
- Monorail
- Parking
- Petrol station
- Skytrain/Subway station
- Taxi
- Train station/Railway
- Tram
- Underground station
- Other Transport

Note: Not all symbols displayed above appear on the maps in this book

Routes
- Tollway
- Freeway
- Primary
- Secondary
- Tertiary
- Lane
- Unsealed road
- Road under construction
- Plaza/Mall
- Steps
- Tunnel
- Pedestrian overpass
- Walking Tour
- Walking Tour detour
- Path/Walking Trail

Boundaries
- International
- State/Province
- Disputed
- Regional/Suburb
- Marine Park
- Cliff
- Wall

Hydrography
- River, Creek
- Intermittent River
- Canal
- Water
- Dry/Salt/Intermittent Lake
- Reef

Areas
- Airport/Runway
- Beach/Desert
- Cemetery (Christian)
- Cemetery (Other)
- Glacier
- Mudflat
- Park/Forest
- Sight (Building)
- Sportsground
- Swamp/Mangrove

MAP INDEX

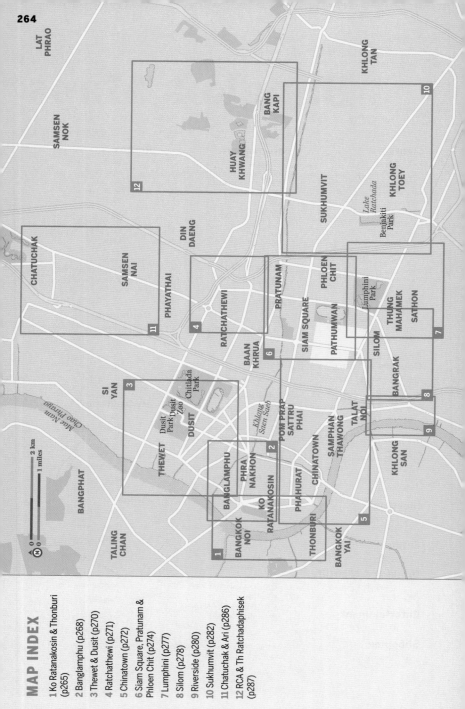

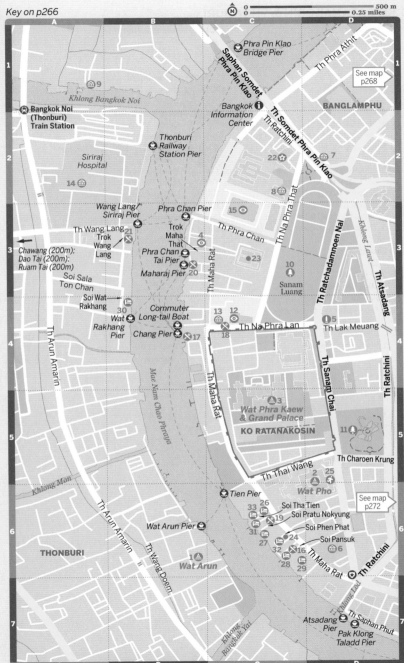

0 500 m
0 0.25 miles

Phra Pin Klao
Bridge Pier

Th Phra Athit

See map
p268

BANGLAMPHU

Saphan Somdet
Phra Pin Klao

Th Somdet Phra Pin Klao

Bangkok
Information
Center

Th Ratchini

9

Khlong Bangkok Noi

Bangkok Noi
(Thonburi)
Train Station

Thonburi
Railway
Station Pier

22

Th Na Phra That

7

Siriraj
Hospital

14

8

Wang Lang/
Siriraj Pier

Phra Chan Pier

15

Th Wang Lang

Trok
Maha
That

Th Phra Chan

Th Na Phra That

Th Ratchadamnoen Nai

Khlong Lawt

Th Atsadang

21
Trok
Wang
Lang

Phra Chan
Tai Pier

4

Chawang (200m);
Dao Tai (200m);
Ruam Tai (200m)

Maharaj Pier

20

23

10

Sanam
Luang

Th Ratchini

Soi Sala
Ton Chan

Soi Wat
Rakhang

30

Wat
Rakhang
Pier

Commuter
Long-tail Boat

13 **12**

5
Th Lak Meuang

Th Ratchini

Th Arun Amarin

Chang Pier

17

18

Th Na Phra Lan

Th Maha Rat

Th Sanam Chai

Mae Nam Chao Phraya

Th Maha Rat

Wat Phra Kaew
& Grand Palace

3

KO RATANAKOSIN

11

Khlong Mon

Th Arun Amarin

THONBURI

Wat Arun Pier

Th Charoen Krung

Th Thai Wang

2 **25**

Wat Pho

See map
p272

Tien Pier

33 **26**

Soi Tha Tien

Soi Pratu Nokyung

19

Th Wang Doem

Wat Arun

1

31

27

32

28 **29**

24

Soi Phen Phat

Soi Pansuk

6

16

Th Maha Rat

Th Ratchini

Atsadang
Pier

Th Saphan Phut

Khlong Lawt

Pak Klong
Taladd Pier

Khlong Bangkok Yai

KO RATANAKOSIN & THONBURI *Map on p265*

◎ Top Sights (p60)
1 Wat Arun B6
2 Wat Pho...D5
3 Wat Phra Kaew & Grand Palace...............C5

◎ Sights (p70)
4 Amulet Market B3
5 Lak Meuang D4
6 Museum of Siam...D6
7 National Gallery..D2
8 National Museum.......................................C2
9 Royal Barges National Museum A1
10 Sanam Luang..C3
11 Saranrom Royal Garden D5
12 Silpakorn University C4
13 Silpakorn University Art Centre..............C4
14 Siriraj Medical Museum A2
15 Thammasat University..............................C3

◎ Eating (p75)
16 Err C6
17 Khunkung...B4
18 Ming Lee...C4
19 Pa Aew..C6
    Sala Rattanakosin Eatery &
    Bar ....(see 33)
20 Savoey...B3
21 Wang Lang Market.....................................B3

◎ Drinking & Nightlife (p77)
    Amorosa...(see 27)
    Roof...(see 33)

◎ Entertainment (p77)
22 National Theatre..C2

◎ Sports & Activities (p77)
23 Center Meditation Wat
    Mahadhatu..C3
24 Chetawan Traditional Massage
    School..C6
25 Massage Pavilions.....................................D5
    Muay Thai Lab...................................(see 20)
    National Museum Tours....................(see 8)

◎ Sleeping (p190)
26 Arom D Hostel C6
27 Arun Residence C6
28 Aurum: The River Place.............................C6
29 Chakrabongse Villas C6
30 Ibrik Resort..B4
31 Inn A Day C6
32 Royal Tha Tien Village...............................C6
33 Sala Ratanakosin.......................................C6

◎ Information (p45)
    Office of the National
    Museum...(see 8)

KO RATANAKOSIN & THONBURI

BANGLAMPHU *Map on p268*

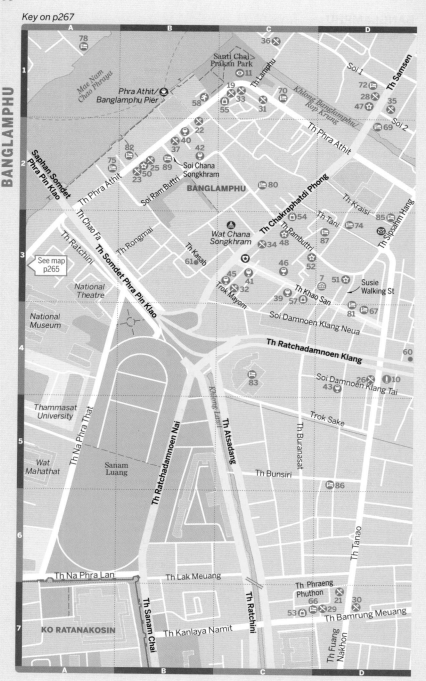

Key on p267

BANGLAMPHU

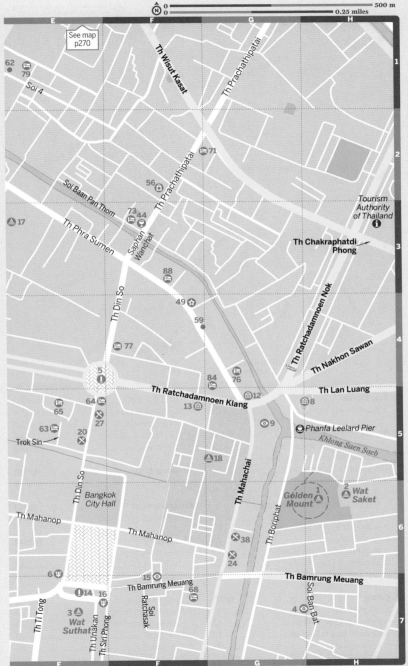

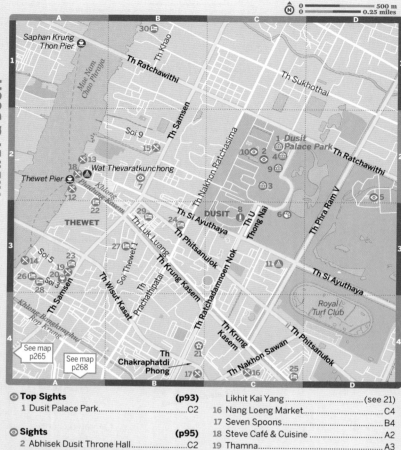

RATCHATHEWI

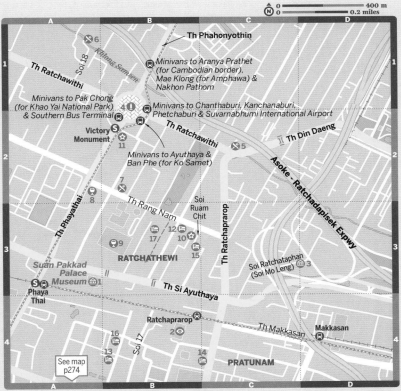

CHINATOWN

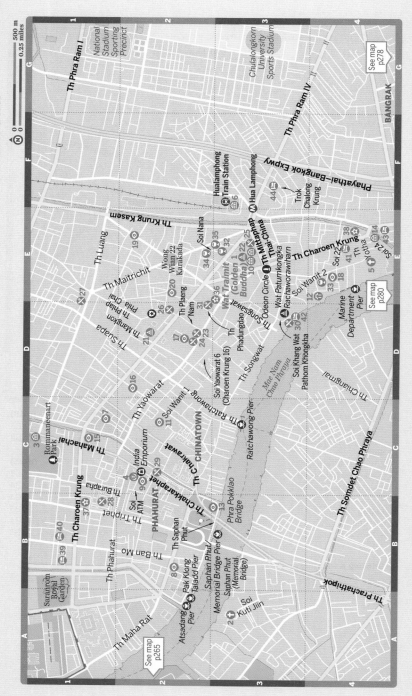

500 m
0.25 miles

See map p278

BANGRAK

Th Phra Ram I

National Stadium Sporting Precinct

Chulalongkorn University Sports Stadium

Th Phra Ram IV

Phayathai–Bangkok Expwy

Hualamphong Train Station

Hua Lamphong

Trok Chalong Krung

Th Krung Kasem

Soi Nana

Th Charoen Krung

Th Mittaphap Thai-China

Th Luang

Th Maitrichit

Wong Wian 22 Karakada

Wat Traimit (Golden Buddha)

Soi Yotha

Th Plaeng Nam

Odeon Circle

Wat Patumkongka Rachaworawiharn

Soi 24

Soi 22

Th

Th Songsawat

Phadungdao

Th Phiap Chai

Th Suapa

Th Mangkon

Soi Wanit 2

Marine Department Pier

Th Chiangmai

Th Yaowarat

Soi Yaowarat 6 (Charoen Krung 16)

Th Songwat

Wat Khang Wat

Soi Khang Wat Pathom Khongkha

See map p280

Romaneenart Park

Th Mahachai

India Emporium

Soi Wanit 1

Th Ratchawong

Th CHINATOWN

Th Chakrawat

Ratchawong Pier

Mae Nam Chao Phraya

Th Somdet Chao Phraya

Saranrom Royal Garden

Th Charoen Krung

Soi ATM

Th Triphet

Th Burapha

PHAHURAT

Th Chakkraphet

Phra Pokklao Bridge

Th Prachathipok

Th Ban Mo

Th Phahurat

Saphan Phut

Pak Klong Taladd Pier

Saphan Phut Pier

Memorial Bridge Pier

Saphan Phut (Memorial Bridge)

Soi Kuti Jiin

Atsadang Pier

Th Maha Rat

See map p265

CHINATOWN

Key on p276

SIAM SQUARE, PRATUNAM & PHLOEN CHIT

A **B** **C** **D**

1

Soi 12

Da-Ru-
Fa-Lah
Mosque

**BAAN
KHRUA**

51

Soi Phaya Nak

30 ☆ 31

25

Ratchathewi Ⓢ

Th Phetchaburi

Soi 15

40

2

11 4

3

1

8 🏛 Jim Thompson
House

Soi Kasem San 3

Soi Kasem San 2

Soi Kasem San 1

62
57

Sapan Hua
Chang Pier

Th Phayathai

Khlong Saen Saeb

Sra
Pathum
Palace

24 ✕

61

60

58

5

National
Stadium Ⓢ

4744

10

36

43

45

12

3

National
Stadium
Sporting
Precinct

38 ☆

32 ☆

29

46

19

Siam Family
Dental Clinic ✚

**SIAM
SQUARE**

Soi 1

Soi 2

Soi 4

Siam Ⓢ

Th Phra Ram I

15 ✕

Soi 5

Soi 6

23

13 ✕

21

37

Soi 9

Soi Chulalongkorn 64

Soi 7

Th Henri Dunant

4

Th Chulalongkorn

5

7

Th Phayathai

Royal
Bangkok
Sports Club

6

PATHUMWAN

Chulalongkorn
University

7

Soi 15

Soi Chulalongkorn 42

See map
p277

A **B** **C** **D**

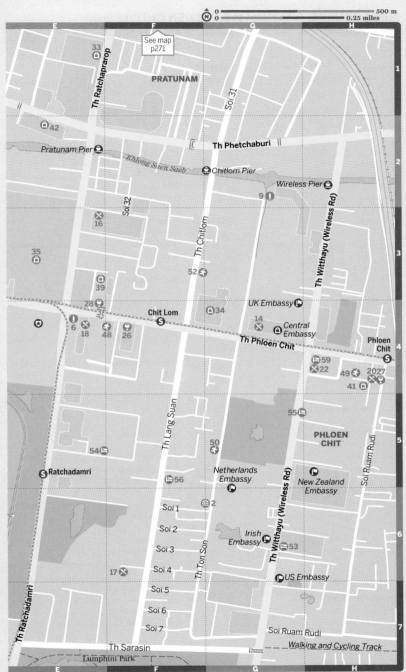

SIAM SQUARE, PRATUNAM & PHLOEN CHIT *Map on p274*

LUMPHINI

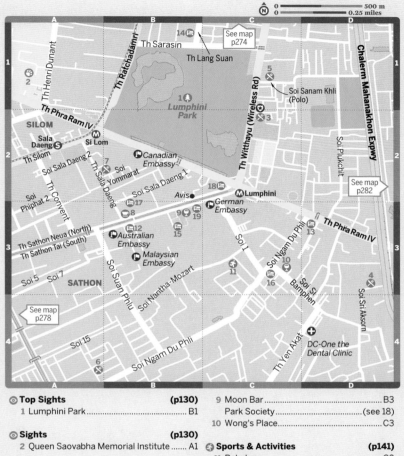

SILOM

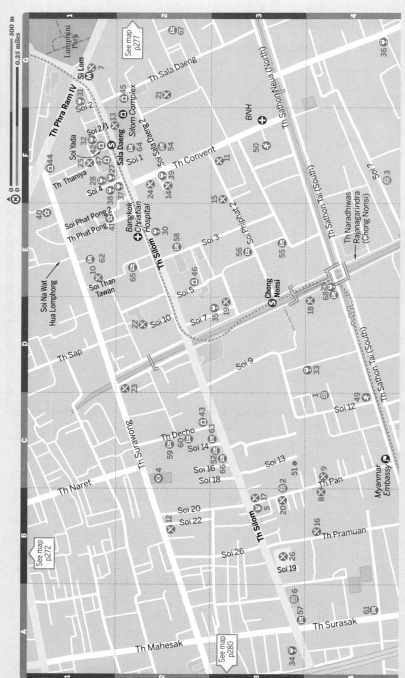

See map p277

See map p272

See map p280

Lumphini Park

Th Phra Ram IV

Si Lom

Th Sala Daeng

Silom Complex

Sala Daeng

Soi 2/1

Soi 2

Soi Yada

Th Thaniya

Soi 4

Soi Phat Pong 2

Th Phat Pong

Soi Na Wat Hua Lomphong

Soi Than Tawan

Th Sap

Th Surawong

Th Naret

Th Mahesak

Th Decho

Soi 14

Soi 16

Soi 18

Soi 20

Soi 22

Soi 26

Soi 19

Th Silom

Soi 1

Th Convent

Th Sala Daeng 2

Bangkok Christian Hospital

Th Silom

Soi 3

Soi 5

Soi 7

Soi 10

Soi 9

Soi 13

Soi 12

BNH

Th Sathon Neua (North)

Th Sathon Tai (South)

Th Naradhiwas Rajanagarindra (Chong Nonsi)

Chong Nonsi

Soi Phiphat 2

Th Pan

Th Pramuan

Th Surasak

Myanmar Embassy

Th Sathon Tai (South)

Soi 7

500 m
0.25 miles

Surasak Ⓢ

Th Sathon Neua (North)

Tawandang German Brewery (3km)

Sensi (250m)

St Louis Hospital

53 🏨

48 ●

◎ **Sights** (p128)

1 H Gallery	C4
2 Kathmandu Photo Gallery	C3
3 MR Kukrit Pramoj House	F4
4 Neilson Hays Library	C2
Number 1 Gallery	(see 6)
5 Sri Mariamman Temple	B3
6 Tang Gallery	A3
Thavibu Gallery	(see 6)

✗ **Eating** (p131)

7 Benjarong	G1
8 Bonita Cafe & Social Club	B4
9 Chennai Kitchen	C4
10 Dai Masu	E1
11 Eat Me	F3
12 Foo Mui Kee	B2
13 iBerry	F1
14 Indigo	F2
15 Jay So	F3
16 Kalapapruek	B4
17 Krua 'Aroy-Aroy'	B3
18 L'Atelier de Joël Robuchon	D4
19 Le Du	D3
20 Mashoor	B3
Nadimos	(see 26)
21 Pizza Massilia	G2
22 Soi 10 Food Centres	D2
23 Somboon Seafood	D2
24 Somtam Convent	F2
25 Sushi Tsukiji	F1
26 Taling Pling	B3
37 Tapas Room	F2
38 Telephone Pub	F1
The Bar	(see 68)
39 Vesper	F2
Vogue Lounge	(see 18)

🍸 **Drinking & Nightlife** (p135)

27 Balcony	G1
28 Bearbie	F1
29 Cé La Vi	E4
30 Cloud 47	E2
Craft	(see 57)
31 DJ Station	G1
Duc de Praslin	(see 13)
32 G Bangkok	F1
33 Hanakaruta	D4
34 Maggie Choo's	A3
35 Namsaah Bottling Trust	D3
36 Smalls	G4

🎭 **Entertainment** (p138)

40 Duangthawee Plaza	E1
41 Patpong	E1

🛍 **Shopping** (p139)

42 Everyday by Karmakamet	E2
43 House of Chao	C2
44 Jim Thompson	F1
45 July	G2
Patpong Night Market	(see 41)
46 Soi Lalai Sap	E2
47 Tamnan Mingmuang	F1

✦ **Sports & Activities** (p141)

48 Blue Elephant Thai Cooking School	A3
49 Health Land	C4
50 Ruen-Nuad Massage Studio	F3
51 Silom Thai Cooking School	C3

🛏 **Sleeping** (p198)

52 Amber	C3
53 Anantara Sathorn	E5
54 Bangkok Christian Guest House	F2
55 Café Ice Residence	E3
56 Glow Trinity Silom	E3
57 Holiday Inn	A3
58 HQ Hostel	E2
59 Lub*d	C2
60 LUXX	C2
61 Saphaipae	A4
62 Siam Heritage	E1
63 Silom Art Hostel	C3
64 Silom One	F2
65 Smile Society	E2
66 Triple Two Silom	C3
67 Urban House	G2
68 W Bangkok	E4

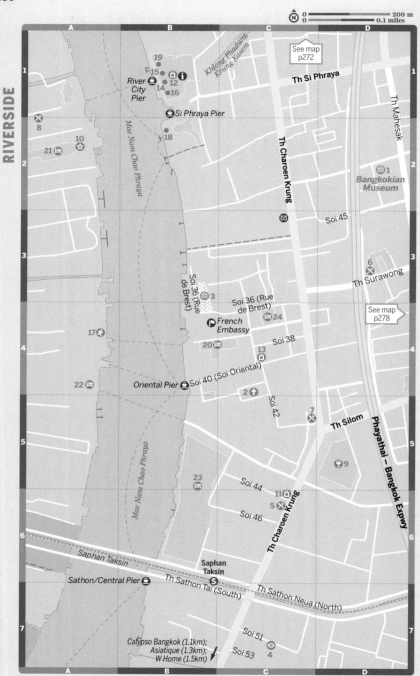

RIVERSIDE

0 — 200 m
0 — 0.1 miles

See map p272

Th Si Phraya

Klong Phadung Krung Kasem

19
15
14 12
16

River City Pier

Si Phraya Pier

18

Mae Nam Chao Phraya

8

21
10

Th Charoen Krung

Soi 45

Th Mahesak

Bangkokian Museum
1

6
Th Surawong

See map p278

Soi 36 (Rue de Brest)

3
Soi 36 (Rue de Brest)

French Embassy

24

17

20

13

Soi 38

22

Oriental Pier
Soi 40 (Soi Oriental)

2

Soi 42

7

Th Silom

9

23

Soi 44
11
5

Soi 46

Mae Nam Chao Phraya

Th Charoen Krung

Phayathai – Bangkok Expwy

Saphan Taksin

Sathon/Central Pier

Saphan Taksin
Th Sathon Tai (South)
Th Sathon Neua (North)

Calypso Bangkok (1.1km);
Asiatique (1.3km);
W Home (1.5km)

Soi 51

Soi 53

4

RIVERSIDE

RIVERSIDE

Key on p284

SUKHUMVIT

Nana Nua Pier
101
Khlong Saen Saeb
Nana Chard Pier
Tourism Authority of Thailand
Phetchaburi
Asoke-Phetchaburi Pier
Prasanmit Pier

Soi 1
Soi 3 (Nana)
Bumrungrad International Hospital

41
65
69
54
59

Soi 3/1
Soi 5
Soi 7
24
80
13
22
115
33
Soi 11
Soi 13
Soi 15

Soi 21 (Asoke)
Soi 23
Soi Prasanmit
Soi 31

71
79
47
42
34
36
Nana
Soi 11/1
84

Nana Plaza
Soi 6
78
89
114
3
23
Soi 8
Soi 10
27
11
97
Soi 12

94

Bangkok Dental Spa
104
Siam Society & Ban Kamthieng
Soi 19
Asok
112
Soi Cowboy
Sukhumvit
1
72
82
74
49
12
57
8

113

Chalerm Mahanakhon Expwy
Soi 2
Soi 4
102

Soi 14
Th Ratchadaphisek
106
55
Soi 16
103
61
Soi 18
31
29
7
73
Soi 22

92
83
25
Soi 27
67
Soi 31
88
5
99

109
110
111
14
38
Soi 33
Soi 31/1
Soi 33/1
25
77
76
19

Lake Ratchada

Benjakiti Park
2
90

45
Soi 20
70

Benjasiri Park

96
86
Soi Aree

KHLONG TOEI

105
Soi Sainumthip 2

See map p277

Soi 10

Queen Sirikit National Convention Centre

Queen Sirikit National Convention Centre

Khlong Toei

Soi Rongnarong Phichai Songkhram
Soi 26
Soi 24

100

Th Phra Ram IV
4

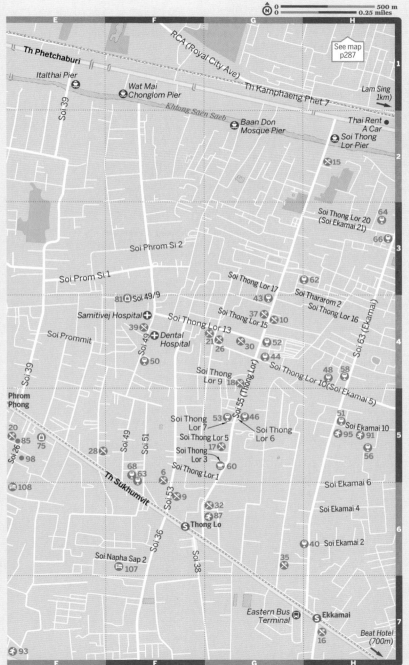

N 0 —————— 500 m
0 —————— 0.25 miles

Th Phetchaburi

RCA (Royal City Ave)

Italthai Pier

Wat Mai
Chonglom Pier

Th Kamphaeng Phet 7

Lam Sing
1km

Khlong Saen Saeb

Baan Don
Mosque Pier

Thai Rent
A Car

Soi Thong
Lor Pier

Soi 39

15

Soi Thong Lor 20
(Soi Ekamai 21)

64

66

Soi Phrom Si 2

Soi Prom Si 1

Soi Thong Lor 17

62

Soi Thararom 2
Soi Thong Lor 16

81 Soi 49/9

43

Samitivej Hospital

Soi Thong Lor 15

37

10

Soi Thong Lor 13

39

Dental
Hospital

Soi 49

Soi Prommit

21
26

30

52

50

44

Soi Thong Lor 10 (Soi Ekamai 5)

48 58

Soi 39

Soi Thong
Lor 9

18

Soi 63 (Ekamai)

Phrom
Phong

20
85
75
26
98

28

Soi 49

Soi 51

Soi Thong
Lor 7

Soi Thong Lor 5

Soi Thong
Lor 3

53

46

Soi Thong
Lor 6

51

95 91

Soi Ekamai 10

56

68
63

6

17

60

Soi Thong Lor 1

108

Th Sukhumvit

Soi 53

9

Soi Ekamai 6

32

87

Soi Ekamai 4

Thong Lo

Soi 36

Soi Ekamai 2

40

Soi Napha Sap 2

Soi 38

35

107

Eastern Bus
Terminal

Ekkamai

Beat Hotel
(700m)

16

93

See map
p287

55 (Thong Lor)

SUKHUMVIT *Map on p282*

58 Nung-Len H4
59 Oskar B2
60 Root Garden G5
61 Scratch Dog C4
62 Shades of Retro H3
63 Studio Lam F5
64 Sugar Ray..................................... H3
65 The District B1
66 Tuba.. H3
67 Walden D4
68 WTF.. F5

🎭 **Entertainment** **(p152)**
69 Apoteka....................................... B2
    Fat Gut'z.................................(see 44)
70 Friese-Green Club........................ D5
    Living Room..........................(see 112)
71 Nana Entertainment Plaza A2
72 Soi Cowboy.................................. C3
73 Titanium...................................... C4

🛍 **Shopping** **(p153)**
74 Almeta... C3
    Another Story....................... (see 77)
75 Dasa Book Café............................ E5
76 Emporium D5
77 Emquartier................................... D4
    Nickermann's....................... (see 79)
78 Raja's Fashions B3
79 Rajawongse A2
80 Ricky's Fashion House A2
    Shop @ TCDC......................(see 76)
81 Sop Moei Arts............................... F4
82 Terminal 21.................................. C3
83 ThaiCraft Fair C3
84 Thanon Sukhumvit Market........... B3
    ZudRangMa Records...........(see 68)

🏃 **Sports & Activities** **(p154)**
85 ABC Amazing Bangkok Cyclists.............. E5
86 Asia Herb Association............................. D5
87 Asia Herb Association............................. G6
88 Asia Herb Association............................. D3
89 Baan Dalah B3
90 Bicycle Hire B5
91 Coran H5
92 Divana Massage & Spa.......................... C3
93 Fun-arium.. E7
94 Health Land C2
95 Health Land H5
96 Krudam Gym.. D5
97 Lavana... B3
98 Phussapa Thai Massage School.............. E5
99 Rakuten.. D3
100 Yunomori Onsen & Spa D7

🛏 **Sleeping** **(p201)**
101 AriyasomVilla.......................................A1
102 Atlanta A3
103 Baan Sukhumvit C4
104 Fusion Suites C3
105 House by the Pond C5
106 Ma Du Zi.. C4
107 Napa Place F6
108 Pause Hostel E6
109 RetrOasis... C4
110 S31.. D4
111 S-Box... D4
112 Sheraton Grande Sukhumvit.................. B3
113 Spa Auberge Eugenia D3
114 Stable Lodge B3
115 Suk 11 .... B2

CHATUCHAK & ARI

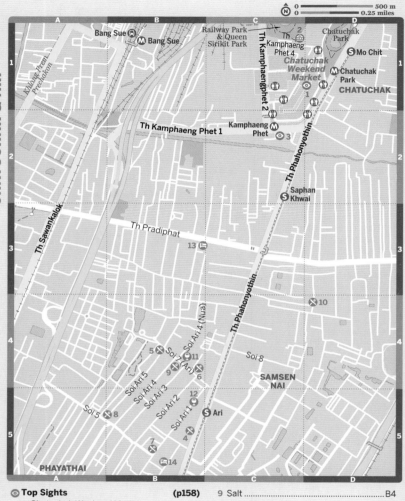

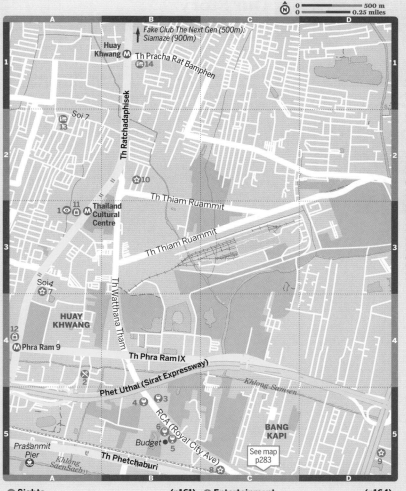

Our Story

A beat-up old car, a few dollars in the pocket and a sense of adventure. In 1972 that's all Tony and Maureen Wheeler needed for the trip of a lifetime – across Europe and Asia overland to Australia. It took several months, and at the end – broke but inspired – they sat at their kitchen table writing and stapling together their first travel guide, *Across Asia on the Cheap*. Within a week they'd sold 1500 copies. Lonely Planet was born.

Today, Lonely Planet has offices in Franklin, London, Melbourne, Oakland, Beijing and Delhi, with more than 600 staff and writers. We share Tony's belief that 'a great guidebook should do three things: inform, educate and amuse'.

Our Writer

Austin Bush

Austin Bush came to Thailand in 1999 as part of a language study program hosted by Chiang Mai University. The lure of city life, employment and spicy food eventually led Austin to Bangkok. City life, employment and spicy food have managed to keep him there ever since. Austin is a native of Oregon, and a writer and photographer who often focuses on food; samples of his work can be seen at www.austinbushphotography.com.

Published by Lonely Planet Publications Pty Ltd
ABN 36 005 607 983
12th edition – September 2016
ISBN 978 1 78657 011 6
© Lonely Planet 2016   Photographs © as indicated 2016
10 9 8 7 6 5 4 3 2 1
Printed in China